INDEX TO ANTHOLOGIES ON POSTSECONDARY EDUCATION, 1960-1978

INDEX TO ANTHOLOGIES ON POSTSECONDARY EDUCATION, 1960-1978

COMPILED BY
RICHARD H. QUAY

GREENWOOD PRESS
WESTPORT, CONNECTICUT LONDON, ENGLAND

Library of Congress Cataloging in Publication Data

Quay, Richard H
Index to anthologies on postsecondary education, 1960-1978.

Includes bibliographical references.
1. Education, Higher—Collected works—Indexes 2. Education, Higher—Bibliography—Indexes. I Title.
LB2305.Q39 016.378 79-8286
ISBN 0-313-21272-4

Library of Congress Catalog Card Number: 79-8286
ISBN: 0-313-21272-4

First published in 1980

Greenwood Press, Inc.
51 Riverside Avenue, Westport, Connecticut 06880

Printed in the United States of America

10 9 8 7 6 5 4 3 2 1

CONTENTS

PREFACE

Professor Howard R. Bowen began the fifth David D. Henry Lecture at the University of Illinois at Chicago Circle in April 1978 by asserting the following:

> When historians reflect on the three decades following World War II, they will, I think, judge the period to be one of the most creative in American history. And they will conclude that a significant and influential feature of this period was the intense interest of the American people in learning and the consequent growth, enrichment, and diversity of our system of higher education.

Certainly, Professor Bowen is accurate in his characterization of this period as one in which higher education has experienced extraordinary attention from the American public. Unfortunately, much of the attention was precipitated by the "student revolution" of the 1960s. This is not to suggest that the students of Berkeley or San Francisco State can be held culpable for the present condition of higher education in America. What they did, however, greatly accelerated the process of evolution which began under much less dramatic circumstances in the late nineteenth century. They also managed to focus intense public debate on many of the traditional ideals and values associated with American higher education. Although we are too close historically to predict the final outcome of this public debate, it is obvious that our institutions of higher education will be significantly different from what they were before the 1960s.

A tangible manifestation of this national debate was the creation of numerous public and private commissions. In turn, these commissions issued literally hundreds of technical reports, monographs, and specific policy recommendations. Many of the changes advocated by these commissions have been put into operation, while others are still being resisted. Some of the resistance to change can be attributed to a lack of consensus on the purposes of higher education and the means available to achieve them. In other cases, the changes are perceived as truly antithetical to the strongly held vision of an autonomous institution dedicated to the pursuit of knowledge and the transmission of culture. This is especially true where specific changes are perceived as an attempt to use higher education as an agent for "reforming society." What emerges, therefore, is a feeling of inadequacy of the standard model of higher education without, at the same time, a clear understanding of what parts of this model should be preserved and what parts should be modified or supplemented to meet desirable social and educational goals.

Today's colleges and universities are confronted with a staggering array of financial, social, educational, and political problems which appear unresolvable within the traditional range of policy options. If these problems are to be resolved new policies must be developed that can accommodate a variety of alternative and, sometimes, unconventional educational structures. These new policies can be realized, I think, by a dispassionate and systematic analysis of the criticism and recommendations included in the literature on higher education published since 1960. Accordingly, I hope both the concept and format of this index will greatly facilitate a representative review of the literature without the burdens inherent in a full-scale research undertaking.

Richard H. Quay
Oxford, Ohio
May 1979

NOTES ON THE SCOPE AND USE OF THIS INDEX

For more than five years I have assisted numerous doctoral candidates in formulating dissertation proposals on topics related to postsecondary education. With few exceptions, the major initial task was the construction of a search strategy that would adequately cover a literature base that has proliferated enormously during the past three decades. For example, in 1976 I prepared a bibliography of bibliographies on higher education which included 572 entries.[1] If I were to revise the bibliography today, I believe it could be expanded by an additional 300 plus entries.

Although bibliographical control has improved substantially during the same period, the investment in time for an exploratory literature review tends, in my judgment, to inhibit some students from attempting research in areas of broad critical concern to the future viability of higher education. For example, the topic "liberal education versus vocational training" as a primary focus in postsecondary education could easily generate a selective bibliography of 2,000 citations representing widely differing views. The bibliography would also involve familiarity with research in economics, public policy, manpower planning and other disciplines outside of the traditional sources of information on postsecondary education. This situation is, of course, greatly exacerbated at the undergraduate level and with others generally unfamiliar with the structure of bibliography in the social sciences.

This index is designed to mitigate the initial literature review problem by providing a highly select cross section of research dealing with a wide variety of topics on postsecondary education. In other words, I hope the index will serve as a microcosm that can be used to sample the literature without a major research commitment. Furthermore, because 87 percent of the essays in this index are original publications, they will not be identifiable through standard sources; therefore, the index serves the added purpose of providing access to an important literature not adequately covered by other reference works.

The 218 anthologies included in this index were identified from sources such as *Subject Guide to Books in Print,* book review sections of key periodicals in higher education, and specialized bibliographies such as those that appear in my 1976 publication. The initial search produced over 300 anthologies which met the subject criteria as represented in the table of contents. From this initial list I excluded those anthologies that dealt exclusively with student activism. This subject has been documented extremely well in other existing sources.[2] I also eliminated the anthologies published by Jossey-Bass under the series title *New Directions.*[3] These excellent anthologies are indexed by author and subject in *Current Index to Journals in Education.* The few remaining exclusions were subjective in the sense of choosing the best anthologies among several in the same general subject area. This was necessary in order to keep the index within reasonable quantitative limits.

The index may be approached in several different ways. Some users may wish to consult one of the broader subject categories in the table of contents. In each case, a typical citation will appear as follows:

Gordon, Margaret, "The Changing Labor Market for College Graduates," IN *Gordon* 1974, 27-81. Original.

The complete bibliographic information on the Gordon book can be found by consulting the List of Anthologies which begins on page xxvii. The term "original" indicates that the essay is published for the first time in the Gordon anthology. If the essay was reprinted from another source, the term "original" would be omitted and the primary source identified by a series of abbreviations which can be located in the List of Abbreviations beginning on page xiii.

The more detailed Subject Index that begins on page 325 may also be approached in several different ways. In some cases a single term such as "Affirmative Action" will be specific enough to meet the user's needs. In other cases the user may wish to interrelate more than one aspect of a specific topic. For example, the user may want to read an essay on "Student Personnel Services" in "Great Britain." In this instance, if the user compares the citation numbers under both subject headings he/she will find that essay number 3313 is common to both and would therefore fulfill the search specification. The terms used in the Subject Index were selected, with minor modifications, from the *Thesaurus of ERIC Descriptors.*[4] Finally, both the author index and subject index are keyed to number citations, not page numbers.

I wish to thank the Committee on Faculty Research, Miami University, for financial assistance during the preparation of this manuscript. I also wish to express my appreciation to Ms. Cindy Wiley for her helpful suggestions and typing assistance. I, of course, assume full responsibility for all errors or omissions.

NOTES

1. Richard H. Quay. *Research in Higher Education: A Guide to Source Bibliographies.* New York: College Entrance Examination Board, 1976.

2. For example see: (a) Philip G. Altbach and David H. Kelly. *American Students: A Selected Bibliography on Student Activism and Related Topics.* Lexington, Massachusetts: Lexington Books, 1973, (b) Bettina Aptheker. *Higher Education and the Student Rebellion in the United States, 1960-1968; A Bibliography.* New York: American Institute for Marxist Studies, 1969, (c) Kenneth Keniston, Mary-Kay Duffield, and Sharon Martinek. *Radicals and Militants: An Annotated Bibliography of Empirical Research on Campus Unrest.* Lexington, Massachusetts: Lexington Books, 1973, and (d) Nedjelko D. Suljak. *Campus Disorder and Cultural Counter-Revolution: A Bibliography.* Davis, California: Institute of Government Affairs, 1970. Essays on issues relating to student activism are not totally absent from this index. These essays can be identified by consulting the *Subject Index* under the heading "Activism."

3. Titles in the *New Directions* series include: (a) *New Directions for Community Colleges,* (b) *New Directions for Higher Education,* and (c) *New Directions for Institutional Research.* Five new titles in this series were begun in 1978 and shortly will be added to the list of serials indexed in *Current Index to Journals in Education.*

4. *Thesaurus of ERIC Descriptors.* 7th ed. New York: Macmillan, 1977. When applicable, I used "identifiers" rather than descriptors as subject headings. The "identifiers" were selected from the *ERIC Identifier Usage Report.* Columbus, Ohio: Information Reference Center (ERIC/SMEAC), The Ohio State University, 1974.

LIST OF ABBREVIATIONS

AAL	Gordon, Milton M. Assimilation in American Life . . . . New York: Oxford University Press, 1964.
AAPWG	Cartter, Alan W., ed. Assuring Academic Progress Without Growth. San Francisco: Jossey-Bass, 1975.
AAUPB	American Association of University Professors Bulletin
ABS	American Behavioral Scientist
AC	Sanford, Nevitt, ed. The American College. New York: Wiley, 1962.
Aca Rev	Jencks, Christopher and David Riesman. The Academic Revolution. New York: Anchor, 1969.
Ac M	Lazarsfeld, Paul F. and Wagner Thielens, eds. The Academic Mind. New York: Free Press, 1958.
ADEI	Glazer, Nathan. Affirmative Discrimination. New York: Basic Books, 1975.
Adol Psy	Feinstein, C. S., P. L. Giovacchini, and A. A. Miller, eds. Adolescent Psychiatry. New York: Basic Books, 1971.
Aff Soc	Galbraith, John K. The Affluent Society. Boston: Houghton Mifflin, 1958.
AGBP	Beyle, Thad and J. Oliver Williams, eds. The American Governor in Behavioral Perspective. New York: Harper and Row, 1972.

AGB Rep	AGB Reports
AGP	Archives of General Psychiatry
AHE	Nason, John W. American Higher Education in 1980--Some Basic Issues. Palo Alto, California: Aspen Institute for Humanistic Studies, 1966.
AIS	Approach to Independent Study. Washington, D.C.: U.S. Government Printing Office, 1965.
AJS	American Journal of Sociology
ALJ	Akron Law Journal
ALM	Gareth, William, T. Blackstone, and D. Metcalf. The Academic Labor Market. New York: Elsevier Scientific Publishers, 1974.
Amer S	American Scholar
Amer Soc	American Sociologist
Amer Univ	Barzun, Jacques. The American University. New York: Harper and Row, 1968.
AMFF	Wolk, Ronald A. Alternative Methods of Federal Funding for Higher Education. Berkeley, California: Carnegie Commission on Higher Education, 1968.
Analysis	Analysis
Annals	American Academy of Political and Social Science. Annals
AOE	Whitehead, Alfred N. The Aims of Education. New York: Macmillan, 1959.
AP	American Psychologist
AR	Antioch Review
AS	Pusey, Nathan N. The Age of the Scholar. Cambridge, Massachusetts: Belknap Press, 1963.
ASQ	Administrative Science Quarterly
ASR	American Sociological Review
AtL	Atlantic Monthly

AW	Bernard, Jessie. Academic Women. University Park, Pennsylvania: Pennsylvania State University Press, 1964.
BA	Halsey, A. H. and Martin Trow. The British Academics. London: Faber and Faber, 1971.
BBSS	Bulletin of the Bureau of School Service (College of Education, University of Kentucky)
BCU	Bulletin of the Association of College Unions
BE	Freeman, Richard B. Black Elite: The New Market for Highly Educated Black Americans. New York: McGraw-Hill, 1976.
BM	Educational Facilities Laboratories. Bricks and Mortarboards: A Report on College Planning and Building. New York: EFL, 1964.
CAC	Sanford, Nevitt, ed. College and Character. New York: Wiley, 1964.
CAS	Moss, Malcolm and Francis E. Rourke. The Campus and the State. Baltimore, Maryland: John Hopkins University Press, 1959.
CBR	College Board Review
CC	Christian Century
CCF	Freeman, Roger A. Crisis in College Finance? Time for New Solutions. Washington, D.C.: Institute for Social Science Research, 1965.
CDUT	Pervin, Lawrence A., Louis E. Reik, and Willard Dalrymple, eds. The College Dropout and the Utilization of Talent. Princeton, New Jersey: Princeton University Press, 1966.
CE	College English
Cen Mag	Center Magazine
Cent Mag	Century Magazine
CF	Carnegie Foundation for the Advancement of Teaching. Annual Report for 1963-1964. New York: Carnegie Foundation, 1964.
CFBR	Bittker, Boris I. The Case for Black Reparations. New York: Random House, 1973.

CFC	Hartman, Robert W. *Credit for College: Public Policy for Student Loans*. New York: McGraw-Hill, 1971.
Change	Change Magazine
Chau	The Chautauquan
CISC	Eddy Jr., Edward D. *The College Influence on Student Character*. Washington, D.C.: American Council on Education, 1959.
CIUO	Gross, Edward and Paul V. Grambsch. *Changes in University Organization, 1964-1971*. New York: McGraw-Hill, 1974.
Civ R D	Civil Rights Digest
Col Law R	Columbia Law Review
College Board	College Entrance Examination Board. *Barriers to Higher Education*. New York: CEEB, 1971.
Col Man	College Management
Comm	Commentary
Common	Commonweal
COS	Goodman, Paul. *The Community of Scholars*. New York: Random House, 1962.
CR	Christian Scholar
CSJ	College Student Journal
CSS	College Student Survey
CU	College and University
CUB	College and University Business
Current 1958	*Current Issues in Higher Education, 1958* Smith, G. Kerry, ed. *Higher Education: Strengthening Quality in the Satellite Age*. Washington, D.C.: Association for Higher Education, 1958.
Current 1963	*Current Issues in Higher Education, 1963* Smith, G. Kerry ed. *Critical Decisions in Higher Education*. Washington, D.C.: Association for Higher Education, 1963.

Current 1964	Current Issues in Higher Education, 1964
	Smith, G. Kerry, ed. Undergraduate Education. Washington, D.C.: Association for Higher Education, 1964.
Current 1965	Current Issues in Higher Education, 1965
	Smith, G. Kerry, ed. Pressures and Priorities in Higher Education. Washington, D.C.: Association for Higher Education, 1965.
CUT	Hartnett, Rodney T. College and University Trustees, Their Background, Roles, and Education. Princeton, New Jersey: Educational Testing Service, 1969.
CVAE	Riesman, David. Constraint and Variety in American Education. Lincoln, Nebraska: University of Nebraska Press, 1956.
CVI	Jacob, Philip E. Changing Values in College. New York: Harper and Row, 1957.
CW	Searle, John R. The Campus War. New York: Thomas Y. Crowell, 1971.
CWA	Committee on College and World Affairs. College and World Affairs. New York: CCWF, 1964.
CWW	Mills, C. Wright. The Causes of World War III. New York: Ballantine Books, 1960.
DA	Roszak, Theodore, ed. The Dissenting Academy. New York: Pantheon Books, 1968.
DAD	O'Neil, Robert M. Discrimination Against Discrimination: Preferential Admissions in the De Funis Case. Bloomington, Indiana: Indiana University Press, 1975.
Dae	Daedalus
DAF	Hofstadter, Richard and Walter P. Metzger. The Development of Academic Freedom in the United States. New York: Columbia University Press, 1955.
DG	Clark, Kenneth B. Dark Ghetto. New York: Harper and Row, 1965.
Dissent	Dissent

DSHE	Hofstadter, Richard and C. DeWitt Hardy. The Development and Scope of Higher Education in the United States. New York: Columbia University Press, 1952.
EAU	Veysey, Laurence R. The Emergence of the American University. Chicago: University of Chicago Press, 1965.
EB	Select Committee on Education. Education at Berkeley. Berkeley, California: Regents of the University of California, 1966.
EBHS	President's Committee on Education Beyond High School. Second Report to the President. Washington, D.C.: U.S. Government Printing Office, 1957.
EC	Maritain, Jacques. Education at the Crossroads. New Haven, Connecticut: Yale University Press, 1943.
EES	Clark, Burton R. Educating the Expert Society. San Francisco: Chandler, 1962.
EFF	Hutchins, Robert M. Education for Freedom. Baton Rouge, Louisiana: Louisiana State University Press, 1943.
EFP	Henry, Nelson B., ed. Education for the Professions. Chicago: University of Chicago Press, 1962.
EJS	European Journal of Sociology
EMU	Emory University Quarterly
En E	Frede, Richard. Entry E. New York: Random House, 1958.
EPAHE	Wilson, Logan ed. Emerging Patterns in American Higher Education. Washington, D.C.: American Council on Education, 1965.
ER	Educational Record
ERHE	Elam, Stanley and Michael H. Moskow, eds. Employment Relations in Higher Education. Bloomington, Indiana: Phi Delta Kappa, 1969.
Ethics	Ethics
Exce	Gardner, John W. Excellence: Can We Be Equal and Excellent Too? New York: Harper and Row, 1961.

FBCC	Garbarino, Joseph W. and Bill Aussieker. Faculty Bargaining: Change and Conflict. New York: McGraw-Hill, 1975.
FCDS	Bowen, Howard R., ed. Freedom and Control in a Democratic Society. New York: American Council of Life Insurance, 1976.
FHE	Bowen, Howard R. Financing Higher Education: The Current State of the Debate. Washington, D.C.: Association of American Colleges, 1974.
FM	Vermilye, Dykeman W., ed. The Future in the Making. San Francisco: Jossey-Bass, 1973.
Forum	The Forum
FSCB	Lunsford, Terry F. The Free Speech Crises at Berkeley, 1964-65 . . . Berkeley, California: The Center for Research and Development in Higher Education, 1965.
GAU	Slosson, Edwin E. Great American Universities. New York: Macmillan, 1938.
GEAA	Mayhew, Lewid B., ed. General Education: An Account and Appraisal. New York: Harper and Row, 1960.
GEFS	Harvard University Committee on General Education. General Education in a Free Society. Cambridge, Massachusetts: Harvard University Press, 1945.
GET	Walters, Everett, ed. Graduate Education Today. Washington, D.C.: American Council on Education, 1965.
Harper's	Harper's Magazine
HE	Higher Education; the International Journal of Higher Education and Educational Planning
HEFS	Chambers, M. M. Higher Education in the Fifty States. Danville, Illinois: Interstate Printers and Publishers, 1970.
HEMD	Goldwin, Robert A., ed. Higher Education and American Democracy . . . Chicago: Rand McNally, 1967.
HER	Harvard Educational Review
HLIA	Veblen, Thorstein. The Higher Learning in America. New York: Sagamore Press, 1957.

IAS	Minter, W. John, ed. The Individual and the System: Personalizing Higher Education. Boulder, Colorado: Western Interstate Commission for Higher Education, 1967.
ICH	Hodgkinson, Harold L. and Myron B. Bloy, Jr., eds. Identity Crisis in Higher Education. San Francisco: Jossey-Bass, 1971.
ICT	Lee, Calvin B. T., ed. Improving College Teaching. Washington, D.C.: American Council on Education, 1967.
IDTPHE	Medsker, Leland L. and James W. Trent. The Influences of Different Types of Public Higher Institutions in College Attendance from Varying Socioeconomic and Ability Levels. Berkeley, California: The Center for the Study of Higher Education, University of California, 1965.
IPOSC	Kirk, Russell. The Intemperate Professor, and Other Cultural Splentics. Baton Rouge, Louisiana: Louisiana State University Press, 1965.
JABS	Journal of Applied Behavioral Science
JACHA	Journal of the American College Health Association
JCJ	Junior College Journal
J Col P	Journal of College Placement
JCP	Journal of Counseling Psychology
J Crit A	Journal of Critical Analysis
JCSP	Journal of College Student Personnel
JEP	Journal of Educational Psychology
JGE	Journal of General Education
JHE	Journal of Higher Education
JLE	Journal of Law and Education
JNASPA	Journal of the National Association of Student Personnel Administrators
JNAWDC	Journal of the National Association of Women Deans and Counselors
JNE	Journal of Negro Education

JP	Journal of Psychology
JPE	Journal of Political Economy
JSI	Journal of Social Issues
LCP	Law and Contemporary Problems
LCSPC	Freeman, Roger A. Last Chance to Save the Private College. Washington, D.C.: The American Conservative Union, 1969.
LE	Liberal Education
LEd	Van Doren, Mark. Liberal Education. Boston: Beacon Press, 1959.
LEDI	Griswold, A. Whitney. Liberal Education and the Democratic Ideal. New Haven, Connecticut: Yale University Press, 1959.
LYGE	Heard, Alexander. The Lost Years in Graduate Education. Atlanta, Georgia: Southern Regional Educational Board, 1963.
Ma	Mademoiselle
McC	McCall's Magazine
MCEO	Baldridge, J. Victor and Terrence Deal. Managing Change in Educational Organizations. Berkeley, California: McCutchan, 1975.
Measure	Measure
MI	Coser, Lewis. Men of Ideas. New York: Free Press, 1975.
Minerva	Minerva
Mot	Motive
NAR	North American Review
Nation	The Nation
NCNB	North Central News Bulletin
New	Newsweek
NG	Michael, Donald N. The Next Generation. New York: Random House, 1965.
NYRB	The New York Review of Books

NYT New York Times

NYTM New York Times Magazine

OBCT Medalia, Nahum Z. On Becoming a College Teacher, A Review of Three Variables. Atlanta, Georgia: Southern Regional Educational Board, 1963.

ODC Clark, Burton R. The Open Door College. New York: McGraw-Hill, 1960.

OFC Knorr, Owen A. and John W. Minter, eds. Order and Freedom on the Campus--The Rights and Responsibility of Faculty and Students. Boulder, Colorado: Western Interstate Commission for Higher Education, 1965.

OVEI Baldridge, J. Victor and Terrence E. Deal. An Organizational View of Educational Innovation. Stanford, California: Center for Research and Development in Teaching, 1974.

PAR Public Administration Review

PDK Phi Delta Kappan

PFA Rockefeller Brothers Fund. Prospect for America. New York: Doubleday, 1961.

PFAC Benewitz, Maurice C., ed. Proceedings, First National Conference, April 1973, National Center for the Study of Collective Bargaining in Higher Education. New York: Baruch College, City University of New York, 1973.

PFHE Southern Regional Education Board. Proceedings: A Symposium on Financing Higher Education. Miami Beach, Florida: SREB, 1969.

PGJ Personnel and Guidance Journal

PHE Nowlan, James D. The Politics of Higher Education: Lawmakers and the Academy in Illinois. Urbana, Illinois: University of Illinois Press, 1975.

PHEC Smelser, Neil J. and Gabriel Almond, eds. Public Higher Education in California. Berkeley, California: University of California Press, 1974.

PI Public Interest

PIP	Telford, Charles W. and Walter T. Plant. The Psychological Impact of the Two-Year College on Certain Non-Intellectual Functions. San Jose, California: San Jose State College, 1963.
PJE	Peabody Journal of Education
POE	Bailey, Stephen K. The Purposes of Education. Bloomington, Indiana: Phi Delta Kappa, 1976.
POHE	Smith, Huston. The Purposes of Higher Education. New York: Harper and Row, 1955.
PUAHE	Ladd Jr., Everett C. and Seymour M. Lipset. Professors, Unions, and American Higher Education. Berkeley, California: Carnegie Commission on Higher Education, 1973.
RATU	Pollard, William G. Religion and the University. Toronto: University of Toronto Press, 1964.
RE	Heath, Roy. The Reasonable Adventurer. Pittsburgh, Pennsylvania: University of Pittsburgh Press, 1964.
RER	Review of Educational Research
RGE	Bell, Daniel. Reforming General Education: The Columbia College Experience in Its National Setting. New York: Columbia University Press, 1966.
RL	Bestor, Arthur. The Restoration of Learning. New York: Random House, 1956.
RP	Howe, Irving, ed. The Radical Papers. New York: Doubleday, 1966.
RR	The Research Reporter
SAA	Lunsford, Terry F., ed. The Study of Academic Administration. Boulder, Colorado: Western Interstate Commission for Higher Education, 1963.
SAOC	Keeton, Morris. Shared Authority on Campus. Washington, D.C.: American Association for Higher Education, 1971.
SAP	Sampson, Edward E., Harold A. Horn and Associates. Student Activism and Protest: Alternatives for Social Change. San Francisco: Jossey-Bass, 1970.

SAY	Johnson, Owen M. Stover at Yale. New York: Grosset and Dunlap, 1912.
SCHE	Berdahl, Robert O. Statewide Coordination of Higher Education. Washington, D.C.: American Council on Education, 1971.
Sch R	School Review
Science	Science
SCM	Piel, Gerard. Science in the Cause of Man. New York: Knopf, 1961.
SCPG	Newcomb, T. M. and E. K. Wilson, eds. The Study of College Peer Groups . . . New York: Social Science Research Council, 1961.
SE	Sociology of Education
SECE	Barton, Allen H. Studying the Effects of College Education . . . New Haven, Connecticut: The Edward W. Hazen Foundation, 1959.
SED	McConnel, T. R., ed. Selection and Educational Differentiation. Berkeley, California: Center for the Study of Higher Education, University of California, 1960.
SEP	Saturday Evening Post
S Ess	Eliot, T. S. Selected Essays. New York: Harcourt, Brace and World, 1964.
SFIAE	Tyler, Ralph W., ed. Social Forces Influencing American Education. Chicago: University of Chicago Press, 1961.
SHE	Committee on the Student in Higher Education. The Student in Higher Education. New Haven, Connecticut: Edward W. Hazen Foundation, 1968.
SI	Sports Illustrated
SL	Woodhall, Maureen. Student Loans: A Review of Experience in Scandinavia and Elsewhere. London: George Harrap, 1970.
SLCS	Abbott, John. Student Life in a Class Society. Oxford: Pergamon Press, 1971.
SM	Scribner's Magazine

Soc I	Sociological Inquiry
Soc P	Social Problems
Soc Th P	Social Theory and Practice
SOHE	Enlau, Heinz and Harold Quinley. State Officials and Higher Education. New York: McGraw-Hill, 1970.
Soundings	Soundings, An Interdisciplinary Journal
SP	Keats, John. The Sheepskin Psychosis. Philadelphia, Pennsylvania: J. B. Lippincott, 1965.
SQ	Sociological Quarterly
SR	Saturday Review
SS	School and Society
SSR	Sociology and Social Research
Stu M	Student Medicine
TCR	Teachers College Record
Time	Time Magazine
TMD	Butz, Otto, ed. To Make a Difference. New York: Harper and Row, 1967.
Tran	Trans-Action
TWC	Havemann, Ernest and Patricia S. West. They Went to College: The College Graduate in America Today. New York: Harcourt, Brace, 1952.
UA	Adams, J. F., ed. Understanding Adolescence. Boston: Allyn and Bacon, 1968.
U Chic Law R	University of Chicago Law Review
UIA	Kerr, Clark. The University in America. Santa Barbara, California: The Center for the Study of Democratic Institutions, 1967.
UIT	Perkins, James A. The University in Transition. Princeton, New Jersey: Princeton University Press, 1966.
ULA	Michie, Alan A., ed. The University Looks Abroad . . . New York: Education and World Affairs, 1966.

Unc	Keniston, Kenneth. The Uncommited. New York: Harcourt, Brace and World, 1962.
Univ	University; a Princeton Quarterly
UOEBHS	Educational Policies Commission. Universal Opportunity for Education Beyond the High School. Washington, D.C.: National Education Association, 1964.
US	Bolton, Charles D. and Kenneth C. W. Kammeyer. The University Student . . . New Haven, Connecticut: College and University Press, 1967.
UU	Kerr, Clark. The Uses of the University. Cambridge, Massachusetts: Harvard University Press, 1963.
VCHE	Smith, John E. Value Convictions and Higher Education. New Haven, Connecticut: The Edward W. Hazen Foundation, 1958.
WGHE	Lee, Calvin B. T., ed. Whose Goals for Higher Education? Washington, D.C.: American Council on Education, 1968.
WGW	Astin, Alexander W. Who Goes Where to College? Chicago: Science Research Associates, 1965.
WPWB	Carnegie Commission on Higher Education. Higher Education: Who Pays? Who Benefits? Who Should Pay? New York: McGraw-Hill, 1973.

LIST OF ANTHOLOGIES

Altbach 1977 — Altbach, Philip G., ed. Comparative Perspectives on the Academic Profession. New York: Praeger, 1977.

Altman 1970 — Altman, Robert A. and Patricia O. Snyder, eds. The Minority Student on the Campus: Expectations and Possibilities. Boulder, Colorado: Western Interstate Commission for Higher Education, 1970.

Altman 1971 — Altman, Robert A. and Carolyn M. Byerly, eds. The Public Challenge and the Campus Response. Boulder, Colorado: Western Interstate Commission for Higher Education, 1971.

Anderson 1971 — Anderson, Charles H. and John D. Murry, eds. The Professors: Work and Life Styles Among Academicians. Cambridge, Massachusetts: Schenkman Publishing, 1971.

Anderson 1976 — Anderson, G. Lester, ed. Land-Grant Universities and Their Continuing Challenge. East Lansing, Michigan: Michigan State University Press, 1976.

Angell 1977 — Angell, George W., Edward P. Kelley, Jr., and Associates. Handbook of Faculty Bargaining. San Francisco, California: Jossey-Bass, 1977.

Archer 1972 — Archer, Margaret S., ed. Students, University and Society: A Comparative Sociological Review. London: Heinemann Educational Books, 1972.

Astin 1976 — Astin, Helen S., ed. Some Action of Her Own--The Adult Woman and Higher Education. Lexington, Massachusetts: Lexington Books, 1976.

Astin 1978 — Astin, Helen S. and Werner Z. Hirsch, eds. The Higher Education of Women: Essays in Honor of Rosemary Parks. New York: Praeger, 1978.

Averill 1971 — Averill, Lloyd J. and William W. Jellema, eds. Colleges and Commitments. Philadelphia, Pennsylvania: The Westminster Press, 1971.

Baade 1964 — Baade, Hans W. and Robinson O. Everett, eds. Academic Freedom, The Scholar's Place in Modern Society. Dobbs Ferry, New York: Oceana Publications, 1964.

Bailey 1977 — Bailey, Stephen K., ed. Higher Education in the World Community. Washington, D.C.: American Council on Education, 1977.

Baldridge 1971 — Baldridge, J. Victor, ed. Academic Governance: Research on Institutional Politics and Decision Making. Berkeley, California: McCutchan, 1971.

Baskin 1965 — Baskin, Samuel, ed. Higher Education: Some Newer Developments. New York: McGraw-Hill, 1965.

Bellman 1962 — Bellman, Samuel I., ed. The College Experience: Material for Analysis. San Francisco, California: Chandler Publishing, 1962.

Bergen 1966 — Bergen, Dan and E. D. Duryea, eds. Libraries and the College Climate of Learning. Syracuse, New York: Syracuse University Press, 1966.

Blain 1961 — Blain Jr., Graham B. and Charles C. McArthur, eds. Emotional Problems of the Student. New York: Appleton-Century-Crofts, 1961.

Bloom 1975	Bloom, Bernard L., ed. Psychological Stress in the Campus Community: Theory, Research, and Action. New York: Behavioral Publications, 1975.
Brann 1972	Brann, James and Thomas A. Emmet, eds. The Academic Department or Division Chairman: A Complex Role. Detroit, Michigan: Belamp Publishing, 1972.
Breneman 1978	Breneman, David W. and Chester E. Finn, Jr., eds. Public Policy and Private Higher Education. Washington, D.C.: The Brookings Institution, 1978.
Brickman 1962	Brickman, William W. and Stanley Lehrer, eds. A Century of Higher Education: Classical Citadel to Collegiate College. New York: Society for the Advancement of Education, 1962.
Brookover 1965	Brookover, Wilbur B., et. al. The College Student. New York: The Center for Applied Research in Education, 1965.
Brown 1960	Brown, Nicholas C., ed. Higher Education: Incentives and Obstacles. Washington, D.C.: American Council on Education, 1960.
Budig 1970	Budig, Gene A., ed. Perceptions in Public Higher Education. Lincoln, Nebraska: University of Nebraska Press, 1970.
Budig 1972	Budig, Gene A., ed. Dollars and Sense: Budgeting for Today's Campus. Chicago: College and University Press, 1972.
Bunnell 1960	Bunnell, Kevin, ed. Faculty Work Load. Washington, D.C.: American Council on Education, 1960.
Burns 1962	Burns, Gerald P., ed. Administrators in Higher Education: Their Functions and Coordination. New York: Harper and Brothers, 1962.
Butcher 1972	Butcher, H. J. and Ernest Rudd, eds. Contemporary Problems in Higher Education; An Account of Research. London: McGraw-Hill, 1972.

Buxton 1975 — Buxton, Thomas H. and Keith W. Prichard, eds. Excellence in University Teaching--New Essays. Columbia, South Carolina: University of South Carolina Press, 1975.

Caffrey 1969 — Caffrey, John, ed. The Future Academic Community--Continuity and Change. Washington, D.C.: American Council on Education, 1969.

Carpenter 1960 — Carpenter, Marjorie, ed. The Larger Learning: Teaching Values to College Students. Dubuque, Iowa: William C. Brown Company Publishers, 1960.

Cohen 1964 — Cohen, Arthur A., ed. Humanistic Education and Western Civilization, Essays for Robert M. Hutchins. New York: Holt, Rinehart and Winston, 1964.

Cohen 1966 — Cohen, Joseph W., ed. The Superior Student in American Higher Education. New York: McGraw-Hill, 1966.

College 1968 — College Entrance Examination Board. College Admissions Policies for the 1970s. New York: College Entrance Examination Board, 1968.

(Also available as ERIC Document #ED 040-660)

College 1970 — College Entrance Examination Board. Financing Equal Opportunity in Higher Education. New York: College Entrance Examination Board, 1970.

(Also available as ERIC Document #ED 046-333)

College 1971 — College Entrance Examination Board. Barriers to Higher Education. New York: College Entrance Examination Board, 1971.

(Also available as ERIC Document #ED 050-694)

College 1974 — College Entrance Examination Board. Who Pays? Who Benefits?--A National Invitational Conference on the Independent Student. New York: College Entrance Examination Board, 1974.

(Also available as ERIC Document #ED 096-924)

College 1975 — College Entrance Examination Board. Perspectives on Financial Aid. New York: College Entrance Examination Board, 1975.

(Also available as ERIC Document #ED 112-807)

Connery 1970 — Connery, Robert H., ed. The Corporation and the Campus. New York: Praeger, 1970.

Cross 1974 — Cross, K. Patricia, John R. Valley, and Associates. Planning Non-Traditional Programs. San Francisco, California: Jossey-Bass, 1974.

DeCoster 1974 — DeCoster, David A. and Phyllis Mable, eds. Student Development and Education in College Residence Halls. Washington, D.C.: American College Personnel Association, 1974.

Deferrari 1961 — Deferrari, Roy J., ed. Quality of College Teaching and Staff. Washington, D.C.: The Catholic University of America Press, 1961.

Dennis 1963 — Dennis, Lawrence E., ed. Education and a Woman's Life. Washington, D.C.: American Council on Education, 1963.

Dennis 1966 — Dennis, Lawrence E. and Joseph H. Kauffman, eds. The College and the Student: An Assessment of Relationships and Responsibilities in Undergraduate Education. Washington, D.C.: American Council on Education, 1966.

Dobbins 1963 — Dobbins, Charles G., ed. Higher Education and the Federal Government: Programs and Problems. Washington, D.C.: American Council on Education, 1963.

Dobbins 1964 — Dobbins, Charles G., ed. The University, The City, and Urban Renewal. Washington, D.C.: American Council on Education, 1964.

Dobbins 1968 — Dobbins, Charles G. and Calvin B. T. Lee, eds. Whose Goals for American Higher Education? Washington, D.C.: American Council on Education, 1968.

Donovan 1962 — Donovan, George F., ed. College and University Student Personnel Services. Washington, D.C.: The Catholic University of America Press, 1962.

Donovan 1964 — Donovan, George F., ed. Selected Problems in Administration of American Higher Education. Washington, D.C.: The Catholic University of America Press, 1964.

Donovan 1965 — Donovan, George F., ed. College and University Interinstitutional Cooperation. Washington, D.C.: The Catholic University of America Press, 1965.

Dressel 1961 — Dressel, Paul, ed. Evaluation in Higher Education. Boston, Massachusetts: Houghton Mifflin, 1961.

Elam 1969 — Elam, Stanley and Michael H. Moskow, eds. Employment Relations in Higher Education. Bloomington, Indiana: Phi Delta Kappa, 1969.

Entwistle 1976 — Entwistle, Noel, ed. Strategies for Research and Development in Higher Education. Amsterdam: Swets and Zeitlinger, 1976.

Eurich 1968 — Eurich, Alvin, ed. Campus 1980: The Shape of the Future in American Higher Education. New York: Delacorte Press, 1968.

Feldman 1972 — Feldman, Kenneth A., ed. College and Student: Selected Readings in the Social Psychology of Higher Education. New York: Pergamon Press, 1972.

<u>Fitzgerald</u> 1970 — Fitzgerald, Laurine E., Walter F. Johnson, and Willa Norris, eds. <u>College Student Personnel: Readings and Bibliography</u>. Boston, Massachusetts: Houghton Mifflin, 1970.

<u>Furniss</u> 1971 — Furniss, W. Todd, ed. <u>Higher Education for Everybody?--Issues and Implications</u>. Washington, D.C.: American Council on Education, 1971.

<u>Furniss</u> 1974 — Furniss, W. Todd and Patricia Aberjerg Graham, eds. <u>Women in Higher Education</u>. Washington, D.C.: American Council on Education, 1974.

<u>Godwin</u> 1972 — Godwin, Winfred L. and Peter B. Mann, eds. <u>Higher Education: Myths, Realities and Possibilities</u>. Atlanta, Georgia: Southern Regional Education Board, 1972.

(Also available as ERIC Document #ED 071-596)

<u>Goldwin</u> 1967 — Goldwin, Robert A., ed. <u>Higher Education and Modern Democracy: The Crisis of the Few and the Many</u>. Chicago: Rand McNally, 1967.

<u>Goodall</u> 1976 — Goodall, Leonard E., ed. <u>State Politics and Higher Education: A Book of Readings</u>. Dearborn, Michigan: LMG Associates, 1976.

<u>Gordon</u> 1974 — Gordon, Margaret S., ed. <u>Higher Education and the Labor Market</u>. New York: McGraw-Hill, 1974.

<u>Gross</u> 1977 — Gross, Barry R., ed. <u>Reverse Discrimination</u>. Buffalo, New York: Prometheus Books, 1977.

<u>Hamelman</u> 1972 — Hamelman, Paul W., ed. <u>Managing the University: A Systems Approach</u>. New York: Praeger, 1972.

<u>Harcleroad</u> 1970 — Harcleroad, Fred F., ed. <u>Issues of the Seventies: The Future of Higher Education</u>. San Francisco, California: Jossey-Bass, 1970.

Harcleroad 1971 — Harcleroad, Fred F. and Jean H. Cornell, eds. Assessment of Colleges and Universities. Iowa City, Iowa: The American College Testing Program, 1971.

(Also available as ERIC Document #ED 058-857)

Harcleroad 1974 — Harcleroad, Fred F., ed. Higher Education: A Developing Field of Study. Iowa City, Iowa: American College Testing Program, 1974.

(Also available as ERIC Document #ED 104-311)

Harris 1960 — Harris, Seymour E., ed. Higher Education in the United States: The Economic Problems. Cambridge, Massachusetts: Harvard University Press, 1960.

Harris 1964 — Harris, Seymour E., ed. Economic Aspects of Higher Education. Paris: Organisation for Economic Co-operation and Development, 1964.

Harrison 1975 — Harrison, Shelley A. and Lawrence M. Stolurow, eds. Improving Instructional Productivity in Higher Education. Englewood Cliffs, New Jersey: Educational Technology Publications, 1975.

Hassenger 1967 — Hassenger, Robert, ed. The Shape of Catholic Higher Education. Chicago: University of Chicago Press, 1967.

Havice 1971 — Havice, Charles W., ed. Campus Values: Some Considerations for Collegians. New York: Charles Scribner's Sons, 1971.

Hawkins 1970 — Hawkins, Hugh, ed. The American University and Industrial America. Lexington, Massachusetts: D. C. Heath, 1970.

Heinlein 1974 — Heinlein, Albert C., ed. Decision Models in Academic Administration. Kent, Ohio: Kent State University Press, 1974.

Heist 1968	Heist, Paul, ed. The Creative College Student: An Unmet Challenge. San Francisco, California: Jossey-Bass, 1968.
Henderson 1968	Henderson, Algo D., ed. Higher Education in Tomorrow's World. Ann Arbor, Michigan: The University of Michigan, 1968.
Henry 1962	Henry, Nelson, B., ed. Education for the Professions. Chicago, Illinois: University of Chicago Press, 1962. (Yearbook of the National Society for the Study of Education, 61st., pt. 2)
Herron 1970	Herron Jr., Orley R., ed. New Dimensions In Student Personnel Administration. Scranton, Pennsylvania: International Textbook Company, 1970.
Heyns 1977	Heyns, Roger W., ed. Leadership for Higher Education, The Campus View. Washington, D.C.: American Council on Education, 1977.
Hobbs 1978	Hobbs, Walter C., ed. Government Regulation of Higher Education. Cambridge, Massachusetts: Ballinger Publishing, 1978.
Hodgkinson 1971	Hodgkinson, Harold L. and Richard Meeth, eds. Power and Authority: Transformation of Campus Governance. San Francisco, California: Jossey-Bass, 1971.
Hodgkinson 1971a	Hodgkinson, Harold L. and Myron B. Bloy, Jr., eds. Identity Crisis in Higher Education. San Francisco, California: Jossey-Bass, 1971.
Holmes 1971	Holmes, Brian, David G. Scanlon, and W. R. Niblett, eds. Higher Education in a Changing World. New York: Harcourt Brace Jovanovich, 1971. (Series: The World Year Book of Education 1971/72)

Hook 1974 — Hook, Sidney, Paul Kurtz, and Miro Todorovich, eds. The Idea of a Modern University. Buffalo, New York: Prometheus Books, 1974.

Hook 1975 — Hook, Sidney, Paul Kurtz, and Miro Todorovich, eds. The Philosophy of the Curriculum: The Need for General Education. Buffalo, New York: Prometheus Books, 1975.

Hook 1978 — Hook, Sidney, Paul Kurtz, and Miro Todorovich, eds. The University and the State: What Role for Government in Higher Education? Buffalo, New York: Prometheus Books, 1978.

Howe 1975 — Howe, Florence, ed. Women and the Power to Change. New York: McGraw-Hill, 1975.

Hughes 1973 — Hughes, Clarence R., Robert L. Underbrink, and Charles O. Gordon, eds. Collective Negotiations in Higher Education: A Reader. Carlinville, Illinois: Blackburn College Press, 1973.

Hughes 1975 — Hughes, John F. and Olive Mills, eds. Formulating Policy in Postsecondary Education: The Search for Alternatives. Washington, D.C.: American Council on Education, 1975.

Hughes 1975a — Hughes, John F., ed. Education and the State. Washington, D.C.: American Council on Education, 1975.

Humphrey 1967 — Humphrey, Richard A., ed. Universities . . . and Development Assistance Abroad. Washington, D.C.: American Council on Education, 1967.

Jellema 1972 — Jellema, William W., ed. Efficient College Management. San Francisco, California: Jossey-Bass, 1972.

Jensen 1964 — Jensen, Gale, A. A. Liveright, and Wilbur Hallenbeck, eds. Adult Education: Outlines of an Emerging Field of University Study. Washington, D.C.: Adult Education Association of the U.S.A., 1964.

Johnson 1969 — Johnson, Charles B. and William G. Katzenmeyer, eds. Management Information Systems in Higher Education: The State of the Art. Durham, North Carolina: Duke University Press, 1969.

Johnson 1974 — Johnson, Roosevelt, ed. Black Scholars on Higher Education in the 70's. Columbus, Ohio: ECCA Publications, 1974.

Juster 1975 — Juster, F. Thomas, ed. Education, Income, and Human Behavior. New York: McGraw-Hill, 1975.

Katz 1976 — Katz, Joseph and Rodney T. Hartnett, eds. Scholars in the Making, The Development of Graduate and Professional Students. Cambridge, Massachusetts: Ballinger Publishing, 1976.

Kaysen 1973 — Kaysen, Carl, ed. Content and Context: Essays on College Education. New York: McGraw-Hill, 1973.

Keene 1975 — Keene, Roland, Franck C. Adams, and John E. King, eds. Money Marbles, or Chalk: Student Financial Support in Higher Education. Carbondale, Illinois: Southern Illinois University Press, 1975.

Keeton 1976 — Keeton, Morris T. and Associates. Experiential Learning: Rationale, Characteristics, and Assessment. San Francisco, California: Jossey-Bass, 1976.

Kent 1972 — Kent, Leonard J. and George P. Springer, eds. Graduate Education Today and Tomorrow. Albuquerque, New Mexico: University of New Mexico Press, 1972.

Kertesz 1971 — Kertesz, Stephen D., ed. The Task of Universities in a Changing World. Notre Dame, Indiana: University of Notre Dame Press, 1971.

Knight 1960 — Knight, Douglas M., ed. The Federal Government and Higher Education. Englewood Cliffs, New Jersey: Prentice-Hall, 1960.

Knorr 1965 — Knorr, Owen A., ed. Long-Range Planning in Higher Education. Boulder, Colorado: Western Interstate Commission for Higher Education, 1965.

(Also available as ERIC Document #ED 026-847)

Knorr 1965a — Knorr, Owen A. and W. John Minter, eds. Order and Freedom on the Campus: The Rights and Responsibilities of Faculty and Students. Boulder, Colorado: Western Interstate Commission for Higher Education, 1965.

(Also available as ERIC Document #ED 032-856)

Kruytbosch 1970 — Kruytbosch, Carlos E. and Sheldon L. Messinger, eds. The State of the University: Authority and Change. Beverly Hills, California: Sage Publications, 1970.

Lawlor 1968 — Lawlor, John, ed. The New University. New York: Columbia University Press, 1968.

Lawlor 1972 — Lawlor, John, ed. Higher Education, Patterns of Change in the 1970's. London: Routledge and Kegan Paul, 1972.

Lawrence 1970 — Lawrence, Ben, George Weathersby, and Virginia W. Patterson, eds. Outputs of Higher Educations: Their Identification, Measurement, and Evaluation. Boulder, Colorado: Western Interstate Commission for Higher Education, 1970.

(Also available as ERIC Document #ED 043-296)

Lee 1967 — Lee, Calvin B. T., ed. Improving College Teaching. Washington, D.C.: American Council on Education, 1967.

Letter 1968 — Letter, Sidney S., ed. New Prospects for the Small Liberal Arts College. New York: Teachers College Press, 1968.

Letter 1970 — Letter, Sidney S., ed. The Time Has Come Today. New York: Teachers College Press, 1970.

Lumsden 1974 — Lumsden, Keith G., ed. Efficiency in Universities: The La Paz Papers. New York: Elsevier Scientific Publishing, 1974.

Lunsford 1963 — Lunsford, Terry F., ed. The Study of Academic Administration. Boulder, Colorado: Western Interstate Commission for Higher Education, 1963.

Lunsford 1963a — Lunsford, Terry F., ed. The Study of College Cultures. Boulder, Colorado: Western Interstate Commission for Higher Education, 1963.

McGrath 1964 — McGrath, Earl J. and L. Richard Meeth, eds. Cooperative Long-Range Planning in Liberal Arts Colleges. New York: Bureau of Publications, Teacher College, Columbia University, 1964.

McGrath 1966 — McGrath, Earl J., ed. Universal Higher Education. New York: McGraw-Hill, 1966.

McGrath 1966a — McGrath, Earl J., ed. The Liberal Arts Colleges's Responsibility for the Individual Student. New York: Teachers College Press, 1966.

McGrath 1967 — McGrath, Earl J., ed. Selected Issues in College Administration. New York: Teachers College Press, 1967.

McGrath 1972 — McGrath, Earl J., ed. Prospect for Renewal, The Future of the Liberal Arts College. San Francisco, California: Jossey-Bass, 1972.

McHenry 1977 — McHenry, Dean E. and Associates. Academic Departments: Problems, Variations, and Alternatives. San Francisco, California: Jossey-Bass, 1977.

McLeod 1973 — McLeod, T. H., ed. Post-Secondary Education in a Technological Society. Montreal: Queen's University Press, 1973.

McMurrin 1976 — McMurrin, Sterling M., ed. On The Meaning of the University. Salt Lake City, Utah: The University of Utah Press, 1976.

Margolis 1969 — Margolis, John D., ed. The Campus in the Modern World. New York: Macmillan, 1969.

Mauer 1976 — Mauer, George J., ed. Crises in Campus Management: Case Studies in the Administration of Colleges and Universities. New York: Praeger, 1976.

Mayhew 1960 — Mayhew, Lewis B., ed. General Education: An Account and Appraisal. New York: Harper and Brothers, 1960.

Mayhew 1967 — Mayhew, Lewis B., ed. Higher Education in the Revolutionary Decades. Berkeley, California: McCutchan, 1967.

Messick 1976 — Messick, Samuel and Associates. Individuality in Learning: Implications of Cognitive Style and Creativity for Human Development. San Francisco, California: Jossey-Bass, 1976.

Milton 1968 — Milton, Ohmer and Edward Joseph Shoben, Jr., eds. Learning and the Professors. Athens, Ohio: Ohio University Press, 1968.

Minter 1966 — Minter, W. John, ed. Campus and Capitol: Higher Education and the State. Boulder, Colorado: Western Interstate Commission for Higher Education, 1966.

(Also available as ERIC Document #ED 025-009)

Minter 1967 — Minter, W. John, ed. The Individual and the System: Personalizing Higher Education. Boulder, Colorado: Western Interstate Commission for Higher Education, 1967.

Minter 1968 — Minter, W. John and Ian M. Thompson, eds. Colleges and Universities as Agents of Social Change. Boulder, Colorado: Western Interstate Commission on Higher Education, 1968.

Minter 1969 — Minter, W. John and Patricia O. Snyder, eds. Value Change and Power Conflict in Higher Education. Boulder, Colorado: Western Interstate Commission for Higher Education, 1969.

Minter 1969a — Minter, John and Ben Lawrence, eds. Management Information Systems: Their Development and Use in the Administration of Higher Education. Boulder, Colorado: Western Interstate Commission for Higher Education, 1969.

(Also available as ERIC Document #ED 042-427)

Mitchell 1974 — Mitchell, Howard E., ed. The University and the Urban Crisis. New York: Behavioral Publications, 1974.

Morison 1966 — Morison, Robert S., ed. The Contemporary University: U.S.A. Boston: Houghton Mifflin, 1966.

(Re-prints, with revisions and additions, the Fall 1964 issue of Daedalus, Journal of the American Academy of Arts and Sciences)

Morris 1970 — Morris, William H., ed. Effective College Teaching: The Quest for Relevance. Washington, D.C.: American Association for Higher Education, 1970.

Murphy 1960 — Murphy, Lois B. and Esther Raushenbush, eds., Achievement in the College Years: A Record of Intellectual and Personal Growth. New York: Harper and Brothers, 1960.

Murphy 1975 — Murphy, Thomas P., ed. Universities in the Urban Crisis. New York: Dunellen Publishing, 1975.

Mushkin 1962 — Mushkin, Selma J., ed. Economics of Higher Education. Washington, D.C.: U.S. Government Printing Office, 1962.

(U.S. Office of Education Bulletin No. 5, 1962 and also available as ERIC Document #ED 096-860)

Newcomb 1966 — Newcomb, Theodore M. and Everett K. Wilson, eds. College Peer Groups: Problems and Prospects for Research. Chicago, Illinois: Aldine Publishing, 1966.

Niblett 1970 — Niblett, W. R., ed. Higher Education: Demand and Response. San Francisco, California: Jossey-Bass, 1970.

Niblett 1972 — Niblett, W. Roy and R. Freeman Butts, eds. Universities Facing the Future: An International Perspective. San Francisco, California: Jossey-Bass, 1972.

Nichols 1970 — Nichols, David C. and Olive Mills, eds. The Campus and the Racial Crisis. Washington, D.C.: American Council on Education, 1970.

OECD 1974 — Organisation for Economic Co-operation and Development. Structure of Studies and Place of Research in Mass Higher Education. Paris: OECD, 1974.

(Also available as ERIC Document #ED 098-903)

OECD 1974a — Organisation for Economic Co-operation and Development. Towards Mass Higher Education, Issues and Dilemmas. Paris: OECD, 1974.

(Also available as ERIC Document #ED 095-809)

Orwig 1971 — Orwig, M. D., ed. Financing Higher Education: Alternatives for the Federal Government. Iowa City, Iowa: The American College Testing Program, 1971.

Packwood 1977 — Packwood, William T., Theodore K. Miller, and Clyde A. Parker, eds. College Student Personnel Services. Springfield, Illinois: Charles C. Thomas, 1977.

Paulsen 1970 — Paulsen, F. Robert, ed. Higher Education: Dimensions and Directions. Tucson, Arizona: The University of Arizona Press, 1970.

Peltason 1978 — Peltason, J. W. and Marcy V. Massengale, eds. Students and Their Institutions: A Changing Relationship. Washington, D.C.: American Council on Education, 1978.

Perkins 1972 — Perkins, James A. and Barbara B. Israel, eds. Higher Education: From Autonomy to Systems. New York: International Council for Educational Development, 1972.

Perkins 1973 — Perkins, James A., ed. The University as an Organization. New York: McGraw-Hill, 1973.

Perry 1971 — Perry, Richard R. and W. Frank Hull IV, eds. The Organized Organization: The American University and Its Administration. Toledo, Ohio: The University of Toledo, 1971.

Pervin 1966 — Pervin, Lawrence A., Louis E. Reik, and Willard Dalrymple, eds. The College Dropout and the Utilization of Talent. Princeton, New Jersey: Princeton University Press, 1966.

Peterson 1977 — Peterson, Vance T., ed. Higher Education and the Law: An Administrator's Overview. Toledo, Ohio: Center for the Study of Higher Education, The University of Toledo, 1977.

(Also available as ERIC Document #ED 142-114)

Pincoffs 1972 — Pincoffs, Edmund L., ed. The Concept of Academic Freedom. Austin, Texas: University of Texas Press, 1972.

Portman 1972 — Portman, David N., ed. Early Reform in American Higher Education. Chicago: Nelson-Hall, 1972.

Rever 1971 — Rever, Philip R., ed. Open Admissions and Equal Access. Iowa City, Iowa: The American College Testing Program, 1971.

Rice 1964 — Rice, James G., ed. General Education, Current Ideas and Concerns. Washinton, D.C.: Association for Higher Education, National Education Association, 1964.

Rice 1977 — Rice, Lois D., ed. Student Loans: Problems and Policy Alternatives. New York: College Entrance Examination Board, 1977.

(Also available as ERIC Document #ED 143-244)

Rich 1963 — Rich, Catherine R. and Thomas A. Garrett, eds. Philosophy and Problems of College Admissions. Washington, D.C.: The Catholic University of America Press, 1963.

Riesman 1973 — Riesman, David and Verne A. Stadtman, eds. Academic Transformation: Seventeen Institutions Under Pressure. New York: McGraw-Hill, 1973.

Riley 1977 — Riley, Gary L. and J. Victor Baldridge, eds. Governing Academic Organizations: New Problems, New Perspectives. Berkeley, California: McCutchan, 1977.

Ritterbush 1972 — Ritterbush, Philip C., ed. The Bankruptcy of Academic Policy. Washington, D.C.: Acropolis Books, 1972.

Robertson 1978 — Robertson, D.B., ed. Power and Empowerment in Higher Education: Studies in Honor of Louis Smith. Lexington, Kentucky: The University Press of Kentucky, 1978.

Rossi 1973 — Rossi, Alice S. and Ann Calderwood, eds. Academic Women on the Move. New York: Russell Sage Foundation, 1973.

Rowland 1977	Rowland, A. Westley, ed. Handbook of Institutional Advancement. San Francisco, California: Jossey-Bass, 1977.
Runkel 1969	Runkel, Philip, Roger Harrison, and Margaret Runkel, eds. The Changing College Classroom. San Francisco, California: Jossey-Bass, 1969.
Sacks 1978	Sacks, Herbert S. and Associates. Hurdles, The Admissions Dilemma in American Higher Education. New York: Atheneum, 1978.
Sanford 1962	Sanford, Nevitt, ed. The American College: A Psychological and Social Interpretation of the Higher Learning. New York: Wiley, 1962.
Seabury 1975	Seabury, Paul, ed. Universities in the Western World. New York: Free Press, 1975.
Shiver 1967	Shiver, Elizabeth N., ed. Higher Education and Public International Service. Washington, D.C.: American Council on Education, 1967.
Siegel 1968	Siegel, Max, ed. The Counseling of College Students--Function, Practice, and Technique. New York: Free Press, 1968.
Smelser 1974	Smelser, Neil J. and Gabriel Almond, eds. Public Higher Education in California. Berkeley, California: University of California Press, 1974.
Smith 1960	Smith, G. Kerry, ed. Platform for Higher Education: Guide Lines for the 60s. Washington, D.C.: Association for Higher Education, 1960. (Series: Current Issues in Higher Education, 1960)
Smith 1961	Smith, G. Kerry, ed. Goals for Higher Education in a Decade of Decision. Washington, D.C.: Association for Higher Education, 1961. (Series: Current Issues in Higher Education, 1961)

Smith 1962 — Smith, G. Kerry, ed. Higher Education in an Age of Revolutions. Washington, D.C.: Association for Higher Education, 1962.

(Series: Current Issues in Higher Education, 1962)

Smith 1963 — Smith, G. Kerry, ed. Critical Decision in Higher Education. Washington, D.C.: Association for Higher Education, 1963.

(Series: Current Issues in Higher Education, 1963)

Smith 1964 — Smith, G. Kerry, ed. Undergraduate Education. Washington, D.C.: Association for Higher Education, 1964.

(Series: Current Issues in Higher Education, 1964)

Smith 1965 — Smith, G. Kerry, ed. Pressures and Priorities in Higher Education. Washington, D.C.: Association for Higher Education, 1965.

(Series: Current Issues in Higher Education, 1965)

Smith 1966 — Smith, G. Kerry ed. Higher Education Reflects--On Itself and on the Larger Society. Washington, D.C.: Association for Higher Education, 1966.

(Series: Current Issues in Higher Education, 1966)

Smith 1967 — Smith, G. Kerry, ed. In Search of Leaders. Washington, D.C.: American Association for Higher Education, 1967.

(Series: Current Issues in Higher Education, 1967)

Smith 1968 — Smith, G. Kerry, ed. Stress and Campus Response. San Francisco, California: Jossey-Bass, 1968.

(Series: Current Issues in Higher Education, 1968)

Smith 1969 — Smith, G. Kerry, ed. Agony and Promise. San Francisco, California: Jossey-Bass, 1969.

(Series: Current Issues in Higher Education, 1969)

Smith 1970 — Smith, G. Kerry, ed. The Troubled Campus. San Francisco, California: Jossey-Bass, 1970.

(Series: Current Issues in Higher Education, 1970)

Smith 1971 — Smith, G. Kerry, ed. New Teaching, New Learning. San Francisco, California: Jossey-Bass, 1971.

(Series: Current Issues in Higher Education, 1971)

Smith 1973 — Smith, Bardwell L. and Associates. The Tenure Debate. San Francisco, California: Jossey-Bass, 1973.

Solmon 1973 — Solmon, Lewis C. and Paul L. Taubman, eds. Does College Matter? Some Evidence on the Impacts of Higher Education. New York: Academic Press, 1973.

Sprague 1960 — Sprague, Hall T., ed. Research on College Students. Boulder, Colorado: Western Interstate Commission for Higher Education, 1960.

Stephens 1975 — Stephens, Michael D. and Gordon W. Roderick, eds. Universities For A Changing World: The Role of the University in the Later Twentieth Century. New York: Halsted Press, 1975.

Stephens 1978 — Stephens, Michael D. and Gordon W. Roderick, eds. Higher Education Alternatives. London: Longman, 1978.

Stickler 1964 — Stickler, W. Hugh, ed. Experimental Colleges, Their Role in American Higher Education. Tallahassee, Florida: Florida State University Press, 1964.

Stone I 1974
Stone II 1974 — Stone, Lawrence, ed. The University in Society. Princeton, New Jersey: Princeton University Press, 1974.

Volume I - Oxford and Cambridge from the 14th. to the Early 19th. Century.

Volume II - Europe, Scotland, and the United States from the 16th. to the 20th. Century.

Strickland 1967 — Strickland, Stephen, ed. Sponsored Research in American Universities and Colleges. Washington, D.C.: American Council on Education, 1967.

Stroup 1966 — Stroup, Thomas B., ed. The University in the American Future. Lexington, Kentucky: University of Kentucky Press, 1966.

Tice 1973 — Tice, Terrence N., ed. Faculty Bargaining in the Seventies. Ann Arbor, Michigan: The Institute of Continuing Legal Education, 1973.

Tice 1976 — Tice, Terrence N., ed. Campus Employment Relations. Ann Arbor, Michigan: Institute of Continuing Legal Education, 1976.

Trow 1975 — Trow, Martin, ed. Teachers and Students: Aspects of American Higher Education. New York: McGraw-Hill, 1975.

Vaccaro 1969 — Vaccaro, Louis C. and James Thayne Covert, eds. Student Freedom in American Higher Education. New York: Teachers College Press, 1969.

Vaccaro 1975 — Vaccaro, Louis C., ed. Reshaping American Higher Education. Irving, Texas: A.M.I. Press, 1975.

Vermilye 1972 — Vermilye, Dyckman W., ed. The Expanded Campus. San Francisco, California: Jossey-Bass, 1972.

(Series: Current Issues in Higher Education, 1972)

Vermilye 1973 — Vermilye, Dyckman W., ed. The Future in the Making. San Francisco, California: Jossey-Bass, 1973.

(Series: Current Issues in Higher Education, 1973)

Vermilye 1974 — Vermilye, Dyckman W., ed. Lifelong Learners--A New Clientele for Higher Education. San Francisco, California: Jossey-Bass, 1974.

(Series: Current Issues in Higher Education, 1974)

Vermilye 1975 — Vermilye, Dyckman W., ed. Learner-Centered Reform. San Francisco, California: Jossey-Bass, 1975.

(Series: Current Issues in Higher Education, 1975)

Vermilye 1976 — Vermilye, Dyckman W., ed. Individualizing the System. San Francisco, California: Jossey-Bass, 1976.

(Series: Current Issues in Higher Education, 1976)

Vermilye 1977 — Vermilye, Dyckman W., ed. Relating Work and Education. San Francisco, California: Jossey-Bass, 1977.

(Series: Current Issues in Higher Education, 1977)

Verreck 1974 — Verreck, W. A., ed. Methodological Problems in Research and Development in Higher Education. Amsterdam: Swets and Zeitlinger, 1974.

Vladeck 1975 — Vladeck, Judith P. and Stephen C. Vladeck, eds. Collective Bargaining in Higher Education--The Developing Law. New York: Practising Law Institute, 1975.

Walters 1965 — Walters, Everett, ed. Graduate Education Today. Washington, D.C.: American Council on Education, 1965.

Warnath 1973	Warnath, Charles F. and Associates. New Directions for College Counselors: A Handbook for Redesigning Professional Roles. San Francisco, California: Jossey-Bass, 1973.
Wasserman 1975	Wasserman, Elga, Arie Y. Lewin, and Linda H. Bleiweis, eds. Women in Academia: Evolving Policies Toward Equal Opportunities. New York: Praeger, 1975.
Wattel 1975	Wattel, Harold L., ed. Planning in Higher Education. Hempstead, New York: Hofstra University, 1975. (Series: Hofstra University Yearbook of Business, Series 11, Number 1)
Weatherford 1960	Weatherford, Willis D., ed. The Goals of Higher Education. Cambridge, Massachusetts: Harvard University Press, 1960.
Willie 1978	Willie, Charles V. and Ronald R. Edmonds, eds. Black Colleges in America: Challenge, Development, Survival. New York: Teachers College Press, 1978.
Wilson 1961	Wilson, Logan, et. al. Studies of College Faculty. Boulder, Colorado: Western Interstate Commission for Higher Education, 1961.
Wilson 1965	Wilson, Logan, ed. Emerging Patterns in American Higher Education. Washington, D.C.: American Council on Education, 1965.
Wilson 1972	Wilson, Logan and Olive Mills, eds. Universal Higher Education: Costs, Benefits, Options. Washington, D.C.: American Council on Education, 1972.
Wingfield 1970	Wingfield, Clyde J., ed. The American University: A Public Administration Perspective. Dallas, Texas: Southern Methodist University Press, 1970.

Yamamoto 1968	Yamamoto, Kaoru, ed. The College Student and His Culture: An Analysis. Boston: Houghton Mifflin, 1968.
Young 1974	Young, Kenneth E., ed. Exploring the Case for Low Tuition in Public Higher Education. Iowa City, Iowa: The American College Testing Program, 1974. (Also available as ERIC Document #ED 096-929)

INDEX TO ANTHOLOGIES ON POSTSECONDARY EDUCATION, 1960-1978

1
HISTORY OF POSTSECONDARY EDUCATION

1. Anonymous, "Chautauqua Local Circles and Summer Assemblies," IN Portman 1972, 193-221. Chau, 10 (October 1889), 102-113.

2. Brickman, William W., "International Relations in Higher Education, 1862-1962," IN Brickman 1962, 208-239. Original.

3. Cowley, W. H., "Critical Decisions in American Higher Education," IN Smith 1963, 13-21. Original.

Dr. Cowley has identified several "key" decisions in the history of American higher education from the 17th. century to the G.I. Bill of Rights in 1945.

4. Engel, Arthur, "Emerging Concepts of the Academic Profession at Oxford 1800-1854," IN Stone I 1974, 305-352. Original.

5. Glazer, Nathan, "City College," IN Riesman 1973, 71-98. Original.

An excellent brief historical and sociological analysis of City College of the City University of New York.

6. Hofstadter, Richard, "The Age of the University," IN Hawkins 1970, 1-9. DSHE (1952).

7. Jarausch, Konrad H., "The Sources of German Student Unrest 1815-1848," IN Stone II 1974, 533-569. Original.

8. Johnson, Owen M., "Dink Stover at Yale, About 1909," IN Bellman 1962, 1-15. SAY (1912).

9. Kagan, Richard L., "Universities in Castile 1500-1800," IN Stone II 1974, 355-405. Original.

10. Kerr, Clark, "Destiny--Not So Manifest," IN Smith 1971, 245-252. Original.

Dr. Clark Provides an historical account of higher education and concludes that we are, in the 1970's, entering a "period of uncertainty."

11. Lyte, Guy F., "Patronage Patterns and Oxford Colleges c. 1300-c. 1530," IN Stone I 1974, 111-149. Original.

12. McConica, James, "Scholars and Commoners in Renaissance Oxford," IN Stone I 1974, 151-181. Original.

13. McLachlan, James, "The Choice of Hercules American Student Societies in the Early 19th Century," IN Stone II 1974, 449-494. Original.

14. Montague, H. Patrick, "The Historical Function of the University," IN Holmes 1971, 15-26. Original.

A concise world history of the university.

15. Morgan, Victor, "Cambridge University and 'The Country,'" IN Stone I 1974, 183-245. Original.

16. Phillipson, N. T., "Culture and Society in the 18th Century Province: The Case of Edinburgh and the Scottish Enlightenment," IN Stone II 1974, 407-448. Original.

17. Piel, Gerard, "The Acceleration of History," IN Smith 1964, 22-32. Original.

18. Raushenbush, Ester, "Three Women: Creators of Change," IN Astin 1978, 29-52. Original.

The impact of three women educators on their institutions: Clara Mayer, Jacqueline Grennan, and Lucy Sprague.

19. Ripley, S. Dillon, "Truth and Institutions: Reflections on the 125th Anniversary of the Smithsonian Institution," IN Ritterbush 1972, 35-40. Original.

20. Rothblatt, Sheldon, "The Student Sub-culture and the Examination System in Early 19th Century Oxbridge," IN Stone I 1974, 247-303. Original.

21. Royce, Josiah, "Present Ideals of American University Life," IN Hawkins 1970, 10-23. SM, 10 (1891), 376-388.

22. Rudy, Willis, "Higher Education in the United States, 1862-1962," IN Brickman 1962, 19-31. Original.

23. Russell, John Dale, "Reflections on 'Reflections,'" IN Smith 1966, 49-55. Original.

Reflections on the dramatic changes in higher education from 1946 (first Annual Conference on Higher Education) to 1966.

24. Slosson, Edwin E., "Great American Universities," IN Hawkins 1970, 60-68. GAU (1938).

25. Smelser, Neil J., "Growth, Structural Change, and Conflict in California Public Higher Education, 1950-1970," IN Smelser 1974, 9-141. Original.

26. Stern, George, "Higher Education in the Mass Society," IN Smith 1964, 112-115. Original.

27. Stewart, Campbell, "The Place of Higher Education in a Changing Society," IN Sanford 1962, 894-939. Original.

28. Stone, Lawrence, "The Size and Composition of the Oxford Student Body 1580-1909," IN Stone I 1974, 3-110. Original.

29. Sullivan, Richard H., "Coordination for the Definition of Goals," IN Dobbins 1968, 197-205. Original.

An historical essay on the relations of the American Council on Education with the federal government.

30. Tead, Ordway, "The History and Philosophy of American Higher Education," IN Burns 1962, 13-27. Original.

31. Turner, R. Stephen, "University Reformers and Professorial Scholarship in Germany 1760-1806," IN Stone II 1974, 495-531. Original.

2
PHILOSOPHY OF POSTSECONDARY EDUCATION

32. Adler, Mortimer J., "The Future of Democracy: A Swan Song," IN Cohen 1964, 30-43. Original.

33. Adler, Mortimer J., "Work, Education, and Leisure," IN Vermilye 1977, 46-54. Original.

34. Bailey, Stephen K., "Education and the Free Self," IN Vermilye 1976, 39-48. POE (1976).

Dr. Bailey suggests that human satisfaction stems from the following: (1) "creating and appreciating beauty, (2) enhancing physical well-being, (3) performing obligations of service, and (4) intensifying intellectual and emotional discovery." This essay shows how education can contribute to the realization of these goals.

35. Beach, Waldo, "Christian Ethical Community as a Norm," IN Averill 1971, 169-185. EMU, 22 (Summer 1967).

36. Bestor, Arthur, "In Defense of Intellectual Integrity," IN Hook 1974, 61-73. Original.

A very strongly presented plea that faculty do not lose sight of the intellectual purpose of the university through a misunderstanding that "the forces that have battered the university represent an irresistible wave of the future . . ."

Commentaries by Robert Nisbet, Oscar Handlin, and Irving Kristol follow on pages 75-91.

37. Bickel, Alexander M., "The Aims of Education and the Proper Standards of the University," IN Seabury 1975, 3-15. Original.

38. Blanshard, Brand, "Democracy and Distinction in American Education," IN McMurrin 1976, 29-49. Original.

39. Blanshard, Brand, "Values: The Polestar of Education," IN Weatherford 1960, 76-98. Original.

40. Borgese, Elisabeth M., "The Universalization of Western Civilization," IN Cohen 1964, 75-86. Original.

41. Bowen, Howard R., "Values, the Dilemmas of Our Time, and Education," IN Vermilye 1977, 22-35. FCDS (1976).

42. Brameld, Theodore, "Wanted: Experimental Centers for the Creation of World Civilization," IN Smith 1961, 30-37. Original.

43. Brewster Jr., Kingman, "New Responsibilities for an Old Generation," IN Dennis 1966, 71-75. Original.

44. Brown, Robert M., "No Promise Without Agony," IN Smith 1969, 265-276. Original.

Violence, power, materialism, and compassion are key terms for Dr. Brown in his analysis of higher education and contemporary society.

45. Callahan, Daniel, "Facts, Values, and Commitments," IN Hodgkinson 1971a, 13-26. Original.

The author is concerned with the supposed distinction between facts and values and how this distinction plays an important part in decision-making concerning contemporary problems that are faced by colleges and universities.

46. Cleveland, Harlan, "Educational Values and National Purposes," IN Dobbins 1963, 8-16. Original.

47. Cohen, Arthur A., "Robert Maynard Hutchins: The Educator as Moralist," IN Cohen 1964, 3-17. Original.

48. Commonger, Barry, "The Dual Crisis in Science and Society," IN Smith 1968, 15-26. Original.

49. Courvoisier, Jaques, "The Quest for Values and Choices," IN Henderson 1968, 147-152. Original.

50. Douglas, William O., "The Society of the Dialogue," IN Cohen 1964, 44-54. Original.

Justice Douglas asserts that "Education is a kind of continuing dialogue . . ." and that a university is a place where the very best people can think of and discuss important issues. This process is extremely important in a free democratic society.

51. Farmer, James, "From Polarization to Pluralism," IN <u>Smith</u> 1969, 59-68. Original.

Mr. Farmer asserts that America must move toward pluralism or it may not survive as a nation.

52. Frankel, Charles, "Epilogue: Reflections on a Worn-out Model," IN <u>Seabury</u> 1975, 279-289. Original.

Professor Frankel suggests that the historical model of the university may no longer meet the social, psychological, and educational needs of the post-1960's.

53. Frankel, Charles, "The Happy Crisis in Higher Education," IN <u>Smith</u> 1961, 3-11. Original.

Professor Frankel sees three critical problem areas in higher education: (1) specialized training without neglecting the broader social issues, (2) maintaining the liberal education tradition, although "essentially aristocratic, within a democratic climate," and (3) managing the tension between "traditional elements in our culture and the scientific elements."

54. Frankl, Viktor E., "The Task of Education in an Age of Meaninglessness," IN <u>Letter</u> 1968, 41-60. Original.

55. Gideonse, Harry D., "The Purpose of Higher Education: A Re-examination," IN <u>Dennis</u> 1966, 23-46. Original.

56. Gilman, Daniel C., "The Idea of a University," IN <u>Portman</u> 1972, 93-109. <u>NAR</u>, 133 (October 1881), 353-367.

57. Greeley, Andrew M., "The Psychedelic and the Sacred," IN <u>Smith</u> 1969, 201-210. Original.

58. Green, Thomas F., "Ironies and Paradoxes," IN <u>Vermilye</u> 1977, 36-45. Original.

Dr. Green presents an excellent essay which attempts to illustrate the conflict between the ways we think of work and its relationship to education.

59. Henderson, Hazel, "A New Economics," IN <u>Vermilye</u> 1977, 227-235. Original.

The author envisions an emerging "countereconomy" in which "selling oneself as a commodity called labor . . . will constitute a much less important fraction of overall productive activity . . ." or, ". . . in other words, this countereconomy is more concerned with labor as self-realization."

60. Herberg, Will, "Biblical Realism as a Norm," IN Averill 1971, 150-167. CR, 36 (December 1953).

Professor Herberg attempts to define the meaning of education in terms "congenial to and spring from Biblical faith . . ."

61. Husain, Zakir, "The Nation-State as a Moral Entity," IN Henderson 1968, 41-48. Original.

Mr. Husain's position is that education prepares for work that, in turn, must be rooted in moral and ethical values.

62. Hutchins, Robert M., "An Appraisal of American Higher Education," IN Brickman 1962, 197-207. Original.

63. Jellema, William W., "Academic Excellence and Moral Value," IN Averill 1971, 137-147. Original.

64. Jessup, Philip C., "International Democracy," IN Cohen 1964, 21-29. Original.

65. Jones, Hardy E., "Academic Freedom as a Moral Right," IN Pincoffs 1972, 37-51. Original.

66. Jones, Howard Mumford, "The Meaning of a University," IN Margolis 1969, 68-77. AtL, 216 (November 1965), 157-160.

67. Keniston, Kenneth, "Commitment Reconstructed," IN Averill 1971, 18-31. Unc (1962), abridged.

Dr. Keniston reviews the need for renewed commitment toward the "goal of human wholeness."

68. Kurtz, Paul, "Excellence and Irrelevance: Democracy and Higher Education," IN Hook 1974, 185-201. Original.

69. Lippmann, Walter, "The University," IN Anderson 1971, 343-350. NR, 154 (May 28, 1966), 17-20.

Mr. Lippmann "expects from academics not only unbiased inquiry but also commitment to a set of values that would continually reshape and redirect knowledge for wise, just, and humane use."

70. Lippmann, Walter, "The University and the Human Condition," IN Dobbins 1968, 233-241. Original.

71. McMurrin, Sterling M., "The Philosophy of Education," IN McMurrin 1976, 1-12. Original.

72. McMurrin, Sterling M., "Reason, Freedom, and the University," IN Kent 1970, 125-138. Original.

73. McMurrin, Sterling M., "The Role of Philosophy in Higher Education," IN Paulsen 1970, 121-136. Original.

74. Martin, Warren B., "Universities and Their Range of Concerns," IN Niblett 1972, 386-397. Original.

75. Mathews, David, "Education and the Future of the Republic," IN Bailey 1977, 215-219. Original.

76. May, Rollo, "Reality Beyond Rationalism," IN Smith 1969, 189-193. Original.

> "The demise of symbol and myth . . . is the surest sign of disunity and trouble."

77. Mayer, Milton, "To Know and to Do," IN Cohen 1964, 206-230. Original.

> Professor Mayer presents a powerful analysis of the moral obligations of an educated person.

78. Mayhew, Lewis B., "Values and the Future," IN Carpenter 1960, 62-78. Original.

79. Niblett, W. R. and Kay Pole, "Objectives in Higher Education," IN Butcher 1972, 35-44. Original.

80. Outler, Albert C., "Discursive Truth and Evangelical Truth," IN Averill 1971, 102-106. Original.

> Professor Outler insists that there are two dimensions of truth; "truth about structure" and "truth about meaning." "Only when both are fully affirmed can it finally be said that 'colleges and universities exist for the pursuit of truth.'"

81. Pippard, A. B., "The Structure of a Morally Committed University," IN Lawlor 1972, 69-87. Original.

82. Pollard, William G., "Natural Order and Transcendent Order," IN Averill 1971, 108-117. RATU (1964).

83. Rozek, Edward J., "Education and a Free Society," IN Hook 1974, 125-131. Original.

84. Schumacher, E. F., "Good Work," IN Vermilye 1977, 55-64. Original.

> A strong condemnation of current higher education as a means of preparing for the world of work, especially a higher education dominated by ". . . the metaphysics of materialistic scientism and the doctrine of mindless evolution."

85. Seaborg, Glenn T., "Education for the Third Revolution," IN Smith 1963, 3-12. Original.

Mr. Seaborg believes that to make sound judgements concerning higher education, we must first understand the nature and forces that shape our world. With this in mind, he suggests two primary objectives for higher education: (1) "expand and accelerate the process of creative evolution" and (2) maintain the "concept of the individual as the focus of human values."

86. Shiflett, James A., "Soul," IN Smith 1969, 194-200. Original.

Mr. Shiflett discusses three new forms of communication: "Happening," "Living Theater," and "Soul." Soul is an experience of ". . . what it means to be whole . . ."

87. Shoben, Edward J., "Thoughts on the Decay of Morals," IN Smith 1968, 134-143. Original.

88. Smith, Huston, "Objectivity vs. Commitment," IN Averill 1971, 34-59. POHE (1955).

The pursuit of scientific objectivity and neutrality helps to explain the philosophy of 'pluralism' which, when applied to higher education institutions, may help to explain why some of our universities are so "non-descript."

89. Smith, Huston, "Values: Academic and Human," IN Carpenter 1960, 1-22. Original.

90. Stassen, Glen, "Amnesty and Fairness: The Power to Educate and the Duty to Dissent," IN Robertson 1978, 107-133. Original.

The author uses the vehicle of amnesty for Vietnam war deserters to illustrate the moral obligation of educational institutions to "challenge the nation's conscience."

91. Travelstead, Chester C., "Excellence: The Evolution of a Concept," IN Paulsen 1970, 41-50. Original.

92. Trow, Martin, "Conceptions of the University: The Case of Berkeley," IN Kruytbosch 1970, 27-44. ABS, 11 (May-June 1968), 14-21.

Dr. Trow uses the student disturbances at Berkeley as a vehicle toward an understanding of the basic character and mission of a university and its various forms of authority and governance.

93. Turnbull, William W., "Dimensions of Quality in Higher Education," IN Furniss 1971, 126-136. Original.

Commentaries by Edward J. Bloustein, Elias Blake, Jr., Vivian W. Henderson, and Frank G. Dickey follow on pages 136-147.

94. Tyson Jr., Ruel W., "Confusions of Culture," IN Hodgkinson 1971a, 27-48. Original.

This essay deals with the historical, philosophical, and psychological bases of the conflict between college students and the values of contemporary society.

95. Veblen, Thorstein, "The Higher Learning in America," IN Hawkins 1970, 46-53. HLIA (1957).

96. Walsh, William, "Education for Life," IN Lawlor 1972, 133-142. Original.

An essay on the place, purpose, and product of higher education.

97. Whitehead, Alfred N., "Universities and Their Functions," IN Margolis 1969, 118-129. AOE (1959).

98. Williams, John D., "The Right to Know," IN Mauer 1976, 139-146. Original.

The author presents a strong endorsement of the proven achievements of higher education and defends its basic purpose against "false prophets and uninformed adversaries."

99. Wilson, O. Meredith, "Our First Priority: A Credible Ethic," IN Harcleroad 1970, 13-25. Original.

100. Wirth, Arthur G., "The Philosophical Split," IN Vermilye 1977, 12-21. Original.

The relationship between education and work, as viewed by Mr. Wirth, relates to broad philosophical issues concerning the type of society we want. The alternative is between a society based on "the unfettered pursuit of profits" or a society based on a "set of values concerned with the wholeness of persons and selfrealization."

101. Yost Jr., Henry T., "Redefining the Ethics of Academia," IN Smith 1967, 21-25. Original.

3
SOCIOLOGY OF POSTSECONDARY EDUCATION

102. Adolfson, L. H. "The Role of Higher Education in Pervasive and Intensifying Urbanization," IN Smith 1963, 120-123. Original.

103. Aiken, Henry D., "How Late Is It?" IN Minter 1969, 23-45. Original.

An extremely interesting reflection on the nature and structure of the university and how it has responded to sometimes conflicting social and educational functions.

104. Aldrich Jr., Daniel G., "University Services in the Face of Conflicting Societal Pressure on Institutions of Higher Education," IN Smith 1966, 126-128. Original.

105. Arnstein, George E., "Feasibility Study on a Computer-Based Manpower and Talent Clearning House (MATCH)," IN Smith 1966, 211-213. Original.

106. Bailey, Duncan and Charles Schotta, "Does Undergraduate Education Really Pay Off for Society?" IN Hamelman 1972, 123-139. Original.

107. Bailey, Stephen K., "International Responsibilities of the Modern University," IN Shiver 1967, 1-9. Original.

108. Baldridge, J. Victor, David V. Curtis, George P. Ecker, and Gary L. Riley, "Diversity in Higher Education: Professional Autonomy," IN Riley 1977, 42-63. Original.

109. Bebout, John E., "Higher Education as a Leader in the Urban Setting," IN Smith 1967, 207-210. Original.

110. Berdie, Ralph F., "Group Membership and Higher Education," IN Brown 1960, 85-90. Original.

A review of social group incentive to attend college.

111. Berdie, Ralph F., "A University is a Many-Faceted Thing," IN Feldman 1972, 165-176. PGJ, 45 (April 1967), 768-775.

Applies the College and University Environment Scales to measure the prevailing campus "atmosphere" as perceived by students.

112. Bereday, George Z. F., "College and Non-College--The Changing Social Values of Education," IN Kertesz 1971, 111-122. Original.

113. Berle Jr., Adolf A., "The Irrepressible Issues of the 60s." IN Smith 1960, 3-8. Original.

Professor Berle believes that 1960 marks the end of an era and the beginning of another which will bring great economic and social pressures to bear on our institutions, especially colleges and universities.

114. Bolton, Charles D. and Kenneth C. W. Kammeyer, "Campus Cultures, Role Orientations and Social Types," IN Feldman 1972, 377-391. US (1967).

115. Boulding, Kenneth E., "The Spotted Reality: The Fragmentation, Isolation, and Conflict in Today's World," IN Smith 1966, 7-16. Original.

116. Boulding, Kenneth E., "The University as an Economic and Social Unit," IN Minter 1968, 75-87. Original.

117. Bowman, Mary Jean, "Selective Remarks and Some Dicta," IN Solmon 1973, 381-391. Original.

The author presents comments on the noncognitive effects of education, higher education in a career perspective, earnings expectations as distributions, and critical comments on the literature of the "costs and benefits" of higher education.

118. Brademas, John, "The University in the 1970's," IN Kertesz 1971, 63-70. Original.

119. Braden, Thomas W., "Pressures on Higher Education," IN Smith 1965, 17-22. Original.

120. Brandl, John E., "Public Service Outputs of Higher Education: An Exploratory Essay," IN Lawrence 1970, 85-91. Original.

121. Brazer, Harvey E. and Martin David, "Social and Economic Determinants of the Demand for Education," IN Mushkin 1962, 21-42. Original.

122. Bridgeman, D. S., "Problems in Estimating the Monetary Value of College Education," IN Harris 1960, 180-184. Original.

123. Bristow, Thelma, "Bibliographic Review of the Literature on Higher Education," IN Holmes 1971, 384-401. Original.

The bibliography includes items published since 1960 generally in the area of the social forces effecting higher education worldwide.

124. Brubacher, John S., "The Autonomy of the University--How Independent Is the Republic of Scholars?" IN Margolis 1969, 84-100. JHE, 38 (May 1967), 237-249.

125. Brubacher, John S., "The Leadership Role of Higher Education in Effecting Basic Societal Change," IN Smith 1966, 60-67. Original.

126. Capelle, Jean, "Mass Education and Quality University," IN Henderson 1968, 59-64. Original.

127. Cerych, Ladislav and Dorotea E. Furth, "On the Threshold of Mass Higher Education," IN Niblett 1972, 14-28. Original.

The direction and characteristics of universal mass higher education on a worldwide basis.

128. Clark, Burton R., "The Culture of the College: Its Implications for the Organization of Learning Resources," IN Bergen 1966, 7-19. Original.

129. Clark, Burton R., "The New University," IN Kruytbosch 1970, 17-26. ABS, 11 (May-June 1968), 1-5.

The author examines the changing social structure of the university and the ideologies of university administrators and faculties that are responsible for the nature of change that is underway.

130. Clark, Kenneth B., "Intelligence, the University and Society," IN Margolis 1969, 234-244. Amer S, 36 (Winter 1966-67), 23-32.

Professor Clark wants to effect some changes in the modern university so that it may assume a position of moral leadership, which he believes has been lost by the decline of organized religion.

131. Clark, Kenneth E., "A Slightly Different Approach," IN Solmon 1973, 317-320. Original.

Professor Clark believes that the "costs and benefits" of higher education should be viewed by its effects on the entire society.

132. Coffin Jr., William Sloane, "The University and the Social Order: A Problem of Ineffectiveness," IN Smith 1964, 86-90. Original.

133. Coleman, James S., "Peer Cultures and Education in Modern Society," IN Newcomb 1966, 244-269. Original.

134. Coleman, James S., "The University and Society's New Demands Upon It," IN Kaysen 1973, 359-399. Original.

135. Collins, LeRoy, "Higher Education in an Age of Revolutions," IN Smith 1962, 3-9. Original.

136. Corson, John J., "Public Service and Higher Education: Compatibility or Conflict?" IN Dobbins 1968, 83-90. Original.

Commentaries by Edward D. Re, Albert N. Whiting, Roger Lehecka, and Harold W. Chase follow on pages 91-102.

137. Cosand, Joseph P., "Setting National Goals and Objectives: Postsecondary Education," IN Hughes 1975a, 28-39. Original.

Commentaries by Laura Bornholdt, Bennett Katz, and Steven Muller follow on pages 40-50.

138. Dahrendorf, Ralf, "The Educational Class," IN Seabury 1975, 47-57. Original.

139. Daniere, Andre, "Social Class Competition in American Higher Education," IN McLeod 1973, 145-159. Original.

140. Davis, Bertram H., "Academic Freedom, Academic Neutrality, and the Social System," IN Pincoffs 1972, 27-36. Original.

141. Davis, Harry R., "Institutional Commitment: A Social Scientist's View," IN Averill 1971, 61-72. Original.

142. der Ryn, Sim Van, "Building a People's Park," IN Smith 1970, 54-71. Original.

The author is critical of the "liberal bureaucracy" who do not seem to be working toward a society built on the "ideals of the Christian-democratic tradition."

143. Drucker, Peter F., "American Higher Education: Cornerstone of Free World Unity," IN Smith 1960, 17-23. Original.

Mr. Drucker believes that "American higher education is rapidly becoming the basic resource of the free world" and attempts to assess the impact of that responsibility on colleges and their faculties and students.

144. Eckland, Bruce K., "Academic Ability, Higher Education, and Occupational Mobility," IN Yamamoto 1968, 427-442. ASR, 30 (October 1965), 735-746.

145. Eddy Jr., Edward D., "The Possible and the Potential," IN Yamamoto 1968, 395-400. CISC (1959).

A sociological inquiry into the conditions that support excellence on a college campus.

146. Ehrlich, Isaac, "On the Relation Between Education and Crime," IN Juster 1975, 313-337. Original.

147. Eliot II, Charles W., "The Implications for Higher Education of the Growing Urbanization and Industrialization of American Society," IN Smith 1961, 201-202. Original.

148. Ellison, Anne and Bennett Simon, "Does College Make a Person Healthy and Wise? A Social-Psychiatric Overview of Research in Higher Education," IN Solmon 1973, 35-63. Original.

149. Esnault, Eric and Jean Le Pas, "New Relations Between Postsecondary Education and Employment," IN OECD 1974a, 105-169. Original.

150. Finch, Robert H., "Challenge and Response in the American Educational Environment," IN Nichols 1970, 299-304. Original.

Mr. Finch states what he believes are the ". . . parameters of the social environment in which the institutional response will take place." He goes on to explain what tasks educational institutions can and should undertake.

151. Fisk, Milton, "Academic Freedom in Class Society," IN Pincoffs 1972, 5-26. Original.

152. Frankel, Charles, "The Educational Impact of American Foreign Policy," IN Smith 1968, 52-63. Original.

153. Frantzreb, Arthur C., "Pressures of Necessity," IN Smith 1966, 145-148. Original.

The author provides his views concerning the main sources of "societal pressures" on institutions of higher education.

154. Freedman, Mervin B., "San Francisco State: Urban Campus Prototype," IN Smith 1969, 82-90. Original.

155. Freeman, Richard B., "On Mythical Effects of Public Subsidization of Higher Education: Social Benefits and Regressive Income Redistribution," IN Solmon 1973, 321-328. Original.

156. Fulbright, J. W., "Higher Education and the Crisis in Asia," IN Smith 1966, 24-30. Original.

157. Gallagher, Buell G., "Mandate for Change," IN Smith 1970, 5-15. Original.

The author relates how the fundamental problems of society are reflected in the difficulties faced by the modern university.

158. Gallagher, Buell G., "Pressures, Priorities, and Progress," IN Smith 1965, 55-62. Original.

President Gallagher addresses his basic concern for higher education by response to the following question: "Can heuristic controversy successfully contain the destructive forces of the eristic, or will the eristic pressures of our time reduce the campus to a brutal struggle for power?"

159. Gallagher, Buell G., "The Vanguard of the Dysphoric Generation," IN Dennis 1966, 368-371. Original.

An historical overview of changes in campus morals.

160. Gambino, Richard, "The Ethnic Revolution and Public Policy," IN Hook 1974, 203-224. Original.

161. Gamson, Zelda F., "Michigan Muddles Through: Luck, Nimbleness, and Resilience in Crisis," IN Riesman 1973, 173-197. Original.

162. Gardner, John W., "Agenda for the Colleges and Universities," IN Eurich 1968, 1-8. JHE, 36 (October 1965), 359-365.

163. Gardner, John W., "The Individual and Society," IN McMurrin 1976, 51-62. Original.

Mr. Gardner discusses the problem of modern man in balancing the claims of individuality with those of community.

164. Gerstl, Joel E., "Leisure, Taste and Occupational Milieu," IN Anderson 1971, 155-173. Soc P, 9 (Summer 1961), 56-68.

165. Grambsch, Paul V., "Conflicts and Priorities," IN Smith 1970, 101-107. Original.

An analysis of four controversies basic to higher education: (1) admissions policy, (2) education vs. training, (3) teaching vs. research, and (4) service to society.

166. Graubard, Stephen R., "The Contemporary University," IN Yamamoto 1968, 29-35. Dae, 93 (Fall 1964), 1027-1032.

167. Green, Robert L., "Urban America and Crucial Issues Facing Higher Education," IN Johnson 1974, 191-214. Original.

168. Grennan, Sister Jacqueline, "The Ecumenical World of Search," IN Dennis 1966, 381-384. Original.

A discussion of the recent "moral revolution" in higher education.

169. Haber, William, "Authority and the Use of Power," IN Kertesz 1971, 52-62. Original.

Mr. Haber reviews some of the important contemporary events that have impacted most heavily on the university.

170. Hamilton, Thomas H., "The Nature and Scope of American Higher Education," IN Burns 1962, 1-12. Original.

171. Hansen, W. Lee, "On External Benefits and Who Should Foot the Bill," IN Solmon 1973, 329-333. Original.

172. Harbinson, Federick, "Development and Utilization of Human Resources: Building a System for Assistance Activities," IN Shiver 1967, 44-57. Original.

An essay on how American universities can assist in foreign policy as relates to training and assistance in manpower projects.

Commentary by Royden C. Dangerfield follows on pages 63-66.

173. Harcleroad, Fred F., "The Relationship of New Technology to the Dehumanization of Education," IN Smith 1966, 98-101. Original.

174. Harrington, Michael, "The University and the Problem of Poverty," IN Smith 1968, 43-51. Original.

175. Harris, Norman C., "What Will be the Demands for Highly Trained Manpower and What Changes Will be Needed in Policies and Programs?" IN Smith 1962, 110-113. Original.

An expanded discussion on manpower needs follows on pages 114-124.

176. Harris, Seymour E., "General Problems in Education and Manpower," IN Harris 1964, 11-95. Original.

177. Hauser, Robert M. "Socioeconomic Background and Differential Returns to Education," IN Solmon 1973, 129-145. Original.

178. Hesburgh, Theodore M., "Legislating Attitudes," IN Hughes 1975a, 246-251. Original.

Father Hesburgh presents a compelling defense for the elimination of structural inequalities through strong legislation.

Commentaries by David B. Frohnmayer, Ruby G. Martin, and Anita Hughes follow on pages 252-266.

179. Hester, James M., "Urbanization and Higher Education," IN Smith 1966, 88-92. Original.

180. Hickman, C. Addison, "Internal Implications of Affluence in Higher Education," IN Smith 1966, 102-105. Original.

The author discusses the impact of affluence "upon goals, values, and attitudes" of various institutions of higher education and the students and faculty within these schools.

181. Hoagland, Hudson, "Mechanisms of Population Control," IN Mayhew 1967, 69-85. Dae, 93 (Summer 1964), 812-829.

182. Hochbaum, Jerry, "Structure and Process in Higher Education," IN Feldman 1972, 5-15. CU, 43 (Spring 1968), 190-202.

A proposed sociological model for the study of higher education.

183. Hodgkinson, Harold L., "The Next Decade," IN Hodgkinson 1971, 139-152. Original.

A critical appraisal of the way social institutions may change in the 1970's and how this change will relate to management of institutions of higher education.

184. Hoggart, Richard, "Higher Education and Personal Life-Changing Attitudes," IN Niblett 1970, 211-230. Original.

Commentary by Edward J. Shoben, Jr. follows on pages 231-242.

185. Holmes, Brian, "Universities, Higher Education and Society," IN Holmes 1971, 1-12. Original.

186. Holmstrom, Engin I., "Higher Education and Social Mobility," IN Vermilye 1976, 148-154. Original.

187. Idzerda, Stanley J., "Building Community in a Pluralistic Society," IN Smith 1969, 39-44. Original.

188. "International Security--The Military Aspect," IN Mayhew 1967, 87-93. PFA (1961).

189. Jackson, Henry M., "Ecological Crisis," IN Smith 1970, 29-36. Original.

190. Jencks, Christopher, "Social Stratification and Higher Education," IN Orwig 1971, 71-111. HER, 38 (Spring 1968), 277-316.

191. Johnson, Harry G., "The University and the Social Welfare: A Taxonomic Exercise," IN Lumsden 1974, 21-49. Original.

192. Juster, F. Thomas, "Education, Income and Human Behavior: Introduction and Summary," IN Juster 1975, 1-43. Original.

193. Kaiser, Edgar F., "Problems as Opportunities," IN Connery 1970, 137-146. Original.

The author reviews some of the major problems facing America in the 1970's and the ways in which these difficulties are reflected in higher education.

194. Kalz, Joseph, "Societal Expectations and Influences," IN Dennis, 1966, 137-140. Original.

195. Kaysen, Carl, "New Directions for Research," IN Solmon 1973, 147-150. Original.

Review of research on the measurement of economic benefits of higher education.

196. Kaysen, Carl, "Setting National Goals for Higher Education: What is College For?" IN Hughes 1975a, 15-27. Original.

Commentaries by Laura Bornholdt, Bennett Katz, and Steven Muller follow on pages 40-50.

197. Keeton, Morris, "The Disenfranchised on Campus," IN Smith 1970, 113-121. Original.

Professor Keeton asserts that current feelings of "pervasive disenfranchisement" among various campus groups can be changed by: (1) realignment of authority among constituent groups, (2) opening new routes of communication, and (3) fostering collaboration through "differentiation of structures and processes."

198. Keniston, Kenneth, "Responsibility for Criticism and Social Change," IN Dobbins 1968, 145-163. Original.

Commentaries by Frederic W. Ness, Paul Danish, and Neil O. Davis follow on pages 164-174.

199. Kerr, Clark, "The Frantic Race to Remain Contemporary," IN Morison 1966, 19-38. Dae, 93 (Fall 1964), 1051-1070.

200. Kerr, Clark, "The Frantic Race to Remain Contemporary," IN Yamamoto 1968, 14-28. Dae, 93 (Fall 1964), 1051-1070.

201. Kerr, Clark, "The Moods of Academia," IN Hughes 1975a, 267-275. Original.

202. Kreps, Juanita M., "Learning and Earning," IN Vermilye 1976, 155-160. Original.

203. Lerner, Abba, "Reflections on the Agonies of the University," IN Hook 1974, 233-237. Original.

This essay outlines the public policy issues that have developed as a consequence of student unrest in the late-1960's and the resulting turmoil within many institutions of higher learning.

204. Lerner, Max, "The Revolutionary Frame of Our Time," IN Dennis 1966, 8-22. Original.

205. Levin, Henry M., "What Are the Returns on a College Education?" IN Peltason 1978, 183-192. Original.

206. Lichtman, Richard, "The University: Mask for Privilege?" IN Margolis 1969, 212-233. Cen Mag, 1 (January 1968), 2-10.

Dr. Lichtman is critical of higher education for not challenging ". . . the student to change the world by giving him a vision of what it might become, but rather to help him understand, accept and adjust to the world as it is."

207. Liveright, A. A., "The Impact of the Emerging City," IN Yamamoto 1968, 482-488. ECHAE (1963).

An analysis of the social and economic forces that effect urban institutions of higher education.

208. Lowenthal, Richard, "The University's Autonomy Versus Social Priorities," IN Seabury 1975, 75-84. Original.

209. Lyman, Richard W., "The Search for Alternatives," IN Hughes 1975, 323-331. Original.

Mr. Lyman suggests several broad responses to the continuing pressure on institutions of higher education to meet sometimes conflicting public demands.

210. Machlup, Fritz, "Perspectives on the Benefits of Postsecondary Education," IN Solmon 1973, 353-363. Original.

211. McConnell, T. R., "Surfeit or Death of Highly Educated People?" IN McMurrin 1976, 63-80. Original.

A review of the social and economic benefits of a college degree, with special emphasis on Great Britain.

212. McHenry, Dean E., "Institutions of Higher Education in the USA--Some Recent Developments," IN Niblett 1970, 123-130. Original.

Commentary by Edward Sheffield follows on pages 131-138.

213. Maeda, Yoichi, "The Problems of Cultural Assimilation," IN Henderson 1968, 153-158. Original.

214. Mallery, David, "Society and the Campus," IN Dennis 1966, 131-136. Original.

215. Mayhew, Lewis B., "American Higher Education and Social Change," IN Mayhew 1967, 3-10. Original.

216. Meyer, John W., "The Effects of the Institutionalization of Colleges in Society," IN Feldman 1972, 109-126. Original.

217. Michael, Robert T., "Education and Consumption," IN Juster 1975, 235-252. Original.

218. Michael, Robert T., "Education and Fertility," IN Juster 1975, 339-364. Original.

219. Miller, Herman P., "Income and Education: Does Education Pay Off?" IN Mushkin 1962, 129-146. Original.

220. Millett, John D., "Value Patterns and Power Conflict in American Higher Education," IN Minter 1969, 1-20. Original.

221. Moynihan, Daniel P., "The Impact on Manpower Development and Employment of Youth," IN McGrath 1966, 65-103. Original.

222. Mundel, David S., "Whose Education Should Society Support? The Appropriate and Effective Bases for Social Support for and Intervention in Undergraduate Education," IN Solmon 1973, 293-315. Original.

223. Nader, Ralph, "Environmental Control," IN Smith 1970, 16-28. Original.

Mr. Nader links environmental problems with violence and tyranny in contemporary society.

224. Nelson, Charles A., "Quantity and Quality in Higher Education," IN Goldwin 1967, 155-185. Original.

The author discusses the "scale of commitments" to higher education in America and the changes that are taking place in response to those commitments.

225. Newcomb, Theodore M., "Administering Studies Among Campus Cultures," IN Lunsford 1963a, 81-94. Original.

226. Nichols, David C., "The Coming of Crisis," IN Nichols 1970, 3-9. Original.

The author outlines several issues that he believes are contributing to a coming crisis in American higher education.

227. O'Neil, Robert M., "Autonomy and Mythology: The Need for Neutral Principles," IN Furniss 1974, 309-324. Original.

Commentary by Bernice Sandler follows on pages 324-327.

228. Osman, John, "The Bias of Urbanization," IN Smith 1963, 116-120. Original.

An excellent overview of the trend toward urbanization and its effect on and reaction by institutions of higher education.

229. O'Toole, James, "Education, Work, and Quality of Life," IN Vermilye 1974, 12-21. Original.

230. Oxtoby, Marie, "The Impact of Higher Education: Socialization and Role-Learning," IN Butcher 1971, 198-210. Original.

231. Pace, C. Robert, "Evaluating the Total Climate or Profile of a Campus," IN Smith 1961, 171-175. Original.

232. Pace, C. Robert, "Interactions Among Academic, Administrative, and Student Subcultures," IN Lunsford 1963a, 55-80. Original.

233. Pace, C. Robert, "Methods of Describing College Culture," IN Yamamoto 1968, 193-205. TCR, 63 (January 1962), 267-277.

234. Park, Rosemary, "Higher Education in California: An Irenic View," IN Smelser 1974, 251-263. Original.

An analysis of the environment in which the modern university exists and how stress from this environment effects internal structures and goals.

235. Parsons, Talcott, "The University 'Bundle': A Study of the Balance Between Differentiation and Integration," IN Smelser 1974, 275-299. Original.

236. Perkins, James A., "The New Conditions of Autonomy," IN Wilson 1965, 8-17. Original.

The author reviews new and developing relationships between society and institutions of higher learning and suggests ways in which these relationships could affect college and university independence.

237. Piel, Gerard, "Consumers of Abundance," IN Mayhew 1967, 43-56. SCM (1961).

The author provides a very interesting analysis of the possible effect on property and work of advances in science and technology.

238. Pinnock, Theo. James, "Human Resources Development--An Emerging Role for Black Professionals in Higher Education," IN Johnson 1974, 301-314. Original.

239. Pitkin, Royce S., "Should Colleges Reflect or Help Change Value Systems of Society?" IN Smith 1960, 213-215. Original.

240. Pusey, Nathan M., "Utility and the American University," IN Yamamoto 1968, 7-13. AS (1963).

241. Ramsay, William R., "Students as Manpower," IN Keene 1975, 89-101. Original.

This essay deals with the economic, social, and educational impacts of part-time working students.

242. Rawlings, V. Lane and Lloyd Ulman, "The Utilization of College-Trained Manpower in the United States," IN Gordon 1974, 195-235. Original.

243. Reder, Melvin W., "Elitism and Opportunity in U.S. Higher Education," IN Gordon 1974, 419-425. Original.

244. Rees, Mina, "The Ivory Tower and the Marketplace," IN McMurrin 1976, 81-101. Original.

245. Renshaw, Jean R., "The Company and the Family," IN Vermilye 1977, 206-217. Original.

An extremely interesting essay on the problems and strains between work demands and family responsibilities.

246. Rice, James G., "The Campus Climate: A Reminder," IN Baskin 1965, 304-317. Original.

247. Riddick, Ed, "A Race With Disaster," IN Smith 1971, 221-226. Original.

Empasizes the direct role higher education can play in changing society.

248. Riesman, David and Christopher Jencks, "The Viability of the American College," IN Sanford 1962, 74-197. Original.

249. Rorty, Amélie O., "Dilemmas of Academic and Intellectual Freedom," IN Pincoffs 1972, 97-110. Original.

250. Rosaz, Theodore, "The Complacencies of the Academy: 1967," IN Margolis 1969, 245-270. NAW, 1 (September 1967), 82-107.

Mr. Rosaz wants to see the American university accept anew its responsibility to society which, he believes, was lost during the crisis of the 1960's.

251. Rosen, Leo, "Myths by Which We Live," IN Smith 1965, 8-16. Original.

A lively review of some prevailing myths (e.g., crime does not pay) and how they reflect on the development of a rational life style.

252. Rossman, Michael, "Learning and Social Change--The Problem of Authority," IN Runkel 1969, 20-32. Original.

253. Sanders, Irwin T., "The University as a Community," IN Perkins 1973, 57-78. Original.

254. Sanford, Nevitt, "Aims of College Education," IN Havice 1971, 10-25. Original.

255. Sanford, Nevitt, "The Contribution of Higher Education to the Life of Society," IN Niblett 1970, 7-20. Original.

Commentary by Bryan Wilson follows on pages 21-33.

256. Sanford, Nevitt, "The Development of Social Responsibility Through the College Experience," IN McGrath 1966a, 22-37. Original.

257. Sanford, Nevitt, "Higher Education as a Social Problem," IN Sanford 1962, 10-30. Original.

258. Sanford, Nevitt, "Loss of Talent," IN Harcleroad 1970, 56-67. Original.

Dr. Sanford is concerned with the human element of this manpower problem and how colleges and universities can contribute to individual needs within broad social goals.

Commentaries by Nevitt Sanford, Donald P. Hoyt, Leonard L. Baird, and Lyle D. Edmison follow on pages 67-68.

259. Schary, Dore, "The Creative Spirit and the Free Society," IN Smith 1960, 24-31. Original.

260. Scherer, Jacqueline, "Changes Influencing the Development of Higher Education in the U.S.A.," IN Holmes 1971, 227-237. Original.

261. Schwartz, Edward, "Toward a Theory of Off-Campus Action," IN Smith 1966, 242-245. Original.

This essay suggests that the "end of education must be to create a class of interested human beings." In turn, it is the responsibility of these individuals to turn this interest into creative solutions to societal problems.

262. Selvin, Hanan C. and Warren O. Hagstrom, "The Empirical Classification of Formal Groups," IN Newcomb 1966, 162-189. ASR, 28 (June 1963), 399-411.

263. Shea, F. X., "Sectarian and Religious Pressures on the University," IN Smith 1965, 97-101. Original.

264. Sherburne, Philip, "Before the Doctor Comes: Conditions of Stress on the Campus," IN Dennis 1966, 342-348. Original.

265. Shils, Edward, "The Academic Ethos Under Strain," IN Seabury 1975, 16-46. Original.

266. Shoben Jr., Edward J., "To Disenthrall Ourselves," IN Milton 1968, 196-212. Original.

The author outlines four reasons for the current pessimism concerning the role of colleges and universities in the United States.

267. Shoben Jr., Edward J., "University and Society," IN Hodgkinson 1971a, 49-74. Original.

268. Siepmann, Charles A., "What Should be the Role of Higher Education in Social Criticism of the Mass Media?" IN Smith 1960, 216-219. Original.

269. Silberman, Charles E., "The Remaking of American Education," IN Smith 1971, 227-233. Original.

270. Smelser, Neil J., "Berkeley in Crisis and Change," IN Riesman 1973, 51-69. Original.

271. Smith, Robert, "San Francisco State Experience," IN Smith 1969, 91-99. Original.

272. Solmon, Lewis C., "The Definition and Impact of College Quality," IN Solmon 1973, 77-105. Original.

The author uses student and instructional quality as features of colleges "that might yield financial payoffs . . . in later life and then testing to see which . . . do add most to the explanatory power of the traditional earnings function."

273. Solmon, Lewis C., "The Relationship Between Schooling and Saving Behavior: An Example of the Indirect Effects of Education," IN Juster 1975, 253-293. Original.

274. Stadtman, Verne A., "Constellations in a Nebulous Galaxy," IN Riesman 1973, 1-11. Original.

The author outlines four broad issues that have dramatically affected many institutions of higher education during the period 1964-1971: (1) students rights issue, (2) war in Vietnam, (3) extending greater opportunities for higher education, and (4) student participation in campus decision making.

275. Stern, Barry and Fred Best, "Cyclic Life Patterns," IN Vermilye 1977, 250-267. Original.

A very interesting sociological analysis of what the authors describe as a "linear life plan," which involves a pattern of education, work, and leisure.

276. Stern, George G., "The Intellectual Climate in College Environments," IN Yamamoto 1968, 205-227. HER, 33 (Winter 1963), 5-41.

277. Taubman, Paul and Terence Wales, "Education as an Investment and a Screening Device," IN Juster 1975, 95-121. Original.

278. Taylor, Harold, "The American Idea," IN Smith 1960, 43-46. Original.

Mr. Taylor states that contemporary American society suffers from a lack of purpose and an overconcern with security, also that debates about education "reflect the aimlessness of our national policy."

279. Taylor, Harold, "Freedom and Authority on the Campus," IN Sanford 1962, 774-804. Original.

280. Taylor, Stuart A., "All In All--Is It Worth It?" IN Peltason 1978, 192-201. Original.

An assessment of the labor market potential for college graduates in the 1970's.

281. Thurow, Lester C., "Measuring the Economic Benefits of Education," IN Gordon 1974, 373-418. Original.

282. Trow, Martin A., "Administrative Implications of Analyses of Campus Cultures," IN Lunsford 1963a, 95-111. Original.

283. Trow, Martin, "Bell, Book and Berkeley," IN Kruytbosch 1970, 295-308. ABS, 11 (May-June 1968), 43-48.

A penetrating review of Daniel Bell's The Reforming of General Education along with a report on education at Berkeley titled Education at Berkeley. Taken together these reports shed light on the differences in institutional perspectives and how these differences are reflected in policy.

284. Trow, Martin, "The Campus Viewed as a Culture," IN Sprague 1960, 105-123. SCPG (1961).

285. Trow, Martin, "Elite and Popular Function in American Higher Education," IN Niblett 1970, 181-201. Original.

Commentary by Ben Morris follows on pages 202-210.

286. Tyler, Ralph W., "The Study of Campus Cultures," IN Lunsford 1963a, 1-10. Original.

287. Wachtel, Paul, "The Returns to Investment in Higher Education: Another View," IN Juster 1975, 151-170. Original.

288. Wescoe, W. Clarke, "Higher Education and Moral Responsibility," IN Dennis 1966, 377-380. Original.

289. Wilcox, Wayne, "The University in the United States of America," IN Stephens 1975, 34-50. Original.

290. Wilson, Joseph C., "Technology and Society," IN Connery 1970, 158-165. Original.

291. Wilson, Logan, "Form and Function in American Higher Education," IN Wilson 1965, 29-37. ER, 45 (April 1964), 299-307.

292. Wilson, Logan, "Myths and Realities of Institutional Independence," IN Wilson 1965, 18-28. Original.

293. Wilson, Logan, "The New Orthodoxies in Higher Education," IN Wilson 1972, 319-324. ER, 53 (Spring 1972), 157-160.

A list of policies, many developed in reaction to the student movement of the 1960's, that Dr. Wilson feels are designed to fetter institutional independence.

294. Wingfield, Clyde J., "Campus Conflict and Institutional Maintenance," IN Wingfield 1970, 3-18. Original.

295. Wise, W. Max, "Changing Societal Values and Their Implications for Students and Institutional Values," IN Smith 1966, 118-121. Original.

296. Wolfe, Dael, "Economies and Educational Values," IN Harris 1960, 178-179. Original.

A short overview of the rate-of-return on a college education.

297. Wolfe, Dael, "To What Extent Do Monetary Returns to Education Vary with Family Background, Mental Ability, and School Quality?" IN Solmon 1973, 65-74. Original.

298. Wright, Stephen J., "Institutional Expectations and Influences," IN Dennis 1966, 123-125. Original.

The author discusses the assumptions which form the foundation for a college's influences over the learning environment.

299. Zinn, Howard, "The Case for Radical Change," IN Goodall 1976, 278-288. SR, 52 (October 18, 1969), 81-82;94-95.

The author recommends that universities should take an active social role in helping to eliminate war, poverty, etc.

4
ECONOMICS OF POSTSECONDARY EDUCATION

300. Adkins, Douglas L., "The American Educated Labor Force: An Empirical Look at Theories of Its Formation and Composition," IN Gordon 1974, 111-145. Original.

301. Alexander, David, "Current Issues in Fund Raising," IN Hughes 1975, 87-97. Original.

302. Alstyne, Carol Van, "Higher Education Among National Budget Priorities," IN Vermilye 1975, 191-202. Original.

303. Alstyne, Carol Van, "Tuition: Analysis of Recent Policy Recommendations," IN Young 1974, 35-103. Original.

304. "An Aggerate View of College Financing," IN Goodall 1976, 192-200. WPWB (1973).

305. Andrews, F. Emerson, "Foundation Influence on Education," IN Perkins 1972, 109-119. ER, 53 (Winter 1972), 23-29.

306. Archibald, G. C., "On the Measurement of Inputs and Outputs in Higher Education," IN Lumsden 1974, 113-130. Original.

307. Arrow, Kenneth J., "Higher Education as a Filter," IN Lumsden 1974, 51-74. Original.

> Professor Arrow develops a model of the economic role of higher education divergent from the common assumptions in human capital theory.

308. Attiyeh, Richard and Keith G. Lumsden, "Educational Production and Human Capital Formation," IN Lumsden 1974, 131-145. Original.

309. Auburn, Norman P., "Tax Support," IN Connery 1970, 94-107. Original.

310. Balderston, F. E., "Financing California's System of Postsecondary Education," IN Smelser 1974, 143-159. Original.

311. Balderston, Frederick E., "Varieties of Financial Crisis," IN Wilson 1972, 87-106. Original.

Commentaries by Joseph A. Kershaw, Herman H. Long, and Peggy Heim follow on pages 106-114.

312. Bates, George E., "Difficulties in Determining Investment Policies," IN Harris 1960, 214-218. Original.

313. Bear, Donald V. T., "The University as a Multi-Product Firm," IN Lumsden 1974, 77-111. Original.

314. Beaton, Albert E., "The Influence of Education and Ability on Salary and Attitudes," IN Juster 1975, 365-396. Original.

315. Bell, Peter D., "Reaffirming the Value of a College Education," IN Peltason 1978, 177-183. Original.

316. Benezet, Louis T., "Is Higher Education a Commodity?" IN Smith 1971, 241-244. Original.

317. Bennett, George F., "Some Examples of Experience with Growth Stocks," IN Harris 1960, 222-223. Original.

318. Blitz, Rudolph C., "The Nation's Educational Outlay," IN Mushkin 1962, 147-169. Original.

319. Bokelman, W. Robert, "Tuition and Costs," IN Harris 1960, 73-74. Original.

320. Bolling, Landrum R., "Public Monies and Independent Colleges," IN Letter 1970, 103-111. Original.

321. Bombach, Gottfried, "Long-Term Requirements for Qualified Manpower in Relation to Economic Growth," IN Harris 1964, 201-221. Original.

322. Bowen, Howard R., "Effective Education at Reasonable Cost," IN Godwin 1972, 20-37. ER, 53 (Summer 1972), 191-200.

323. Bowen, Howard R., "Finance and the Aims of American Higher Education," IN Orwig 1971, 155-170. Original.

324. Bowen, Howard R., "Financial Needs of the Campus," IN Connery 1970, 75-93. Original.

325. Bowen, Howard R., "Financing Higher Education: The Current State of the Debate," IN Young 1974, 11-31. FHE (1974).

326. Bowen, Howard R., "The Financing of Higher Education: Issues and Prospects," IN Caffrey 1969, 205-219. Original.

Commentaries by H. Thomas James, Clarence Scheps, Alice M. Rivlin, and John W. Lederle follow on pages 220-232.

327. Bowen, Howard R., "Where are the Dollars for Higher Education Coming From?" IN Smith 1960, 9-16. Original.

328. Bowen, Howard R., "Who Pays the Higher Education Bill?" IN Orwig 1971, 281-298. PFHE (1969).

329. Bowen, Howard R. and Gordon K. Douglass, "Cutting Instructional Costs," IN Jellema 1972, 79-92. Original.

330. Bowen, William G., "Assessing the Economic Contribution of Education: An Appraisal of Alternative Approaches," IN Harris 1964, 177-200. Original.

331. Bowles, Frank H., "The High Cost of Low-Cost Education," IN Harris 1960, 199-202. Original.

332. Bowman, Mary Jean, "Economics of Education," IN Orwig 1971, 37-70. RER, 39 (December 1969), 641-670.

333. Bowman, Mary Jean, "Human Capital: Concepts and Measures," IN Mushkin 1962, 69-92. Original.

334. Boyd, Joseph D., "History of State Involvement in Financial Aid," IN College 1975, 118-149. Original.

335. Brady, Joseph J., "Strategies for Grant Development," IN Rowland 1977, 199-216. Original.

336. Brainard, William C., "Private and Social Risk and Return to Education," IN Lumsden 1974, 241-265. Original.

337. Breneman, David W. and Sharon Collins, "The Special Problems of Graduate Student Loan Finance," IN Rice 1977, 164-169. Original.

338. Breneman, David W. and Chester E. Finn, Jr., "An Uncertain Future," IN Breneman 1978, 1-61. Original.

The authors provide an excellent overview of the debate concerning public support for private higher education, plus statistics and comments on the current federal and state role.

339. Bromery, Randolph W., "Doing Well With Less," IN Heyns 1977, 149-155. Original.

340. Browne, Michael B., "At What Price the Cost Per Credit Hour?" IN Mauer 1976, 160-165. Original.

341. Bucklin, Leonard W., "Deferred Giving," IN Rowland 1977, 217-235. Original.

342. Budig, Gene A., "Building a Budget for the 1970's," IN Budig 1972, 13-30. Original.

343. Budig, Gene A., "A Prerequisite to Budgeting," IN Budig 1972, 1-10. Original.

344. Bump, Boardman, "Objectives of Investment Policies," IN Harris 1960, 219-221. Original.

345. Bundy, McGeorge, "In Praise of Candor," In Dobbins 1968, 214-219. Original.

Mr. Bundy discusses the problems faced by the academic community in trying to explain themselves in economic terms.

346. Burson, Ruth F., "Student Employment and the Off-Campus Employer," IN Keene 1975, 102-114. Original.

347. Cabot, Paul C., "Should Harvard Borrow?" IN Harris 1960, 239-241. Original.

348. Cain, J. Harvey, "Recent Trends in Endowment," IN Harris 1960, 242-244. Original.

349. Cameron Jr., Ben F., "How Can Local Institutional Policies and Practices on Student Aid Serve Individual Needs More Effectively?" IN Smith 1960, 165-166. Original.

The author presents a series of recommendations on student financial aid.

Commentary by Rodney J. Harrison follows on pages 167-168.

350. "Carnegie Commission Recommendations on Tuition and Finance," IN Goodall 1976, 201-206. WPWB (1973).

351. Cartter, Allan M., "The Future Financing of Higher Education," IN Hughes 1975a, 51-70. Original.

Commentaries by Howard R. Bowen, Harold L. Enarson, and Robert W. Hartman follow on pages 70-85.

352. Cartter, Allan M., "Private Institutions in Peril," IN Godwin 1972, 139-148. Original.

353. Chambers, Charles M., "An Institutional View of the Costs of Government Regulation," IN Hook 1978, 123-132. Original.

354. Chambers, M. M., "Financing Higher Education in the Decades Ahead," IN Paulsen 1970, 51-62. Original.

355. Cheshire, Richard D., "The State of the Art (for Fund Raising)," IN Rowland 1977, 121-128. Original.

356. Chiswick, Barry R., "Schooling, Screening, and Income," IN Solmon 1973, 151-158. Original.

357. Cootner, Paul H., "Economic Organization and Inefficiency in the Modern University," IN Lumsden 1974, 217-240. Original.

358. Corbally Jr., John E., "A Quid pro Quo Approach to Tuition," IN Hughes 1975, 118-123. Original.

359. Curtis, Grant E., "Who Should Support the Nontraditional Aid Applicant?" IN College 1974, 73-79. Original.

360. Cyert, Richard M., "The Market Approach to Higher Education," IN Hughes 1975, 123-132. Original.

361. Daniere, Andre, "Economics of Higher Education: The Changing Scene," IN Solmon 1973, 365-379. Original.

362. Dannells, Michael, "Financial Aid," IN Packwood 1977, 51-73. Original.

A very thorough overview of college student financial aid programs and services with an extensive bibliography.

363. David, Henry, "Pressures on Higher Education from the Changing Economy," IN Smith 1965, 72-79. Original.

364. Deitch, Kenneth, "Some Observations on the Allocation of Resources in Higher Education," IN Harris 1960, 192-198. Original.

365. DeJarnett, Raymond P., "The Organization of Student Support Programs in Institutions of Higher Learning," IN Keene 1975, 206-213. Original.

366. Dent, Richard A., "Student Resources," IN College 1975, 150-167. Original.

An overview of the various ways students find to support their education through personal funds.

367. Dewitt, Nicholas, "Soviet and American Higher Education: Magnitude, Resources and Costs," IN Harris 1964, 133-152. Original.

368. Donham, Dennis E. and Les E. Stege, "Grants, Loans, and Scholarships," IN Keene 1975, 67-79. Original.

369. Dresch, Stephen P., "Blindered Economics: Higher Education and Public Policy," IN Solmon 1973, 335-340. Original.

370. Drucker, Peter F., "The Financial Basis of the Independent College," IN Letter 1968, 12-24. Original.

371. Eckaus, Richard S., "Education and Economic Growth," IN Mushkin 1962, 102-128. Original.

372. Eckaus, Richard S., Ahmad El Safty, and Victor D. Norman, "An Appraisal of the Calculations of Rates of Return to Higher Education," IN Gordon 1974, 333-371. Original.

373. Eckstein, Otto, "The Problem of Higher College Tuition," IN Harris 1960, 61-72. Original.

374. Eddy, Edward D., "The Future of Voluntary Donations," IN Heyns 1977, 72-77. Original.

375. Eggers, Melvin A., "Autonomy and Accountability in a Shrinking Enterprise," IN Bailey 1977, 175-182. Original.

376. Enarson, Harold L., "A University President: Where Do We Go From Here?" IN Young 1974, 157-162. Original.

Speculation on achieveing low tuition levels through various reforms suggested by several national study groups.

377. Eurich, Alvin C., "Increasing Productivity in Higher Education," IN Harris 1960, 185-188. Original.

378. Farrell, Robert L. and Charles J. Andersen, "General Federal Support for Higher Education: An Analysis of Five Formulas," IN Orwig 1971, 219-268. (Originally published by The American Council on Education in 1968)

379. Fey, John T., "Motivating Business to Support Education," IN Peltason 1978, 115-121. Original.

380. "Financing Reports and the Attack on Low Tuition," IN Goodall 1976, 210-218.

A statement of the American Association of State Colleges and Universities, 1974.

381. Finney Jr., Robert J., "Patterns of Private Support of American Higher Education," IN Vaccaro 1975, 110-122. Original.

382. Fogel, Walter and Daniel J. B. Mitchell, "Higher Education Decision Making and the Labor Market," IN Gordon 1974, 453-502. Original.

383. Folsom, Marion B., "Who Should Pay for American Higher Education?" IN Mushkin 1962, 195-201. Original.

384. Fram, Eugene H., "Marketing Higher Education," IN Vermilye 1973, 56-67. Original.

385. Freeman, Roger A., "Last Chance to Save Private Colleges," IN Orwig 1971, 201-218. LCSPC (1969).

386. Freeman, Roger, "Needed: Another Seven to Eleven Billion Dollars," IN Mayhew 1967, 281-296. CCF (1965).

387. Fuller, Bruce, "Addressing Costs and Questioning Benefits," IN Peltason 1978, 33-42. Original.

> Mr. Fuller examines the question of who should pay for a college education and what are the priorities and values a state government should consider in determining their share of the financial burden.

388. Fuller, Stephen H., "Corporations and Colleges: Their Mutual Expectations," IN Peltason 1978, 124-128. Original.

389. Fulton, Richard A., "Differentiated Aid Programs for Today's Emancipated Students," IN Hughes 1975, 180-188. Original.

390. Galbraith, John Kenneth, "The Dependence Effect," IN Mayhew 1967, 13-18. Aff Soc (1958).

391. German, Kathleen, "The Financial Drain on the Average-Income Student," IN College 1970, 20-21. Original.

392. Ghez, Gilbert R., "Education, the Price of Time, and Life-Cycle Consumption," IN Juster 1975, 295-312. Original.

393. Godzicki, Ralph J., "A History of Financial Aids in the United States," IN Keene 1975, 14-21. Original.

394. Goode, Richard, "Educational Expenditures and the Income Tax," IN Mushkin 1962, 281-304. Original.

395. Gordon, Margaret, "The Changing Labor Market for College Graduates," IN Gordon 1974, 27-81. Original.

396. Griffin, John R. and Cherie D. Lenz, "The On-Campus Student Work Program," IN Keene 1975, 80-88. Original.

397. Gross, Stanley J., "A Critique of Practice in the Administration of Financial Aid," IN Fitzgerald 1970, 263-272. JCSP, 7 (March 1966), 78-85.

398. Grossman, Michael, "University Fund Raising Planning," IN Wattel 1975, 314-434. Original.

399. Hall, J. Parker, "Unorthodox Investing," IN Harris 1960, 235-238. Original.

400. Hansen, W. Lee, "The Financial Implications of Student Independence," IN College 1974, 10-26. Original.

401. Hansen, W. Lee and Suzanne C. Feeney, "New Directions in State Loan Programs for Postsecondary Students," IN Rice 1977, 48-67. Original.

Commentaries by William Ihlanfeldt and Jay W. Evans follow on pages 67-73.

402. Hansen, W. Lee and Burton A. Weisbrod, "A New Approach to Higher Education Finance," IN Orwig 1971, 117-142. Original.

The authors recommend a "Higher Education Opportunity Program" for direct state grants to low income students.

403. Harris, Seymour E., "Financing of Higher Education: Broad Issues," IN Keezer 1959, 35-78. Original.

404. Harris, Seymour E., "Higher Education: Resources and Finance (U.S.A.)," IN Harris 1964, 109-116. Original.

405. Hartman, Robert W., "Federal Options for Student Aid," IN Breneman 1978, 231-279. Original.

406. Hartman, Robert W., "Financing the Opportunity to Enter the 'Educated Labor Market,'" IN Gordon 1974, 427-451. Original.

407. Hartman, Robert W., "The National Bank Approach to Solutions," IN Rice 1977, 74-89. Original.

An overview of the history and feasibility of a National Student Loan Bank.

Commentaries by Edward A. Fox and Martin A. Kramer follow on pages 89-93.

408. Hartman, Robert W., "Student Loans for Higher Education," IN Orwig 1971, 177-199. CFC (1971).

409. Hauptman, Arthur M., "Student Loan Defaults: Toward a Better Understanding of the Problem," IN Rice 1977, 125-155. Original.

Commentaries by Robert F. Lyke and J. Wilmer Mirandon follow on pages 155-163.

410. Hause, John C., "Ability and Schooling as Determinants of Lifetime Earnings, or If You're So Smart, Why Aren't You Rich?" IN Juster 1975, 123-149. Original.

411. Heim, Peggy, "Financing Private Higher Education: Assessment and Suggestions," IN Hughes 1975, 97-107. Original.

412. Henderson, Algo D., "How High Can Tuitions Go?" IN McGrath 1964, 50-61. Original.

413. Henderson, Algo D., "The Economic Aspects (of Higher Education)," IN McGrath 1966, 193-217. Original.

414. Henry, Joe B., "Student Financial Need Analysis," IN Keene 1975, 195-205. Original.

415. Hicks, John W., "Selling the Budget," IN Budig 1972, 33-54. Original.

416. Holderman, James B., "State Coordination and Student Support," IN Keene 1975, 187-194. Original.

417. Houston, Livingston W., "Broadway," IN Harris 1960, 232-234. Original.

The usefullness of small investments, in this case real estate, to provide institutional income.

418. Huff, Robert P., "Institutional Financial Aid Resources: Their Nature, Utilization, and Development," IN College 1975, 168-179. Original.

419. Hurd, T. N. and Donald Axelrod, "The Governor's Role in the Budget Process," IN Budig 1972, 57-94. Original.

420. Jacobs, Donald P., "Knowledge of Financial Institutions as the Basis for National Policy on Financial Structure and Regulation," IN Ritterbush 1972, 74-77. Original.

421. Jellema, William W., "Financial Status," IN Jellema 1972, 107-121.

A survey of the financial status of private colleges.

422. Jenny, Hans H., "Higher Education Finance: Health and Distress," IN Hughes 1975, 108-117. Original.

423. Jenny, Hans H., "The Management of Resources," IN Rowland 1977, 498-507. Original.

424. Johnson, Eldon L., "Is the Low-Tuition Principal Outmoded?" IN Harris 1960, 44-47. CBR, 38 (Spring 1959), 16-18.

425. Johnstone, D. Bruce, "Federally Sponsored Student Loans: An Overview of Issues and Policy Alternatives," IN Rice 1977, 16-42. Original.

Commentaries by Colin C. Blaydon and Chester E. Finn, Jr. follow on pages 42-47.

426. Johnstone, D. Bruce, "Tidying Up the Policy Space," IN Peltason 1978, 25-33. Original.

An essay on the limits to public policy alternatives regarding the financing of higher education.

427. Jones, Howard L., "The Future of Educational Fund Raising," IN Rowland 1977, 265-272. Original.

428. Jones, Sherman J. and George B. Weathersby, "Financing the Black College," IN Willie 1978, 100-131. Original.

Includes many detailed statistical tables.

429. Kaysen, Carl, "Some General Observations on the Pricing of Higher Education," IN Harris 1960, 55-60. Original.

430. Keeney, Barnaby C., "A College Administrator Views the Tuition Problem," IN Harris 1960, 40-43. Original.

431. Knight, Douglas M., "National Goals and Federal Means," IN Knight 1960, 176-199. Original.

432. Kohnstamm, Max, "The Common Market and Atlantic Partnership," IN Smith 1963, 47-55. Original.

433. Kohr, Russell V., "Capital Campaigning," IN Rowland 1977, 236-264. Original.

434. Kreps, Juanita M., "Higher Education in a Low-Growth, High Inflation Economy," IN Hughes 1975, 58-67. Original.

435. Lawrence, G. Ben, "Policy Proposals for Financing," IN Vermilye 1974, 153-161. Original.

This essay deals with the necessity to adjust financial policies to the realities of the 1970's, but at the same time to continue a commitment to educate the poor and minorities.

436. Lees, Dennis S., "Financing Higher Education in the United States and in Great Britain," IN Mushkin 1962, 328-342. Original.

437. Leslie, Larry L. and Gary P. Johnson, "Equity and the Middle Class," IN Young 1974, 105-137. Original.

The authors address the question: "Is there equity, by income level, in the recently proposed schemes for altering present patterns of financing American higher education?"

438. Levi, Julian, "Issues of Accountability," IN Furniss 1974, 282-305. Original.

Commentary by Carolyn S. Bell follows on pages 305-308.

439. McAnally, Stanley R., "Annual Giving," IN Rowland 1977, 181-198. Original.

440. McCoy, Charles B., "Criteria for Corporate Aid," IN Connery 1970, 166-174. Original.

441. McGill, William J., "Means and Ways in Private Universities," IN Wilson 1972, 115-121. Original.

442. McPherson, Michael S., "The Demand for Higher Education," IN Breneman 1978, 143-196. Original.

An analysis of declining enrollments and the current labor market situation as they impact on colleges and universities.

443. Magnussen, Olav, "The Cost and Finance of Post-Secondary Education," IN OECD 1974a, 171-227. Original.

444. May, William F., "Corporate Support of Higher Education," IN Connery 1970, 147-152. Original.

445. Meadows, Dennis L. and Lewis Perelman, "Limits to Growth," IN Vermilye 1973, 111-127. Original.

446. Meck, John F., "Investment Possibilities," IN Harris 1960, 229-231. Original.

447. Meck, John F., "The Tax-Credit Proposal," IN Harris 1960, 93-95. Original.

448. Meeth, L. Richard, "Restrictive Practices in Formula Funding," IN Vermilye 1975, 174-190. Original.

Professor Meeth describes the ways in which state funding formulas work against nontraditional programs.

449. Miller Jr., James L., "Coordination Versus Centralized Control," IN Vermilye 1972, 237-244. Original.

An essay on the merits of statewide coordination of higher education.

450. Millett, John D., "The Pressures of Increasing Operating Costs," IN Smith 1965, 145-147. Original.

451. Millett, John D., "Who Should Pay for the Major Costs of Higher Education, Society or the Individual?" IN Smith 1960, 145-147. Original.

Commentary by Miller Upton follows on pages 147-149.

452. Mincer, Jacob, "Education, Experience, and the Distribution of Earnings and Employment: An Overview," IN Juster 1975, 71-93. Original.

453. Mitau, G. Theodore, "Needed: A National Cost Adjustment Factor for Higher Education," IN Hughes 1975, 133-139. Original.

454. Mitau, G. Theodore, "A State Chancellor: Some Preliminary Comments on Postsecondary Tuition Levels," IN Young 1974, 153-156. Original.

455. Mitchell, Maurice B., "Encouraging Private Support," IN Heyns 1977, 67-72. Original.

456. Moon Jr., Rexford G., "History of Institutional Financial Aid in the United States," IN College 1975, 1-10. Original.

457. Moon Jr., Rexford G., "Equalizing Opportunity Under Higher Charges," IN Harris 1960, 52-54. Original.

458. Morse, John F., "Higher Fees and the Position of Private Institutions," IN Harris 1960, 48-51. Original.

459. Morse, John F., "How We Got Here From There--A Personal Reminiscense of the Early Days," IN Rice 1977, 3-15. Original.

An essay on the evolution of the federal student loan programs.

460. Mushkin, Selma J., "Public Financing of Higher Education," IN Wilson 1972, 153-178. Original.

Commentaries by Harold Orlans, Allan W. Ostar, and Albert H. Quie follow on pages 178-188.

461. Nelson, James E., "The Cost of a College Education: Getting the Word Out," IN Peltason 1978, 19-25. Original.

462. Nelson, Susan C., "Financial Trends and Issues," IN Breneman 1978, 63-142. Original.

An excellent overview of private and public financial support for higher education (especially private higher education), plus extensive statistical tables.

463. Nowlan, James D., "The Lawmakers Budget for Higher Education: The Case of Illinois," IN Goodall 1976, 146-175. PHE (1975).

464. Oates Jr., James F., "The Corporation and the Community," IN Connery 1970, 153-157. Original.

465. Patterson, Frederick D., "The College Endowment Funding Plan," IN Heyns 1977, 77-84. Original.

466. Payton, Robert L., "They Say You Can't Do It, But Sometimes That Doesn't Always Work," IN Peltason 1978, 122-124. Original.

Guidelines for raising funds from corporations are presented.

467. Phillips, John D., "Don't Forget the 'Student' in Student Assistance," IN Hughes 1975, 140-148. Original.

468. Pitchell, Robert J., "Corporate Support of Higher Education," IN Mushkin 1962, 250-267. Original.

469. Pitchell, Robert J., "Financing Part-Time Students," IN Vermilye 1974, 40-46. Original.

470. Post, A. Alan, "The Legislative Expectations of the Budget," IN Budig 1972, 97-114. Original.

471. Pray, Francis C., "What Financial Aid Practices Are Emerging for Privately Supported Institutions of Higher Education, and What New Ones Should be Developed?" IN Smith 1962, 158-160. Original.

472. Psacharopoulos, George, "The Profitability of Higher Education: A Review of the Experience in Britain and the United States," IN Butcher 1972, 361-371. Original.

473. Ramsden, Richard J., "GSLP and NDSL--In Search of Synthesis," IN Rice 1977, 94-111. Original.

The author provides a synthesis of the two major national student loan programs--Guaranteed Student Loan (GSLP) and National Direct Student Loan (NDSL).

Commentaries by Stephen P. Dresch, Carol Wennerdahl, and Thomas R. Wolanin follow on pages 112-122.

474. "Recommendations of the Committee for Economic Development," IN Goodall 1976, 207-209.

Recommendations of the Committee concerning the financing of higher education as published by the Committee in their 1973 report.

475. "Recommendations on State Support for Private Higher Education in Illinois," IN Goodall 1976, 219-224.

Taken from a report of The Commission to Study Non-Private Higher Education in Illinois published by the Illinois Board of Higher Education in 1969.

476. Reder, Melvin W., "A Suggestion for Increasing the Efficiency of Universities," IN Lumsden 1974, 207-216. Original.

Efficiency is defined as a variable of quantity and quality of output.

477. Rexford Jr., G. Moon, "Beating the High Cost of Low Ratios," IN Jellema 1972, 73-78. Original.

478. Rice, Lois D., "Federal Student Assistance: Title IV Revisited," IN Hughes 1975, 149-168. Original.

479. Rivlin, Alice M., "Research in the Economics of Higher Education: Progress and Problems," IN Mushkin 1962, 357-383. Original.

480. Rivlin, Alice M. and June O'Neill, "Growth and Change in Higher Education," IN Connery 1970, 66-74. Original.

481. Rosenberg, Herbert H., "Research and the Financing of Higher Education," IN Mushkin 1962, 305-327. Original.

482. Russell, John D., "Dollars and Cents: Some Hard Facts," IN Baskin 1965, 273-303. Original.

483. Russell, John D., "What Financial Aid Practices are Emerging for Publicly Supported Institutions of Higher Education and What New Ones Should be Developed?" IN Smith 1962, 253-256. Original.

484. Scheps, Clarence, "Federal Programs of Loans and Grants for Capital Improvements," IN Dobbins 1963, 45-54. Original.

485. Scheps, Clarence, "Systematic Financial Analysis and Budgetary Planning as Aids in the Attainment of College and University Purposes," IN Smith 1961, 185-188. Original.

486. Schultz, Theodore W., "Resources for Higher Education: An Economist's View," IN Orwig 1971, 13-36. JPE, 76 (May-June 1968), 327-347.

487. Schultz, Theodore W., "Rise in the Capital Stock Represented by Education in the United States, 1900-57," IN Mushkin 1962, 93-101.

488. Schuster, Jack H., "The Federal Government and Student Financial Aid: Some Reflections on 'Clout'," IN College 1970, 12-14. Original.

489. Schwartz, John J., "Role and Selection of Professional Counsel," IN Rowland 1977, 152-165. Original.

The author notes the importance of selecting a professional coordinator for large fund raising drives.

490. Shea, James M., "Organization and Structure," IN Rowland 1977, 475-484. Original.

Pertains to the conditions best suited for the operation and organization of the fund raising activity.

491. Silber, John R., "Financing the Independent Sector," IN Vermilye 1976, 107-117. Original.

492. Smith, G. T., "The Development Program," IN Rowland 1977, 142-151. Original.

493. Smith, Hayden W., "Prospects for Voluntary Support," IN Connery 1970, 120-136. Original.

494. Smith, Hayden W., "Voluntary Support: Retrospect and Prospect," IN Peltason 1978, 128-145. Original.

495. Smith, Virginia B., "Assessing and Improving Productivity in Higher Education," IN Godwin 1972, 38-53. Original.

496. Smith, Virginia B., "More for Less: Higher Education's New Priority," IN Wilson 1972, 122-141. Original.

Commentaries by C. Arnold Hanson, Paul C. Reinert, and Clarence Scheps follow on pages 142-149.

497. Spencer, Lyle M., "The New Social-Industrial Complex," IN Mayhew 1967, 431-441. Original.

498. Svennilson, Ingvar, "Targets for the Development of Society," IN Henderson 1968, 109-115. Original.

499. Thackrey, Russell I., "The Case Against the Wisconsin Voucher Plan," IN Smith 1971, 121-128. Original.

500. Thackrey, Russell I., Financing Higher Education: Society's Responsibility," IN Godwin 1972, 149-163. Original.

501. Tollett, Kenneth S., "Higher Education and the Public Sector," IN Lawrence 1970, 61-72. Original.

502. Tonsor, Stephen, "Rationalizing the Financing of Higher Education," IN Hook 1974, 253-254. Original.

503. Treece, Raymond J., "Institutional Financial Planning," IN Donovan 1964, 173-193. Original.

504. Tripp, Hulbert W., "Growth and Income," IN Harris 1960, 224-228. Original.

505. Umbeck, Sharvy G., "New Approaches to Finance," IN Jellema 1972, 122-128. Original.

506. Underhill, Robert M., "Special Problems in Public Institutions," IN Harris 1960, 245-247. Original.

The legal and political considerations in the development of investment policy of state universities.

507. Van Dusen, William D., "Toward a Philosophy of Financial Aid Programs," IN Fitzgerald 1970, 273-276. JNASPA, 4 (July 1966), 3-7.

508. Vickrey, William, "A Proposal for Student Loan," IN Mushkin 1962, 268-280. Original.

509. Vogelnik, Dolfe, "A Comparison Between the Financing of Higher Education in the United States and Yugoslavia," IN Harris 1964, 117-132. Original.

510. Volpe, Edmond J., "Retrenchment: The Case at CUNY," IN Heyns 1977, 155-166. Original.

511. Walkup, J. Lawrence and William G. Hoyt, "The Institution as an Agency of Student Support," IN Keene 1975, 45-53. Original.

Deals with the impact of student aid programs on the institutions that must administer them.

512. Weathersby, George B., "Grants for Students Based on Their Own Income," IN Hughes 1975, 169-179. Original.

513. Weathersby, George B., "Institutional Versus Student Aid," IN Vermilye 1976, 118-129. Original.

514. Wharton Jr., Clifton R., "Citizens' Bill of Educational Entitlement," IN Vermilye 1975, 212-221. Original.

515. Wilson, Logan, "Analyzing and Evaluating Costs in Higher Education," IN Fitzgerald 1970, 147-154. ER, 42 (April 1961), 99-105.

516. Wilson, Logan, "Higher Education and the National Interest," IN Eurich 1968, 23-42. Original.

517. Wolfe, Alan, "Hard Times on Campus," IN Anderson 1971, 143-151. Nation, 210 (May 25, 1970), 623-627.

This essay describes some of the consequences that flow from the labor surplus in academia.

518. Wolk, Ronald A., "Revenue Sharing and Aid to the States," IN Orwig 1971, 269-280. AMFF (1968).

519. Woodhall, Maureen, "Methods of Financing Higher Education," IN Butcher 1972, 347-360. SL (1970).

Reviews trends in the financing of higher education with special emphasis on various schemes of student loans and grants.

520. Wooldridge, Roy L., "Cooperative Education as a Means of Financial Aid in Higher Education," IN Keene 1975, 125-134. Original.

521. Wootton, Richard T., "Business Management and Data Systems for Financial Aid Offices," IN Keene 1975, 229-242. Original.

522. Wright, Stephen J., "The Financing of Equal Opportunity in Higher Education: The Problem and the Urgency," IN College 1970, 1-5. Original.

523. York Jr., E. T., "Managing Under Depressed Funding," IN Heyns 1977, 166-175. Original.

524. Zimny, Joseph D. and Lyle B. Williams, Jr., "Veterans' and Special Programs," IN Keene 1975, 149-158. Original.

5
INTERNATIONAL AND COMPARATIVE POSTSECONDARY EDUCATION

525. Abu-Merhy, Nair Fortes, "Emerging National Policies for Higher Education in Brazil," IN Holmes 1971, 334-347. Original.

526. Aidoo, Agnes A., "The African Case: Problems and Prospects," IN Bailey 1977, 12-17. Original.

An essay on the history of development and support of African universities.

527. Alexander, W. Boyd, "England's New Seven, An American View," IN Lawlor 1968, 27-48. Original.

An overview of the development of the seven new universities created by British Parliament in the late 1950's.

528. Alexandrov, Alexandr D., "Promoting Mutual Understanding," IN Henderson 1968, 142-146. Original.

529. Anderson, D. S., "Post-Secondary Education and Manpower Planning in Australia," IN McLeod 1973, 73-87. Original.

530. Annan, Lord, "The University in Britain," IN Stephens 1975, 19-33. Original.

531. Antoine, Gerald, "An Innovative University in France--Orleans--La Source: A Stocktaking," IN Niblett 1972, 195-206. Original.

532. Archer, Margaret S., "France," IN Archer 1972, 127-153. Original.

A review of French higher education with special emphasis on the sixties, especially since the student movement as a result of the Algerian crisis.

533. Archer, Margaret S., "Introduction to Student, University and Society," IN Archer 1972, 1-35. Original.

A comprehensive overview of social, economic, and political development of higher education with special emphasis on Europe.

534. Armytage, W. H. G., "The Polytechnic Tradition in England," IN Holmes 1971, 62-74. Original.

535. Armytage, W. H. G., "Thoughts After Robbins," IN Lawlor 1968, 79-100. Original.

A review of British higher education in the early 1960's as compared with the recommendations of the Robbins Commission.

536. Ballantine, Duncan S., "Goals for International Support of Emerging Universities," IN Bailey 1977, 17-29. Original.

537. Becher, Anthony, "United Kingdom," IN Entwistle 1976, 183-201. Original.

538. Bela, Ramón, "Spanish Educational Reform--Three Views," IN Kertesz 1971, 353-369. Original.

539. Beloff, Max, "The Independent Alternative," IN Stephens 1978, 116-126. Original.

Mr. Beloff relates the history of the relatively new University College at Buckingham (England) to both internal and external forces that effect policy and direction.

540. Belyaev, S. T. and Taukoed Golenpolsky, "The State University of Novosibirsk (USSR): Experience and Problems," IN Niblett 1972, 255-265. Original.

541. Bienaymé, Alain, "France," IN Perkins 1972, 151-158. Original.

542. Bissell, Claude T., "Canada," IN Perkins 1972, 175-184. Original.

543. Bissell, Claude, "Institutions of Higher Education in Canada--Some Recent Developments," IN Niblett 1970, 139-151. Original.

Commentary by Paul A. Miller follows on pages 152-158.

544. Blandy, Richard J., "Flinders University and the Pressure to Conform," IN Niblett 1972, 235-242. Original.

545. Blegvad, Mogens and Steen L. Jeppesen, "Danish Universities in Transition," IN Seabury 1975, 181-194. Original.

546. Boulding, Kenneth E., "The Role of the University in the Development of a World Community," IN Henderson 1968, 135-141. Original.

547. Bourricaud, Francois, "The French University as a 'Fixed Society' or, the Futility of the 1968 'Reform,'" IN Seabury 1975, 232-245. Original.

548. Bowden, Lord, "English Universities--Problems and Prospects," IN Kertesz 1971, 235-258. Original.

549. Brest, de Romero Gilda L., "Ten Years of Change at the University of Buenos Aires, 1956-66: Innovations and the Recovery of Autonomy," IN Niblett 1972, 124-136. Original.

550. Briggs, Asa, "Development in Higher Education in the United Kingdom: Nineteenth and Twentieth Centuries," IN Niblett 1970, 95-116. Original.

Commentary by Arnold Nash follows on pages 117-121.

551. Briggs, Asa, "The Role of the International Intellectual Community," IN Bailey 1977, 183-191. Original.

552. Brosan, G. S., "Some Aspects of Post-Secondary Education in the United Kingdom," IN McLeod 1973, 111-127. Original.

553. Brothers, Joan, "Residence in British Higher Education," IN Butcher 1971, 186-197. Original.

554. Bruecher-Hamm, Hildegard, "Towards the Comprehensive University in Germany," IN Niblett 1972, 325-335. Original.

555. Burgess, Johanna, "Emerging Concepts of Universities in Britain," IN Holmes 1971, 75-89. Original.

556. Burn, Barbara B., "Comparative Lessons on National Systems," IN Perkins 1972, 243-253. Original.

557. Burn, Barbara B., "Comparisons of Four Foreign Universities," IN Perkins 1973, 79-103. Original.

558. Busch, Alexander, "The Vicissitudes of the Privatdozent: Breakdown and Adaptation in the Recruitment of the German University Teacher," IN Kruytbosch 1970, 225-245. Minerva, 1 (Spring 1963), 319-341.

559. Buttgereit, Michael, "An Information System for the Field of the Further Education in the Federal Republic of Germany," IN Verreck 1974, 426-439. Original.

560. Byrnes, Robert F., "Cultural Relations Between Ideologically Divided Countries," IN Kertesz 1971, 217-231. Original.

561. Canipel, Jacqueline, "France," IN Entwistle 1976, 220-236. Original.

562. Carneiro Jr., David, "The University in Brazil: Expansion and the Problem of Modernization," IN Niblett 1972, 115-123. Original.

563. Choh-Ming Li, "Tomorrow's Universities in Today's Developing Countries," IN Henderson 1968, 65-71. Original.

564. Chorley, Lord, "Academic Freedom in the United Kingdom," IN Baade 1964, 217-241. LCP, 28 (Summer 1963), 647-671.

565. Chye, Toh Chin, "A Regional Institute of Higher Education and Development in South-East Asia," IN Niblett 1972, 174-179. Original.

566. Conway, Jill, "Academic Change and Crisis, Canadian Style," IN Riesman 1973, 343-366. Original.

A review of change and internal response at the University of Toronto.

567. Coombs, Philip H., "The Role of International Organizations in the Field of Higher Education," IN Perkins 1972, 257-264. Original.

568. Cowen, Robert, "The Utilitarian University," IN Holmes 1971, 90-107. Original.

This essay addresses itself to the "linkage between universities and their host society in England, France, the USA and the USSR."

569. Cowen, Zelman, "Higher Education in Australia," IN Holmes 1971, 357-367. Original.

570. Crouch, Colin, "Britain," IN Archer 1972, 196-211. Original.

A review of recent developments in British higher education stemming from the student revolts and other left/liberal activities.

571. Daalder, Hans, "The Dutch Universities Between the 'New Democracy' and the 'New Management,'" IN Seabury 1975, 195-231. Original.

572. Dennis, Lawrence E., "Internationalizing the Outlook of Institutions of Higher Learning," IN Smith 1966, 82-85. Original.

573. Dogan, Mattei, "Causes of the French Student Revolt in May 1968," IN Kertesz 1971, 306-322. Original.

574. Donovan, George F., "International Affairs as a Problem Area in the Administration of American Higher Education," IN Donovan 1964, 81-94. Original.

575. Dreyfus, F. G., "Problems of the French University," IN Kertesz 1971, 287-305. Original.

576. Dundonald, James, "Advice to an Alderman," IN Lawlor 1968, 103-126. Original.

A critical overview of the prospects for further (1960's and beyond) development of the British university system.

577. Duster, Troy, "Student Interests, Student Power, and the Swedish Experience," IN Kruytbosch 1970, 191-206. ABS, 11 (May-June 1968), 21-27.

578. Edding, Friedrich, "The Planning of Higher Education in the Federal Republic of Germany," IN Harris 1964, 153-176. Original.

579. Edwards, Reginald, "Emerging National Policies for Higher Education in Canada," IN Holmes 1971, 317-333. Original.

580. Eide, Kjell, "Some Aspects of Post-Secondary Education in Norway," IN McLeod 1973, 101-110. Original.

581. Einaudi, Luigi, "University Autonomy and Academic Freedom in Latin America," IN Baade 1964, 206-216. LCP, 28 (Summer 1963), 636-646.

582. Ekgolm, Igor, "Higher Education in the Soviet Union," IN Holmes 1971, 284-297. Original.

583. Ely, Richard T., "American Colleges and German Universities," IN Portman 1972, 77-91. Harper's, 61 (July 1880), 253-260.

584. Ferguson, John, "The Open University in Britain," IN Niblett 1972, 373-385. Original.

585. Floud, Jean, "Studying Students in Britain and America: Contrasting Approaches to Comparable Problems," IN Lunsford 1963a, 113-127. Original.

586. Fowler, Gerald T., "The Binary Policy in England and Wales," IN Niblett 1972, 268-280. Original.

Describes the dual system of private and public financial support by type of institution.

587. Fowler, G. T., "Present Trends and Future Policies," IN Stephens 1978, 156-169. Original.

A project of the course and factors effecting the development of higher education in Great Britain.

588. Froese, Leonhard, "University Reform: A Comparative Analysis of the American, Russian and German Universities," IN Holmes 1971, 135-146. Original.

589. Frondizi, Risieri, "The Role of Private and Voluntary Organizations in the Field of Higher Education," IN Perkins 1972, 265-276. Original.

An overview of major organizations dealing with international education.

590. Fusé, Toyomasa, "Japan," IN Archer 1962, 212-245. Original.

A social and historical review of Japanese higher education from 1868 to the late 1960's.

591. Garibay, G. Luis, "Autonomy and Accountability in Latin America," IN Bailey 1977, 160-168. Original.

The evolution of university and state government relations in Latin America.

592. Gass, James R., "Lifelong Learning in Europe," IN Vermilye 1974, 22-28. Original.

593. Giner, Salvador, "Spain," IN Archer 1962, 103-126. Original.

An essay on trends and modernization of higher education in Spain since 1939.

594. Glowka, Detlef, "Soviet Higher Education Between Government Policy and Self-Determination--A German View," IN Holmes 1971, 175-185. Original.

595. Goldman, Ronald and A. W. Martin, "La Trobe--A Case Study of a New Australian University," IN Niblett 1972, 220-234. Original.

596. Goldschmidt, Dietrich, "West Germany," IN Archer 1972, 154-166. Original.

A review of issues that have had the most significant effect on West German higher education since the early 1950's.

597. Goldschmidt, Dietrich and Sibylle Hübner, "Changing Concepts of the University in Society: The West Germany Case," IN Holmes 1971, 265-283. Original.

598. Goodrich, Peter S., "Manchester's (England) Urban Univer-City," IN Murphy 1975, 161-178. Original.

599. Grant, Nigel, "U.S.S.R.," IN Archer 1972, 80-102. Original.

An essay on the structure and function of higher education in the Soviet Union.

600. Granzow, Hermann, "Post Secondary Education in the Federal Republic of Germany," IN McLeod 1973, 89-100. Original.

601. Graubard, Stephen R., "Barriers to Internationalism," IN Bailey 1977, 191-196. Original.

602. Halsey, A. H., "The English Idea of a University," IN Lunsford 1963a, 151-169. EJS, 3 (October 1962), 85-101.

603. Harasymiw, Bohdan, "Post-Secondary Education in the USSR," IN McLeod 1973, 129-143. Original.

604. Harrison, John P., "The Latin American University--Present Problems Viewed Through the Recent Past," IN Kertesz 1971, 414-432. Original.

605. Harrison, Wilfrid, "Some Problems of New Universities in England," IN Lawlor 1968, 51-75. Original.

606. Hauner, Milan, "Czechoslovakia," IN Archer 1972, 36-56. Original.

An overview of the development of higher education in Czechoslovakia mainly from 1945 to the late 1960's.

607. Haviland Jr., H. Field, "Federal Programs of International Education," IN Dobbins 1963, 76-88. Original.

608. Hester, James M., "To Illuminate Tomorrow: Higher Education in an Interdependent World," IN Bailey 1977, 1-11. Original.

609. Hewett, Stanley, "Contextual Change in the Education of Teachers--England and Wales," IN Holmes 1971, 240-250. Original.

610. Hewlett, Sylvia, "The University in Latin America," IN Stephens 1975, 129-142. Original.

611. Hilliard, John F., "A Perspective on Internation Development," IN Humphrey 1967, 180-196. Original.

612. Hochleitner, Ricardo D., "Spain," IN Perkins 1972, 195-198. Original.

613. Holmström, L. G., "Description and Evaluation of Roskilde University Centre a University Pedogogic Innovation," IN Verreck 1974, 105-129. Original.

614. Hu, C. T., "The Chinese People's University: Bastion of Marxism-Leninism," IN Niblett 1972, 63-74. Original.

615. Husén, Torsten, "The Community: Its Nature and Responsibilities," IN Bailey 1977, 197-206. Original.

An international community of scholarship and cooperation is recommended.

616. Husén, Torsten, "Sweden," IN Entwistle 1972, 202-219. Original.

617. Jackson, Stanley P., "The University in South Africa," IN Stephens 1975, 114-128. Original.

618. Jobling, R. G., "The New Universities," IN Butcher 1972, 325-334. Original.

The "new universities" is a term that generally applies to all the colleges in Great Britain which received a Royal Charter during the 1960's and the early 1970's.

619. Karmel, Peter, "Flinders: A Case-Study of New University Development in Australia," IN Lawlor 1968, 129-156. Original.

620. Kato, Ichiro, "Japanese Universities: Student Revolt and Reform Plans," IN Seabury 1975, 257-263. Original.

621. Kean, Andrew M., "Trinity and All Saint's Colleges, Leeds, England," IN Niblett 1972, 347-360. Original.

622. Kettle, Arnold, "The Open University and the Problem of Inter-disciplinary Education," IN Lawlor 1972, 51-65. Original.

623. Khusro, Ali Mohammed, "Education: An Economic Necessity to Developing Countries," IN Bailey 1977, 82-88. Original.

624. Kirpal, Prem, "Higher Education in India: Priorities and Problems," IN Niblett 1972, 147-159. Original.

625. Klauw, Cor Van der and J. J. W. M. Wagemakers, "The Netherlands," IN Entwistle 1976, 237-248. Original.

626. Knoll, Joachim H., "The University in West Germany," IN Stephens 1975, 143-159. Original.

627. Kobayashi, Tetsuya, "Changing Policies in Higher Education--The Japanese Case," IN Holmes 1971, 368-375. Original.

628. Kohlbrenner, Bernard J., "Some Aspects of Higher Education in the Philippines," IN Kertesz 1971, 455-469. Original.

629. Kothari, D. S., "India," IN Perkins 1972, 199-207. Original.

630. Kwapong, Alex A., "Ghana," IN Perkins 1972, 185-193. Original.

631. Laves, Walter H. C., "University Leadership in Transnational Educational Relationships," IN Humphrey 1967, 18-27. Original.

632. Leussink, Hans, "The Federal Republic of Germany," IN Perkins 1972, 143-150. Original.

633. Lewis, Brian, "The British Open University: Concepts and Realities," IN Harrison 1975, 202-227. Original.

Commentary by Stephen Yelon follows on pages 228-231.

634. Limiti, G., "The Italian University," IN Holmes 1971, 27-35. Original.

635. Lindop, Norman, "Hatfield (England) Polytechnic Today," IN Niblett 1972, 281-296. Original.

636. McAuley, James, "The Condition of Australian Universities," IN Seabury 1975, 264-267. Original.

637. McConnell, T. R., "The University and the State: A Comparative Study," IN Minter 1966, 88-118. Original.

Compares the internal/external relationships of Cambridge and Oxford with those of American universities.

638. MacRae, Donald, "The British Position," IN Seabury 1975, 176-180. Original.

Presents a view of the organizational climate of British universities in the late 1960's.

639. Maksimovic, Ivan, "The State and Major Contemporary Problems of Higher Education in Yugoslavia," IN Kertesz 1971, 370-380. Original.

640. Mancilla H., Ramón, "Professional Manpower Needs in Venezuela," IN Bailey 1977, 105-111. Original.

641. Mancini, Federico, "The Italian Student Movement--From Reform to Adventure," IN Kertesz 1971, 323-335. Dissent, 16 (September-October 1969), 413-422.

642. Martinotti, Guido, "Italy," IN Archer 1972, 167-195. Original.

An essay on Italian higher education with emphasis on university organization, students, faculty, and curricula.

643. Marvel, William W., "The University in World Affairs: An Introduction," IN Mayhew 1967, 139-146. ULA (1966).

644. Mathur, M. W., "Tasks of Universities in India," IN Kertesz 1971, 471-485.

645. Michael, Ian and Felix Mnthali, "Political Influence and Higher Education in Malawi," IN Holmes 1971, 348-356. Original.

646. Migoya, Francisco, "Universidad Iberoamericana, Mexico: The Ongoing Reform," IN Niblett 1972, 137-146. Original.

647. Miller, Paul A., "The Development of Coordination Planning for International Educational Endeavors," IN Shiver 1967, 115-121. Original.

648. Miller, Paul A., "Expanding Opportunities in International Education," IN Smith 1967, 166-169. Original.

649. Moncada, Alberto, "Directions of Development in Higher Education in Spain," IN Niblett 1972, 207-219. Original.

650. Mukherjee, K. C., "The Indian Universities," IN Holmes 1971, 376-383. Original.

651. Munroe, David, "Post-Secondary Education in Canada: A Survey of Recent Trends and Development," IN McLeod 1973, 31-49. Original.

(Also printed in French)

652. Nagai, Michio, "University Problems in Japan," IN Kertesz 1971, 433-444. Original.

653. Najman, Dragoljub, "Functions for International Organizations in Higher Education," IN Bailey 1977, 52-62. Original.

654. Narita, K., "The University in Japan," In Stephens 1975, 174-185. Original.

655. Nicol, Davidson, "African Universities and the State--Academic Freedom and Social Responsibility," IN Kertesz 1971, 405-413. Original.

656. Nimmanheminda, Nai Sukich, "Higher Education in Thailand," IN Kertesz 1971, 445-454. Original.

657. Nipperdy, Thomas, "The German University in Crisis," IN Seabury 1975, 119-142. Original.

658. Njoku, Eni, "The Modernization of the New Nations," IN Henderson 1968, 120-124. Original.

659. Nuttgens, Patrick, "The New Polytechnics: Their Principles and Potential," IN Lawlor 1972, 37-47. Original.

660. Oliver, W. H., "A Society and Its Universities--The Case of New Zealand," IN Lawlor 1968, 159-195. Original.

661. Passin, Herbert, "Japan," IN Perkins 1972, 219-227. Original.

662. Pearlman, Samuel, "Aspects of Campus Mental Health Outside of the United States and Canada," IN Bloom 1975, 153-182. Original.

663. Perkin, Harold J., "A British University Designed for the Future: Lancaster," IN Niblett 1972, 183-194. Original.

664. Perkins, James A., "The International Dimension in Higher Education," IN Bailey 1977, 207-214. Original.

665. Perry, Walter, "Britain's Open University," IN Godwin 1972, 97-106. Original.

666. Perry, Walter, "Britain's Open University," IN Wilson 1972, 287-292. Original.

667. Perry, Walter, "Developments at the Open University," IN Stephens 1978, 127-138. Original.

668. Peterson, A. D. C., "English Higher Education: The Issues Involved," IN McGrath 1966, 218-234. Original.

669. Posthumus, Kornelis, "The Netherlands," IN Perkins 1972, 209-217. Original.

670. Pratt, John, "Higher Education and the State," IN Holmes 1971, 161-174. Original.

This essay deals with the relationship between higher education and the state in Great Britain.

671. Price, R. F., "The University in China," IN Stephens 1975, 186-201. Original.

672. Reed, Howard A., "Intercultural or Non-Western Studies in General Education," IN Rice 1964, 51-60. Original.

673. Reeves, Marjorie, "The European University from Medieval Times (with special reference to Oxford and Cambridge)," IN Niblett 1970, 61-84. Original.

Commentary by Warren B. Martin follows on pages 85-93.

674. Rhodes, Herbert D. and William L. Gaines, "Gustave Erlt and African Education," IN Kent 1970, 152-160. Original.

A case study of the African Graduate Fellowship Program as sponsored, in part, by the Council of Graduate Schools.

675. Sartori, Giovanni, "The Italian University System," IN Seabury 1975, 246-256. Original.

676. Scheffknecht, J. J., "Permanent Education: A European Framework for Higher Education," IN Stephens 1978, 91-115. Original.

677. Schutte, Donald G. W., "The University of Dar es Salaam: A Socialist Enterprise," IN Niblett 1972, 75-96. Original.

A case study of the development of the University of Dar es Sallaam in Tanzania, Africa.

678. Segerstedt, Torgny T., "The Situation of Swedish Universities," IN Kertesz 1971, 277-286. Original.

679. Sherlock, Philip, "The Caribbean," IN Perkins 1972, 159-173. Original.

680. Shimbori, Michiya, "Hiroshima University in Evolution: The Question of Autonomy," IN Niblett 1972, 160-173. Original.

681. Shuster, George, "The Exchange of Persons and the Cultural Policy of Nations," IN Kertesz 1971, 208-216. Original.

682. Singh, Amrik, "The University in India," IN Stephens 1975, 71-81. Original.

683. Sommerkorn, Ingrid N., "The Free University of Berlin: Case Study of an Experimental Seminar (1968-69)," IN Niblett 1972, 336-346. Original.

684. Smith, R. C., "The Open University of the United Kingdom," IN McLeod 1973, 171-173. Original.

685. Smuckler, Ralph H., "The American University and Its International Relations," IN Bailey 1977, 45-51. Original.

686. Stewart, W. A. C., "Rediscovering Identity in Higher Education," IN Lawlor 1972, 107-129. Original.

A review of the pattern of development of higher education in Great Britain.

687. Suchodolski, Bogdan, "The East European University," IN Holmes 1971, 120-134. Original.

688. Sutton, F. X., "African Universities and the Process of Change in Middle Africa," IN Kertesz 1971, 383-404. Original.

689. Taggart, Glen L., "Association for International Cooperation in Higher Education and Research," IN Bailey 1977, 97-105. Original.

690. Thompson, Kenneth W., "Public and Private Organizations: Their Differing Roles," IN Bailey 1977, 34-45. Original.

Problems and prospects of large public international organizations in support of higher education.

691. Thompson, Kenneth W., "Universities and the Developing World," IN Kertesz 1971, 153-161. Original.

692. Tierney, James F., "Higher Education in Latin America in an Era of Change," IN Niblett 1972, 97-114. Original.

693. Tokoyama, Tsunesaburo, "The Japanese System of Indirect Support to Private Institutions," IN Bailey 1977, 168-175. Original.

694. Tollefson Jr., Bert M., "Co-operation Between Universities of Developed and Developing Countries," IN Kertesz 1971, 162-173. Original.

695. Tomiak, J. J., "The University in the Soviet Union," IN Stephens 1975, 160-173. Original.

696. Vaughan, Michalina, "Poland," IN Archer 1972, 57-79. Original.

An overview of the development and expansion of higher education in Poland since World War II.

697. Venables, Ethel and Peter Venables, "The Study of Higher Education in Britain," IN Butcher 1972, 17-34. Original.

698. Verney, Douglas V., "The Government and Politics of a Developing University--A Canadian Experience," IN Kertesz 1971, 259-276. Original.

699. Vimont, Claude, "Methods of Forecasting Employment in France and Use of These Forecasts to Work Out Official Educational Programmes," IN Harris 1964, 223-246. Original.

700. Wagley, Charles W., "Latin America," IN Perkins 1972, 229-241. Original.

701. Wahlbäck, Krister, "University Autonomy in Sweden," IN Seabury 1975, 268-278. Original.

702. Walker, W. G., "The University in Australia," IN Stephens 1975, 51-70. Original.

703. Weiler, Hans N., "Evaluation of Purpose in Emerging Universities," IN Bailey 1977, 29-33. Original.

704. Wildenmann, Rudolf, "Higher Education in Transition--The Case of the Universities in the Federal Republic of Germany," IN Kertesz 1971, 336-352. Original.

705. Williams, Eric, "Higher Education Alternatives in Developing Countries," IN Stephens 1978, 42-67. Original.

706. Williams, Eric, "The University in the Caribbean," IN Stephens 1975, 83-113. Original.

707. Williamson, Ann, "Innovations in Higher Education: French Experience Before 1968," IN Holmes 1971, 250-264. Original.

708. Willson, F. M. G., "Department, College, or Inter-disciplinary School: A British Perspective," IN McHenry 1977, 170-184. Original.

709. Wolfenden, John Sir, "British University Grants and Government Relations," IN Dobbins 1968, 206-213. Original.

710. Wolfenden, John F., "Great Britain," IN Perkins 1972, 133-141. Original.

711. Wright, Douglas T., "Recent Development in Higher Education in Ontario," IN Niblett 1972, 297-309. Original.

712. Young, Herrick B., "A Reassessment of Overseas Student Exchange Programs: Guidelines for the Further Development of Policies and Programs," IN Smith 1962, 69-71. Original.

6
THE UNIVERSITY

713. Anderson, G. Lester, "Land-Grant Universities and Their Continuing Challenge," IN Anderson 1976, 1-10. Original.

714. Arrowsmith, William, "Toward a New University," IN Letter 1970, 1-23. Original.

715. Barbe, Richard H. and Roy M. Hall, "The Metropolitan State University: On Becoming an Operating Center," IN Mauer 1976, 43-52. Original.

716. Barzun, Jacques, "College to University--And After," IN Margolis 1969, 148-155. Amer S, 33 (Spring 1964), 212-219.

717. Bennis, Warren G., "Great Expectations," IN Mitchell 1974, 19-27. Original.

Inaugural address, University of Cincinnati, November 5, 1971.

718. Birenbaum, William, "Cities and Universities: Collision of Crises," IN Eurich 1968, 43-63. Original.

719. Brick, Holmes, "The University in the U.S.A.," IN Holmes 1971, 36-61. Original.

An excellent concise history of American universities that documents some of the major European influences.

720. Brubacher, John S., "A Century of the State University," IN Brickman 1962, 67-79. Original.

721. Clark Jr., Joseph S., "The Task of the Urban University," IN Dobbins 1964, 40-45. Original.

722. Dash, Roger E., and Gary L. Riley, "The Evolution of an Urban University," IN Riley 1977, 145-158. Original.

723. Dickey, Frank G., "Aligning Priorities in Public, Comprehensive Universities," IN Smith 1965, 182-184. Original.

724. Dorsey, Gray L., "Rationality in the Contemporary University," IN Hook 1974, 119-120. Original.

725. Doxiadis, Constantinos A., "Cities in Crisis and the University," IN Caffrey 1969, 305-327. Original.

726. Duhl, Leonard J., "The University and the Urban Crisis," IN Mitchell 1974, 177-189. Original.

727. Ellis, Elmer, "The Functions of a State University in a State System of Higher Education," IN Donovan 1965, 64-72. Original.

728. Folger, John K., "Urban Sprawl in the Academic Community," IN Mayhew 1967, 181-190. JHE, 34 (November 1963), 450-457.

729. Gardner, John W., "The University and the Cities," IN Caffrey 1969, 184-190. ER, 50 (Winter 1969), 5-8.

730. Goddard, David R. and Linda C. Koons, "A Profile of the University of Pennsylvania," IN Riesman 1973, 225-248. Original.

731. Harvill, Richard A., "The American State University," IN Paulsen 1970, 1-15. Original.

732. Healy, Timothy S., "The City University of New York," IN Niblett 1972, 361-372. Original.

733. Heimberger, Frederic, "The State Universities," IN Morison 1966, 51-76. Dae, 93 (Fall 1964), 1083-1108.

734. Hoffman, Robert, "The Irrelevance of Relevance," IN Hook 1974, 107-118. Original.

> Mr. Hoffman states that the common objective of the university is to pursue knowledge, not to solve major social problems or to foster student interests by teaching them "what they want to learn."

735. Howard, George F., "The State University of America," IN Portman 1972, 121-138. AtL, 67 (March 1891), 332-342.

736. Jackson, Samuel C., "Is the University Superfluous in the Urban Crisis?" IN Murphy 1975, 3-13. Original.

737. Johnson Jr., Henry C., "Are Our Universities Schools?" IN Milton 1968, 158-174. HER, 35 (Spring 1965), 165-177.

738. Keast, William R., "Aligning Priorities in Independent Comprehensive Universities," IN Smith 1965, 185-188. Original.

739. Kerr, Clark, "Conservatism, Dynamism, and the Changing University," IN Eurich 1968, 299-321. UU (1963).

740. Kerr, Clark, "Toward the More Perfect University," IN Margolis 1969, 298-312. UIA (1967).

741. Kristol, Irving, "What Business is a University In?" IN Goodall 1976, 289-299. NYTM, (March 22, 1970), 30-31; 106; 108; 111.

Mr. Kristol suggests that universities are "asking for trouble" if they assume a more political role and stray from their "traditional and historical" activities.

742. Lipset, Seymour M., "The American University--1964-1974: From Activism to Austerity," IN Seabury 1975, 143-156. Original.

743. McConnell, T. R., "Can the Elite University Survive," IN Goodall 1976, 264-277. RR, 3 (1973), 1-7.

744. McCormick, Richard P., "Rutgers, The State University," IN Riesman 1973, 271-286. Original.

745. Madsen, David, "The Land-Grant University: Myth and Reality," IN Anderson 1976, 23-48. Original.

746. Maritain, Jacques, "The University," IN Margolis 1969, 288-297. EC (1943).

747. Maucker, J. W., "Aligning Priorities in State Colleges and Medium-Sized Universities," IN Smith 1965, 179-181. Original.

748. Millett, John D., "Similarities and Differences Among Universities of the United States," IN Perkins 1973, 39-56. Original.

749. Mitchell, Howard E., "The Human Resources Center of the University of Pennsylvania," IN Mitchell 1974, 35-68. Original.

750. Morison, Robert S., "Foundations and Universities," IN Morison 1966, 77-109. Dae, 93 (Fall 1964), 1109-1141.

751. Morris, Charles, "The University and the Modern Age," IN Stroup 1966, 52-75. Original.

752. Murphy, Thomas P., "Urban Governmental Manpower," IN Murphy 1975, 49-70. Original.

753. Murphy, Thomas P. and M. Gordon Seyffert, "The Future Urban University," IN Murphy 1975, 381-400. Original.

754. Nash, Paul, "The American University," IN Holmes 1971, 298-316. Original.

A very perceptive assessment of the forces that are influencing change within the American university.

755. Nichols, David C., "Federal City College: A Model for New Urban Universities?" IN Anderson 1976, 205-222. Original.

756. Nichols, David C., "Land-Grant University Services and Urban Policy," IN Anderson 1976, 223-236. Original.

757. Perkins, James A., "Missions and Organization: A Redefinition," IN Perkins 1973, 247-260. Original.

Dr. Perkins presents arguments for and against removing certain "missions from the organization" in order to make multimission university more "manageable."

758. Perkins, James A., "The Search for Internal Coherence," IN Margolis 1969, 179-196. UIT (1966).

The author provides specific suggestions concerning curriculum and the distribution of power within the university in response to contemporary demands.

759. Peterson, Richard E., "The Regional University and Comprehensive College: Some Ideas," IN Perry 1971, 73-95. Original.

760. Pinner, Frank, "The Crisis of the State Universities: Analysis and Remedies," IN Sanford 1962, 940-971. Original.

761. Rosenbaum, Patricia L., "Facts About Philadelphia and Its Institutions of Higher Learning," IN Mitchell 1974, 193-206. Original.

762. Ross, Earle D., "Contributions of Land-Grant Colleges and Universities to Higher Education," IN Brickman 1962, 94-109. Original.

763. Seyffert, M. Gordon, "The University as an Urban Neighbor," IN Murphy 1975, 137-159. Original.

764. Van Hise, Charles R., "Inaugural Address (University of Wisconsin, 1904)," IN Hawkins 1970, 23-34. Science, 20 (1904), 194-205.

In his inaugural address President Van Hise calls for a multi-purpose university that serves the needs of both basic and applied research in addition to the other more traditional forms of service.

765. Veysey, Laurence R., "The Price of Structure," IN Hawkins 1970, 79-87. EAU (1965).

A view of the university in the 1890's that emphasizes the development of "bureaucratic standards."

766. Wallis, W. Allen, "Centripetal and Centrifugal Forces in University Organization," IN Morison 1966, 39-50. Dae, 93 (Fall 1964), 1071-1082.

767. Wells, Herman B., "The Growth and Transformation of State Universities in the United States Since World War II," IN Kertesz 1971, 12-22. Original.

7
COLLEGES (FOUR-YEAR) AND JUNIOR/COMMUNITY COLLEGES

768. Averill, Lloyd J., "A Singular Model," IN Averill 1971, 202-229. Original.

An overview of the distinct features of the church-related college.

769. Beckes, Isaac K., "The Impact of Public Junior Colleges on Private Institutions," IN Letter 1970, 92-102. Original.

770. Bennett, Mary Woods, "Changes Within the Liberal Arts Colleges," IN Wilson 1965, 62-73. Original.

771. Bestor, Arthur, "The College of Liberal Arts and Sciences," IN Margolis 1969, 130-147. RL (1956).

772. Blum, Virgil C., "The Future Role of the Church-Related College," IN Smith 1961, 207-209. Original.

Commentary by John D. Mosely follows on pages 210-213.

773. Bogue, Jesse P. and Norman Burns, "Legal and Extralegal Influences for Improving Junior Colleges," IN Henry 1965, 232-246. Original.

774. Bolman Jr., Frederick deW., "Feast or Famine for the Liberal Arts College? Reflections on Intellectual Economy and Polity," IN McGrath 1964, 80-89. Original.

775. Boroff, David, "Smith: A College for ARG's (All-Round Girls) with High IQ's," IN Bellman 1962, 147-159. Ma, 52 (March 1961), 122-125; 182-187.

776. Bowen, Howard R., "Does Private Education Have a Future?" IN Jellema 1972, 136-149. Original.

777. Bushnell, David S., "Community College: Organizing for Change," IN Smith 1971, 78-88. Original.

778. Chapman, Charles E., "Aligning Priorities in Junior and Community Colleges," IN Smith 1965, 167-170. Original.

779. Cosand, Joseph P., "The Community College in 1980," IN Eurich 1968, 134-148. Original.

780. Cosand, Joseph P., "The Two-Year College's Contribution to Curriculum Development," IN Dennis 1966, 192-195. Original.

781. Devane, William C., "The College of Liberal Arts," IN Morison 1966, 1-18. Dae, 93 (Fall 1964), 1033-1050.

782. Dixon, James P., "Aligning Priorities in Liberal Arts Colleges Over 1,000," IN Smith 1965, 175-178. Original.

783. Doherty, George P., "Case Study: The Bell and Howell Schools," IN Vermilye 1973, 182-189. Original.

784. Erickson, Clifford G., "Community Colleges and the Immediacy of Community Pressures," IN Smith 1966, 141-144. Original.

785. Erickson, Clifford G., "Recruitment of Faculty for the Community and Junior Colleges," IN Smith 1967, 249-252. Original.

786. Eskow, Seymour, "Community College," IN Smith 1969, 51-55. Original.

787. Evans, John W., "Catholic Higher Education on the Secular Campus," IN Hassenger 1967, 275-293. Original.

788. Ford, Charles E., "Where Next: The Future of Catholic Higher Education," IN Smith 1967, 162-165. Original.

789. Fortmann, Henry R., Jerome K. Pasto, and Thomas B. King, "Colleges of Agriculture Revisited," IN Anderson 1976, 49-78. Original.

790. Foster, Julian, "Some Effects of Jesuit Education: A Case Study," IN Hassenger 1967, 163-190. Original.

791. Friedrichs, Robert W., "Limited Cognition and Ultimate Cognition," IN Averill 1971, 119-124. Mot, (April 1966).

> "How might church and university reciprocate within the format of the church college while each maintains its separate integrity?"

792. Garrison, Roger H., "Unique Problems of Junior Colleges," IN Smith 1967, 227-231. Original.

793. Gleason, Philip, "American Catholic Higher Education: A Historical Perspective," IN Hassenger 1967, 15-53. Original.

794. Gleazer Jr., Edmund J., "Recognizing the Expanding Role of Junior Colleges in Higher Education," IN College 1968, 66-83. Original.

795. Godard, James M., "Federal Aid and the Governance of Church Colleges," IN Smith 1964, 242-245. Original.

796. Hassenger, Robert, "College and Catholics: An Introduction," IN Hassenger 1967, 3-13. Original.

797. Hassenger, Robert, "The Future Shape of Catholic Higher Education," IN Hassenger 1967, 295-334. Original.

798. Hassenger, Robert, "The Impact of Catholic Colleges," IN Hassenger 1967, 103-161. Original.

799. Hassenger, Robert, "Portrait of a Catholic Women's College," IN Hassenger 1967, 83-100. Original.

800. Hassenger, Robert and Gerald Rauch, "Some Problem Areas in Catholic Higher Education--The Student," IN Hassenger 1967, 213-221. Original.

801. Hill, Alfred T., "Cooperation Among Small Colleges," IN Donovan 1965, 34-46. Original.

802. Hill, A. T., "Effective Means of Evaluating Programs in Small Colleges and Developing Long-Range Plans with Limited Resources for Planning Are Available," IN Smith 1961, 176-180. Original.

803. Hillway, Tyrus, "Historical Development of the Junior and Community College," IN Brickman 1962, 110-123. Original.

804. Huitt, Ralph K., "What's Ahead for the Land-Grant Colleges?" IN Anderson 1976, 11-22. Original.

805. Hungate, Thad L., L. Richard Meeth, and William R. O'Connell, Jr., "The Quality and Cost of Liberal Arts College Programs: A Study of Twenty-Five Colleges," IN McGrath 1964, 8-36. Original.

806. Jellema, William W., "The Identity of the Christian College," IN Averill 1971, 86-99. Original.

807. John, Ralph C., "The Private College and the Church-State Issue," IN Mauer 1976, 219-225. Original.

808. Jones, Jack H., "Proprietary Schools as a National Resource," IN Vermilye 1973, 177-181. Original.

809. Kerns, Francis E., "Social Consciousness and Academic Freedom in Catholic Higher Education," IN Hassenger 1967, 223-249. Original.

810. Leo, John, "Some Problem Areas in Catholic Higher Education--The Faculty," IN Hassenger 1967, 193-201. Original.

811. Lerner, Max, "Colleges and the Urban Crisis," IN Harcleroad 1970, 26-44. Original.

812. McCoy, Pressley C., "Qualities of Institutional Excellence in a Liberal Arts College," IN McGrath 1964, 90-106. Original.

813. McGrath, Earl J., "Continuing Study of the Liberal Arts College," IN McGrath 1964, 1-7. Original.

814. McGrath, Earl J., "Rescuing the Small College: A Bold Approach," IN McGrath 1972, 127-151. Original.

815. McNamara, Robert J., "Some Problem Areas in Catholic Higher Education--The Priest-Scholar," IN Hassenger 1967, 203-212. Original.

816. Marvel, William W., "The Small College and World Affairs," IN Letter 1968, 108-125. Original.

817. Mayhew, Lewis B., "The New Colleges," IN Baskin 1965, 1-26. Original.

818. Medsker, Leland L., "The American Community College: Its Contribution to Higher Education," IN Niblett 1972, 314-324. Original.

819. Medsker, Leland L., "Changes in Junior Colleges and Technical Institutes," IN Wilson 1965, 79-84. Original.

820. Medsker, Leland L., "What is the Most Constructive Role for the Junior Colleges?" IN Smith 1960, 194-196. Original.

821. Mount, Sister Teresa A., "The Catholic Junior College Movement," IN Donovan 1964, 36-65. Original.

822. Pattillo, Manning M., "Church-Related Colleges: Where Next?" IN Smith 1967, 158-161. Original.

823. Pfnister, Allan O., "A Century of the Church-Related College," IN Brickman 1962, 80-93. Original.

824. Reiss, Paul L., "The Catholic College: Some Built-In Tensions," IN Hassenger 1967, 253-273. Original.

825. Reynolds, James W., "The Future Goals of the Junior College," IN Smith 1961, 203-206. Original.

826. Reynolds, James W., "The Junior College: What Next?" IN Smith 1967, 223-226. Original.

827. Reynolds, James W., "Needed Changes in Purposes and Programs of Community Colleges," IN McGrath 1966, 104-121. Original.

828. Richardson Jr., Richard C., "Departmental Leadership in the Two-Year College," IN Smith 1967, 244-248. Original.

829. Sanford, Nevitt, "What is an Excellent Liberal Arts College," IN Letter 1968, 25-40. Original.

830. Schmidt, George P., "A Century of Liberal Arts College," IN Brickman 1962, 50-66. Original.

831. Sherry, Paul H., "The Policy-Making Role of Trustees in Church-Related Colleges," IN Smith 1967, 139-143. Original.

832. Stewart, Blair, "Cooperation by Small Groups of Liberal Arts Colleges," IN Wilson 1965, 207-210. Original.

833. Stewart, Blair, "Experimentation and the Liberal Arts College," IN Harris 1960, 156-159. Original.

834. Swett, David E., "A Model for an Upper-Division Urban College," IN Vermilye 1972, 211-224. Original.

835. Telford, Charles W. and Walter T. Plant, "The Psychological Impact of the Public Junior College," IN Yamamoto 1968, 390-394. PIP (1963).

836. Wattenbarger, James L., "The Expanding Roles of the Junior and Community Colleges," IN Smith 1963, 132-135. Original.

837. Weigle, Richard D., "Aligning Priorities in the Small College," IN Smith 1965, 171-174. Original.

838. Weiss, Robert F., "The Environment for Learning on the Catholic College Campus," IN Hassenger 1967, 57-82. Original.

839. Wilms, Wellford W., "Profile of Proprietary Students," IN Vermilye 1974, 34-39. Original.

8

NON-TRADITIONAL INSTITUTIONS, PROGRAMS, AND CLIENTELE

840. Abrams, Irwin, "Overseas Travel-Study Programs in U.S. Higher Education," IN Smith 1961, 220-223. Original.

841. Adams, Donald V., "Living and Learning Centers," IN Herron 1970, 128-138. Original.

842. Adams, Frank C., "Innovation in Student Support: Undergraduate Credit for Work Experience at One University," IN Keene 1975, 135-148. Original.

843. Anderson, Adolph G., "Higher Education and the University-Sponsored Experimental College," IN Smith 1967, 215-217. Original.

844. Arbolino, Jack N., "A Plan for External Degrees," IN Smith 1971, 65-69. Original.

845. Bailey, Stephen K., "Flexible Time-Space Programs: A Plea for Caution," IN Vermilye 1972, 172-176. Original.

846. Beckman, George M., "Guidelines for an Experimental Curriculum with Major Emphasis on Non-Western Cultures," IN Smith 1964, 168-171. Original.

847. Bernardo, Aldo S., "New Beginnings in General Education," IN Hook 1975, 257-259. Original.

> A case study and rationale of innovation at Verrazzano College which attempts to provide a student directed curriculum without traditional academic departments.

848. Bevan, John M., "Florida Presbyterian College: New Adventure in Education," IN Stickler 1964, 91-105. Original.

849. Blackman, Edward B., "Residence Halls as an Integral Part of the Learning Environment," IN Smith 1966, 250-252. Original.

850. Bouwsma, Franklin G., "Instructional Delivery Systems and Open Learning," IN Hughes 1975, 284-294. Original.

851. Boyer, Ernest L., "Breaking Up the Youth Ghetto," IN Vermilye 1974, 4-11. Original.

Dr. Boyer suggests that American higher education must stop its heavy reliance on the younger student and seek to develop "new constituencies" especially among older citizens.

852. Caldwell, Oliver J., "The New Humanism--International and Intercultural Programs in the State Universities of Illinois," IN Kertesz 1971, 198-207. Original.

853. Caldwell, Oliver J., "Some Comments on Possible Experimental Curricula with Major Emphasis on Non-Western Cultures," IN Smith 1964, 172-176. Original.

854. Campbell, Jean W., "The Nontraditional Student in Academe," IN Furniss 1974, 192-199. Original.

855. Carpenter, Marjorie, "The Role of Experimental Colleges in American Higher Education," IN Stickler 1964, 1-14. Original.

856. Christ-Janer, Arland F., "Credit by Examination," IN Vermilye 1972, 160-171. Original.

857. Coleman, James S., "Differences Between Experiential and Classroom Learning," IN Keeton 1976, 49-61. Original.

858. Coleman, John R. and Paul E. Wehr, "Off-Campus Involvement Programs," IN Mitchell 1974, 107-120. Original.

859. Cross, K. Patricia and John R. Valley, "Non-Traditional Study: An Overview," IN Cross 1974, 1-10. Original.

860. Cytrynbaum, Solomon and Richard D. Mann, "Community as Campus--Project Outreach: University of Michigan," IN Runkel 1969, 266-289. Original.

A case study of a social action program as an outgrowth of the attempt to reorganize an introductory psychology course.

861. Dennis, Lawrence E., "The Other End of Sesame Street," IN Smith 1971, 57-64. Original.

Dr. Dennis presents a model for a new university based on the concept reflected in the British Open University.

862. Dennis, Lawrence E., "The Proper Role of Higher Education in the Development of the Peace Corps," IN Smith 1961, 214-219. Original.

863. Dressel, Paul L., "Educational Innovation at Michigan State University," IN Stickler 1964, 121-132. Original.

864. Driscoll, William J., "Independent Study: A New Emphasis for the 1970's," IN Buxton 1975, 232-238. Original.

865. Dubois, Eugene E. and Frederick A. Ricci, "Non-Traditional Study: A Burgeoning Force in Reshaping American Higher Education," IN Vaccaro 1975, 28-42. Original.

866. Dunn Jr., John A., "Old Westbury I and Old Westbury II," IN Riesman 1973, 199-224. Original.

> The history and development of an experimental college within the SUNY system.

867. Forrest, Aubrey, Joan E. Knapp, and Judith Pendergrass, "Tools and Methods of Evaluation," IN Keeton 1976, 161-188. Original.

> The essay deals with some of the problems associated with the assessment of experiential learning.

868. Friedman, Neil, "Experiment on a Black Campus--Miles College," IN Runkel 1969, 52-66. Original.

869. Fuchs, Lawrence H., "The Peace Corps and American Institutions--The Not So Hidden Agenda," IN Kertesz 1971, 174-197. Original.

870. Furniss, W. Todd, "Developments in Off-Campus Learning," IN Godwin 1972, 126-136. Original.

871. Gardner, John W., "College and the Alternatives," IN Margolis 1969, 328-340. Exce (1961).

872. Gould, Samuel B., "New Arrangements for Learning," IN Godwin 1972, 87-96. Original.

873. Grant, Gerald, "A Network of Antiochs," IN Riesman 1973, 13-49. Original.

874. Gruber, Howard E., "The Uses and Abuses of Negative Results," IN Milton 1968, 49-60. AIS (1965).

> A report of an extended investigation of "self-directed study."

875. Gustad, John W., "New College: A Minus Five Months," IN Stickler 1964, 49-56. Original.

876. Hayward, Sumner, "Five Experimental Programs in Undergraduate Liberal Arts," IN Smith 1964, 66-69. Original.

877. Hefferlin, J. B. Lon, "Avoiding Cut-Rate Credits and Discount Degrees," IN Cross 1974, 148-174. Original.

The author addresses the problems associated with maintaining quality in awarding credits in non-traditional programs.

878. Houle, Cyril O., "Deep Traditions of Experimental Learning," IN Keeton 1976, 19-33. Original.

879. Hunt, Mary R., "How Important and How Valid Are Off-Campus Learning Experiences, Both Formal and Informal?" IN Smith 1966, 246-249. Original.

880. Iversen, Robert W., "The Peace Corps Challenge to Higher Education," IN Smith 1967, 201-206. Original.

881. Johnson, B. Lamar, "Behold, You Have Creative A New Thing: Summary and Critique," IN Stickler 1964, 173-185. Original.

An overview of the trends and problems of experimental colleges.

882. Jones, Phillip E., "Accommodating the Nontraditional Student," IN Heyns 1977, 100-104. Original.

883. Keats, John, "Some Reasonable Alternatives," IN Margolis 1969, 341-354. SP (1965).

The author provides some alternatives to attendance at college for further learning.

884. Keeton, Morris, "The Case for Experimental Education," IN Vermilye 1976, 188-191. Original.

885. Keeton, Morris T., "Credentials for the Learning Society," IN Keeton 1976, 1-18. Original.

An overview of the Cooperative Assessment of Experimental Learning (CAEL) project and of the rationale for experimental learning in higher education.

886. Kelley, Samuel E. and Karen L. Morell, "Administrators of Change: The Development and Administration of Campus Centers for Offenders," IN Mauer 1976, 178-194. Original.

A case study of the institutional impact of a highly unusual innovation involving a prison release program to attend college.

887. Kormondy, Edward J., "The Evergreen State College: An Alternative," IN Hughes 1975, 202-206. Original.

888. Lehmann, Timothy, "Evaluating Contract Learning," IN Vermilye 1975, 126-136. Original.

889. Lewis, Caleb A., "Courses by Newspaper," IN Vermilye 1974, 67-70. Original.

890. Leyden, Ralph C., "The Stephens College Program," IN Stickler 1964, 33-47. Original.

891. Lichtman, Jane, "Free Universities," IN Vermilye 1972, 149-159. Original.

892. London, Herbert L., "Questions of Viability in Non-traditional Education," IN Hook 1975, 221-226. CSJ, 7 (September-October 1973), 90-93.

893. Longsworth, Charles R., "Academic Organization by Schools at Hampshire College," IN McHenry 1977, 117-146. Original.

894. McCann, Charles J., "Academic Administration Without Departments at the Evergreen State College," IN McHenry 1977, 147-169. Original.

895. McCann, Charles J., "Vital Undergraduate Studies: What's the Right Climate?" IN Brann 1972, 118-126. Original.

896. McCollum, Sylvia G., "College for Prisoners," IN Vermilye 1975, 98-106. Original.

897. McHenry, Dean E., "The University of California, Santa Cruz," IN Stickler 1964, 133-144. Original.

898. Mahler, William A., "An Annotated Bibliography with Overviews," IN Cross 1974, 175-218. Original.

Annotated bibliography on non-traditional educational programs plus related subjects.

899. Mangone, Gerard J., "How Can We Better Educate Americans to Work and to Study Abroad?" IN Smith 1960, 119-123. Original.

900. Martin, Warren B., "A Pluralistic Model," IN Averill 1971, 187-200. SR, 50 (January 21, 1967), 68-69.

Dr. Martin argues for the "cluster college" as a means toward organizational and value diversity.

901. Mayeske, Betty Jo, "Open University in America," IN Vermilye 1974, 76-81. Original.

902. Meskill, Victor P., "Weekend College," IN Vermilye 1975, 107-112. Original.

903. Meyer, Samuel L., "The University of the Pacific and Its 'Cluster Colleges,'" IN Stickler 1964, 73-89. Original.

904. Mood, Alexander M., "Another Approach to Higher Education," IN Wilson 1972, 293-310. Original.

A "radical rearrangement" of higher education that calls for changing residence requirement, emphasis on lifelong learning, and home use of academic video cassettes.

Commentaries by David Mathews, Leonard A. Lecht, and John W. Macy, Jr. follow on pages 310-318.

905. Morgan, George A., "A New Interdisciplinary Curriculum," IN Smith 1971, 70-77. Original.

A case study of the integrated curriculum at Hiram College. This new curriculum emphasizes interdisciplinary studies with increased student freedom and responsibility.

906. Morrison, Donald H., "The Dartmouth Experience," IN Harris 1960, 146-151. Original.

An innovative calendar plan which permits independent study and individualized curricula.

907. Mortimer, Kenneth P. and Mark D. Johnson, "External Degree Programs: The Current Educational Frontier," IN Anderson 1976, 286-308. Original.

908. Murphy, Thomas P., "Free Universities and Urban Higher Education," IN Murphy 1975, 113-135. Original.

909. Nolan, Donald J., "Toward an Examining University: New York Regents External Degree," IN Hughes 1975, 260-272. Original.

910. Oglesby, R. R., "Proposed New College for the Florida State University," IN Stickler 1964, 157-171. Original.

911. Oldt, Esther A., "Antioch College as an Experimental Institution," IN Stickler 1964, 15-32. Original.

912. O'Neil, Robert M., "Pros and Cons of Learner-Centered Reform," IN Vermilye 1975, 4-13. Original.

913. Pitkin, Royce S. and George Beecher, "Extending the Educational Environment: The Community as a Resource for Learning," IN Baskin 1965, 174-195. Original.

914. Radest, Howard B., "On Interdisciplinary Education," IN Hook 1975, 227-233. Original.

915. Read, Joel Sr., "A Degree by Any Other Name . . . The Alverno Program," IN Hughes 1975, 214-226. Original.

This essay outlines the rationale and development of a non-traditional degree program at Alverno College in California.

916. Reed, Howard A., "Trends in Non-Western Studies in U.S. Liberal Arts Colleges," IN Smith 1964, 177-179. Original.

917. Rettaliata, John T., "Aligning Priorities in Professional, Technical, and Other Specialized Institutions," IN Smith 1965, 189-191. Original.

918. Ross, Woodburn O., "Monteith College of Wayne State University," IN Stickler 1964, 145-156. Original.

919. Ruyle, Janet and Lucy A. Geiselman, "Non-Traditional Opportunities and Programs," IN Cross 1974, 53-94. Original.

920. Sanford, Nevitt, "Theories of Higher Education and the Experimental College," IN Harris 1960, 152-155. Original.

921. Shoben Jr., Edward J., "Another Pass at Academic Organization and the Curriculum at the Evergreen State College," IN Brann 1972, 127-136. Original.

922. Shriver, R. Sargent, "The Peace Corps--A Report to Higher Education," IN Smith 1962, 37-43. Original.

923. Stephenson, John B. and Robert F. Sexton, "Experimental Education and Revitalization of the Liberal Arts," IN Hook 1975, 177-196. Original.

924. Stirton, W. E., "The University of Michigan Dearborn Campus," IN Stickler 1964, 107-120. Original.

925. Sutton, Lee, "Parsons College: Experiment as the Art of the Possible," IN Stickler 1964, 57-71. Original.

926. Sweet, David E., "Minnesota Metropolitan State College," IN Godwin 1972, 107-125. Original.

927. Tumin, Melvin, "Valid and Invalid Rationales," IN Keeton 1976, 41-48. Original.

The author develops what he believes are the valid arguments to support change and experiment within the traditional school curricula.

928. Warren, Jonathan R., "Alternatives to Degrees," IN Vermilye 1975, 137-143. Original.

929. Weathersby, George and Armand J. Henault, Jr., "Cost-Effectiveness of Programs," IN Keeton 1976, 131-149. Original.

An assessment of the economics of experiential learning.

930. Weidner, Edward W., "The University of Wisconsin-Green Bay: Man and His Evnironment," IN Niblett 1972, 243-254. Original.

931. Weinberg, Alvin M., "The Think Tank and the University," IN Smith 1968, 27-39. Original.

932. Whitaker, Urban G., "Assessors and Their Qualifications," IN Keeton 1976, 189-223. Original.

933. Willingham, Warren W., "Critical Issues and Basic Requirements for Assessment," IN Keeton 1976, 224-244. Original.

934. Winkie, Joy D., "Responsibility and Cooperative Education," IN Havice 1971, 133-144. Original.

935. Zarnowiecki, James and Thomas P. Murphy, "University Without Walls," IN Murphy 1975, 241-258. Original.

9
COLLEGE AND COMMUNITY RELATIONSHIPS

936. Apodaca, Jerry, "The Public and the University: A Decade of Difficulty," IN Peltason 1978, 15-18. Original.

937. Bailey, Richard P., "A Presidential Editorial Column," IN Mauer 1976, 202-210. Original.

President Bailey relates some of the "fun" and public reaction to his column, published irregularly, in the Minneapolis Star.

938. Ballard, Doris R., "Research, Records, and Reporting," IN Rowland 1977, 166-180. Original.

An overview of research, records, and reporting as fundamental activities relating to fund raising and alumni affairs.

939. Beld, Gordon G., "Photography for Institutional Relations," IN Rowland 1977, 109-118. Original.

940. Boyer, Ernest L., "Rebuilding Confidence," IN Vermilye 1973, 32-40. Original.

An essay on the need to rebuild public confidence in higher education as a result of the 1960's, etc.

941. Brandon, Arthur L., "What Public Information Programs Dealing with Higher Education Should Be Produced Over National Commercial TV and Radio?" IN Smith 1962, 165-168. Original.

942. Brooks, Oliver, "University Circle and Community Relations," IN Dobbins 1964, 32-36. Original.

A case study of school and community relations in largescale planning for a "higher education" complex in Cleveland, Ohio.

943. Cahill, Edward E. and Yvonne S. Perry, "Developing Indigenous Community Leadership: A Challenge to Urban Universities," IN Mitchell 1974, 69-86. Original.

944. Christenson, Wesley J., "News Services," IN Rowland 1977, 60-77. Original.

945. Ciervo, Arthur V., "Professionalism, Performance, and Productivity," IN Rowland 1977, 13-29. Original.

The author presents what he feels are the qualities necessary for an effective college public relations officer.

946. Corbett, Frank J. and Murray Levine, "University Involvement in the Community," IN Mitchell 1974, 137-162. Original.

947. Crawford, Anne R., "Organizing the Publications Program," IN Rowland 1977, 389-398. Original.

Ms. Crawford provides an overview of the development and production of college related publications and of the professional staff used by many colleges and universities to operate a publications office.

948. Crawford, Anne R., "Production of Publications," IN Rowland 1977, 408-412. Original.

949. Crawford, Anne R., "Publications for Key Audiences," IN Rowland 1977, 424-438. Original.

950. Cuthbertson, Kenneth M., "Ways in Which American Higher Education Can Better Inform the Public of Its Goals, Values, Needs, and Opportunities," IN Smith 1961, 197-200. Original.

951. Enarson, Harold L., "Higher Education and Community Services," IN Nichols 1970, 241-254. Original.

Commentaries by Barbara Fisler, Gerard J. Mangone, Joseph F. Kauffman, and Joseph P. Cosand follow on pages 255-268.

952. Fitzpatrick, B. T., "Procedures for Campus Participation in Urban Renewal," IN Dobbins 1964, 16-19. Original.

953. Frantzreb, Arthur C., "Management of Volunteers," IN Rowland 1977, 129-141. Original.

Problems and guidance in the management of volunteer help for various college related projects.

954. Gould, Samuel B., "Bridging the Interpretation Gap," IN Smith 1971, 234-240. Original.

Dr. Gould advocates better communication between the university and the general public.

955. Granshaw, Terry F., "Alumni," IN Packwood 1977, 428-449. Original.

A history and overview of college alumni affairs.

956. Heyse, Margaret F., "Extending the Laboratory Into the Community," IN Mauer 1976, 211-218. Original.

957. Humphrey, Hubert, "The Challenge to American Educators," IN Smith 1966, 31-41. Original.

Mr. Humphrey is encouraging the higher education community toward greater participation in community and world affairs.

958. Johnson, Eldon L., "The Tightening Tension: The University's External Relations," IN Minter 1968, 41-56. Original.

959. Lammer, Francis J., "Municipal Concern for Campus Development," IN Dobbins 1964, 22-25. Original.

960. Libby, Winthrop C., "The Public Be Damned," IN Mauer 1976, 226-230. Original.

An analysis of how an "issue," in this case abortion, can cause difficulties in college-community relations without skillful and responsible judgement on and off campus.

961. Lubell, Samuel, "Counsel for the Future," IN Hook 1974, 267-268. Original.

A brief essay on the question of public service responsibilities of the university.

962. Molinaro, Leo, "The Union of University and Community Resources to Serve Philadelphia," IN Dobbins 1964, 36-39. Original.

963. Moscoso, Theodoro, "The University's Role with Business and Industry," IN Henderson 1968, 116-119. Original.

964. Murphy, Thomas P. and James Zarnowiecki, "The Urban Observatory: A University-City Research Venture," IN Murphy 1975, 15-47. Original.

965. Nickell Jr., Thomas P., "Public Relations in Higher Education," IN Smith 1963, 190-193. Original.

966. Niebuhr, Herman, "Temple University and the Community Development Evolution," IN Mitchell 1974, 121-134. Original.

967. "Press Reaction to University Autonomy," IN Goodall 1976, 33-38.

Editorials from Detroit Free Press (May 27, 1973), Detroit News (December 9, 1971) and Kalamazoo Gazette (May 21, 1973).

968. Reichley, Robert A., "Alumni Clubs and Reunions," IN Rowland 1977, 316-325. Original.

969. Reichley, Robert A., "The Alumni Movement: An Overview," IN Rowland 1977, 275-285. Original.

970. Reichley, Robert A., "Alumni Programs," IN Rowland 1977, 304-315. Original.

971. Reichley, Robert A., "Alumni Publications," IN Rowland 1977, 335-338. Original.

972. Reichley, Robert A., "The Staff in Transition," IN Rowland 1977, 295-303. Original.

The development and activities of professional alumni staff affairs personnel.

973. Reichley, Robert A., "Student Programs," IN Rowland 1977, 326-332. Original.

The concept of student programs that involve alumni staff and volunteers.

974. Reichley, Robert A., "Volunteers: Who Are They?" IN Rowland 1977, 286-294. Original.

An essay on how alumni volunteers can be effective in an active development program.

975. Reinert, Paul C., "The Role of Higher Education in Restoring Urban Centers: What We Have Learned," IN Smith 1964, 196-199. Original.

976. Rosenberg, Richard L., "Higher Education: The Public Interest," IN Minter 1969, 47-54. Original.

977. Round, George S., "Public Relations," IN Budig 1970, 123-133. Original.

978. Rydar, Kathleen, "Special Events," IN Rowland 1977, 96-108. Original.

Planning for news coverage of college special events.

979. Rydell, Ernest E., "External Relations," IN Rowland 1977, 47-59. Original.

980. Sherriffs, Alex C., "A Changing Relationship Between Public and Campus," IN Altman 1971, 3-18. Original.

981. Simmons, Althea T. L., "Public Service: The Role of Black Professionals and Black College and University Personnel in Public Service," IN Johnson 1974, 293-299. Original.

982. Smith, Virginia B., "The City and the Campus," IN Hughes 1975a, 120-133. Original.

Commentaries by David E. Sweet, Peter Masiko, Jr., and Charles Z. Wilson follow on pages 133-144.

983. Spear, George E., "The University Public Service Mission," IN Murphy 1975, 95-111. Original.

984. Stober, J. Arthur, "Broadcasting for Broad Services," IN Rowland 1977, 78-95. Original.

985. Sundberg, Norman D., "The Community Concern of the University," IN Paulsen 1970, 157-169. Original.

986. Sussman, Leonard R., "The Scholar-News-Media Gap and Public Education," IN Hook 1974, 269-278. Original.

987. Tate, James, "The Philadelphia Urban Renewal Story," IN Dobbins 1964, 20-21. Original.

988. Terrell, Glenn, "Dual Roles for Public and Campus," IN Altman 1971, 89-93. Original.

989. Turner, Fred H., "The Impact of Local and Community Organizations and Agencies," IN Donovan 1962, 197-216. Original.

990. Volkmann, M. Fredric, "Cost-Saving Devices," IN Rowland 1977, 413-423. Original.

Cost effective suggestions are made for the production of college publications.

991. Williams, Franklin H., "The Community and the Campus," IN Connery 1970, 28-37. Original.

992. Wilson, Logan, "The College or University in Its Environment: External Constraints," IN Lunsford 1963, 99-112. Original.

993. Wines, Leonard R., "What Public Information Programs Dealing with Higher Education Should be Established at the Local Level?" IN Smith 1962, 169-172. Original.

994. Wood, Robert C. and Harriet A. Zuckerman, "The Urban Crisis," IN Connery 1970, 1-14. Original.

Mr. Wood suggests roles and problems of the modern university in assisting communities to correct urban decay.

10
PRESIDENTS, TRUSTEES, AND GOVERNING BOARDS

995. Benezet, Louis T., "The Office of the President," IN Burns 1962, 99-110. Original.

996. Bennis, Warren G., "Who Sank the Yellow Submarine? Eleven Ways to Avoid Mistakes in Taking Over a University Campus and Making Great Changes," IN Riley 1977, 110-122. PT, 6 (November 1972), 112-120.

997. Bloustein, Edward J., "College Presidents as Political Activists," IN Vermilye 1973, 154-159. Original.

998. Bode, Roy R., "Alumni: Intellectual Challenges," IN Donovan 1964, 164-172. Original.

999. Bolman, Frederick de W., "The University President," IN Smith 1970, 240-247. Original.

1000. Carman, Harry J., "Boards of Trustees and Regents," IN Burns 1962, 79-98. Original.

1001. Coons, Arthur G., "How Should the President of a College Divide His Time Among Various Duties?" IN McGrath 1967, 56-70. Original.

1002. Distler, Theodore A., "College Administration: Relationship of President to Trustees, Faculty, and Students," IN Donovan 1964, 72-80. Original.

1003. Dodds, Harold W., "Academic Freedom and the Academic President," IN Baade 1964, 172-182. LCP, 28 (Summer 1963), 602-612.

1004. Donovan, Alfred D., "The Policy-Making Role of Trustees in Church-Related Colleges," IN Smith 1967, 135-138. Original.

1005. Drucker, Peter F., "What Principles of Management Can the President of a Small College Use to Improve the Efficiency of His Institution," IN McGrath 1967, 71-83. Original.

1006. Enarson, Harold L., "What Is Left to Govern?" IN Vermilye 1974, 162-169. Original.

Dr. Enarson lists all the forces that are at work eroding the capacity of university presidents to lead and the prospect for the future.

1007. Fellman, David, "The Departmental Chairman," IN Smith 1967, 240-243. Original.

1008. Fey, John T., "The New England Board of Higher Education," IN Wilson 1965, 196-198. Original.

1009. Fidler, William P., "Presidential Authority in Academic Governance," IN McGrath 1967, 33-43. Original.

1010. Freedman, Mervin B., "Studies of College Alumni," IN Sanford 1962, 847-886. Original.

1011. Gould, Samuel B., "Trustees and the University Community," IN Perkins 1973, 215-228. Original.

1012. Hartnett, Rodney T., "College and University Trustees: Their Background, Roles, and Educational Attitudes," IN Kruytbosch 1970, 47-71. Original.

This is an abridged version of the author's monograph, same title, published by the Educational Testing Service in 1969.

1013. Hartnett, Rodney T., "Trustee Power in America," IN Hodgkinson 1971, 25-38. Original.

1014. Hartnett, Rodney T., "Trustees: Backgrounds, Roles, and Educational Attitudes," IN Baldridge 1971, 124-149. CUT (1969).

1015. Heady, Ferrel, "The Role of the President Today," IN Wingfield 1970, 69-82. Original.

1016. Henderson, Algo D., "The Role of the Governing Board," IN Baldridge 1971, 98-123. AGB Rep, 10 (October 1967), 3-31.

1017. Hesburgh, Theodore M., "The Presidency: A Personalist Manifesto," IN Heyns 1977, 1-11. Original.

1018. Hetzel, Ralph, "What are the Central Responsibilities of the Trustees Which Apply Both to Publicly and to Privately Supported Institutions?" IN Smith 1960, 153-156. Original.

1019. Howe II, Harold, "The President's Role," IN Heyns 1977, 18-26. Original.

1020. Johnson, Elizabeth H., "Role of Statewide Boards in Program Review," IN Vermilye 1975, 37-50. Original.

1021. Knapp, David C., "Pressures on Governing Boards," IN Smith 1965, 163-166. Original.

1022. McGrath, Earl J., "The President as an Innovator," IN McGrath 1967, 1-16. Original.

1023. Menke, Robert, "Frisky Horses and Frisky Trustees," IN Smith 1967, 153-157. Original.

1024. Merrill, Charles, "The Board of Trustees and the Black College," IN Willie 1978, 167-174. Original.

1025. Merry, Robert W., "The Role of the Board of Trustees in the Determination of Institutional Policy," IN Smith 1966, 218-221. Original.

1026. Oswald, John W., "Pressures on Heads of Institutions," IN Smith 1965, 159-162. Original.

1027. Perkins, James A., "Conflicting Responsibilities of Governing Boards," IN Perkins 1973, 203-214. Original.

1028. Pray, Francis C., "Trustees Revisited," IN Vaccaro 1975, 93-109. Original.

1029. Rauh, Morton A., "Governing Boards: A Redefinition," IN Smith 1971, 151-155. Original.

1030. Rauh, Morton A., "Internal Organization of the Board," IN Perkins 1973, 229-243. Original.

1031. Ray, Joseph M., "In the Middle of the Stream" IN Wingfield 1970, 89-98. Original.

A former university president presents his views on the relationship between the office of president and the general continuity of institutional planning and development.

1032. Riesman, David, "Predicaments in the Career of the College President," IN Kruytbosch 1970, 73-86. Original.

1033. Riley, Gary L., "The Changing Role of Trustees in Academic Governance," IN Riley 1977, 228-238. Original.

1034. Robinson, Prezell R., "Effective Management of Scarce Resources: Presidential Responsibility," IN Willie 1978, 155-166. Original.

This essay deals mainly with the fiscal management of black colleges.

1035. Soshnik, Joseph, "The Campus Presidency," IN Budig 1970, 3-17. Original.

1036. Tate, Willis M., "The Ground on Which I Stand," IN Wingfield 1970, 83-88. Original.

A college president presents what he believes are the most important issues facing higher education.

1037. Tolley, William P., "Organizing and Energizing the Board for Effective Action," IN McGrath 1967, 24-32. Original.

1038. Ward, John W., "The College President as Citizen," IN Vermilye 1973, 147-153. Original.

1039. Willie, Charles V. and Marlene Y. MacLeish, "The Priorities of Presidents of Black Colleges," IN Willie 1978, 132-148. Original.

11
DEANS, DEPARTMENTAL CHAIRPERSONS, AND OTHER ADMINISTRATIVE PERSONNEL

1040. Ahmann, J. Stanley, "The Emerging Role of the Department Chairman: Be an Administrative Activist," IN Brann 1972, 186-197. Original.

1041. Andersen, Kay J., "In Defense of Departments," IN McHenry 1977, 1-11. Original.

1042. Bailey, Dudley, "The Academic Department," IN Budig 1970, 55-66. Original.

1043. Beck, Norman E. and Donald R. Ryan, "How an Institutional Aid Office Really Works," IN College 1975, 38-83. Original.

1044. Benezet, Louis T., "Uses and Abuses of Departments," IN McHenry 1977, 34-52. Original.

1045. Bidwell, Charles E., "Librarian, Administrator, and Professor: Implications of Changing College Social Structures," IN Bergen 1966, 61-81. Original.

1046. Booth, David, "Some Reflections for Prospective Chairmen of Academic Departments," IN Brann 1972, 73-76. Original.

1047. Brandon, Arthur L., "The Vice-President or Director of Public Relations," IN Burns 1962, 156-169. Original.

1048. Brann, James, "The Chairman: An Impossible Job About to Become Tougher," IN Brann 1972, 5-27. Original.

1049. Brown, J. Douglas, "Departmental and University Leadership," IN McHenry 1977, 185-209. Original.

1050. Bursch II, Charles W., "The Vice-President or Dean of Students," IN Burns 1962, 141-155. Original.

1051. Clark, Thomas D., "The Academic Hierarchy and the Department Head," IN Robertson 1978, 41-57. Original.

1052. Davis, John R., "The College Dean," IN Budig 1970, 39-52. Original.

1053. Delahanty, James, "What do Faculty Want in a Departmental Chairman?" IN Brann 1972, 221-226. Original.

1054. Dilley, Frank B., "The Department Chairman as Academic Planner," IN Brann 1972, 28-36. Original.

1055. Edwards, Eunice L. and James E. Ingle, "Organizational Structure of a Financial Aid Office," IN College 1975, 23-37. Original.

1056. Enarson, Harold, "The Academic Vice-President or Dean," IN Burns 1962, 111-124. Original.

1057. Erfft, Kenneth R., "The Vice-President for Business Affairs," IN Burns 1962, 125-140. Original.

1058. Fullen, John B., "The Alumni Director," IN Burns 1962, 206-217. Original.

1059. Gould, John W., "Pressures on Deans and Other Administrators," IN Smith 1965, 156-158. Original.

1060. Haas, Eugene and Linda Collen, "Administrative Practices in University Departments," IN Baldridge 1971, 193-207. ASQ, 8 (June 1963), 44-60.

1061. Harrington, Fred H., "Shortcomings of Conventional Departments," IN McHenry 1977, 53-62. Original.

1062. Heimler, Charles H., "The College Departmental Chairman," IN Brann 1972, 198-207. ER, 48 (Spring 1967), 158-163.

1063. Henle, R. J., "The Structure of Academic Administration," IN Brann 1972, 227-237. Original.

1064. Hill, Winston W. and Wendell L. French, "Perceptions of the Power of Department Chairmen by Professors," IN Baldridge 1971, 208-233. ASQ, 2 (March 1967), 548-574.

1065. Hoffmann, Wayne W., "Student Personnel Administrators and the Campus Ministry," IN Herron 1970, 120-127. Original.

1066. Johnston, W. Noel, "The Vice-President or Director of Development," IN Burns 1962, 170-184. Original.

1067. Kastner, Elwood C., "The Registrar and Director of Admissions," IN Burns 1962, 185-205. Original.

1068. Koehnline, William A. and Clyde E. Blocker, "The Division Chairman in the Community College," IN Brann 1972, 146-152. JCJ, 40 (February 1970), 9-12.

1069. Lee, Calvin B. T., "Relationship of the Department Chairmen to the Academic Dean," IN Brann 1972, 54-62. Original.

1070. Lindahl, Charles, "The Registrar and Administrative Relationships in Higher Education," IN Fitzgerald 1970, 134-139. CU, 41 (Winter 1966), 173-179.

1071. Lloyd, Wesley P., "Graduate Deans as Administrators," IN Kent 1970, 56-68. Original.

1072. McArthur, Charles C. and Kenneth T. Dinklage, "The Role of the Psychologist in a College Health Service," IN Blain 1961, 29-53. Original.

1073. MacDonald, Robert L., "The Director of Placement and Student Personnel Services," IN Donovan 1962, 143-160. Original.

1074. McHenry, Dean E., "Toward Departmental Reform," IN McHenry 1977, 210-224. Original.

1075. McKeachie, Wilbert J., "Memo to New Department Chairmen," IN Brann 1972, 43-53. ER, 49 (Spring 1968), 221-227.

1076. Magner, James A., "Role of the Non-Academic Personnel," IN Donovan 1964, 17-24. Original.

Reverend Magner identifies the importance of non-academic staff to the achievement of educational goals.

1077. Magrath, C. Peter, "The Dean of Faculties," IN Budig 1970, 21-36. Original.

1078. Mahoney, Eva, "The Role of the Dean of Women in the Student Personnel Services," IN Donovan 1962, 19-28. Original.

1079. Mahoney, John F., "Chairman as Messmaker," IN Brann 1972, 180-185. Original.

1080. Mauer, George J., "The Chairmanship: One Invitation to Disaster," IN Mauer 1976, 119-129. Original.

1081. Meder Jr., Albert E., "The Place of the Admissions Officer in the Academic Family," IN Rich 1963, 23-35. Original.

1082. Monson Jr., Charles H., "The University of Utah's Department Chairmen Training Program," IN Brann 1972, 37-42. Original.

1083. Morgan, Don A., "Instructional Deans and Chairmen in the Community College: A New Identity Crisis on an Old Theme," IN Brann 1972, 162-172. Original.

1084. Murray, Robert K., "On Departmental Development: A Theory," IN Brann 1972, 63-72. JGE, 16 (October 1964), 227-236.

1085. North, Walter, "Role and Functions of the Financial Aid Officer," IN College 1975, 11-22. Original.

1086. O'Shaughnessy, Terence, "The Role of the Chaplain in the Student Personnel Service Program," IN Donovan 1962, 62-71. Original.

1087. Parish, H. Carroll, "Professional Associations--Genesis and Development," IN Keene 1975, 54-64. Original.

The development and professionalization of the position of Financial Aid Officer.

1088. Price, Philip, "The Dean of Men and Student Personnel Services," IN Donovan 1962, 29-42. Original.

1089. Reister, Russell W., "Campus Personnel Administration," IN Tice 1976, 37-49. Original.

1090. Rich, Catherine R., "The Registrar-Admissions Officer and Student Personnel," IN Donovan 1962, 43-53. Original.

1091. Ross, G. Robert, "The Dean of Students," IN Budig 1970, 87-103. Original.

1092. Rowland, Howard R., "Campus Ombudsman," IN Smith 1970, 122-130. Original.

1093. Schneiders, Alexander A., "The Role of the Health Staff in Student Personnel," IN Donovan 1962, 72-83. Original.

1094. Shoben Jr., Edward J., "Departments vs. Education," IN Brann 1972, 78-94. Original.

1095. Smith, Glenn W., "The Budget Director," IN Budig 1970, 151-162. Original.

1096. Tansil, Rebecca C., "The Admissions Officer: Professional Status," IN Rich 1963, 177-194. Original.

1097. Thiry, James R., "Non-Faculty Bargaining," IN Tice 1976, 105-112. Original.

An overview of contract provisions for non-faculty collective bargaining agreements at institutions of higher education.

1098. Trow, Martin, "The American Academic Department as a Context for Learning," IN Entwistle 1976, 89-106. Original.

1099. Trow, Martin, "Departments as Contexts for Teaching and Learning," IN McHenry 1977, 12-33. Original.

1100. Underwood, David, "The Chairman as Academic Planner," IN Brann 1972, 153-161. Original.

1101. Van Hoogstrate, Sister Dorothy J., "The Office of Academic Dean and Student Personnel," IN Donovan 1962, 217-230. Original.

1102. Walters, Richard L., "Implications of Student Independence on Student Financial Aid Administration," IN College 1974, 80-88. Original.

1103. Weidner, Edward W., "Problem-Based Departments at the University of Wisconsin-Green Bay," IN McHenry 1977, 63-85. Original.

1104. Wicke, Myron F., "Deans: 'Men in the Middle,'" IN Lunsford 1963, 53-70. Original.

1105. Willging, Eugene, "The College Librarian and Student Personnel Services," IN Donovan 1962, 54-61. Original.

1106. Yanitelli, Victor R., "Qualifications of Student Personnel Staff," IN Donovan 1962, 128-142. Original.

12
FACULTY

1107. Adelson, Joseph, "The Teacher as a Model," IN Sanford 1962, 396-417. Original.

1108. Allen, Lucile, "Faculty Expectations, Satisfactions, and Morale," IN Wilson 1961, 65-81. Original.

1109. Alstyne, Arvo Van, "Tenure System at the University of Utah," IN Smith 1973, 74-96.

(This essay is based upon the Final Report of the University of Utah Commission to study Tenure issued in May, 1971.)

1110. Alstyne Van, William W., "Tenure and Collective Bargaining," IN Smith 1971, 210-217. Original.

1111. Altbach, Philip G., "In Search of Saraswati: The Ambivalence of the Indian Academic," IN Altbach 1977, 145-165. HE, 6 (May 1977), 255-275.

1112. Anderson, Charles H., "The Intellectual Subsociety Hypothesis: An Empirical Test," IN Anderson 1971, 229-245. SQ, 9 (Spring 1968), 77-83.

See: Milton M. Gordon for original hypothesis.

1113. Anderson, Charles H., "Marginality and the Academic," IN Anderson 1971, 205-218. Soc I, 39 (Winter 1969), 77-83.

An extensive review of the literature concerning the social status of intellectuals.

1114. Anderson, Charles H. and John D. Murray, "Kitsch and the Academics," IN Anderson 1971, 175-183. SSR, 51 (July 1967), 445-451.

A study of how academics use their leisure time in pursuit of such activities as television viewing, etc.

1115. Angell, George W., "Knowing the Scope of Bargaining," IN Angell 1977, 126-139. Original.

1116. Angell, George W., "Shaping and Amending Collective Bargaining Legislation," IN Angell 1977, 38-57. Original.

1117. Angell, George W., "Understanding Collective Bargaining as a Constructive Process in University Leadership," IN Angell 1977, 7-23. Original.

1118. Astin, Helen S., "Factors Affecting Women's Scholarly Productivity," IN Astin 1978, 133-157. Original.

1119. Axen, Richard, "Faculty Response to Student Dissent," IN Smith 1968, 106-112. Original.

1120. Axt, Richard G., "Assumptions Underlying Present Ways of Measuring Faculty (Work) Load," IN Bunnell 1960, 12-16. Original.

1121. Baldridge, J. Victor, "Faculty Activism and Influence Patterns in the University," IN Baldridge 1971, 293-313. Original.

1122. Baldridge, J. Victor and Frank R. Kemerer, "Academic Senates and Faculty Collective Bargaining," IN Riley 1977, 327-347. JHE, 47 (July-August 1976), 391-411.

1123. Baldridge, J. Victor and Frank R. Kemerer, "Images of Governance: Collective Bargaining versus Traditional Models," IN Riley 1977, 252-271. Original.

1124. Balyeat, Ralph E., "Institutional Practice Concerning Faculty Status and Rewards," IN Smith 1966, 265-268. Original.

1125. Barzun, Jacques, "Scholars in Orbit," IN Anderson 1971, 93-104. Amer Univ (1968).

1126. Beach, Leonard B., "What Should be the Role of the Master's Degree in the Preparation of College Teachers?" IN Smith 1960, 187-189. Original.

1127. Begin, James P., Theodore C. Settle, and Paula B. Alexander, "The Emergence of Faculty Bargaining," IN Tice 1976, 129-153. Original.

An excellent case study of faculty bargaining in the state of New Jersey.

1128. Belcher, Lee A., "Labor-Management Relations in Higher Education," IN Hughes 1973, 73-93. Original.

1129. Benewitz, Maurice C., "Contract Provisions and Procedures," IN Vladeck 1975, 275-295. Original.

1130. Benewitz, Maurice C., "Grievance and Arbitration Procedures," IN Tice 1973, 143-174. Original.

1131. Bernard, Jessie, "Teachers and Professors: Subject Matter Areas," IN Anderson 1971, 45-60. AW (1964).

1132. Berry, Mary F., "Faculty Governance," IN Heyns 1977, 27-30. Original.

1133. Bess, James L., "New Life for Faculty and Institutions," IN Vermilye 1974, 146-152. Original.

The author outlines " . . . a scheme for redirecting surplus or dissatisfied faculty into new careers that would benefit not only them but their institutions and society."

1134. Bienfang, Ralph, "On Being a Professor," IN Buxton 1975, 55-61. Original.

1135. Blackstone, Tessa and Gareth Williams, "Structural Aspects of the Academic Profession in a Period of Expansion," IN Butcher 1972, 291-304. ALM (1974).

1136. Blake, J. Herman and Ronald W. Saufley, "A Case Study in Faculty Development," IN Vermilye 1976, 97-106. Original.

1137. Blee, Myron R., "The Use of Faculty (Work) Load Data in Interinstitutional Analysis," IN Bunnell 1960, 45-52. Original.

1138. Bond, Linda, "Impact of Collective Bargaining on Students," IN Vermilye 1974, 131-135. Original.

1139. Bornholdt, Laura, "Professional Ethics on Campus," IN Vermilye 1972, 93-104. Original.

1140. Bowker, Albert H., "Managing the Faculty Resource in the Steady State," IN Hughes 1975, 77-83. Original.

1141. Boyd, William B., "Collective Bargaining in Academe: Causes and Consequences," IN Hughes 1973, 11-28. LE, 57 (October 1971), 306-318.

1142. Brown, David G., "Climbing the Ivory Tower," IN Smith 1966, 93-97. Original.

Dr. Brown provides an economic analysis of the relationship between "promotion rates and salary levels to the academic marketplace."

1143. Brown, James W., "Student Response Systems," IN Smith 1963, 98-101. Original.

The author strongly supports a system of close teacher-student interaction.

1144. Brown, Kenneth I., "Identifying Early the Potentially Good College Teacher and Encouraging Him to Enter a Career of Scholarship and Teaching," IN Smith 1961, 105-108. Original.

1145. Brown Jr., Ralph S., "Rights and Responsibilities of Faculty," IN Knorr 1965a, 11-21. Original.

1146. Bucklew, Neil S., "Collective Bargaining and Policy-making," IN Vermilye 1974, 136-141. Original.

1147. Bucklew, Neil S., "Fiscal Implications of Collective Bargaining," IN Jellema 1972, 52-58. Original.

1148. Buckley, Neil S., "Controlling the Costs of Bargaining," IN Angell 1977, 520-537. Original.

1149. Bunzel, John H., "Collective Bargaining in Higher Education," IN Hook 1974, 157-178. Original.

1150. Burkhardt, Frederick H., "The Changing Role of the Professor," IN Dennis 1966, 206-210. Original.

1151. Burn, Barbara B., "Exchange Opportunities in a No-Growth Period," IN Bailey 1977, 89-96. Original.

An essay that explores the many possibilities in faculty exchange programs, especially when finances permit few permanent increases in staff.

1152. Bush, Ronald W., "Preparing for Arbitration," IN Angell 1977, 390-405. Original.

1153. Caplow, Theodore, "The Dynamics of Faculty (Work) Load Studies," IN Bunnell 1960, 65-79. Original.

1154. Caplow, Theodore, "Faculty Pay and Institutional Extravagance," IN Harris 1960, 122-124. Original.

1155. Carl, Mary K., "Responsive and Responsible Faculty Committees as a Means of Participation in College Governance Within a University," IN Mauer 1976, 92-103. Original.

1156. Cartter, Allan M., "The Academic Labor Market," IN Gordon 1974, 281-307. Original.

1157. Cartter, Allan M., "Faculty Manpower Planning," IN Smith 1970, 231-239. Original.

1158. Cartter, Allan M., "Future Faculty: Needs and Resources," IN Lee 1967, 113-135. Original.

Commentaries by Bernard Berelson, A. W. Dent, and Carl W. Borgmann follow on pages 136-145.

1159. Centra, John A., "Evaluating College Teaching: The Rhetoric and the Research," IN Vermilye 1972, 225-236. Original.

1160. Chait, Richard and Andrew T. Ford, "Affirmative Action, Tenure, and Unionization," IN Vermilye 1974, 123-130. Original.

1161. Chanin, Robert H., "Teacher Organizations in Higher Education Negotiations," IN Vladeck 1975, 115-151. Original.

1162. Chomsky, Noam, "The Responsibility of Intellectuals," IN Anderson 1971, 315-324. NYRB, 8 (February 23, 1967), 16-26.

1163. Clark, Burton R., "Faculty Culture," IN Lunsford 1963a, 39-54. Original.

1164. Clark, Burton R., "Faculty Organization and Authority," IN Lunsford 1963, 37-52. Original.

1165. Clark, Burton R., "Faculty Organization and Authority," IN Baldridge 1971, 236-250. ODC (1960).

1166. Clark, Burton R., "Faculty Organization and Authority," IN Riley 1977, 64-78. SAA (1963).

1167. Clark, Kenneth E., "Studies on Faculty Evaluation," IN Wilson 1961, 35-52. Original.

1168. Cole, Charles W., "Faculty Problems in the Liberal Arts College," IN Harris 1960, 111-114. Original.

1169. Cooper, Russell M., "Faculty Development Programs," IN Smith 1967, 232-235. Original.

1170. Coser, Lewis, "Academic Intellectuals," IN Anderson 1971, 71-91. MI (1965).

1171. Cottle, Thomas J., "Pains of Permanence," IN Smith 1973, 9-33. Original.

A personal story of the ordeal to achieve tenure at Harvard.

1172. Cummings, William K. and Ikau Amano, "The Changing Role of the Japanese Professor," IN Altbach 1977, 43-67. HE, 6 (May 1977), 209-234.

1173. Dalrymple, Willard, "Faculty Counseling and Referral," IN Blain 1961, 17-28. Original.

1174. David, Henry, "What are the Basic Problems in the Preparation of College Teachers?" IN Smith 1960, 179-182. Original.

1175. Davis, Bertram H., "'Policing' Academic Responsibility," IN Smith 1971, 195-201. Original.

1176. Deferrari, Roy J., "Appointments and Promotions," IN Deferrari 1961, 167-178. Original.

1177. Deferrari, Roy J., "Duties and Powers of the Teaching Staff," IN Deferrari 1961, 243-254. Original.

1178. Doi, James, "The Proper Use of Faculty (Work) Load Studies," IN Wilson 1961, 53-64. Original.

1179. Doi, James, "The Use of Faculty (Work) Load Data Within an Institution," IN Bunnell 1960, 40-44. Original.

1180. Dolan-Green, Colleen, Frank C. Gerry, and Edward P. Kelley, Jr., "Responding Constructively to Strikes and Threats of Strikes," IN Angell 1977, 346-369. Original.

1181. Donovan, George F., "Fringe Benefits for the College Teaching Staff," IN Deferrari 1961, 223-242. Original.

1182. Duff, John B., "Problems Faced in Reducing the Number of Faculty," IN Mauer 1976, 130-138. Original.

1183. Duffey, Joseph D., "Future of the Professoriate," IN Vermilye 1975, 166-173. Original.

1184. Duperre, Maurice R., "Faculty Organizations as an Aid to Employment Relations in Junior Colleges," IN Elam 1969, 181-215. Original.

1185. Durham, G. Homer, "The Uses and Abuses of Faculty (Work) Load Data," IN Bunnell 1960, 53-61. Original.

1186. Duryea, E. D. and Robert S. Fisk, "Impact of Unionism on Governance," IN Vermilye 1972, 105-115. Original.

1187. Eble, Kenneth E., "The College Teacher--Anguished Middleman," IN Goldwin 1967, 31-48. Original.

1188. Eble, Kenneth E., "Tenure and Teaching," IN Smith 1973, 97-110. Original.

1189. Edwards, Harry T., "Legal Aspects of the Duty to Bargain," IN Tice 1973, 21-37. Original.

1190. Elmore, Joe E., "Developing Faculty Leadership," IN Heyns 1977, 30-37. Original.

1191. Emerson, Thomas I. and David Haber, "Academic Freedom of the Faculty Member as Citizen," IN Baade 1964, 95-142. LCP, 28 (Summer 1963), 525-572.

1192. Enochs, James B., "Problems of Defining Faculty (Work) Load," IN Bunnell 1960, 17-25. Original.

1193. Epstein, Noel, "Academic Hypocrisy: A Media View," IN Vermilye 1976, 161-169. Original.

Mr. Epstein, a Washington Post reporter, suggests that academics are being subjected to criticism concerning the apparent contradiction between words and deeds as illustrated in a growing consumer protection movement in higher education. Examples are provided such as the student who sued a university for $400 over a course she believed was "worthless."

1194. Etzioni, Amitai, "Faculty Response to Racial Tensions," IN Nichols 1970, 206-223. Original.

Commentaries by Douglas F. Dowd, Deborah P. Wolfe, and Robert D. Cross follow on pages 224-237.

1195. "Faculty Participation in Strikes," IN Hughes 1974, 157-171. AAUPB, 54 (June 1968), 155-159.

1196. Fellman, David, "The Academic Community: Who Decides What?" IN Dobbins 1968, 105-121. Original.

Commentaries by Arnold M. Grant, John W. Oswald, Edward N. Robinson, and J. Broward Culpepper follow on pages 122-133.

1197. Ferguson, Tracy H., "Recent NLRB Decisions," IN Tice 1973, 39-52. Original.

1198. Ferguson, Tracy H. and Alan J. Septimus, "Recent Labor Board Rulings (National Labor Relations Board Jurisdiction and Faculty Status)," IN Tice 1976, 53-86. Original.

1199. Ferguson, Tracy H., William L. Bergan, and Jeffrey L. Braff, "Labor Board Jurisdictional and Unit Determinations," IN Vladeck 1975, 171-201. Original.

1200. Finch, Jeremiah S., "Responsibilities of the Individual Faculty Member and His Institution for Increasing Ability and Professional Stature," IN Smith 1961, 109-111. Original.

1201. Fleming, Robben W., "Collective Bargaining on Campus," IN Tice 1976, 13-20. Original.

1202. "The Flight From Teaching," IN Mayhew 1967, 305-314. Original.

1203. Fryer Jr., Thomas W., "New Policies for the Part-Time Faculty," IN Heyns 1977, 50-59. Original.

1204. Fuchs, Ralph F., "Academic Freedom--Its Basic Philosophy, Function, and History," IN Baade 1964, 1-16. LCP, 28 (Summer 1963), 431-446.

1205. Fulkerson Jr., William M., "Resolving Retrenchment Problems Within Contractual Agreements," IN Angell 1977, 406-427. Original.

1206. Fulton, Oliver and Martin Trow, "Students and Teachers: Some General Findings of the 1969 Carnegie Commission Survey," IN Trow 1975, 1-38. Original.

An analysis of the extensive Carnegie sponsored national survey of faculty and student opinion. A technical report of the survey is included as Appendix A on pages 297-414.

1207. Gaff, Jerry G., "Faculty Development: The State of the Art," IN Vermilye 1976, 62-69. Original.

1208. Gaff, Jerry G. and Robert C. Wilson, "Faculty Values and Improving Teaching," IN Smith 1971, 39-46. Original.

1209. Gamson, Zelda F., "Performance and Personalism in Student-Faculty Relations," IN Feldman 1972, 237-260. SE, 40 (Fall 1967), 279-301.

1210. Garbarino, Joseph W., "Creeping Unionism and the Faculty Labor Market," IN Gordon 1974, 309-332. Original.

1211. Garbarino, Joseph W., "Faculty Unions, Senates, and Institutional Administrations," IN Hughes 1975, 11-17. FBCC (1975).

1212. Garbarino, Joseph W. and Bill Aussieker, "Collective Bargaining: Evaluating the Issues," IN Riley 1977, 272-294. FBCC (1975).

1213. Gardner, John W., "The Flight from Teaching," IN Milton 1968, 12-24. CF (1964).

1214. Garmezy, Norman, "Pressures on Faculty--1965," IN Smith 1965, 152-155. Original.

1215. Gemmell, James, "Protecting Campus Autonomy and Responsibility Within Statewide Bargaining," IN Angell 1977, 466-485. Original.

1216. Gianopulos, John, "Collective Bargaining: What Part Should College Presidents Play?" IN Hughes 1973, 109-122. CUB, 49 (September 1970), 71-72.

1217. Glazer, Nathan, "The Torment of Tenure," IN Hook 1974, 247-250. Original.

1218. Goodwin, Harold L., "The Impact of Unions and Collective Bargaining on American Higher Education," IN Vaccaro 1975, 66-77. Original.

1219. Gordon, Margaret and Clark Kerr, "University Behavior and Policies: Where are the Women and Why?" IN Astin 1978, 113-132. Original.

A nationwide overview of women on university faculties.

1220. Gordon, Milton M., "The Intellectual Subsociety," IN Anderson 1971, 219-225. AAL (1964).

1221. Graybeal, William S., "Current Faculty Salaries and Practices," IN Smith 1966, 209-210. Original.

1222. Grede, John F., "Negotiating the First Contract," IN Angell 1977, 158-173. Original.

1223. Groty, Keith, "Managing Between Contract Negotiations: An Arbitrator's View," IN Tice 1976, 235-241. Original.

1224. Gusfield, Joseph and David Riesman, "Faculty Culture and Academic Careers," IN Yamamoto 1968, 271-291. SE, 37 (Summer 1964), 281-305.

1225. Gustad, John W., "The American College Teacher: An Appraisal and Critique of Research on College Faculty Members," IN Wilson 1961, 111-124. Original.

1226. Gustad, John W., "Man in the Middle: Conditions of Work of College and University Faculty Members," IN Elam 1969, 102-131. Original.

1227. Gustad, John W., "Preparation for College Teaching," IN Smith 1963, 194-197. Original.

1228. Haag, Ernest van den, "Academic Freedom in the United States," IN Baade 1964, 85-94. LCP, 28 (Summer 1963), 515-524.

1229. Halsey, A. H. and Martin Trow, "The British University Teacher," IN Butcher 1972, 271-290. BA (1971).

1230. Hankin, Joseph N., "Preparing for Table Negotiations," IN Angell 1977, 142-157. Original.

1231. Hanley, Dexter L., "Issues and Model for Collective Bargaining in Higher Education," IN Hughes 1973, 144-156. LE, 57 (March 1971), 5-14.

1232. Hanly, Charles, "Problems of Academic Freedom in Canada," IN Seabury 1975, 157-175. Original.

1233. Harman, Grant, "Academic Staff and Academic Drift in Australian Colleges of Advanced Education," IN Altbach 1977, 68-91. HE, 6 (August 1977), 313-336.

1234. Hexter, J. H., "Publish or Perish--A Defense," IN Anderson 1971, 124-142. PI, 17 (Fall 1969), 60-77.

1235. Heyns, Roger W., "The Nature of the Academic Community," IN Lee 1967, 45-54. Original.

1236. Hicks, John W., "Faculty Work Load--An Overview," IN Bunnell 1960, 3-11. Original.

1237. Hill, Forest G., "The Faculty Senate and Educational Policy-Making," IN Smith 1967, 236-239. Original.

1238. Hind, Robert R., "Analysis of a Faculty: Professionalism, Evaluation, and the Authority Structure," IN Baldridge 1971, 264-292.

(This essay was taken from the author's dissertation, Evaluation and Authority in a University Faculty, Stanford University, 1968.)

1239. Hirsch, Hilde E. and Werner Z. Hirsch, "Intellectual Quality: The Symbols and the Substance," IN Astin 1978, 161-165. Original.

A concise statement concerning the identification and measurement of scholarly productivity.

1240. Hjort, Barry L., "Involving Students in Bargaining," IN Angell 1977, 258-273. Original.

1241. Hobbs, Nicholas, "The Art of Getting Students Into Trouble," IN Dennis 1966, 202-205. Original.

Dr. Hobbs presents several hypotheses that define ". . . what it is about the professor-student relationship that makes a difference in the lives of both."

1242. Hodgkinson, Harold L., "Assessment and Reward Systems," IN Smith 1971, 47-54. Original.

Professor Hodgkinson examines the nature of the reward system for the college professor.

1243. Hodgkinson, Harold L., "Faculty Reward and Assessment Systems," IN Smith 1973, 111-119. Original.

1244. Hodgkinson, Harold, "Unlock the Doors: Let Your Colleagues in Faculty Reward and Assessment Systems," IN Brann 1972, 208-215. Original.

1245. Hook, Sidney, "The Academic Mission and Collective Bargaining," IN Vladeck 1975, 17-31. PFAC (1973).

1246. Hornbeck, David W., "Improving Educational Services Through Statewide Bargaining," IN Angell 1977, 442-465. Original.

1247. Horowitz, Irving L., "Young Radicals and Professorial Critics," IN Anderson 1971, 333-341. Common, 98 (January 31, 1969), 552-556.

1248. Howe, Ray A., "The Bloody Business of Bargaining," IN Hughes 1973, 94-108. CUB, 48 (March 1970), 63-67.

1249. Howe, Ray A., "The Dramatic Action of Bargaining," IN Tice 1973, 95-111. Original.

1250. Howe, Ray A., "The Omega/Alpha Syndrome," IN Tice 1976, 193-208. Original.

A concise step-by-step analysis of the development and implementation of a faculty collective bargaining agreement.

1251. Howe, Ray A., "Roles of Faculty," IN Hodgkinson 1971, 126-138. Original.

1252. Howlett, Robert G., "Developments in Public Employment Relations," IN Tice 1976, 21-35. Original.

1253. Howlett, Robert G., "New Contract Arbitration in the Public Sector," IN Tice 1976, 243-250. Original.

1254. Hughes, Everett C., "Non-Economic Aspects of Academic Morale," IN Harris 1960, 118-121. Original.

1255. Hughes, Graham, "Tenure and Academic Freedom," IN Pincoffs 1972, 170-179. Original.

1256. Hutchison, William R., "Yes, John, There are Teachers on the Faculty," IN Milton 1968, 36-48. Amer S, 35 (Summer 1966), 430-441.

1257. Iffert, Robert E., "The College Teachers Shortage," IN Deferrari 1961, 153-166. Original.

1258. Iffert, Robert E., "Some Statistical Aspects," IN Harris 1960, 125-128. Original.

A comparative analysis of faculty salaries during 1958-59.

1259. Jencks, Christopher and David Riesman, "The Art of Teaching," IN Anderson 1971, 61-70. Aca Rev (1964).

1260. Jencks, Christopher and David Riesman, "The Triumph of Academic Man," IN Eurich 1968, 92-116. Aca Rev (1964).

1261. Joughin, Louis, "Criteria and Procedures in Decisions Regarding the Reappointment of Probationary Faculty Members," IN Smith 1964, 212-214. Original.

1262. Joyner, Thomas E., "Mediation and Fact-Finding in the Academic Setting," IN Tice 1973, 129-142. Original.

1263. Kadish, Sanford H., "The Strike and the Professoriate," IN Hughes 1973, 172-199. AAUPB, 54 (June 1968), 160-168.

1264. Kahn, Kenneth F., "Faculty Bargaining Units," IN Vladeck 1975, 203-221. Original.

1265. Kelley Jr., Edward P., "State and Federal Legislation," IN Tice 1976, 87-102. Original.

An extensive analysis of state and federal legislation relating to postsecondary institutions organizing for the purpose of collective bargaining.

1266. Kelley Jr., Edward P., "Taking the Initiative During Organizing and Election Campaigns," IN Angell 1977, 80-95. Original.

1267. Kelley Jr., Edward P., "Writing Contract Language to Avoid Grievances," IN Angell 1977, 218-231. Original.

1268. Kelley Jr., Edward P. and Frank C. Gerry, "Negotiating Management Rights and Other Special Contract Clauses," IN Angell 1977, 311-325. Original.

1269. Kerr, J. David, "Preparations for Bargaining," IN Tice 1973, 79-94. Original.

1270. Knapp, Robert H., "Changing Functions of the College Professor," IN Sanford 1962, 290-311. Original.

1271. Knapp, Royce H., "The Professor," IN Budig 1970, 69-84. Original.

1272. Kolb, William L., "The College Teacher as Professional Man Plus," IN Smith 1968, 173-176. Original.

1273. Kristeller, Paul O., "Scholarship and the Humanistic Tradition," IN Hook 1974, 255-256. Original.

1274. Kugler, Israel, "Collective Bargaining for the Faculty," IN Hughes 1973, 61-71. LE, 56 (March 1970), 75-85.

1275. Kugler, Israel, "The Union Speaks for Itself," IN Hughes 1973, 200-209. ER, 49 (Fall 1968), 414-418.

1276. Ladd Jr., Everett C. and Seymour M. Lipset, "Effects of Unionism on Higher Education," IN Riley 1977, 295-326. PUAHE (1973).

1277. Laumann, Edward O., "The New Breed of Faculty," IN Smith 1966, 198-202. Original.

1278. Lazarsfeld, Paul F. and Wagner Thielens, Jr., "The Vulnerability and Strengths of the Superior College," IN Baldridge 1971, 478-506. Ac M (1958).

The authors identify how a college's characteristics affect faculty apprehension.

1279. Lefkowitz, Jerome, "Collective Bargaining on the Campus--Contract Dispute Resolution," IN Vladeck 1975, 247-272. Original.

1280. Lemmer, William P., "The Bargaining Unit," IN Tice 1973, 53-62. Original.

1281. Leslie, David W., "Faculty in Governance: A Rationale," IN Tice 1976, 171-191. Original.

1282. Leslie, David W. and Ronald P. Satryb, "Writing Grievance Procedures on the Basis of Principle," IN Angell 1977, 188-217. Original.

1283. Lewis, Lionel S., "On Prestige and Loyalty of University Faculty," IN Baldridge 1971, 251-263. ASQ, 2 (March 1967), 629-642.

1284. Lewis, Lionel S., "University Faculty and Students: A Profile," IN Feldman 1972, 371-375. CU, 42 (Spring 1967), 345-350.

1285. Lewis, Lionel S. and Michael N. Ryan, "The American Professoriate and the Movement Toward Unionization," IN Altbach 1977, 191-214. HE, 6 (May 1977), 139-164.

1286. Lichtenstein, David S., "The Alienated Intellectual and Government Bureaucracy," IN Hook 1978, 249-264. Original.

1287. Lieberman, Myron, "Representational Systems in Higher Education," IN Elam 1969, 40-101. Original.

1288. Lipset, Seymour M., "Who is the Enemy?" IN Hook 1974, 243-246. Original.

Professor Lipset discusses the problem of faculty politization and its consequences.

1289. Livingston, John C., "Academic Senate Under Fire," IN Smith 1969, 161-172. Original.

1290. Livingston, John C., "Tenure Everyone?" IN Smith 1973, 54-73. Original.

1291. Long, Louis, "Why Evaluate?" IN Smith 1967, 118-122. Original.

Lists the possible purposes of a faculty evaluation program.

1292. Loughin, Louis, "Faculty Participation in University or College Governance," IN Smith 1966, 203-206. Original.

1293. Lozier, G. Gregory, "Negotiating Retrenchment Provisions," IN Angell 1977, 232-257. Original.

1294. Lumsden, Keith G., "The Information Content of Student Evaluation of Faculty and Courses," IN Lumsden 1974, 175-204. Original.

1295. Lunine, Myron J., "Alternative to Tenure," IN Vermilye 1974, 142-145. Original.

1296. McCain, James A. and Arthur D. Weber, "The Faculty Expatriate," IN Humphrey 1967, 78-109. Original.

> The paper discusses "how and why overseas service affects the faculty member and his university" and what can be done to "strengthen the faculty expatriate's contributions to academic programs and . . . community."

1297. McConnell, T. R., "Faculty Government," IN Hodgkinson 1971, 98-125. Original.

1298. McConnell, T. R., "Faculty Interests in Value Change and Power Conflict," IN Minter 1969, 57-85. Original.

1299. McCoy, Ramelle and Martin J. Morand, "Establishing Constructive Relationships Between Administrators and Faculty Unions," IN Angell 1977, 25-37. Original.

1300. McGee, Reece, "Constructive Ways in Which the Effectiveness and Ethics of the Academic Market Place Can be Improved," IN Smith 1961, 115-119. Original.

1301. McGill, William J., "Government Regulation and Academic Freedom," IN Hook 1968, 139-154. Original.

> Commentaries by Allan Bloom and George W. Bonham follow on pages 155-166.

1302. McGill, William J., "The Role of Faculties," IN Altman 1971, 107-118. Original.

1303. McHugh, William F., "Collective Bargaining and the College Student," IN Hughes 1973, 131-143. JHE, 42 (March 1971), 175-185.

1304. McHugh, William F., "Effects of Bargaining on Tenure and Other Academic Policies," IN Tice 1973, 113-128. Original.

1305. McHugh, William F., "Faculty Unionism," IN Smith 1973, 129-177. Original.

1306. McHugh, William F., "Tenure and Collective Bargaining," IN Vladeck 1975, 53-77. Original.

1307. McKeefrey, William J., "The Impact of Effective Utilization of Faculty and Facilities on the Changing Role of the Professor," IN Smith 1966, 226-231. Original.

1308. McKeefery, William J., "The Participation of the Faculty in Departmental Decision Making and in Campus Governance," IN Brann 1972, 216-220. Original.

1309. McLaughlin, Daniel R., "Training Administrative Personnel for Collective Bargaining," IN Angell 1977, 96-125. Original.

1310. McQuade, Vincent A., "Non-Teaching Responsibilities," IN Deferrari 1961, 72-87. Original.

An overview of faculty activities outside of classroom teaching.

1311. Mager, James A., "Salary Policies and Practices in Higher Education," IN Deferrari 1961, 198-209. Original.

1312. Magid, Joel G., "Promotion and Good Teaching," IN Smith 1973, 120-128. Original.

1313. Mannix, Thomas M., "Drafting Bargaining Contracts," IN Tice 1976, 113-128. Original.

1314. Marmion, Harry A., "Faculty Organizations in Higher Education," IN Elam 1969, 1-39. Original.

The essay centers on economic negotiations by national faculty organizations such as AAUP and AAHE.

1315. Marmion, Harry A., "Unions and Higher Education," IN Baldridge 1971, 344-356. ER, 49 (Winter 1968), 41-48.

1316. Martinotti, Guido and Alberto Giasanti, "The Robed Baron: The Academic Profession in the Italian University," IN Altbach 1977, 23-42. HE, 6 (May 1977), 189-208.

1317. Marty, Myron A., "Disciplinary Associations and Faculty Development," IN Vermilye 1976, 78-86. Original.

1318. Mayhew, Lewis B., "Faculty Demands and Faculty Militance," IN Hughes 1973, 44-60. JHE, 39 (May 1969), 337-350.

1319. Mayhew, Lewis B., "Faculty in Campus Governance," IN Smith 1969, 145-160. Original.

1320. Mayhew, Lewis, "The Organization of the Profession," IN Morris 1970, 133-147. Original.

1321. Mazur, Allan, "The Socialization of Jews into the Academic Subculture," IN Anderson 1971, 265-287.

This essay was taken from the author's doctoral dissertation, Johns Hopkins University, 1969. See: Milton M. Gordon for original hypothesis.

1322. Medalia, Nahum Z., "On Becoming a College Teacher," IN Yamamoto 1968, 292-300. OBCT (1963).

1323. Menard, Arthur P. and Nicholas Di Giovanni, Jr., "Preparing for Unit Representation Hearing Before Labor Boards," IN Angell 1977, 58-79. Original.

1324. Metzger, Walter P., "Academic Freedom: An Analysis of a Recent Case," IN Knorr 1965a, 23-31. Original.

A case study involving Mr. Leo Koch at the University of Illinois.

1325. Metzger, Walter P., "Academic Freedom and Big Business," IN Hawkins 1970, 69-78. DAF (1955).

1326. Metzger, Walter P., "The Academic Profession and Its Critics," IN Altman 1971, 71-87. Original.

1327. Miles, Leland, "Coordinating Faculty Bargaining with Other University Processes," IN Angell 1977, 553-563. Original.

1328. Miller, Richard L., "Prescribing Faculty Workloads," IN Smith 1971, 202-209. Original.

1329. Mills, C. Wright, "The Cultural Default," IN Anderson 1971, 307-313. CWW (1960).

Mills charges some scholars with "cultural default" because of their "uncritical acceptance of official definitions of world reality."

1330. Moog, Florence, "Tenure Is Obsolete," IN Vermilye 1972, 130-138. Original.

1331. Morand, Martin J. and Edward R. Purcell, "Grievance and Arbitration Processing," IN Vladeck 1975, 297-330. Original.

1332. Morenthau, Hans J., "Student-Faculty Participation in National Politics," IN Smith 1969, 5-9. Original.

1333. Morrow, Glenn R., "The Decline of Professional Morale," IN Hook 1974, 225-228. Original.

1334. Mortimer, Kenneth P. and Mark D. Johnson, "Faculty Bargaining in State Systems," IN Tice 1976, 155-170. Original.

1335. Mortimer, Kenneth P. and T. R. McConnell, "Faculty Participation in University Governance," IN Kruytbosch 1970, 111-131. Original.

1336. Murphy, Thomas P., "Minority Faculty Recruitment," IN Murphy 1975, 325-351. Original.

1337. Murray, John D., "Catholic Academicians and the Intellectual Subsociety Hypothesis," IN Anderson 1971, 247-263.

This essay was taken from the author's doctoral dissertation, University of Massachusetts, 1969. See: Milton M. Gordon for original hypothesis.

1338. Murray, John D., "Religious Orthodoxy Among Catholic Academicians," IN Anderson 1971, 291-303.

This essay was taken from the author's doctoral dissertation, University of Massachusetts, 1969.

1339. Naples, Caesar J., "Preparing to Negotiate the Next Contract," IN Angell 1977, 428-441. Original.

1340. Naples, Caesar J. and Joseph M. Bress, "Collective Bargaining--Its Scope," IN Vladeck 1975, 223-245. Original.

1341. Neff, William J. and John D. Forsyth, "Costing Union Demands," IN Angell 1977, 274-293. Original.

1342. Ness, Frederic W., "Faculty Recruitment and Orientation in Four-Year Colleges and Universities," IN Smith 1967, 144-147. Original.

1343. Newman, Harold R., "Using Neutrals to Help Solve Impasses," IN Angell 1977, 326-345. Original.

1344. Newton, David, "Faculty Attitudes and Collective Bargaining in Higher Education," IN Vladeck 1975, 97-113. Original.

1345. Nisbet, Robert A., "Conflicting Academic Loyalities," IN Lee 1967, 12-34. Original.

An excellent essay on the sometimes conflicting roles of faculty in higher education.

Commentaries by John T. Caldwell, Pauline Tompkins, Clark Byse, and Charles Cogen follow on pages 35-44.

1346. Nisbet, Robert A., "The Permanent Professors: A Modest Proposal," IN Anderson 1971, 105-121. PI, 1 (Fall 1965), 37-50.

The "case" for academic tenure is presented by the result it accomplishes for the university, not for the privilege it gives to a certain class of individuals.

1347. Novotny, Henry R., "Academic Freedom and Authoritarianism," IN Hook 1974, 133-142. Original.

1348. Novotny, Henry R., "The New Class, and 'Professor Bill,'" IN Hook 1978, 277-285. Original.

The author explores the relationship between higher education and the federal government by using the concept of power as expressed by two faculty social groups. The first group he calls "workaday academic" and the second "new class"--from a term coined by Milovan Djilas.

1349. Oberer, Walter E., "Faculty Participation in Academic Decision Making: As to What Issues, By What Forms, Using What Means of Persuasion?" IN Elam 1969, 132-180. Original.

1350. Odegaard, Charles E., "Organizing an Effective Student-Faculty Dialogue," IN Dennis 1966, 173-176. Original.

1351. O'Neil, Robert M., "Tenure Under Attack," IN Smith 1973, 178-199. Original.

1352. Orgel, Stephen and Alex Zwerdling, "On Judging Faculty," IN Morison 1966, 217-241. Original.

1353. Orze, Joseph J., "Working with the Faculty Senate in a Bargaining Context," IN Angell 1977, 504-519. Original.

1354. Osborne, Woodley B., "The AAUP and Collective Bargaining," IN Vladeck 1975, 153-168. Original.

1355. Ostroff, Anthony, "Economic Pressure and the Professor," IN Sanford 1962, 445-462. Original.

1356. Padberg, John W., "Student Faculty Interaction In and Outside the Classroom," IN Smith 1966, 186-189. Original.

1357. Parsons, Talcott, "New Roles for Academic Faculties," IN Smith 1966, 190-197. Original.

1358. Pelczar, Richard, "The Latin American Professoriate: Progress and Prospects," IN Altbach 1977, 125-144. HE, 6 (May 1977), 235-254.

1359. Pettit, Lawrence K., "Bargaining Educational Diversity in a Centralized State System," IN Angell 1977, 486-501. Original.

1360. Piper, David Warren, "Muddlemuch: Staff Development in Universities," IN Verreck 1974, 143-160. Original.

This essay places staff development in the context of staff training for the infusion of innovation.

1361. Powell, Walter H., "Making the Contract a Beneficial Instrument of University Governance," IN Angell 1977, 374-389. Original.

1362. Rabkin, Jakov M. and Thomas O. Eisemon, "Multiple Professional Roles of the Academic: A Canadian Case Study," IN Altbach 1977, 114-124. Original.

1363. Rehmus, Charles M., "Final Offer Arbitrations: The U.S. Experience," IN Tice 1976, 251-259. Original.

1364. Richardson Jr., Richard C., "Tenure, Promotion and Career Development," IN Tice 1976, 211-222. Original.

1365. Ritchie, Alexander, "Tenure and Academic Freedom," IN Pincoffs 1972, 159-169. Original.

1366. Rogers, James F., "Colleges and Universities Look at Their Need for Professional Staff," IN Smith 1966, 207-208. Original.

A statistical analysis and projection (period 1963 to 1969) of professional staff.

1367. Rosenhaupt, Hans, "How Can the Independent Liberal Arts College Attract Top Quality Faculty Members?" IN McGrath 1967, 44-55. Original.

1368. Roszak, Theodore, "On Academic Delinquency," IN Anderson 1971, 325-332. DA (1968).

Professor Roszak is extremely critical of scholars for their neglect of "exposing" misuse of power, etc. in favor of the "utilitarian service of . . . monied interests . . ."

1369. Sagen, H. Bradley, "Faculty Evaluation for Accountability," IN Vermilye 1976, 70-77. Original.

1370. Sanford, Nevitt, "New Values and Faculty Response," IN McGrath 1972, 30-49. Original.

1371. Sartorius, Rolf, "Tenure, Academic Freedom, and the Nature of the University," IN Pincoffs 1972, 184-188. Original.

1372. Sartorius, Rolf, "Tenure and Academic Freedom," IN Pincoffs 1972, 133-158. Original.

1373. Scarfe, Janet and Edward Sheffield, "Notes on the Canadian Professoriate," IN Altbach 1977, 92-113. HE, 6 (August 1977), 337-358.

1374. Schmitt, Richard, "Academic Freedom: The Future of a Confusion," IN Pincoffs 1972, 111-124. Original.

1375. Seabury, Paul, "The Affirmative-Action Program of HEW," IN <u>Hook</u> 1974, 179-183. Original.

1376. Searle, John R., "The Role of the Faculty," IN <u>Hook</u> 1974, 147-156. Original.

1377. Searle, John R., "Two Concepts of Academic Freedom," IN <u>Pincoffs</u> 1972, 86-96. <u>CW</u> (1971).

> Discusses academic freedom as both an institutional and societal right.

1378. Seeman, Melvin, "The Intellectual and the Language of Minorities," IN <u>Anderson</u> 1971, 187-203. <u>AJS</u>, 64 (July 1958), 25-35.

> A study, using the social problem of minority status, to determine how intellectuals deal with their "identity" and further to determine "what difference it may make if this identity is handled in different ways."

1379. Silber, John R., "Tenure in Context," IN <u>Smith</u> 1973, 34-53. Original.

1380. Simpson, Thomas K., "Liberal Scholarship and the College Teacher," IN <u>Goldwin</u> 1967, 49-71. Original.

1381. Smith, Bardwell L., "Academic Freedom, Tenure, and Countervailing Forces," IN <u>Smith</u> 1973, 200-222. Original.

1382. Smith, Bardwell L., "What Price Tenure?" IN <u>Smith</u> 1973, 1-8. Original.

1383. Snyder, Benson R., "How Does the Educator Under Stress Align His Personal and Professional Priorities," IN <u>Smith</u> 1965, 40-48. Original.

1384. Snyder, Richard C., "What Faculty Members Can Do on the Issue of War and Peace," IN <u>Smith</u> 1961, 224-227. Original.

1385. Spurr, Stephen H., "Faculty Power Versus Student Power," IN <u>Hughes</u> 1973, 124-130. <u>PJE</u>, 48 (October 1970), 37-41.

1386. Spurr, Stephen H., "New Degrees for College Teachers," IN <u>Smith</u> 1967, 106-109. Original.

1387. Stakenas, Robert G., "Student-Faculty Contact and Experimental Program for College Freshmen," IN <u>Feldman</u> 1972, 463-471. Original.

1388. Stanton, Frank, "Freedom for the Press and Academic Freedom," IN <u>Wilson</u> 1972, 337-342. Original.

1389. Stearns, Charles E., "Alternatives to 'Up or Out,'" IN Smith 1967, 114-117. Original.

1390. Stecklein, John E., "Methods of Analyzing, Expressing, and Reporting Faculty (Work) Load Data," IN Bunnell 1960, 26-35. Original.

1391. Stecklein, John E., "Research on Faculty Recruitment and Motivation," IN Wilson 1961, 11-34. Original.

1392. Steinbach, Sheldon E., "Collective Bargaining on Private Campuses," IN Vermilye 1972, 116-129. Original.

1393. Steinberg, Stephen, "Religious Involvement and Scholarly Productivity Among American Academics," IN Trow 1975, 85-112. Original.

1394. Stickler, W. Hugh, "Working Material and Bibliography on Faculty (Work) Load," IN Bunnell 1960, 80-97. Original.

1395. Stull, Harriet C., "Faculty Reorganization at Western Illinois University," IN Lunsford 1963, 71-81. Original.

1396. Sumberg, Alfred D., "Collective Bargaining," IN Smith 1970, 139-145. Original.

1397. Sumberg, Alfred, "The Impact of Government Regulation on the Academic Occupation," IN Hobbs 1978, 73-83. Original.

1398. Sumberg, Alfred D., "Legislated Bargaining Rights and Academic Self-Government," IN Tice 1973, 7-20. Original.

1399. Tice, Terrence N., "Faculty Bargaining: Varieties and Alternatives," IN Tice 1973, 63-75. Original.

1400. Tice, Terrence N., "The Situation in the States," IN Tice 1973, 177-238. Original.

A state-by-state rundown of legal provisions for collective bargaining.

1401. Tice, Terrence N., "The Situation in the States," IN Tice 1976, 319-357. Original.

A state-by-state rundown of legal provisions for collective bargaining.

1402. Tobias, Sheila, "Government Regulation, Institutional Self-Regulation, and Access to Academic Employment," IN Hobbs 1978, 85-95. Original.

1403. Tobias, Sheila and Margaret L. Rumbarger, "Full-Status Part-Time Faculty," IN Furniss 1974, 128-137. Original.

1404. Todorovich, Miro M. and Howard A. Glickstein, "Discrimination in Higher Education A Debate on Faculty Employment," IN Gross 1977, 12-40. Civ R D, 7 (Spring 1975), 3-21.

1405. Tollett, Kenneth S., "The Faculty and the Government," IN Hughes 1975a, 211-231. Original.

This essay deals with faculty tenure, unionization, and affirmative action.

Commentaries by Cyrena N. Pondrom, Dexter L. Hanley, and William W. Van Alstyne follow on pages 232-245.

1406. Tonsor, Stephen, "Some Things We Need," IN Hook 1974, 121-122. Original.

The author suggests that changing faculty appointment and tenure policies may help to create a more "open" university.

1407. Trow, Martin, "The Distribution of Academic Tenure in American Higher Education," IN Smith 1973, 223-250. Original.

1408. Tuohy, Sister Vincent T., "Teachers' Work Loads," IN Deferrari 1961, 210-222. Original.

1409. Tyler, Gus, "The Faculty Joins the Proletariat," IN Hughes 1973, 29-43. Change, 3 (Winter 1971-72), 40-45.

1410. Veblen, Thorstein, "The Academic Personnel," IN Anderson 1971, 31-44. HLIA (1957).

1411. Walker, Donald E., David Feldman, and Gregory O. Stone, "Achieving Institutional Goals Through Collective Bargaining," IN Angell 1977, 174-187. Original.

1412. Wallerstein, Immanuel, "Academic Freedom and Collective Expressions of Opinion," IN Smith 1971, 189-194. Original.

1413. Walworth, William R. and George W. Angell, "Improving Bargaining Processes Through Self-Evaluation," IN Angell 1977, 538-551. Original.

1414. Weissman, Myrna M., Katherine Nelson, Judith Hackman, Cynthia Pincus, and Brigitte Prusoff, "The Faculty Wife: Her Academic Interests and Qualifications," IN Rossi 1973, 187-195. Original.

1415. Wellemeyer Jr., J. Fletcher, "Sources of New Teachers, Full- and Part-Time," IN Deferrari 1961, 179-189. Original.

1416. Werdell, Philip R., "Student Participation in Effective Programs of Faculty Evaluation," IN Smith 1967, 182-185. Original.

1417. West, Andrew F., "What is Academic Freedom?" IN Portman 1972, 61-75. NAR, 140 (May 1885), 432-444.

1418. Williams, Gareth, "Gentlemen and Players: The Changing British Professoriate," IN Altbach 1977, 9-22. Original.

1419. Wilson, Logan, "The Academic Man Revisited," IN Wilson 1961, 1-9. Original.

1420. Wilson, Logan, "Freedom and Responsibility in Higher Education," IN Dennis 1966, 333-339. Original.

1421. Wilson, Logan, "The Professor and his Roles," IN Lee 1967, 99-109. Original.

1422. Wilson, O. Meredith, "Some Issues of Supply and Productivity," IN Harris 1960, 115-117. Original.

A survey of issues on faculty supply and productivity.

1423. Wilson, Robert C. and Jerry G. Gaff, "Student Voice--Faculty Response," IN Kruytbosch 1970, 181-188. RR, 4 (1969), 1-4.

1424. Witkin, Herman A., "Cognitive Style in Academic Performance and in Teacher-Student Relations," IN Messick 1976, 38-72. Original.

Commentaries by Seymour Wapner and Arthur W. Chickering follow on pages 73-89.

1425. Wollett, Donald H., "Government Regulation and the Staying Power of the Professoriate," IN Hobbs 1978, 97-101. Original.

1426. Wollett, Donald H., "Self-Governance and Collective Bargaining for Higher Education Faculty: Can the Two Systems Coexist?" IN Vladeck 1975, 33-51. Original.

1427. Woodburne, Lloyd S., "Guidelines for Student Ratings of Faculty," IN Smith 1966, 269-272. Original.

1428. Yuker, Harold E., "Faculty Workloads and Productivity," IN Tice 1976, 223-233. Original.

1429. Zeller, Bella, "Why Faculties Organize," IN Vladeck 1975, 81-95. Original.

13
STUDENTS

1430. Abbott, Joan, "The Effects of Social Class on Student Life," IN Butcher 1972, 170-185. SLCS (1971).

1431. Abrams, Irwin, "The Student Abroad," IN Baskin 1965, 78-103. Original.

1432. Adams, Donald V., "Residential Learning Opportunities," IN De Coster 1974, 87-94. Original.

1433. Allport, Gordon W., "Uniqueness in Students," IN Weatherford 1960, 57-75. Original.

1434. Anderson, C. Arnold, "Interdisciplinary Research on Outcomes of Higher Education," IN Solmon 1973, 393-401. Original.

1435. Astin, Alexander W., "Measurement and Determinants of the Outputs of Higher Education," IN Solmon 1973, 107-127. Original.

1436. Astin, Alexander W., "Measuring Student Outputs in Higher Education," IN Lawrence 1970, 75-83. Original.

1437. Astin, Alexander W., "Undergraduate Achievement and Institutional 'Excellence,'" IN Feldman 1972, 193-209. Science, 161 (August 16, 1968), 661-668.

1438. Averill, Lloyd J., "The Climate of Valuing," IN Smith 1963, 67-73. Original.

> Professor Averill considers the role of higher education in helping students to achieve "worthy and enduring values."

1439. Bacon, Emery F., "What Will be the Implication for American Higher Education of the Growing Concentration on the Superior Student?" IN Smith 1962, 189-192. Original.

Commentary by James H. Robertson follows on pages 193-196.

1440. Barton, Allen H., "Studying the Effects of College Education," IN Yamamoto 1968, 326-329. SECE (1959).

1441. Bay, Christian, "A Social Theory of Intellectual Development," IN Sanford 1962, 972-1005. Original.

1442. Beardslee, David C. and Donald D. O'Dowd, "Students and the Occupational World," IN Sanford 1962, 597-626. Original.

1443. Becker, Howard S., "Student Culture," IN Lunsford 1963a, 11-25. Original.

1444. Becker, Howard S., "What Do They Really Learn at College?" IN Feldman 1972, 103-108. Tran, 1 (May 1964), 14-17.

1445. Berdie, Ralph F., "Student Ambivalence and Behavior," IN Dennis 1966, 359-366. Original.

1446. "The Berkeley Student," IN Mayhew 1967, 315-340. EB (1966).

1447. Bien, Peter, "Metaphysics, Myth, and Politics," IN Buxton 1975, 157-188. Original.

An excellent essay which attempts to establish a philosophical understanding of the student movement in the 1960's and to discern what changes could best meet the student's needs.

1448. Black, Bernard R., "Student Needs and Orientation Directors' Aspirations," IN Fitzgerald 1970, 188-196. JCSP, 6 (December 1964), 102-108.

1449. Blackman, Edward B., "The Campus Environment and Student Freedom," IN Vaccaro 1969, 1-30. Original.

1450. Blaine Jr., Graham B., "College Students and Moral Values," IN Dennis 1966, 372-376. Original.

1451. Blaine Jr., Graham B., "Therapy," IN Blain 1961, 232-248. Original.

This essay describes the use of short-term psychotherapy with college students.

1452. Blaine Jr., Graham B. and Charles C. McArthur, "Basic Character Disorders and Homosexuality," IN Blain 1961, 100-115. Original.

1453. Blaine Jr., Graham B. and Charles C. McArthur, "Problems (Emotional) Connected with Studying," IN Blain 1961, 76-99. Original.

1454. Blewett, John, "Student Movements: East Asian and American Patterns," IN Vaccaro 1969, 155-165. Original.

1455. Block, Jeanne H., Norma Haan, and M. Brewster Smith, "Activism and Apathy in Contemporary Youth," IN Feldman 1972, 393-407. UA (1968).

1456. Bloland, Paul A., "Emerging Patterns in Student Activity Programs," IN Fitzgerald 1970, 215-218. JCSP, 8 (November 1967), 390-392.

1457. Bloy Jr., Myron B., "A Spiritual Taxonomy," IN Hodgkinson 1971a, 162-176. Original.

Mr. Bloy believes that students, especially through their participation in the civil rights demonstrations, have developed a "new vision" based on religious principles, integrity, and commitment.

1458. Bolder, Dorothy A., "Summer and Vacation Employment for College Students," IN Keene 1975, 115-124. Original.

1459. Bossard, James H. S. and Eleanor S. Boll, "Campus Marriages--For Better or for Worse," IN Bellman 1962, 59-68. NYTM, 108 (April 5, 1959), 59; 83; 85-86; 88.

1460. Bowers, William J., "Confronting College Cheating," IN Havice 1971, 72-87. Original.

1461. Bradshaw, Ted K., "The Impact of Peers on Student Orientations to College: A Contextual Analysis," IN Trow 1975, 265-296. Original.

1462. Britt, Laurence V., "Some Concepts of Student Academic Freedom," IN Dennis 1966, 284-287. Original.

1463. Brouder, Kathleen and Lucy Miller, "Legislative Initiatives on Students and Academic Bargaining," IN Tice 1976, 283-297. Original.

1464. Brown, Donald R., "Personality, College Environment, and Academic Productivity," IN Sanford 1962, 536-562. Original.

1465. Brown, Robert D., "Manipulation of the Environmental Press in a College Residence Hall," IN Feldman 1972, 319-327. PGJ, 46 (February 1968), 555-560.

1466. Brown, Robert D., "Student Development and Residence Education: Should It Be Social Engineering?" IN De Coster 1974, 41-54. Original.

1467. Bucklew, Neil S., "Students and Concerted Action," IN Vladeck 1975, 357-377. Original.

The author provides an analysis of the nature of student activity, especially in the 1960's, and suggests some possible consequences.

1468. Burns, Tom, "The Revolt of the Privileged," IN Butcher 1972, 245-257. Original.

1469. Bushnell, John H., "Student Culture at Vassar," IN Sanford 1962, 489-514. Original.

1470. Bushnell, John, "Student Values: A Summary of Research and Future Problems," IN Carpenter 1960, 45-61. Original.

1471. Butler, William R., "Student Involvement in the Decision-Making Process," IN Fitzgerald 1970, 67-73. JCSP, 7 (November 1966), 331-335.

1472. Butts, Porter, "The (College) Union Mission," IN Fitzgerald 1970, 236-240. BCU, 34 (December 1966), 6-7.

1473. Campbell, David P., "The Right College," IN Harcleroad 1970, 85-94. Original.

An essay on the process of college selection by students.

Commentaries by Tom G. Sexton, Joseph D. Boyd, and Ted R. Robinson follow on pages 95-97.

1474. Carskadon, Thomas G., "Help-Seeking in the College Student: Strength or Weakness?" IN Bloom 1975, 125-152. Original.

1475. Cartter, Allan M., "Student Financial Aid," IN Wilson 1972, 189-204. Original.

Commentaries by Edward Sanders and Valerie A. Riddick follow on pages 205-209.

1476. Cassidy, Sally W., "The Name of the Game is the Student," IN McGrath 1972, 50-61. Original.

1477. Chang, T. M., "A Method for Analysing Cognitive Skills," IN Verreck 1974, 383-396. Original.

1478. Chickering, Arthur W., "Education and Identity: Implications for Residence Hall Living," IN De Coster 1974, 76-86. Original.

1479. Chickering, Arthur W., "Institutional Objectives and Student Development in College," IN Feldman 1972, 89-102. JABS, 3 (July/September 1967), 287-304.

1480. Clark, Burton R., "The College as Determinant," IN Yamamoto 1968, 255-269. EES (1962).

An essay on the effect of college on student attitudes and behavior.

1481. Clark, Burton R. and Martin Trow, "The Organizational Context," IN Newcomb 1966, 17-70. Original.

The organization of colleges as it effects student attitudes and behavior.

1482. Clemans, William V., "Evaluation of Student Achievement," IN Smith 1966, 257-260. Original.

1483. Coelho, George V., David A. Hamburg, and Elizabeth B. Murphey, "Coping Strategies in a New Learning Environment," IN Yamamoto 1968, 331-344. AGP, 9 (November 1963), 433-443.

The psychological stress of the transfer from high school to college is examined in this essay.

1484. Cole, Fred C., "Intercollegiate Athletics and Higher Education," IN Smith 1961, 193-196. Original.

1485. Collins, Mary, "The College Experience Through the Eyes of the Students," IN Murphy 1960, 58-90. Original.

1486. Commager, Henry S., "Give the Games Back to the Students," IN Bellman 1962, 83-91. NYTM, (April 16, 1961), 27; 120-121.

A study of intercollegiate athetics.

1487. Committee on the Student in Higher Education, "The Student in Higher Education: Recommendations," IN Feldman 1972, 443-452. SHE, (1968).

1488. Conant, James B., "Preparing Students for Study in the University," IN Henderson 1968, 72-77. Original.

1489. Conley, William H., "Pressures from Students for Emancipation from Institutional Controls--and Vice Versa," IN Smith 1965, 88-91. Original.

1490. Conns, Frederick W., "The Developmental Tasks of the College Student," IN De Coster 1974, 3-20. Adol Psy (1971).

1491. Coon, Gaylord P., "Acute Psychosis, Depression, and Elation," IN Blain 1961, 116-132. Original.

1492. Cottle, Thomas J., "The Effects of College on Individuals," IN Solmon 1973, 175-224. Original.

1493. Crane, Robert M., "Student Governance and the Issue of Student Freedom," IN Vaccaro 1969, 49-62. Original.

1494. Cross, K. Patricia, "New Students in a New World," IN Vermilye 1973, 87-95. Original.

1495. Cutler, Richard L., "The New Role of the Student in the Academic Society," IN Smith 1966, 154-157. Original.

1496. Dakak, Fred, "Problems of Foreign Students," IN Keene 1975, 159-169. Original.

1497. Daley, Wayne W., "Off-Campus Housing at Universities and Colleges with 2,500 or More Student Enrollment," IN Fitzgerald 1970, 209-214. JACHA, 13 (April 1965), 502-510.

1498. Dannells, Michael, "Discipline," IN Packwood 1977, 232-278. Original.

> A thorough history and overview of student discipline in American colleges with an extensive bibliography.

1499. Daughtry, Alex A., "The Kansas Surveys of Postgraduate Activities of High School Seniors," IN Brown 1960, 52-57. Original.

1500. Davis, James M., "The Most Effective and Helpful Means of Educating and Dealing with the Increasing Number of Foreign Students Attending American Colleges and Universities," IN Smith 1961, 101-104. Original.

1501. De Coster, David A. and Phyllis Mable, "Residence Education: Purpose and Process," IN De Coster 1974, 21-40. Original.

> An historical, philosophical, and pedagogical overview of the potential for student development within the context of residence halls.

1502. Deinhardt, Barbara, "'Mother of Men,'" IN Furniss 1974, 66-69. Original.

> A view of coeducation by a female student at Yale University.

1503. De Jouvenel, Bertrand, "Academic Youth and Social Revolution," IN Caffrey 1969, 150-168. Original.

> Commentaries by Gresham M. Sykes, Glenn E. Brooks, Hugh W. Lane, Malcolm Moos, and Robert Boguslaw follow on pages 169-183.

1504. Demos, George D., "Problem of Integrating the Commuter College Student to the College Campus," IN Fitzgerald 1970, 229-233. JACHA, 15 (April 1967), 291-294.

1505. Dennis, Lawrence E., "On Discovering College Students," IN Dennis 1966, 1-5. Original.

1506. "A Dialogue on Creativity," IN Heist 1968, 3-17. Original.

1507. Dixon, James P., "The Student's Role in Educational Policy," IN Dennis 1966, 164-168. Original.

1508. Donald Jr., T. Williams, "Students Assess Their Colleges and Universities Historical Backgrounds," IN Harcleroad 1971, 13-20. Original.

1509. Dressel, Paul L. and Irvin J. Lehmann, "The Impact of Higher Education on Student Attitudes, Values, and Critical Thinking Abilities," IN Milton 1968, 105-124. ER, 46 (Summer 1965), 248-258.

1510. Drever, James, "The Place of Academic Aptitude Testing in the British System of Higher Education," IN Butcher 1972, 49-58. Original.

1511. Driessel, Diane K., "A Student's View of Freedom in the Multiversity," IN Vacarro 1969, 73-83. Original.

1512. Duncan, James P., "Emphasis on the Education in Coeducational Living," IN De Coster 1974, 95-104. Original.

1513. Eddy Jr., Edward D., "Some Suggestions for Student Involvement in Educational Policy," IN Dennis 1966, 169-172. Original.

1514. Ellison, Jerome, "American Disgrace: College Cheating," IN Bellman 1962, 177-187. SEP, 232 (January 9, 1960), 13; 58-60.

1515. Entwistle, N. J., "Students and Their Academic Performance in Different Types of Institutions," IN Butcher 1972, 59-70. Original.

1516. Ericksen, Stanford C., "The Teacher, The Book, and the Student's Private Knowledge," IN Minter 1967, 83-99. Original.

1517. Erickson, F. Martin, "How Can the Undergraduate College Channel to Constructive Ends the Present Climate of Student Criticism and Desire of Independence?" IN Smith 1964, 83-86. Original.

1518. "The Etiquette of Pinning," IN Bellman 1962, 55-58. McC, 86 (March 1959), 22-23.

1519. Fairchild, Ellen, "Evaluating Residence Halls Through Trifocals," IN Fitzgerald 1970, 197-203. JCSP, 4 (March 1963), 171-176.

1520. Falk, David, "Campus Environments, Student Stress, and Campus Planning," IN Bloom 1975, 25-41. Original.

1521. Farnsworth, Dana L., "The Liberal Arts College's Responsibility for the Emotional Stability of Students," IN McGrath 1966a, 1-21. Original.

1522. Farnsworth, Dana L., "Student Power: Some Reflections on Decision Making in Colleges and Universities," IN Letter 1970, 50-58. Original.

1523. Farris, Theodore N., "Social Role Limitations of the Student as an Apprentice," IN Vaccaro 1969, 39-47. Original.

1524. Feldman, Kenneth A., "The Assessment of College Impacts," IN Feldman 1972, 211-225.

(ACT Research Report, No. 34, 1970)

1525. Feldman, Kenneth A., "Difficulties in Measuring and Interpreting Change and Stability During College," IN Feldman 1972, 127-142. Original.

1526. Ferguson, Marie A., "Adult Students in an Undergraduate University," IN Fitzgerald 1970, 345-350. JCSP, 7 (November 1966), 345-348.

1527. Ferrer, Terry, "Religion in Our Colleges," IN Bellman 1962, 109-116. New, 49 (April 22, 1957), 115-116; 118; 120.

1528. Finney, Ben C., "The Peer Program: An Experiment in Humanistic Education," IN Bloom 1975, 185-195. Original.

1529. Fitzgerald, Laurine E., "The Future for College Residence Halls," IN De Coster 1974, 267-278. Original.

1530. Fitzgerald, Laurine E. and Shirley B. Evans, "Orientation Programs: Foundation and Framework," IN Fitzgerald 1970, 180-184. CU, 38 (Apring 1963), 270-275.

1531. Flacks, Richard, "The Liberated Generation: An Exploration of the Roots of Student Protest," IN Baldridge 1971, 390-415. JSI, 23 (July 1967), 52-75.

1532. Folger, John K., "Student Pressures on Colleges and Universities," IN Smith 1965, 84-87. Original.

1533. Ford, Donald H. and Hugh B. Urban, "College Dropouts: Successes or Failures?" IN Pervin 1966, 83-106. Original.

1534. Ford, Robert S., "Foreign Students," IN Walters 1965, 153-170. Original.

1535. Fox, David E., "Presentation of Attrition Study," IN McGrath 1966a, 86-120. Original.

1536. Frank, Alan, "Patterns of Student Stress," IN Dennis 1966, 354-358. Original.

1537. Frankel, Charles, "Rights and Responsibilities in the Student-College Relationship," IN Dennis 1966, 232-251. Original.

1538. Frede, Richard, "The College Weekend," IN Bellman 1962, 160-166. En E (1958).

Excerpts from a novel on college life.

1539. Freedman, Mervin B., "Pressures on Students," IN Smith 1965, 148-151. Original.

1540. "Football and the Faculty," IN Bellman 1962, 101-105. SI, 12 (November 16, 1959), 51.

1541. Frye, Northrop, "The University and Personal Life: Student Anarchism and the Educational Contract," IN Niblett 1970, 35-51. Original.

Commentary by James Jarrett follows on pages 52-59.

1542. Funkenstein, Daniel H., "What Does Higher Education Need to Know About the Student in Today's Changing Society?" IN Smith 1960, 160-164. Original.

1543. Gagnon, John H., "The Uses of Failure," IN Feldman 1972, 283-287. Change, 1 (May-June 1969), 27-31.

An exploration into the social-psychological consequences of failure, especially academic failure, with suggestions for positive application in the university.

1544. Garrity, Donald L., "Response to Student Demands for Relevance," IN Smith 1968, 214-219. Original.

1545. Getman, Lisa, "From Conestoga to Career," IN Furniss 1974, 63-66. Original.

A view of coeducation by one of the first female students admitted to Yale University.

1546. Goldberg, Maxwell H. and Norman D. Kurland, "The Abler Student," IN Baskin 1965, 104-127. Original.

1547. Goldsen, Rose K., "High Hopes and Campus Realities," IN Dennis 1966, 117-122. Original.

Dr. Goldsen presents an interesting essay on the conflicts of interest and orientation between faculty and students when they attempt to resolve a "serious" question concerning curriculum or governance.

1548. Gomez-Millas, Juan, "The Student in Tomorrow's University," IN Henderson 1968, 87-93. Original.

1549. Goodstein, Leonard, "Institutional Research on Students," IN Sprague 1960, 124-132. Original.

1550. Gordon, David M., "'Rebellion' in Context: A Student's View of Students," IN Morison 1966, 292-314. Original.

1551. Gottlieb, David, "College Climate and Student Subcultures," IN Brookover 1965, 78-99. Original.

1552. Gottlieb, David and Benjamin Hodgkins, "College Student Subcultures," IN Yamamoto 1968, 238-255. Sch R, 71 (Fall 1963), 266-289.

1553. Gracey, Colin B., "Tobacco, Alcohol, Drugs: and Allied Substances," IN Havice 1971, 55-71. Original.

1554. Grant, W. Harold, "Humanizing the Residence Hall Environment," IN De Coster 1974, 71-75. Original.

1555. Greene, Theodore P., "John Cotton, Anne Hutchinson, and the Student Power Movement," IN Smith 1968, 99-105. Original.

1556. Greenleaf, Elizabeth A., "Coeducational Residence Halls: An Evaluation," IN Fitzgerald 1970, 203-208. JNAWDA, 25 (April 1962), 106-111.

1557. Grier, Daniel J., "Orientation: Tradition or Reality?" IN Fitzgerald 1970, 184-188. JNASPA, 3 (January 1966), 37-41.

1558. Gummere Jr., Richard M., "America's Wandering Scholars," IN Bellman 1962, 42-51. Harper's, 222 (May 1961), 73-76.

A study of student migration.

1559. Haggard, Ernest A., "Personality Dynamics and Intellectual Achievement," IN Murphy 1960, 116-133. Original.

1560. Hall, Douglas K., "Student Freedom and the Development of Creative Education," IN Vaccaro 1969, 147-154. Original.

1561. Hall, Mary Jo, "Academic Freedom for Students: Some Thoughts on the Current Debate," IN Vaccaro 1969, 63-72. Original.

1562. Hall, Thomas S., "In What Ways Can the College Best Assist the Student in Developing His Basic Pattern of Values?" IN Smith 1960, 157-159. Original.

1563. Halleck, Seymour L., "Emotional Problems of the Graduate Student," IN Katz 1976, 161-176. Original.

1564. Halleck, S. L., "Twelve Hypotheses of Student Unrest," IN Smith 1968, 115-133. Original.

1565. Hannah, William, "Dropouts: Recent Studies--Implications and Observations," IN Herron 1970, 156-178. Original.

1566. Harcleroad, Fred F., "Assessment of College and Universities," IN Harcleroad 1971, 3-10. Original.

The primary concern of this essay is with the assessment of colleges and universities by students.

1567. Hardee, Melvene D., "Politics, Pluralities, and the Student Development Perspective," IN De Coster 1974, 255-266. Original.

The impact of student politics on residence hall and other student personnel services are discussed.

1568. Hartshorn, Kay, "A Day in the Life of a Graduate Student," IN Katz 1976, 177-193. Original.

1569. Harvey, William A., "Identity and Depression in Students Who Fail," IN Pervin 1966, 223-236. Original.

1570. Hassenger, Robert, "A Campus Sexual Revolution?" IN Vaccaro 1969, 125-145. Original.

1571. Hatch, Stephen, "Change and Dissent in the Universities, An Examination of the Source of Protest," IN Butcher 1971, 224-232. Original.

1572. Haverman, Ernest and Patricia S. West, "Motorboards Come in All Sizes," IN Bellman 1962, 209-218. TWC (1952).

A biographical and sociological overview of students who attend college.

1573. Havice, Charles W., "Creative Criticism," IN Havice 1971, 106-116. Original.

The author provides several rational alternatives for handling criticism, especially from the students.

1574. Havice, Charles W., "Religion on Campus," IN Havice 1971, 117-129. Original.

1575. Heath, Douglas H., "Better Educated: Less Educable?" IN Letter 1970, 35-49. Original.

The author presents two theses: (1) that although today's college freshmen are better educated they may be less educable than previous generations and (2) the proper goal of education is "not to help students become better educated but to help them become more educable."

1576. Heath, Mark, "Religion on Campus," IN Donovan 1964, 132-154. Original.

1577. Heath, Roy, "The Reasonable Adventurer," IN Yamamoto 1968, 345-352. RE (1964).

The impact of a university on the lives of its students.

1578. Hechinger, Grace and Fred Hechinger, "The Case for Campus Life," IN Bellman 1962, 167-174. NYTM, 108 (March 29, 1959), 11; 31-32; 34.

1579. Hefferlin, J. B. Jon, "Recent Research on College Students," IN McGrath 1966a, 80-85. Original.

1580. Heinich, Robert, "Technology and the Student," IN Harcleroad 1970, 154-163. Original.

Commentaries by Robert C. Snider, O. W. Hascall, and Lee W. Cochran follow on pages 163-165.

1581. Heist, Paul, "Considerations in the Assessment of Creativity," IN Heist 1968, 208-223. Original.

1582. Heist, Paul, "Creative Students: College Transients," IN Heist 1968, 35-55. Original.

1583. Heist, Paul, "Intellect and Commitment: The Faces of Discontent," IN Knorr 1965a, 61-69. Original.

An historical and sociological analysis of the student movement.

1584. Heist, Paul, "The Student," IN Henry 1962, 211-234. Original.

A study of the characteristics of students in professional schools.

1585. Heist, Paul, "Uneasy Youth: Four Sketches," IN Heist 1968, 18-32. Original.

1586. Heist, Paul and Robert Wilson, "Curricular Experiences for the Creative," IN Heist 1968, 190-207. Original.

1587. Henderson, Algo D., "San Francisco State College: A Tale of Mismanagement and Disruption," IN Riesman 1973, 287-302. Original.

1588. Herriott, Robert E., "Some Social Determinants of Educational Aspiration," IN Yamamoto 1968, 105-122. Original.

1589. Hettlinger, Richard F., "Portrait of the Freshman as a Sexual Being," IN Havice 1971, 37-54. Original.

1590. Heyns, Roger W., "Today's Problems and Tomorrow's Students," IN Henderson 1968, 78-86. Original.

1591. Higgins, John J., "The Use of Self-Suggestion with Deep Concentration as Preparation for Examinations," IN Smith 1964, 94. Original.

1592. Hodgkinson, Harold L., "Regional Examining Institutes," IN Vermilye 1974, 97-102. Original.

1593. Holland, John L. and Robert C. Nichols, "A Longitudinal Study of Change in Major Field of Study," IN Feldman 1972, 269-281. PGJ, 43 (November 1964), 235-242.

1594. Hughes, Everett C., Howard S. Becker, and Blanche Geer, "Student Culture and Academic Effort," IN Sanford 1962, 515-530. Original.

1595. Huntley, C. W., "Changes in Values During the Four Years of College," IN Feldman 1972, 261-268. CSS, 1 (1967), 43-48.

1596. Iffert, Robert E., "Summary of Reports on College-Going Plans of High School Students," IN Brown 1960, 74-84. Original.

1597. Impellizzeri, Irene, "The Personality of the College Student," IN Siegel 1968, 15-42. Original.

1598. Isotta, Jo, "Facts, Values and Thinking: A First-Year Student's View," IN Entwistle, 1976, 27-31. Original.

1599. Jackson, Ronald E. A., "Responsible Individual Expression," IN Havice 1971, 100-105. Original.

An analysis of college student demands for greater opportunity to express their needs within the existing power structure.

1600. Jacob, Philip E., "Changing Values in College," IN Yamamoto 1968, 309-316. CVI (1957).

1601. Jahoda, Marie and Neil Warren, "The Myths of Youth," IN Yamamoto 1968, 70-81. SE, 38 (Winter 1965), 138-149.

1602. Jelly, Katherine L., "Coeducation: One Student's View," IN Furniss 1977, 61-63. Original.

1603. Jencks, Christopher, "Politics Is for Other People," IN Bellman 1962, 129-134. NR, 143 (October 3, 1960), 14-15.

An essay on student attitudes on politics and politicians.

1604. Jencks, Christopher S. and David Riesman, "Patterns of Residential Education: A Case Study of Harvard," IN Sanford 1962, 731-773.

1605. Johnston, Robert, "Student Culture and Student Power," IN Hodgkinson 1971, 85-97. Original.

1606. Juola, Arvo J., "Selection, Classification, and Placement of Students," IN Dressel 1961, 301-329. Original.

1607. Katz, Joseph, "Coeducational Living: Effects Upon Male-Female Relationships," IN De Coster 1974, 105-116. Original.

1608. Katz, Joseph, "Development of the Mind," IN Katz 1976, 107-126. Original.

> "This chapter addresses . . . the question of the processes and conditions of the development of the mind of the graduate and professional student."

1609. Katz, Joseph, "Psychodynamics of Development During the College Years," IN Bloom 1975, 43-75. Original.

1610. Katz, Joseph and Nevitt Sanford, "The New Student Power and Needed Reforms," IN Yamamoto 1968, 411-417. PDK, 47 (April 1966), 397-401.

1611. Katz, Joseph, Seymour Halleck, and Nevitt Sanford, "Psychological Stress in the Campus Community," IN Bloom 1975, 247-276. Original.

1612. Kauffman, Joseph F., "The Student in Higher Education," IN Dennis 1966, 141-162. ER, (1964), 291-298; 355-364.

1613. Kauffman, Joseph F., "The Time of the Student: Shall We Overcome?" IN Dennis 1966, 385-390. CU, 40 (Summer 1965), 377-383.

1614. Kaun, David E., "The College Dropout and Occupational Choice," IN Gordon 1974, 147-193. Original.

1615. Kaye, Phyllis, "Resolving Conflict Through Mediation," IN Smith 1971, 163-171. Original.

> This essay strongly supports the idea of mediation to resolve campus conflicts.

1616. Keeton, Morris, "A Productive Voice for Students," IN Letter 1968, 90-107. Original.

1617. Keniston, Kenneth, "The Faces in the Lecture Room," IN Morison 1966, 315-349. Original.

1618. Keniston, Kenneth, "Social Change and Youth in America," IN Yamamoto 1968, 40-60. Dae, 91 (Winter 1962), 145-171.

1619. Keniston, Kenneth, "The Sources of Student Dissent," IN Baldridge 1971, 358-389. JSI, 23 (July 1967), 108-137.

1620. King, Stanley H., "Emotional Problems of College Students," IN Yamamoto 1968, 353-361. AAUPB, 50 (Winter 1964), 327-332.

1621. Knoell, Dorothy M., "A Critical Review of Research on the College Dropout," IN Pervin 1966, 63-81. Original.

1622. Knoell, Dorothy M., "Institutional Research on Retention and Withdrawal," IN Sprague 1960, 41-65. Original.

A review of research on student dropouts.

1623. Knowles, Asa S. and Chester W. Storey, "Campus Activism and You," IN Havice 1971, 26-36. Original.

1624. Kolb, William L., "Changing the Collegiate Culture," IN Dennis 1966, 67-70. Original.

1625. Kraus, Irving, "Educational Aspirations of Working-Class Youth," IN Yamamoto 1968, 83-104. ASR, 29 (December 1964), 867-879.

1626. Kruytbosch, Carlos E., "Campus Radicalization: Notes on the Buildup at Buffalo," IN Kruytbosch 1970, 363-375. Original.

1627. Kubie, Lawrence S., "The Ontogeny of the Dropout Problem," IN Pervin 1966, 23-35. Original.

1628. Kuusisto, Allan A., "What Are the Most Effective Methods of Dealing With Larger Numbers of Students?" IN Smith 1962, 173-176. Original.

1629. Lehmann, Irvin J., "American College Students and the Socialization Process," IN Brookover 1965, 58-77. Original.

1630. Lehmann, Irvin J., "Changes from Freshman to Senior Years," IN Yamamoto 1968, 376-389. JEP, 54 (1963), 305-315.

1631. Lenning, Oscar T., Leo A. Munday, and E. James Maxey, "Student Educational Growth During the First Two Years of College," IN Feldman 1972, 81-88. CU, 44 (Winter 1969), 145-153.

1632. Levenson, Edgar A., "Some Socio-Cultural Issues in the Etiology and Treatment of College Dropouts," IN Pervin 1966, 189-206. Original.

1633. LeVine, Robert A., "American College Experience as a Socialization Process," IN Newcomb 1966, 107-132. Original.

1634. Libscomb, Greg, "A Student Looks at Academic Freedom," IN Dennis 1966, 288-292. Original.

1635. Liebert, Roland, "Finding and Developing Student Leaders: New Needs and an Old Despair," IN Smith 1967, 189-194. Original.

1636. Little, J. Kenneth, "Wisconsin Study of Academically Talented High School Graduates: Their College Plans and Progress," IN Brown 1960, 57-63. Original.

1637. Lloyd-Jones, Susan S., "Student Interests in Value Change and Power Conflict," IN Minter 1969, 87-97. Original.

1638. Loewy, Becky W., "Exploitation of College Students," IN Fitzgerald 1970, 397-400. JCSP, 4 (March 1963), 159-161; 164.

1639. London, Howard B., "The Perils of Opportunity: The Working-Class Community College Student in Sociological Perspective," IN Sacks 1978, 145-192. Original.

1640. Lozoff, Marjorie M., "Interpersonal Relations and Autonomy," IN Katz 1976, 141-159. Original.

The author describes "personality characteristics of graduate students and the effects of the graduate experience on their development."

1641. Lunsford, Terry F., "Activism, Privatism, and the Moral Advantage," IN Smith 1968, 91-98. Original.

1642. Lunsford, Terry, "The Berkeley Case," IN Knorr 1965a, 41-59. Original.

A transcript of a panel discussion of the student protest movement at Berkeley. The panel consisted of Terry Lunsford, David Kolodney, Sheldon Wolin, and Martin Malia.

1643. Lunsford, Terry F., "Some Suggested Directions for Research," IN Kruytbosch 1970, 309-346. FSCB (1965).

Suggested areas for research relating to student protests and institutional responses.

1644. McArthur, Charles C., "Distinguishing Patterns of Student Neuroses," IN Blain 1961, 54-75. Original.

1645. McCabe, Sheridan P., "Religious Commitment and Student Freedom on the Church-Related Campus," IN Vaccaro 1969, 115-123. Original.

1646. McCain, James A., "Unrest on the Campus," IN Harcleroad 1970, 131-136. Original.

Commentaries by Nancy S. Cole, Robert L. Ewigleben, and Robert B. Thompson follow on pages 137-139.

1647. McCann, Carolyn J., "Major Issues in Advising Foreign Students: A Review," IN Fitzgerald 1970, 363-369. JNAWDC, 27 (Summer 1964), 172-178.

1648. McConnell, T. R. and Paul Heist, "The Diverse College Student Population," IN Sanford 1962, 225-252. Original.

1649. MacGregor, Archie, "Student Activities Programs," IN Siegel 1968, 153-187. Original.

1650. MacKinnon, Donald W., "Educating for Creativity," IN Heist 1968, 147-160. Original.

1651. MacNeil, Robert, "Role of the Fourth Estate," IN Smith 1969, 45-50. Original.

Mr. MacNeil asserts that the media has presented a somewhat distorted view of what American college students stand for.

1652. Magrath, C. Peter, "Student Participation: What Happens When We Try It?" IN Caffrey 1969, 97-118. Original.

Commentaries by Joseph Whaley, Joseph M. Hendricks, Robert D. Clark, and Martha Peterson follow on pages 138-149.

1653. Malleson, Nicolas, "Student Wastage in the United Kingdom," IN Butcher 1972, 83-99. Original.

A review of research on the problem of student academic failure and student dropouts.

1654. Martin, Bernice, "The Mining of the Ivory Tower," IN Seabury 1975, 98-115. Original.

This essay attempts to establish the "student revolution" as only one part of a general cultural movement sometimes called the avant-garde or counterculture.

1655. Martin, David, "Mutations: Religio-Political Crisis and the Collapse of Puritanism and Humanism," IN Seabury 1975, 85-97. Original.

A review of the political attitudes in the student movement and their religious significance.

1656. Martin, Warren B., "Student Participation in Academic Governance," IN Smith 1967, 173-177. Original.

1657. Marton, Ference, "What Does it Take to Learn? Some Implications of an Alternative View of Learning," IN Entwistle 1976, 32-43. Original.

1658. Mayhew, Lewis B., "Campus Conflict and Confluence," IN Mayhew 1967, 457-466. Original.

1659. Medsker, Leland L. and James W. Trent, "Factors Related to Type of College Selected," IN Feldman 1972, 41-50. IDTPHE (1965).

1660. Meyer, Marshall W., "After the Bust: Student Politics at Harvard, 1969-1972," IN Riesman 1973, 127-153. Original.

1661. Meyerson, Martin, "The Ethos of the American College Student: Beyond the Protests," IN Goldwin 1967, 1-29. Original.

1662. Meyerson, Martin, "The Ethos of the American College Student: Beyond the Protests," IN Morison 1966, 266-291. HEMD (1967).

1663. Middlebrook, Samuel, "No Panecea for College Cheating," IN Bellman 1962, 188-195. NYTM, 110 (April 9, 1961), 17; 96-98.

1664. Millett, John D., "Student Charges," IN Connery 1970, 108-119. Original.

1665. Monypenny, Philip, "A Teacher Looks at Student Academic Freedom," IN Dennis 1966, 293-297. Original.

1666. Monypenny, Philip, "Toward a Standard for Student Academic Freedom," IN Baade 1964, 195-205. LCP, 28 (Summer 1963), 625-635.

1667. Moon Jr., Rexford G., "Student Aid and the Federal Government," IN Dobbins 1963, 30-44. Original.

1668. Moore, Marv, John E. Hinkle, and Carl Clarke, "Intervention with Married College Students," IN Bloom 1975, 219-229. Original.

1669. Morgan, Arthur E., "Developing Community Responsibility," IN Weatherford 1960, 99-119. Original.

A review of the nature of faculty and student participation in the development of college programs and policy.

1670. Moye, Alfred L., "Institutional Response to Students' Rights," IN Heyns 1977, 85-92. Original.

1671. Murphy, Lois B., "The Student's Experience of Growth," IN Murphy 1960, 91-115. Original.

1672. Murphy, Raymond O. and Charles W. Havice, "Extracurricular Activities," IN Havice 1971, 88-99. Original.

1673. Muskie, Edmund S., "Open the Door to Participation," IN Smith 1969, 245-250. Original.

Senator Muskie appeals for greater student participation in institutional decision-making.

1674. Newcomb, Theodore, "Exploiting Student Resources," IN Sprague 1960, 6-20. SCPG (1961).

1675. Newcomb, Theodore M., "The General Nature of Peer Group Influence," IN Newcomb 1966, 2-16. Original.

1676. Newcomb, Theodore M., "Research on Student Characteristics: Current Approaches," IN Dennis 1966, 101-116. Original.

1677. Newcomb, Theodore M., "Student Peer Group Influence," IN Yamamoto 1968, 230-238. AC (1962).

1678. Newcomb, Theodore M., "Student Peer Group Influences," IN Sanford 1962, 469-488. SCPA (1961).

1679. "The No-Nonsense Kids," IN Bellman 1962, 219-226. Time, 70 (November 18, 1957), 51-52; 54.

A review of attitudes and interests of the U.S. college student in 1957.

1680. Nowlis, Helen H., "Marihuana," IN Smith 1969, 113-122. Original.

1681. Nowlis, Helen H., "Responsibility of the Institution for Developing Student Maturity," IN Smith 1966, 222-225. Original.

1682. O'Hara, James G., "A Congressman's Views on Student Assistance and on Civil Rights Obligations," IN Hughes 1975, 316-322. Original.

1683. Olson, Layton, "The Student's Views on Independence," IN College 1974, 89-92. Original.

1684. Oppelt, Norman T., "Characteristics and Activities of Married College Students," IN Fitzgerald 1970, 356-362. JCSP, 6 (June 1965), 228-231.

1685. Otten, C. Michael, "Ruling Out Paternalism: Students and Administrators at Berkeley," IN Krutybosch 1970, 207-222. ABS, 11 (May-June 1968), 28-33.

1686. Pace, C. Robert, "New Concepts in Institutional Goals for Students," IN McGrath 1966a, 38-47. Original.

1687. Pace, C. Robert, "Perspectives on the Student and His College," IN Dennis 1966, 76-100. Original.

1688. Pace, C. Robert and Leonard Baird, "Attainment Patterns in the Environmental Press of College Subcultures," IN Newcomb 1966, 215-242. Original.

1689. Packwood, William T., "Union," IN Packwood 1977, 179-205. Original.

A very thorough overview of the college union with an extensive bibliography.

1690. Page, Ellis B., "Effects of Higher Education: Outcomes, Values, or Benefits," IN Solmon 1973, 159-172. Original.

1691. Pearlman, Samuel, "College Mental Health," IN Siegel 1968, 241-282. Original.

1692. Pearson, Richard, "What Should Society Do With Rejects from Higher Education?" IN Smith 1966, 86-87. Original.

1693. Pervin, Lawrence A., "The Later Academic, Vocational, and Personal Success of College Dropouts," IN Pervin 1966, 37-62. Original.

1694. Pervin, Lawrence A., "Reality and Nonreality in Student Expectations of College," IN Feldman 1972, 51-65. JP, 64 (September 1966), 41-48.

1695. Pervin, Lawrence A., Louis E. Reik, and Willard Dalrymple, "The Dropout in Conflict with Society," IN Pervin 1966, 3-21. Original.

1696. Pervin, Lawrence A., Louis E. Reik, and Willard Dalrymple, "The Dropout in Conflict with Society," IN Mayhew 1967, 265-279. CDUT (1966).

1697. Pervin, Lawrence A., Louis E. Reik, and Willard Dalrymple, "Personal Determinants and Their Interaction with Environment," IN Pervin 1966, 111-130. Original.

The authors address the idea that personality factors are not always involved in a student's decision to drop out of college.

1698. Peske, Michael A. and Robert L. Arnstein, "Readmission to College After Psychiatric Medical Leave," IN Pervin 1966, 131-153. Original.

1699. Peterson, Martha, "What Principles Should Govern Decisions When Students Disavow Institutional Policies?" IN Smith 1964, 91-93. Original.

1700. Poling, James, "How Pure Can a Game Get?" IN Bellman 1962, 92-100. SI, 13 (December 5, 1960), 32; 35-38; 41-42.

1701. Potter, Paul, "Student Discontent and Campus Reform," IN Knorr 1965a, 71-88. Original.

1702. Potter, Paul, "Student Discontent and Campus Reform," IN Mayhew 1967, 247-264. OFC (1965).

1703. Powell Jr., Robert S., "Evaluation: Student Viewpoints," IN Brann 1972, 137-144. Original.

1704. Powell Jr., Robert S., "More Than a Number," IN Harcleroad 1970, 71-82. Original.

A student perspective on problems and possibilities in higher education in the 1970's.

Commentaries by Lowell Heiny, Carl Varner, and Arthur E. Smith follow on pages 82-84.

1705. Powell Jr., Robert S., "Student Power and Educational Goals," IN Hodgkinson 1971, 65-84. Original.

1706. Pruitt, Wilton, "Leadership Training for Student Groups," IN Fitzgerald 1970, 224-229. JNASPA, 3 (Summer 1965), 35-39.

1707. Ratterman, P. H., "The New Breed of Student," IN Smith 1966, 158-163. Original.

1708. Ratterman, Patrick H., "Student Values--A New Approach," IN Herron 1970, 76-85. Original.

1709. Raushenbush, Esther, "And Among Other Things, Students Say . . .," IN Smith 1963, 186-189. Original.

1710. Reik, Louis E., "The College Dropout in Clinical Perspective," IN Pervin 1966, 177-187. Original.

1711. Reik, Louis E., "Today's Student and the College Psychiatrist," IN Havice 1971, 145-160. Original.

1712. Reubens, Beatrice G., "College and Jobs: International Problems," IN Vermilye 1977, 182-194. Original.

1713. Richards, Robert, "The College Student in Changing America," IN Brookover 1965, 3-18. Original.

1714. Riesman, David, "Coeducation and the Imitation of Life," IN Bellman 1962, 227-231. CVAE (1956).

1715. Riesman, David, "Commentary and Epilogue," IN Riesman 1973, 409-474. Original.

A summary of origins and impact of the campus turmoil of the late 1960's.

1716. Riesman, David, "Where Is the College Generation Headed?" IN Bellman 1962, 232-248. AtL, 207 (April 1961), 39-45.

1717. Riley, Gary L., "Student Participation in Governance: A Review of the Literature," IN Riley 1977, 239-250. Original.

1718. Robertson, James H., "The Superior Student: Characteristics, Aspirations, and Needs, IN Cohen 1966, 50-74. Original.

1719. Rodriguez, Grisel, "Coeds View an Undergraduate Campus," IN Furniss 1974, 69-71. Original.

1720. Rossi, Peter H., "Research Strategies in Measuring Peer Group Influences," IN Newcomb 1966, 190-214. Original.

1721. Rudd, Ernest, "Student Unrest--Can We Get the Facts Straight?" IN Butcher 1972, 233-244. Original.

1722. Rudolph, Frederick, "Neglect of Students as a Historical Tradition," IN Dennis 1966, 47-58. Original.

1723. Sanford, Nevitt, "The College Student in the World Today," IN Yamamoto 1968, 131-143. BBSS, 36 (June 1964), 6-19.

1724. Sanford, Nevitt, "The College Student of 1980," IN Eurich 1968, 176-199. Original.

1725. Sanford, Nevitt, "Developmental Status of the Entering Freshman," IN Sanford 1962, 253-282. Original.

1726. Sanford, Nevitt, "Ends and Means in Higher Education," IN Smith 1962, 10-20. Original.

> The topic of Dr. Sanford's essay is the "development of the individual personality as a major objective of societies."
>
> Commentaries by Fred Harvey Harrington and William C. Fels follow on pages 21-24.

1727. Sanford, Nevitt, "Personality Development and Creativity in the Soviet Union," IN Heist 1968, 161-189. Original.

1728. Schafer, Roy, "Talent as Danger: Psychoanalytic Observations on Academic Difficulty," IN Pervin 1966, 207-222. Original.

1729. Scheele, Adele M., "Successful Careering," IN Vermilye 1977, 195-205. Original.

1730. Schlossberg, Nancy K., "An Ombudsman for Students," IN Fitzgerald 1970, 79-82. JNASPA, 5 (July 1967), 31-33.

1731. Schmidt, Marlin R. and Betty Blaska, "Student Activities," IN Packwood 1977, 153-178. Original.

> A very thorough history and overview of college student activities programs with an extensive bibliography.

1732. Schrag, Peter, "Stirrings on the Campus," IN Bellman 1962, 135-143. NR, 144 (April 17, 1961), 9-11.

1733. Scott, Joseph W. and Mohamed El-Assal, "Multiversity, University Size, University Quality, and Student Protest: An Empirical Study," IN Baldridge 1971, 448-460. ASR, 34 (October 1969), 702-709.

1734. Selvin, Hanan C., "The Impact of University Experiences on Occupational Plans," IN Feldman 1972, 289-299. Sch R, 71 (Autumn 1963), 317-329.

1735. Shark, Alan R., "Students at the Faculty Bargaining Table," IN Tice 1976, 273-281. Original.

1736. Sindler, Allan P., "A Case Study in Student-University Relations," IN Caffrey 1969, 119-137. Original.

Commentaries by Joseph Whaley, Joseph M. Hendricks, Robert D. Clark, and Martha Peterson follow on pages 138-149.

1737. Skager, Rodney, John L. Holland, and Larry A. Braskamp, "Changes in Self-Ratings and Life Goals Among Students at Colleges with Different Characteristics," IN Feldman 1972, 177-191.

(ACT Research Report, No. 14, 1966)

1738. Smith, John E., "Value Convictions and Higher Education," IN Yamamoto 1968, 317-325. VCHE (1958).

1739. Smith, Robert B., "Neighborhood Context Affects College Plans," IN Feldman 1972, 23-39. Original.

1740. Snow, R. J., "The Political Involvement of Students: Where Freedom Begins and Ends," IN Vaccaro 1969, 85-103. Original.

1741. Snyder, Benson R., "Adaptation, Education, and Emotional Growth," IN Pervin 1966, 155-175. Original.

1742. Snyder, Benson R., "The Invisible Curriculum," IN Dennis 1966, 349-353. Original.

A medical doctor's views of the potential for psychological problems caused by stress within the college environment.

1743. Snyder, Benson R., "Student Stress," IN Lunsford 1963a, 27-38. Original.

1744. Solmon, Lewis C., "Prerequisites for Further Research on the Effects of Higher Education," IN Solmon 1973, 403-409. Original.

1745. Solmon, Lewis C., "Schooling and Subsequent Success: The Influence of Ability, Background, and Formal Education," IN Solmon 1973, 13-34. Original.

1746. Solmon, Lewis C., "Too Many College Graduates," IN Vermilye 1977, 172-181. Original.

1747. Solomon, Robert J., "The Forward Look in Testing Students," IN McGrath 1966a, 61-71. Original.

1748. Spike, Paul, "Phenomenology of Today's Students," IN Hodgkinson 1971a, 153-161. Original.

The author believes that a "generation gap" is developing among college students in terms of the perceptual patterns of students and adults.

1749. Spindt, H. A., "How Can the Parents, the College, the High School, and the Student Himself Collaborate Most Effectively for His Guidance and Development?" IN Smith 1960, 175-178. Original.

1750. Spohn, Herbert, "Vocational Orientation and Growth," IN Murphy 1960, 134-155. Original.

1751. Stager, David, "Implications of the Changing Employment Patterns," IN Bailey 1977, 120-125. Original.

1752. Stalnaker, John M., "Climate of Opinion," IN Brown 1960, 123-152. Original.

A survey of the development and use of the National Merit Scholarship Program.

1753. Stam, James and J. Victor Baldridge, "The Dynamics of Conflict on Campus: A Study of the Stanford 'April Third Movement,'" IN Baldridge 1971, 556-579. Original.

1754. Stanton, Charles M., "The Committed Student--A New and Rare Breed," IN Smith 1966, 164-168. Original.

1755. Stark, Matthew, "Human Relations Programs: Social Reconstruction Through Collegiate Extracurricular Activities," IN Fitzgerald 1970, 233-236. JNAWDC, 30 (Winter 1967), 82-85.

1756. Steinhaus, Arthur H., "Research Findings on Teaching Neuromuscular Relaxation," IN Smith 1964, 95-96. Original.

1757. Steinzor, Bernard, "The Development of Intellectual Qualities Through the College Years," IN Murphy 1960, 156-194. Original.

1758. Stern, George G., "The Book on Bardot's Bottom," IN Bergen 1966, 1-5. Original.

A humorous, but serious essay concerning the nature of contemporary (1965) higher education and the aspirations of incoming freshmen.

1759. Stern, George G., "Campus Environments and Student Unrest," IN Smith 1969, 123-135. Original.

1760. Stern, George G., "On Bardot and the State of Our Colleges," IN Smith 1966, 180-185. Original.

A review of student attitudes and values by use of the College Characteristics Index.

1761. Stern, George, "Student Values and Their Relationship to the College Environment," IN Sprague 1960, 67-104. Original.

1762. Stewart, Lawrence H., "Change in Personality Test Scores During College," IN Yamamoto 1968, 363-375. JCP, 11 (Fall 1964), 211-219.

1763. Stewart, Lawrence H., "Change in Personality Test Scores During College," IN Feldman 1972, 67-79. JCP, 11 (Fall 1964), 211-219.

1764. Stewart, Ward, "What Do Major Employer Groups Find Most and Least Important in the Educational Backgrounds of Recently Employed College Graduates," IN Smith 1964, 208-211. Original.

1765. Stice, Glen, "The School Attrition Studies at ETS," IN Brown 1960, 37-43. Original.

1766. Stickgold, Arthur, "The Social and Psychological Implications of Student Independence," IN College 1974, 45-72. Original.

1767. Stimpson, Richard and Lou Anna Kimsey Simon, "Accountability for the Residence Program," IN De Coster 1974, 234-254. Original.

1768. Stringer, Peter, "Student Personality," IN Butcher 1972, 159-169. Original.

1769. Stroup, Francis, "Factors Related to Educational Discontinuance of Arkansas High School Seniors," IN Brown 1960, 63-66. Original.

1770. Stroup, Herbert, "Society and Values: Students and Citizens," IN Siegel 1968, 385-418. Original.

1771. Stroup, Herbert, "The Touchables," IN Bellman 1962, 196-205. CC, 78 (March 22, 1961), 352-354.

A review of the literature on the moral and intellectual quality of college age youth.

1772. Stuner, William F., "The College Environment," IN Vermilye 1973, 71-86. Original.

1773. Summerskill, John, "Dropouts from College," IN Sanford 1962, 627-657. Original.

1774. Summerskill, John, "Dropouts from College," IN Yamamoto 1968, 423-426. CAC (1964).

1775. Super, Donald E., "Career Attitudes: Their Nature and Correlates in Ninth Grade," IN Brown 1960, 44-51. Original.

1776. Taubman, Paul and Terence Wales, "Mental Ability and Higher Educational Attainment in the Twentieth Century," IN Juster 1975, 47-70. Original.

1777. Taylor, Anne R., "Becoming Observers and Specialists," IN Katz 1976, 127-140. Original.

> This essay deals with occupational identity, interpersonal relations and other consequences of "doing graduate work."

1778. Taylor, Harold, "Student Unrest," IN Harcleroad 1970, 108-128. Original.

1779. Temby, William D., "Suicide," IN Blain 1961, 133-152. Original.

1780. Thaden, John R., "The Changing College Student Population," IN Brookover 1965, 19-40. Original.

1781. Thompson, Benjamin, "Student Alienation," IN Smith 1970, 94-100. Original.

1782. Thompson, Hugo W., "College Students and the Church," IN Bellman 1962, 117-126. CC, 78 (March 22, 1961), 355-357.

1783. Thompson, Ian M., "The Children of Nuremberg," IN Minter 1967, 73-81. Original.

> An essay on the forces that have shaped the values and goals of the student generation in the last 25 years.

1784. Tice, Terrence N., "Student Participation in Academic Decision Making," IN Tice 1976, 263-272. Original.

1785. Tigar, Michael E., "Student Participation in Academic Governance," IN Smith 1966, 169-174. Original.

1786. Timmons, Frank R., "Research on College Dropouts--A Critical Look," IN Bloom 1975, 99-123. Original.

1787. Trent, James W., "Revolution, Reformation, and Reevaluation," IN Baldridge 1971, 416-447. SAP (1970).

1788. Trow, Martin, "Some Lessons from Berkeley," IN Dennis 1966, 126-130. Original.

1789. Truitt, John W., "Diverse Views that Contain the Basis for Student Unrest and Agitation," IN Herron 1970, 61-75. Original.

1790. Truitt, John W., "The Image of Today's Student," IN Herron 1970, 29-42. Original.

1791. Truitt, John W., "University Posture and Student Protest--The Second Round," IN Herron 1970, 43-60. Original.

1792. Tyler, Ralph W., "The Impact of Students on Schools and Colleges," IN Yamamoto 1968, 403-410. SFIAE (1961).

1793. Underwood, Kenneth, "What Responsibility Does the College or University Have in Developing Public Leaders?" IN Smith 1960, 209-212. Original.

1794. Vaccaro, Louis C., "The New Student Subculture and the Search for Meaning," IN Vaccaro 1969, 31-38. Original.

1795. Vaccaro, Louis C. and Thomas E. Wolf, "Student Rights and Academic Due Process," IN Vaccaro 1969, 105-113. Original.

1796. Vaughan, George B., "A New Focus for Administrators," IN Heyns 1977, 93-99. Original.

President Vaughan suggests that a series of national and local issues have created a new awareness that the relationship between a college and its students is changing, thus creating new kinds of obligations.

1797. Vener, Arthur M., "College Education and Vocational Career," IN Brookover 1965, 100-116. Original.

1798. Vetter, Betty M., "Too Many College Graduates for Traditional Jobs," IN Bailey 1977, 112-120. Original.

1799. Vreeland, Rebecca and Charles Bidwell, "Organizational Effects on Student Attitudes: A Study of the Harvard Houses," IN Feldman 1972, 301-317. SE, 38 (Spring 1965), 233-250.

1800. Wagoner, Walter D., "The Campus and the Communication Gap," IN Havice 1971, 3-9. Original.

1801. Wallace, Walter L., "Institutional and Life-Cycle Socialization of College Freshmen," IN Feldman 1972, 343-363. AJS, 70 (November 1964), 303-318.

1802. Walsh, John, "Stanford's Search for Solutions," IN Riesman 1973, 303-322. Original.

1803. Walters Jr., Paul A., "Student Apathy," IN Blain 1961, 153-171. Original.

1804. Walters Jr., Roy W., "Employer Expectations for College Graduates," IN Smith 1966, 129-135. Original.

1805. Wankowski, J. A. "Academic Degrees and Personality of Students in One British University," IN Verreck 1974, 352-382. Original.

1806. Wankowski, J. A. "Student Wastage: The Birmingham (England) Experience," IN Butcher 1972, 71-82. Original.

A study of student academic failure.

1807. Wattenbarger, James L., "Student Fees and Public Responsibility," IN Orwig 1971, 143-153. Original.

1808. Webster, Harold, Mervin Freedmann, and Paul Heist, "Personality Changes in College Students," IN Sanford 1962, 811-846. Original.

1809. Weinberg, Ian and Kenneth N. Walker, "A Typology of Student Politics and Political Systems," IN Feldman 1972, 427-433. AJS, 75 (July 1969), 77-96.

1810. Willerman, Ben, "Field Experiments in the Study of Peer Groups," IN Newcomb 1966, 134-161. Original.

1811. William Jr., Moore, "Student Groups Assessing Their Colleges and Universities," IN Harcleroad 1971, 23-31. Original.

1812. Williams, B. R., "Student Problems," IN Holmes 1971, 13-190. Original.

1813. Williams, Don E. and Robert R. Reilley, "The Impact of Residence Halls on Students: The Research," IN De Coster 1974, 211-233. Original.

1814. Williamson, E. G., "Institutional Policy in Relation to Student Rights in Controversial Situations," IN Smith 1961, 93-96. Original.

1815. Williamson, E. G., "Student's Rights Modified by Correlative Responsibilities," IN Knorr 1965a, 33-39. Original.

1816. Williamson, E. G., "Training Student Leaders," IN Smith 1967, 186-188. Original.

1817. Williamson, E. G. and John L. Cowan, "Academic Freedom for Students: Issues and Guidelines," IN Dennis 1966, 252-283. ER, 46 (Fall 1965), 351-372.

1818. Wilson, Everett K., "The Entering Student: Attributes and Agents of Change," IN Newcomb 1966, 71-106. Original.

1819. Wilson, Everett K., "Teachers and Peers as Agents of Change," IN Feldman 1972, 365-370.

1820. Wilson, Logan, "Is the Student Becoming the 'Forgotten Man?'" IN Dennis 1966, 59-66. Original.

1821. Wirtz, Willard, "Education for What?" IN Vermilye 1977, 268-275. Original.

The author describes a three-dimensional education-work policy that attempts to address the problem of underemployment of fully qualified college graduates.

1822. Wolff, Robert P., "The College as Rat Race," IN Margolis 1969, 271-281. RP (1966).

This paper focuses on the competitive atmosphere of student life and the "tyranny of testing."

1823. Wolin, Sheldon and John Schaar, "Berkeley: The Battle of People's Park," IN Kruytbosch 1970, 349-361. NYRB, 12 (June 19, 1969), 24-31.

1824. Wood Jr., Frederic C., "New Sexual Attitudes," IN Smith 1969, 105-112. Original.

1825. Wood, Martha C., "Sororities: I'm Glad I Joined," IN Bellman 1962, 70-73. Ma, 37 (August 1953), 244+.

1826. Wrenn, Robert L., "The Authority Controversy and Today's Student," IN Fitzgerald 1970, 219-224. PGJ, 46 (June 1968), 949-953.

1827. Wright, Wendell W., "Why Capable Indiana High School Students Do Not Continue Their Schooling," IN Brown 1960, 67-73. Original.

1828. Yanitelli, Victor R., "Student Life Issues (Students, Society, and Change)," IN Donovan 1964, 120-131. Original.

1829. Yegge, Robert B., "Emerging Legal Rights for Students," IN Smith 1968, 77-88. Original.

1830. "Zeta Beta Kaput?" IN Bellman 1962, 74-79. New, 57 (March 27, 1961), 82-83.

14
GOVERNANCE AND ADMINISTRATION

1831. Anderson, G. Lester, "The New Breed of Administrator," IN Smith 1966, 232-234. Original.

1832. Anderson, G. Lester, "The Organizational Character of American Colleges and Universities," IN Lunsford 1963, 1-20. Original.

1833. Anderson, G. Lester and Kenneth P. Mortimer, "Governance and Control of Tomorrow's University: Whose Values?" IN Anderson 1976, 326-349. Original.

1834. Axelrod, Joseph, "New Organizational Patterns in American Colleges and Universities," IN Mayhew 1967, 157-179. EPAHE (1965).

(Note: The title of this essay in the original source is: "New Patterns of Internal Organization.")

1835. Axelrod, Joseph, "New Patterns of Internal Organization," IN Wilson 1965, 40-61. Original.

1836. Babbidge Jr., Homer D., "Leadership, Legitimacy, and Academic Governance," IN Murphy 1975, 315-324. Original.

1837. Bailey, Stephen K., "A Comparison of the University with a Government Bureau," IN Perkins 1973, 121-136. Original.

1838. Baldridge, J. Victor, "Environmental Pressure, Professional Autonomy, and Coping Strategies in Academic Organizations," IN Baldridge 1971, 507-529. Original.

A study of external environmental pressure on complex organizations.

1839. Baldridge, J. Victor, "Models of University Governance-Bureaucratic, Collegial, and Political," IN Baldridge 1971, 1-19. Original.

1840. Baldridge, J. Victor, David V. Curtis, George P. Ecker, and Gary L. Riley, "Alternative Models of Governance in Higher Education," IN Riley 1977, 2-25. Original.

1841. Baughman, George W. and Ronald Brady, "Towards a Theory of University Management," IN Johnson 1969, 3-28. Original.

1842. Beach, Mark, "Professional Versus Professorial Control of Higher Education," IN Hawkins 1970, 98-108. ER, 49 (Summer 1968), 263-273.

1843. Bell, Daniel, "By Whose Right?" IN Hodgkinson 1971, 153-172. Original.

> The author's thesis is ". . . that the controlling problem of the governance of universities in the 1970s will be the resolution of a crisis in legitimacy."

1844. Besse, Ralph M., "A Comparison of the University with the Corporation," IN Perkins 1973, 107-120. Original.

1845. Biles, Fay R., "The Management of Personnel," IN Rowland 1977, 485-497. Original.

1846. Blocker, Clyde E., "Decision Making in the Internal Operation of an Institution," IN Smith 1963, 164-166. Original.

1847. Blumen, Isadore, "The Need for Coalition and Proper Strategy," IN Hook 1974, 265-266. Original.

> Mr. Blumen stresses the need for faculty and administration to work together in solving institutional problems.

1848. Boland, Walter R., "Size, Organization, and Environmental Mediation: A Study of Colleges and Universities," IN Baldridge 1971, 58-74. Original.

1849. Bolman Jr., Frederick de W., "The Administrator as Leader and Statesman," IN Smith 1968, 177-184. Original.

1850. Bolman Jr., Frederick de W., "Can We Prepare Better College and University Administrators?" IN Smith 1964, 230-233. Original.

1851. Bolling, Landrum R., "Relating the Administration to the Individual Student," IN McGrath 1966a, 48-60. Original.

1852. Bonus, Thaddeus M., "The Domain of the Manager," IN Rowland 1977, 448-454. Original.

1853. Bowen, Howard R., "Governance and Educational Reform," IN Smith 1969, 173-186. Original.

1854. Bowen, Howard R., "Where Numbers Fail," IN Vermilye 1976, 8-17. Original.

A critique of "business management" principles as applied to higher education.

1855. Boyer, Ernest L., "Reconciling Contradictions: The Task of Creative Management," IN Hughes 1975, 30-38. Original.

1856. Brown, David G. and Thomas E. Wenzlau, "A View From the Campus," IN Breneman 1978, 389-410. Original.

The views of college administrators toward financial and other public policy issues on higher education.

1857. Campbell, Roald F., "Evaluation of College Administrators," IN Smith 1966, 235-237. Original.

1858. Chaney, John F., "Organizing for Administrative-Systems-Analysis Data Processing," IN Johnson 1969, 42-58. Original.

1859. Cheek Jr., King V., "Reflections and Notes on Styles and Attitudes in Higher Education Administration," IN Johnson 1974, 353-370. Original.

1860. Cheit, Earl F., "The Management Systems Challenge: How to be Academic Though Systematic," IN Hughes 1975a, 147-173. Original.

Commentaries by Robert B. Mautz, Paul C. Reinert, and James F. Kelley follow on pages 173-183.

1861. Clark, Burton R., "The Alternatives: Paranoia or Decentralization," IN Smith 1968, 196-200. Original.

Professor Clark recommends a decentralization of university governance to better promote "collegial authority."

1862. Clark, Burton R., "Faculty Organization and Authority," IN Hawkins 1970, 88-97. SAA (1963).

1863. Clark, Burton, "The Mass College," IN Baldridge 1971, 462-477. SAA (1963).

This essay provides the means to develop a profile of organizational character through an understanding of the complex set of relationships between an institution (college) and its environment.

1864. Clark, Burton R., "The Organizational Saga in Higher Education," IN Riley 1977, 99-109. ASQ, 17 (June 1972), 178-184.

1865. Clark, Burton R., "The Role of Faculty in College Administration," IN Wilson 1961, 83-102. Original.

Commentary by Frank Abbott follows on pages 103-110.

1866. Corson, John J., "New Developments in Governance," IN Smith 1971, 179-185. Original.

1867. Corson, John J., "Perspectives on the University Compared with Other Institutions," IN Perkins 1973, 155-169. Original.

1868. Cowen, Zelman, "The Governance of the Universities," IN Seabury 1975, 58-74. Original.

1869. De Burlo Jr., Comegys R., "Decision Making in the Maintenance of Institutional Integrity," IN Smith 1963, 171-174. Original.

1870. Dehner Jr., W. Joseph, "Creative Tension and Home Rule," IN Smith 1971, 156-162. Original.

Mr. Dehner suggests that university tensions can be a force for progress and that problems must be solved through community decision-making. From these two points, he evolves an idea of university governance as "participatory democracy."

1871. Dilley, Frank B., "Comments on Administration: A Position Paper," IN Brann 1972, 95-103. Original.

A reflection on administrative style and leadership in higher education governance.

1872. Dixon, James P., "The Authority Structure: Legality and Reality," IN Lunsford 1963, 21-36. Original.

1873. Donovan, George F., "Selected Problems of Administration in American Higher Education: A Challenge," IN Donovan 1964, 3-16. Original.

1874. Duryea, E. D. "Decision Making Through Allocation of Responsibility," IN Smith 1963, 157-159. Original.

1875. Duryea, E. D., "Evolution of University Organization," IN Perkins 15-37. Original.

1876. Duryea, E. D., "The Theory and Practice of Administration," IN Burns 1962, 28-44. Original.

1877. Dusseldrop, Ralph Van, "Some Principles for the Development of Management in Information Systems," IN Johnson 1969, 29-41. Original.

1878. Eddy, Edward D., "The Student Views the College Administrator," IN Smith 1967, 195-197. Original.

1879. Edwards, Harry, "Pressures, Power, and Priorities in American Institutions of Higher Education," IN Altman 1970, 91-106. Original.

> The author suggests a "radical restructuring of institutions of higher education" to include the "introduction of students into every level of the decision-making process."

1880. Eliot, Thomas H., "Administrative Response to Campus Turmoil," IN Nichols 1970, 181-194. Original.

> Commentaries by Morris B. Abram, Elizabeth D. Scobell, Wesley L. Harris, Sr., and Robert W. Whitmore follow on pages 195-205.

1881. Elliott, Lloyd H., "Changing Internal Structures: The Relevance of Democracy," IN Caffrey 1969, 44-55. Original.

> Commentaries by Lincoln Gordon, Robert Johnston, M. K. Curry, Jr., Bertram H. Davis, and Douglass Cater follow on pages 68-87.

1882. Fogarty, Robert S., "The Good Place or No Place: Communication on the Campus," IN Smith 1967, 148-152. Original.

1883. Freedman, Mervin B., "New Alignments of Power and Authority in Colleges and Universities," IN Smith 1966, 149-153. Original.

1884. French, Sidney J., "The Role as Seen by the Faculty and Administration," IN Smith 1963, 182-185. Original.

1885. Fuchs, Ralph F., "Decision Making Through Allocation of Responsibility," IN Smith 1963, 160-163. Original.

1886. Gallagher, Buell G., "Who Runs the Institution?" IN Knorr 1965a, 89-96. Original.

1887. Gibb, Jack R., "Dynamics of Leadership," IN Smith 1967, 55-66. Original.

1888. Glenny, Lyman A., "Institutional Autonomy for Whom?" IN Smith 1970, 153-160. Original.

> With the advent of centralized control, colleges and universities, according to Dr. Glenny, run some risk in losing their autonomy. He hopes that this situation will cause others to look very closely at this issue.

1889. Gordon, Lincoln, "University Governance and the Public Interest," IN Nichols 1970, 269-284. Original.

Commentaries by W. Bradford Wiley, A. Leroy Willis, and John J. Budds follow on pages 285-292.

1890. Gould, Samuel B., "Damn the Torpedoes--Full Speed Ahead!" IN Furniss 1971, 261-270. Original.

A statement on leaders and leadership theory in higher education.

1891. Gove, Samuel K. and Carol E. Floyd, "Research on Higher Education Administration and Policy: An Uneven Report," IN Goodall 1976, 300-317. PAR, 35 (January-February 1975), 111-118.

1892. Gross, Edward and Paul V. Grambsch, "Power Structures in Universities and Colleges," IN Riley 1977, 26-41. CIUO (1974).

1893. Gustad, John W., "What Significant Changes Need to be Made in Present Conditions of Work for Faculty and Administrators?" IN Smith 1960, 138-140. Original.

Several commentaries follow on pages 140-144.

1894. Henderson, Algo D., "Effective Models of University Governance," IN Smith 1967, 78-82. Original.

1895. Henderson, Algo D., "Improving Decision Making Through Research," IN Smith 1963, 153-156. Original.

1896. Henneman, H. J., "Goals and Techniques of Business, Industry, and Government That May be Applicable to the Administration of Higher Education," IN Smith 1961, 181-184. Original.

1897. Hertzfeld, Kurt M., "Decision Making in the Internal Operation of an Institution," IN Smith 1963, 167-170. Original.

1898. Hewett, W. T., "University Administration," IN Portman 1972, 139-162. AtL, 50 (October 1882), 505-518.

1899. Heyns, Roger W., "Renewal, Financing, Cooperation: Tasks for Today," IN Furniss 1974, 328-336. Original.

The author outlines some major tasks facing higher education and comments on the nature and quality of leadership to meets these tasks.

1900. Heyns, Roger W., "Stress and Administrative Authority," IN Smith 1968, 163-172. Original.

1901. Hilberry, Conrad, "Growing New Leaders," IN Smith 1967, 92-95. Original.

1902. Hodgkinson, Harold, "Finding the Levers: The Folkways and Mores of Campus Governance," IN Morris 1970, 148-157. Original.

1903. Hodgkinson, Harold L., "Who Decides--Who Decides?" IN Smith 1969, 139-144. Original.

1904. Horn, Francis H., "The Organization of Colleges and Universities," IN Burns 1962, 45-78. Original.

1905. Huckfeldt, Vaughn E., "Change in Higher Education Management," IN Heinlein 1974, 1-11. Original.

1906. Huitt, Ralph K., "Governance in the 1970s," IN Hodgkinson 1971, 173-186. Original.

1907. Hull IV, W. Frank, "The University Administrator: From Where Has He Come?" IN Perry 1971, 11-24. Original.

1908. Jacobson, Harvey K., "The Role of Evaluation and Research in Management," IN Rowland 1977, 508-521. Original.

1909. Jagow, Elmer, "Management Talents Required for the Steady State," IN Hughes 1975, 67-76. Original.

1910. Jastrow, Joseph, "The Academic Career as Affected by Administration," IN Hawkins 1970, 34-45. Science, 23 (1906), 561-574.

1911. Kauffman, Joseph F., "The Professor-Administrator," IN Harcleroad 1974, 9-12. Original.

1912. Keene, C. Mansel, "Administration of System-Wide Faculty and Staff Affairs," IN Wingfield 1970, 53-65. Original.

1913. Keeton, Morris, "The Constituencies and Their Claims," IN Riley 1977, 194-210. SAOC (1971).

1914. Knight, Douglas M., "The Changing Academic Society: New Roles and Relationships for Administrators," IN Smith 1966, 214-217. Original.

1915. Koster, Francis P., "Ombudsman," IN Vermilye 1973, 25-29. Original.

1916. Krampf, Robert F. and Albert C. Heinlein, "The Effectiveness of Simulation Models in Academic Administration," IN Heinlein 1974, 91-96. Original.

1917. Leavitt, Harold J., "Entrepreneurs, Mark II," IN Smith 1967, 67-77. Original.

The author wishes to see "conscious planned education for entrepreneurship" and for the management of institutions by "entrepreneurial college presidents and faculties."

1918. Lees, Robert B., "Information Theory in Communication Studies," IN Smith 1963, 233-236. Original.

1919. Lieberman, Myron, "Representational Systems in Higher Education," IN Baldridge 1971, 314-343. ERHE (1969).

1920. Litchfield, Edward H., "Organization in Large American Universities: The Administration," IN Baldridge 1971, 150-168. JHE, 30 (December 1959), 489-504.

1921. Livingston, John C., "Faculty and Administrative Roles in Decision Making," IN Smith 1968, 187-195. Original.

1922. Lowry, W. McNeil, "A Comparison of the University with a Large Foundation," IN Perkins 1973, 137-153. Original.

1923. Lunsford, Terry F., "Authority and Ideology in the Administered University," IN Kruytbosch 1970, 87-107. Original.

1924. McConnell, John W., "Autocracy Versus Democracy in Top Administration," IN Smith 1967, 83-87. Original.

1925. McConnell, T. R., "The Individual in the Organized University," IN Perry 1971, 97-117. Original.

1926. McConnell, T. R., "Needed Research in College and University Organization and Administration," IN Lunsford 1963, 113-131. Original.

1927. McGrath, Earl J., "Who Should Have the Power?" IN Hodgkinson 1971, 187-205. Original.

1928. McHenry, Dean E., "Academic Organizational Matrix at the University of California, Santa Crux," IN McHenry 1977, 86-116. Original.

1929. Margenau, Henry, "Organization and Administration of a University: A Philosopher's Perspective," IN Perry 1971, 51-72. Original.

1930. Mattfeld, Jacquelyn A., "Many Are Called, But Few Are Chosen," IN Furniss 1974, 121-127. Original.

An essay dealing with the qualifications and selection procedures for administrators in higher education, with comments on the paucity of women in administration.

1931. Mauer, George J., "Higher Education Administration: An Overview and Analytical Approach," IN Mauer 1976, 3-16. Original.

1932. Mayhew, Lewis B., "A Rendering of Accounts," IN Smith 1968, 144-156. Original.

The author is concerned over the apparent inability of leaders in higher education to overcome "the enormous discrepancy between our current (late 1960's) activity and the ideals we proclaim."

1933. Meeth, L. Richard, "Administration and Leadership," IN Hodgkinson 1971, 39-53. Original.

1934. Michael, Donald N., "The Next Generation," IN Yamamoto 1968, 466-470. NG (1963).

The author believes that university administration will become more decentralized to meet the needs of the number and characteristics of future students.

1935. Miller, James G., "Some Implications of Communication Theory for Higher Education," IN Smith 1963, 237-240. Original.

1936. Moodie, Graeme C., "University Government," IN Butcher 1972, 261-270. Original.

1937. Mooney, Ross L., "The Problem of Leadership in the University," IN Milton 1968, 175-195. HER, 33 (Winter 1963), 42-57.

1938. Moran, William E., "A Systems View of University Organization," IN Hamelman 1972, 3-12. Original.

1939. Morris, James G. and J. Randall Brown, "The Application of Mathematical Models to Academic Decision Making," IN Heinlein 1974, 131-135. Original.

1940. Murphy, Franklin D., "Some Reflections on Structure," IN Caffrey 1969, 88-94. Original.

1941. Murphy Thomas P., "University Bureaucracy and the Urban Thrust," IN Murphy 1975, 287-313. Original.

1942. Ness, Frederic W., "Campus Governance and Fiscal Stability," IN Jellema 1972, 39-51. Original.

1943. O'Neil, Robert M., "Paradoxes of Campus Power," IN Smith 1971, 172-178. Original.

1944. Pace, C. Robert, "Five College Environments," IN Milton 1968, 91-104. CBR, 41 (Spring 1960), 24-28.

1945. Packwood, William T., "Security," IN Packwood 1977, 279-297. Original.

An excellent and concise history of security programs and problems on college campuses.

1946. Park, Rosemary, "Value Change and Power Conflict: The Administrative Interest," IN Minter 1969, 115-128. Original.

1947. Perkins, James A., "The Future of Coordination," IN Perkins 1972, 279-286. Original.

1948. Perkins, James A., "Organization and Functions of the University," IN Perkins 1973, 3-14. Original.

1949. Perry, Richard R., "Restructuring the University," IN Perry 1971, 119-132. Original.

1950. Peterson, Richard E., "The Institutional Functioning Inventory: Development and Uses," IN Letter 1970, 78-91.

1951. Platt, Gerald M. and Talcott Parsons, "Decision-Making in the Academic System: Influence and Power Exchange," IN Kruytbosch 1970, 133-180. Original.

1952. Radock, Michael, "Overview of Executive Management," IN Rowland 1977, 441-447. Original.

1953. Renne, Roland R., "Decision Making in the Maintenance of Institutional Integrity," IN Smith 1963, 175-178. Original.

1954. Roberts, Millard G., "Management and Higher Education," IN Smith 1966, 238-241. Original.

1955. Robinson, Daniel D., "Who's Managing?" IN Harcleroad 1970, 140-150. Original.

Commentaries by John J. Coffelt, Oluf M. Davidsen, and Philip G. Hubbard follow on pages 151-153.

1956. Rourke, Francis E. and Glenn E. Brooks, "The 'Managerial Revolution' in Higher Education," IN Baldridge 1971, 169-192. ASQ, 9 (September 1964), 154-181.

1957. Rowland, Howard R., "Internal Relations," IN Rowland 1977, 30-46. Original.

1958. Rudolph, Frederick, "Changing Patterns of Authority and Influence," IN Knorr 1965a, 1-10. Original.

A short history and trend analysis of the nature of order and freedom on the college campus.

1959. Sanford, Nevitt, "On Filling a Role and on Being a Man: Leadership to Improved Conditions for Learning and Research," IN Smith 1967, 10-20. Original.

1960. Sanford, Terry, "Cooperative Leadership," IN Heyns 1977, 11-17. Original.

1961. Sanford, Terry, "Or Time Will Waste Us," IN Furniss 1971, 271-278. Original.

An essay on how colleges and universities should react to slander and criticism.

1962. Sawyer, G. M., "Factoring the Concept of Creative Management," IN Hughes 1975, 39-48. Original.

1963. Schenkel, Walter, "Who Has Been in Power?" IN Hodgkinson 1971, 1-24. Original.

An essay on the historical development of governance in the American university.

1964. Schroeder, Roger G., "Four Approaches for the Use of Management Science in University and College Administration: A Comparison," IN Heinlein 1974, 29-37. Original.

1965. Schroeder, Roger G., "A Survey of Management Science in University Operations," IN Heinlein 1974, 13-28. Original.

1966. Schwartz, Edward, "Student Power--In Response to the Questions," IN Caffrey 1969, 56-67. Original.

Commentaries by Lincoln Gordon, Robert Johnston, M. K. Curry, Jr., Bertram H. Davis, and Douglass Cater follow on pages 68-87.

1967. Scott, Ann, "Management as a Political Process: Overt Versus Covert," IN Hughes 1975, 49-57. Original.

1968. Sheats, Paul H., "Decision Making in the Maintenance of Institutional Integrity," IN Smith 1963, 179-181. Original.

1969. Shotzberger, Martin L., "Some Reflections on Higher Education," IN Hamelman 1972, 13-22. Original.

A projection of forces that could influence administrative decision making in the 1980's.

1970. Sigworth, Heather, "Issues in Nepotism Rules," IN Furniss 1974, 110-120. Original.

1971. Smith, Robert R., "Competing Internal Groups in the Governance of Colleges and Universities," IN Smith 1965, 92-96. Original.

1972. Stone Jr., Jesse N., "Achieving Broad-Based Leadership," IN Heyns 1977, 38-42. Original.

1973. Tarcher, Martin, "Leadership: Organization and Structure," IN Smith 1967, 263-271. Original.

1974. Thorsrud, Einar, "Breaking Down Bureaucracy," IN Vermilye 1977, 218-226. Original.

A case study of how a bureaucracy works and some innovative ways of developing alternatives to traditional superior-subordinate relationships.

1975. Tierney, Michael L., "Administration: The Impact of Management Information Systems on Governance," IN Riley 1977, 211-227. Original.

1976. Tuchman, Barbara W., "The Missing Element: Moral Courage," IN Smith 1967, 3-9. Original.

The author is concerned with the "abdication of moral leadership in the sense of a general unwillingness to state standards."

1977. Walker, Donald E., "New Policies for Changed Institutions," IN Heyns 1977, 60-66. Original.

Dr. Walker uses faculty unionism as an example to demonstrate that "old" personnel policies are not working well. He then appeals for new policies that are flexible enough to meet changing needs.

1978. Wallhaus, Robert A., "Modeling for Higher Education Administration and Management," IN Johnson 1969, 125-144. Original.

1979. Watts II, Charles H., "Problems of Academic Governance," IN Hughes 1973, 2-10. SS, 98 (November 1970), 405-408.

1980. Wert, Robert J., "Leadership: The Integrative Factor," IN Lunsford 1963, 83-97. Original.

1981. Wise, W. Max, "New Configurations in Governance," IN Smith 1970, 131-136. Original.

The author identifies major changes in college and university governance during the past few years.

1982. Wise, W. Max, "Thoughts About the Collapse of Academic Government and the Possibilities for Its Revival," IN Perry 1971, 25-49. Original.

1983. Zebot, Cyril, "A Case Study--May 1970," IN Hook 1974, 239-241. Original.

A case study of student-university confrontation and the resulting turmoil and action by the administration which caused the author to recommend a greater faculty role in the university's governance.

1984. Ziegler, Martin L., "The Organization, Economics, and Allocation of Resources to Administrative Systems Analysis," IN Johnson 1969, 59-75. Original.

15
PLANNING AND POLICY DEVELOPMENT

1985. Adams, Joseph J., "The Management of Planning," IN Rowland 1977, 455-463. Original.

1986. Aldrich Jr., Daniel G., "Maintaining Institutional Identity and Autonomy in Coordinated Systems," IN Rice 1966, 16-25. Original.

1987. Allen Jr., James E., "The New York State System," IN Wilson 1965, 110-116. Original.

1988. Allen, John S., "Planning the Nation's Newest State University," IN Smith 1960, 36-39. Original.

An overview of the major planning elements that went into the creation of the University of South Florida.

1989. Anderson, Robert C., "The Southern Regional Education Board," IN Wilson 1965, 191-195. Original.

1990. Andrew, Gary M. and Madelyn D. Alexander, "The Minnesota and Colorado Experiences with the Campus Planning Systems," IN Heinlein 1974, 65-68. Original.

1991. Armstrong, Jack L. and H. Bradley Sagen, "Changes in Calendar and Concept: Small Changes/Large Consequences," IN Vaccaro 1975, 18-27. Original.

1992. Ashby, Eric, "The Great Reappraisal: A Progress Report on the Work of the Carnegie Commission on Higher Education in the USA," IN Niblett 1972, 29-44. Original.

1993. Babbidge, Homer D., "Design and Change in American Higher Education," IN Knorr 1965, 1-6. Original.

1994. Balderston, F. E., "Thinking About the Outputs of Higher Education," IN Lawrence 1970, 11-16. Original.

1995. Baldridge, J. Victor, "Images of the Future and Organizational Change: The Case of New York University," IN Baldridge 1971, 532-555. Original.

This paper deals with problems of policy planning as they relate to long-range goals and strategies of an organization.

1996. Baselice, Francis J., "Budgeting for Effective Planning and Control," IN Wattel 1975, 218-313. Original.

1997. Baughman, George W., "Evaluating the Performance and Effectiveness of University Management Information Systems," IN Minter 1969a, 1-7. Original.

1998. Benezet, Louis T., "College Groups and the Claremont Example," IN Wilson 1965, 199-203. Original.

1999. Berdahl, Robert O., "Types of Statewide Coordinating Boards," IN Goodall 1976, 228-231. SCHE (1971).

2000. Boyer, Ernest L., "Interinstitutional Cooperation and the Exchange of Instructional Materials," IN Smith 1967, 281-285. Original.

2001. Brossman, W. R., "The Management of Priorities," IN Rowland 1977, 470-474. Original.

2002. Brown, David G., "Allocating Limited Resources," IN Nichols 1970, 156-169. Original.

Dr. Brown addresses the topic: "What alternative investments of university resources will be most productive in solving the racial crisis?"

Commentaries by Stuart A. Taylor, Sandy English, and Nils Y. Wessell follow on pages 170-180.

2003. Brown, David G., "A Scheme for Measuring the Output of Higher Education," IN Lawrence 1970, 27-38. Original.

2004. Brown, Edmund G., "Public Higher Education in California," IN Wilson 1965, 104-109. Original.

2005. Browne, Arthur D., "The Institution and the System: Autonomy and Coordination," IN Knorr 1965, 39-51. Original.

2006. Bunnell, Kevin P. and Eldon L. Johnson, "Interinstitutional Cooperation," IN Baskin 1965, 246-272. Original.

2007. Cahow, Clark R., Joe McDonald, and Roger Wilkins, "A Simulation Modeling Approach to a Scheduling Problem," IN Johnson 1969, 163-179. Original.

2008. Caldwell, John T., "The North Carolina State System," IN Wilson 1965, 117-120. Original.

2009. Chaney, John F., "Data Management and Interrelated Data Systems for Higher Education," IN Minter 1969a, 17-27. Original.

2010. Church, Martha E., "The Dwindling Enrollment Pool: Issues and Opportunities," IN Peltason 1978, 146-153. Original.

2011. Cole Jr., Charles C., "How Can a Campus Climate be Created, for Favorable Development of Quality Programs, by Involving the Participation of Faculty, Students, and Administrators?" IN Smith 1960, 132-134. Original.

Several commentaries follow on pages 134-137.

2012. Conger Jr., Louis H., "College and University Enrollment: Projections," IN Mushkin 1962, 3-20. Original.

2013. Connick, George P., "Cooperative Approach," IN Vermilye 1974, 71-75. Original.

A case study of inter-institutional cooperation in Maine.

2014. Cordes, David C., "Project Prime*: A Test Implementation of the Campus Simulation Model," IN Hamelman 1972, 77-105. Original.

*Planning Resources in Minnesota Education

2015. Cuthbertson, Kenneth M., "Long-Range Financial Planning," IN Knorr 1965, 65-77. Original.

2016. Dearing, Bruce, "Coordination--A View from the Campus," IN Perkins 1972, 53-63. Original.

2017. DeMott, Benjamin, "Equality, Excellence, and a Missing Link," IN Vermilye 1976, 29-38. Original.

2018. Doi, James, "Pressures to Increase Educational Productivity in Institutions," IN Smith 1965, 112-114. Original.

2019. Donovan, George F., "Organization of Campus Facilites and Resources," IN Donovan 1962, 84-97. Original.

2020. Donovan, George F., "The Philosophy of Interinstitutional Cooperation in American Higher Learning," IN Donovan 1965, 3-18. Original.

2021. Dressel, Paul L. and Margaret F. Lorimer, "Institutional Self-Evaluation," IN Dressel 1961, 393-432. Original.

2022. Drews, Theodore and Shelia Drews, "HEGIS: A Report on Status and Plans," IN Johnson 1969, 79-99. Original.

HEGIS, or Higher Education General Information Survey is a single package data gathering survey of higher education institutions developed by the U.S. Office of Education.

Commentary by George W. Baughman follows on pages 99-108.

2023. Dyer, James S., "Academic Resource Allocation Models at UCLA," IN Heinlein 1974, 109-119. Original.

2024. Ellis, Elmer, "Coordination of Higher Education in Missouri," IN Wilson 1965, 155-158. Original.

2025. Enarson, Harold L., "Higher Education in New Mexico," IN Wilson 1965, 121-128. Original.

2026. Enteman, Willard F., "Creative Planning," IN Vermilye 1975, 203-211. Original.

2027. Enthoven, Alain C., "Measures of the Outputs of Higher Education: Some Practical Suggestions for Their Development and Use," IN Lawrence 1970, 51-58. Original.

2028. Enzer, Hyman A., "Information, Symbols and Social Forces in Planning," IN Wattel 1975, 71-145. Original.

This essay includes two appendices: a. Information for Planning by Gerd Hemminger and b. A Partial Checklist of External Information Important for Planning by Harold L. Wattel.

2029. Fearn, Robert H. and Loren A. Ihnen, "An Economist's View of Planning Problems in Community College Systems," IN Hamelman 1972, 107-121. Original.

2030. Fitzroy, Herbert W. K., "Regional Cooperation Programs Twenty-Four Virginia Institutions," IN Donovan 1965, 111-125. Original.

2031. Folger, John K., "Three Questions About Statewide Planning," IN Hughes 1975, 227-235. Original.

2032. Foreman, Les, "Impact of the Campus Model on Decision Processes in the Ontario Community Colleges," IN Heinlein 1974, 47-64. Original.

2033. Gavin, James M., "Our Domestic Crises," IN Smith 1969, 251-264. Original.

Mr. Gavin outlines three important problem areas in higher education: "efficiency versus responsiveness," "compensatory treatment versus equal opportunity," and "knowledge gap" (in problem solving).

2034. Gladfelter, Millard E., "The Pennsylvania Way," IN Wilson 1965, 159-164. Original.

A review of coordination and support of higher education in Pennsylvania.

2035. Glenny, Lyman A., "Diversification and Quality Control," IN Godwin 1972, 3-19. Original.

This essay includes an analysis of major trends effecting higher education; followed by a list of eight "myths" concerning "cost savings and quality in educational programs," and concluding with suggestions for "optimizing resources for programs and their management."

2036. Glenny, Lyman A., "Institutional Autonomy for Whom?" IN Goodall 1976, 232-240. Original.

2037. Glenny, Lyman A., "State Systems and Plans for Higher Education," IN Wilson 1965, 86-103. Original.

2038. Glenny, Lyman A., "State-Wide Coordination of Higher Education: Plans, Surveys, and Progress to Date," IN Smith 1962, 242-244. Original.

Commentary by Sebastain V. Martorana follows on pages 245-248.

2039. Godwin, Winfred L., "Regional Dimensions of Planning and Coordination," IN Hughes 1975, 236-246. Original.

2040. Godwin, Winfred L., "The Southern Regional Education Board--A Public Regional System," IN Perkins 1972, 67-74. Original.

2041. Goodall, Leonard E., "Intercampus Relations in Multicampus Universities," IN Mauer 1976, 53-65. Original.

2042. Gould, Samuel B., "New York--The State System," IN Perkins 1972, 15-21. Original.

2043. Gwynn, John, "The Data Base Approach to a Management Information System," IN Minter 1969a, 9-15. Original.

2044. Hanson, Harold P., "From the Expanding University to the Steady State University," IN Mauer 1976, 21-32. Original.

2045. Harrington, Fred H., "The Compact for Education," IN Minter 1966, 74-87. Original.

Reviews the influence of James B. Conant and Terry Sanford on the development of a nationwide higher education policy through the Compact for Education and the Education Commission of the States.

2046. Hathaway, Dale E., "What is the Responsibility of the Faculty in Instructional Long-Range Planning?" IN Smith 1960, 124-127. Original.

2047. Hecquet, I., "Demographic Change as a Factor Influencing the Development of Higher Education," IN Holmes 1971, 149-160. Original.

2048. Henderson, Algo D., "A Critical Look at Year-Round Operations of Institutions," IN Smith 1962, 161-164. Original.

2049. Hill, Warren G., "To Keep from Being King," IN Hughes 1975, 246-252. Original.

Presents the dynamics of decision making and regional planning within a given state.

2050. Hitch, Charles J., "California's Master Plan: Some Kind of Education for Nearly Everybody," IN Furniss 1971, 23-25. Original.

2051. Hobson, Jesse E., "A Case Study in Institutional Planning," IN Knorr 1965, 15-38. Original.

2052. Hodgkinson, Harold L., "Changes in Enrollment: The Consequences," IN Peltason 1978, 154-161. Original.

2053. Hollander, T. Edward, "Enrollment Trends and State Coordinating Boards," IN Peltason 1978, 161-176. Original.

2054. Holroyd, P. and D. J. Loveridge, "Industry and Higher Education Alternatives," IN Stephens 1978, 68-76. Original.

The authors believe that higher education should play a major role in providing skilled personnel to meet constantly changing and highly technical manpower needs. This responsibility is one that is shared with industry and other facets of a highly interdependent society.

2055. Horn, Francis H., "Private Higher Education and State Coordination," IN Perkins 1972, 35-42. LE, 57 (December 1971), 500-508.

2056. Hough, Robbin R., "The Outputs of Undergraduate Education," IN Lawrence 1970, 93-103. Original.

2057. Jackson, Frederick H., "The Committee on Institutional Cooperation--A Private Regional System," IN Perkins 1972, 75-86. Original.

2058. Jensen, Ronald L., Martin L. Levin, William W. Pendleton, and Norman P. Uhl, "The Use of a Scheduling Algorithm in a Gaming Environment for Administrative Planning," IN Johnson 1969, 180-191. Original.

2059. Johnson, Donald A., "The Influence of Consortia in Reshaping American Higher Education," IN Vaccaro 1975, 43-52. Original.

2060. Judy, Richard W., "Systems Analysis for Efficient Resource Allocation in Higher Education," IN Minter 1969a, 41-58. Original.

2061. Kallen, D., "Higher Education: No Limits to Growth?" IN Stephens 1978, 139-155. Original.

2062. Keeton, Morris T., "Networks and Quality," IN Vermilye 1974, 103-107. Original.

The author believes that resource sharing (networks) has a good possibility of increasing opportunities for learning and enhancing the quality of learning.

2063. Keller, John, "Higher Education Objectives: Measures of Performance and Effectiveness," IN Minter 1969a, 79-84. Original.

2064. Kerr, Clark, "Policy Concerns for the Future," IN Vermilye 1972, 3-21. Original.

Dr. Kerr reviews the prospects in higher education that are subject to policy control. This review was written when the Carnegie Commission had completed about two-thirds of its work.

2065. Kerr, Clark, "Toward a Nationwide System of Higher Education," IN Wilson 1965, 258-262. Original.

2066. King, John E., "Changes in the State College System," IN Wilson 1965, 74-78. Original.

2067. Knight, Douglas M., "Purpose and Policy in Higher Education," IN Knight 1960, 6-28. Original.

2068. Koenig, Herman E., "A Systems Model for Management, Planning, and Resource Allocation in Institutions of Higher Education," IN Minter 1969a, 29-40. Original.

2069. Kornfeld, Leo L., "Advanced Applied Management Information Systems in Higher Education: Three Case Studies," IN Minter 1969a, 85-93. Original.

2070. Kroepsch, Robert H., "Regional Cooperation in Higher Education," IN Paulsen 1970, 109-120. Original.

2071. Kroepsch, Robert H. and M. Stephen Kaplan, "Interstate Cooperation and Coordination in Higher Education," IN Wilson 1965, 174-190. Original.

2072. Lawrence, Ben, "The Western Interstate Commission for Higher Education Management Information Systems Program," IN Johnson 1969, 109-122. Original.

2073. Lawrence, Ben, "The WICHE* Planning and Management Systems Program: Its Nature, Scope, and Limitations," IN Hamelman 1972, 49-75. Original.

*Western Interstate Commission for Higher Education

2074. Levine, Jack B., "The Implementation of CAMPUS* Simulation Models for University Planning," IN Minter 1969a, 59-67. Original.

*CAMPUS--Comprehensive Analytical Methods for Planning in University Systems

2075. Lippitt, Ronald, "Planning as a Continuing Leadership Process," IN Smith 1967, 96-100. Original.

2076. Lipson, Joseph I., "Needed: A Collaborative Open University Network," IN Harrison 1975, 20-30. Original.

2077. Little, Clarence, "Evaluation and Control in an Academic Setting," IN Wattel 1975, 435-481. Original.

2078. Lucey, Patrick J., "The Political Requirements of Higher Education Coordination," IN Goodall 1976, 51-61. Original.

2079. McCain, James A., "Cooperation Among American Universities in (Foreign) Technical Assistance Programs," IN Wilson 1965, 204-206. Original.

2080. McConnell, T. R., "The Coordination of State Systems of Higher Education," IN Wilson 1965, 129-140. Original.

2081. McConnell, T. R., "Flexibility, Quality, and Authority in Coordinated Systems of Higher Education," IN Smelser 1974, 170-190. Original.

2082. McCune, Shannon, "The New College Plan," IN Harris 1960, 140-145. Original.

An experiment in cooperation among four colleges in the Connecticut Valley--Amherst, Mt. Holyoke, Smith, and the University of Massachusetts.

2083. McGannon, J. Barry, "Guide to Academic Planning--St. Louis University," IN Brann 1972, 269-296. Original.

2084. McHenry, Dean E., "Planning in the College or University," IN Knorr 1965, 7-13. Original.

2085. McMeekin Jr., Robert W., "Alternative Approaches to Planning and Policy in Higher Education," IN Ritterbush 1972, 70-73. Original.

2086. Mackey, Cecil and Stephen Wenzel, "Educational Leadership or Institutional Reflex?" IN Heyns 1977, 181-185. Original.

Institutional obstacles to compliance with federal directives are discussed in this essay.

2087. Marien, Michael, "Proposal: A Census of Education and Learning," IN Ritterbush 1972, 77-83. Original.

The author recommends a national "Census of Education and Learning" as a means to acquire essential information on which to base a more fully informed educational policy-making process.

2088. Martin, Warren B., "Institutional Priorities," IN Jellema 1972, 20-30. Original.

2089. Marvel, William W., "A Dilemma for Our Colleges and Universities--Domestic Demands and Overseas Needs," IN Smith 1963, 128-131. Original.

The author provides several suggestions for weighing problems of conflict between institutional needs versus demands for expertise, especially by developing countries overseas.

2090. Medsker, Leland L., "Resources for Planning: A Resumé," IN Knorr 1965, 119-127. Original.

2091. Mendelsohn, Harold, "Marketing and Higher Education: Perspectives for Planning," IN McGrath 1972, 115-126. Original.

The author draws a parallel between marketing research and the development of services (products) by the liberal arts college.

2092. Messersmith, James C., "Consortia and Related Interinstitutional Arrangement," IN Wilson 1965, 142-154. Original.

2093. Messersmith, James C., "Ideas and Patterns for Future Programs of Interinstitutional Cooperation," IN Smith 1962, 150-153. Original.

2094. Messersmith, James C., "Role of the Executive Director," IN Donovan 1965, 53-63. Original.

A role analysis of the chief executive officer of a college consortium or cooperative arrangement.

2095. Miller, James W., "Voluntary Cooperation and Coordination of Higher Education in Michigan," IN Wilson 1965, 165-171. Original.

2096. Miller, Kenneth A., "Quantitative Decision Techniques in College and University Planning," IN Wattel 1975, 482-620. Original.

2097. Millett, John D., "The Management of State Systems of Higher Education," IN Perkins 1972, 43-51. Original.

2098. Moore, Raymond S., "Interinstitutional Cooperation," IN Smith 1967, 272-276. Original.

2099. Moore, Raymond S., "Interinstitutional Cooperation," IN Letter 1968, 73-89. Original.

2100. Morris, Delyte W., "Pressures for Expansion of Educational Services Coming from Industry, Labor, and Business," IN Smith 1965, 126-129. Original.

2101. Nelson, Charles A., "Observations on the Scope of Higher Education Planning in the United States," IN Hamelman 1972, 31-47. Original.

2102. Norris, Donald M., "Speculating on Enrollments," IN Vermilye 1976, 139-147. Original.

2103. Odiorne, George S., "Subordinating Management to Policy," IN Ritterbush 1972, 65-70. Original.

2104. O'Dowd, Donald D., "The College Plan at Wesleyan," IN Harris 1960, 163-165. Original.

An analysis of the development and implementation of a physical and administrative reorganization plan at Wesleyan College.

2105. Ostar, Allan W., "Higher Education and National Policy," IN Smith 1969, 25-36. Original.

2106. Parden, Robert J., "Planning, Programming, and Budgeting Systems," IN Jellema 1972, 11-19. Original.

2107. Pellegrin, Jean-Pierre, "Quantitative Trends in Post-Secondary Education," IN OECD 1974a, 9-61. Original.

2108. Perkins, James A., "Coordinating Federal, State, and Institutional Decisions," IN Hughes 1975a, 184-197. Original.

Commentaries by Ernest Boyer, S. V. Martorana, and Richard M. Millard follow on pages 197-207.

2109. Perkins, James A., "The Drive for Coordination," IN Perkins 1972, 3-12. UIT (1966).

2110. Perkins, James A., "The Dynamics of University Growth," IN Mayhew 1967, 113-125. UIT (1966).

2111. Perl, Lewis J., "The Use of Production Functions to Evaluate Educational Technology," IN Minter 1969a, 69-77. Original.

2112. Quehl, Gary H., "Autonomy and Control in Voluntary Consortia," IN Vermilye 1972, 250-259. Original.

2113. Rankin, Alan C., "The Trimester Plan at the University of Pittsburgh," IN Smith 1961, 167-170. Original.

2114. Richardson, Elliot L., "Public Policy for a Pluralistic System of Higher Education," IN Hughes 1975, 311-315. Original.

2115. Richardson Jr., Richard C., "Reaction to the Commission (Carnegie) Recommendations," IN Vermilye 1972, 22-27. Original.

2116. Riesman, David, "Some Problems of Assessing (And Improving) the Quality of a College," IN Harris 1960, 173-177. Original.

2117. Ritterbush, Philip C., "Regaining the Policy Initiative in the Modern University," IN Ritterbush 1972, 41-62. Original.

2118. Rosenbaum, Allen, "University Reorganization in Wisconsin," IN Goodall 1976, 62-83. AAUPB, 59 (September 1973), 298-309.

2119. Rowan, Carl T., "Assessing Colleges and Universities: The Alternatives," IN Harcleroad 1971, 89-97. Original.

2120. Ryans, David G., "System Analysis in Planning," IN Knorr 1965, 79-117. Original.

2121. Scott, Robert W., "Comprehensive and Creative State Planning," IN Godwin 1972, 167-171. Original.

2122. "Second Report to the President," IN Mayhew 1967, 237-245. EBHS (1975).

Report of Presidential Commission on Education Beyond High School.

2123. Sindlinger, Walter E., "Involving Faculty Members in Institutional Policy Formulation," IN McGrath 1964, 71-79. Original.

2124. Slater, J. Marlowe, "Time to Assume a Professional Posture in Educational Staffing," IN Smith 1965, 141-144. Original.

2125. Smelser, Neil J., "California--Three Layers and Coordination," IN Perkins 1972, 23-34. Original.

2126. Smith, Robert D. and John J. Anderson, "Rational Planning Crisis in Higher Education," IN Heinlein 1974, 39-46. Original.

2127. Solberg, J. W., "From a Categorical to a Comprehensive Educational System: Implications for Test Development," IN Verreck 1974, 324-337. Original.

2128. Splete, Allen P., "The Role of the Academic Planning Officer in Innovation," IN Ritterbush 1972, 92-96. Original.

2129. Stewart, Blair, "Establishing and Maintaining Cooperative Programs Between Institutions of Higher Education, IN Smith 1961, 189-192. Original.

2130. Stickler, W. Hugh and Milton W. Carothers, "The Year-Round Calendar in Operation: Status, Trends, Problems, and Future," IN Smith 1964, 193-195. Original.

2131. Stoke, Stuart M., "Cooperation at the Undergraduate Level," IN Donovan 1965, 98-110. Original.

2132. Thorp, Willard L., "Some Problems at Amherst," IN Harris 1960, 160-162. Original.

A case study of decision-making concerning the control of growth at Amherst.

2133. Totaro, Joseph V., "Can Order be Achieved in the Academic Market Place?" IN Smith 1962, 197-201. Original.

An essay on the institutional impact of increases in the number of students seeking admission to college.

2134. Tucker, James F., "Organizational Considerations in Educational Planning," IN Hamelman 1972, 23-29. Original.

2135. Unruh, Jesse M., "California Higher Education: A Report from the Underground," IN Smith 1967, 29-34. Original.

A statement concerning the politics of leadership and the problems inherent in the control and administration of a large state system of higher education.

2136. Vaizey, John, "The Outputs of Higher Education--Their Proxies, Measurement, and Evaluation," IN Lawrence 1970, 19-23. Original.

2137. Varner, D. B., "Planning the New College of the 60s," IN Smith 1960, 40-42. Original.

2138. Vasconcellos, John and Patrick Callan, "The Public and Higher Education in California," IN Riley 1977, 160-167. PHEC (1974).

This essay presents the ". . . conflict between egalitarianism and competitive excellence and the implications . . . for planning of California higher education."

2139. Wallhaus, Robert A., "A Resource Allocation and Planning Model for Higher Education," IN Heinlein 1974, 97-107. Original.

This paper was published in 1971 by the National Center for Higher Education Management Systems.

2140. Wallis, W. Allen, "Institutional Coherence and Priorities," IN Dobbins 1968, 175-183. Original.

Commentaries by Robert S. Powell, Jr., Mrs. Henry B. Owen, James E. Allen Jr., and John William Padberg follow on pages 184-194.

2141. Wattel, Harold L., "Introduction (to Planning in Higher Education)," IN Wattel 1975, 1-70. Original.

2142. Weathersby, George B., "Purpose, Persuasion, Backbone, and Spunk," IN Jellema 1972, 3-10. Original.

The author draws a distinction between leadership and management and suggests how PPBS can be used to facilitate the integration of the "manager's data system . . . with the leader's planning concerns."

2143. Weidner, Edward W., "Master Planning at Green Bay," IN Smith 1970, 197-200. Original.

2144. West, Elmer D., "Opportunities and Problems for Leadership Through Local and Regional Consortia," IN Smith 1967, 277-280. Original.

2145. Williams, Gareth, "Computable Models for Planning Education," IN Butcher 1972, 372-381. Original.

2146. Williams, Jack K., "Perscription: Health Coordinating Boards," IN Godwin 1972, 172-175. Original.

The author advocates strong state level coordinating boards to provide a wide variety of curricula, but with controls on cost and duplication.

2147. Wilson, Logan, "Basic Premises for a National Policy in Higher Education," IN Wilson 1965, 263-271. Original.

2148. Wilson, O. Meredith, "Institutional Quality and Effectiveness," IN Harcleroad 1971, 79-86. Original.

2149. Wilson, O. Meredith, "When Master Plans," IN Smelser 1974, 161-168. Original.

An excellent summary of the strengths and weaknesses of the "master plan" as a major instrument in university planning and policy development.

2150. Wolfbein, Seymour L., "The Need for Professional Personnel," IN Mushkin 1962, 43-46. Original.

2151. Wolfe, Alan, "The Carnegie Commission: Voice of the Establishment," IN Vermilye 1972, 28-38. Original.

2152. Wood, Herbert H., "Financial Aspects of Cooperation Among Institutions," IN Jellema 1972, 59-72. Original.

2153. Wood, John W., "The Reorganization of the University," IN Goodall 1976, 84-92. CUB, 51 (November 1971), 50-54; 62.

2154. Woodhall, Maureen, "Forecasting Demand for Qualified Manpower: Some Problems and Difficulties," IN Holmes 1971, 216-226. Original.

16
POLITICS OF POSTSECONDARY EDUCATION

2155. Adams, Walter and Adrian Jaffe, "Government, the Universities, and International Affairs: A Crisis in Identity," IN Shiver 1967, 73-97. Original.

Commentary by Jacob Cantor follows on pages 98-100.

2156. Allen Jr., James E., "Higher Education--A View from Washington," IN Nichols 1970, 305-309. Original.

2157. Alstyne, Carol Van, "The Costs to Colleges and Universities of Implementing Federally Mandated Social Programs," IN Hook 1978, 115-122. Original.

2158. Altbach, Philip G., "The Campagne University in the Beer State: Notes on Wisconsin's Crisis," IN Riesman 1973, 383-408. Original.

2159. An, Nack Young, "Comparative Politics of Education in Four Industrial Nations," IN Robertson 1978, 135-152. Original.

2160. Andringa, Robert C., "Congressional Staff and Higher Education Policy," IN Vermilye 1973, 13-20. Original.

2161. Andringa, Robert C., "A View from Capitol Hill," IN Hook 1978, 133-136. Original.

The viewpoint of Representative Andringa concerning the relations between the higher education community and Congress.

2162. Bailey, Stephen K., "Education and the State," IN Hughes 1975a, 1-12. Original.

2163. Bailey, Stephen K., "Higher Educational Leadership in Developing Federal Policies," IN Smith 1967, 41-45. Original.

2164. Bailey, Stephen K., "The Peculiar Mixture: Public Norms and Private Space," IN Hobbs 1978, 103-112. Original.

A short history of federal regulation and higher education with comments concerning future prospects.

2165. Baumann, Fred, "Is the University a Special Case?" IN Hook 1978, 237-244. Original.

The author presents an excellent, yet concise analysis of the arguments for and against federal government intervention (regulation) in higher education.

2166. Benson, Charles S., "The Effects of Federal Support on Allocation of Campus Resources," IN Minter 1966, 62-72. Original.

2167. Berdahl, Robert O., "The Politics of State Aid," IN Breneman 1978, 321-352. Original.

2168. Birnbaum, Norman, "Students, Professors, and Philosopher Kings," IN Kaysen 1973, 401-490. Original.

An excellent essay on the political implications of university activity both internally and externally. Although the university cannot impose new values on a society, it can raise "society's consciousness" and attempt to demonstrate "alternative definitions of reality."

2169. Blaydon, Colin C., "State Policy Options," IN Breneman 1978, 353-388. Original.

An overview of state level options for the financial support of institutions and students, plus extensive statistical tables.

2170. Bloland, Harland, "Politicization of Higher Education Organizations," IN Smith 1969, 10-17. Original.

2171. Boling, Edward, "What Should be the Relationship Between the State Government and the Publicly Supported Institution of Higher Education?" IN Smith 1960, 220-222. Original.

Commentary by Albert N. Jorgensen follows on pages 222-224.

2172. Bolling, Landrum R., "How Best Can the Undergraduate College Fulfill Its Purposes in the Face of Pressures Exerted by Sources of Financial Support and Outside Interest Groups," IN Smith 1964, 234-237. Original.

2173. Bork, Robert H., "The Limits of Governmental Regulation," IN Hook 1978, 169-175. Original.

Commentary by John R. Searle follows on pages 205-213.

2174. Boyd, Joseph D., "State Programs of Financial Aid," IN Keene 1975, 34-44. Original.

2175. Brewster Jr., Kingman, "Politics of Academia," IN Hodgkinson 1971, 54-64. Original.

2176. Buchanan, Scott, "The Conjugation of a Greek Verb: Persuasion and the Life of Politics," IN Cohen 1964, 87-96. Original.

2177. Budig, Gene A., "State Government in Higher Education," IN Budig 1970, 107-119. Original.

2178. Bundy, McGeorge, "Of Winds and Windmills: Free Universities and Public Policy," IN Dobbins 1963, 89-98. Original.

The author comments on the role and responsibility of government in support of higher education.

2179. Caldwell, Lynton K., "The University-Government Relationship," IN Humphrey 1967, 28-56. Original.

2180. Caldwell, Oliver J., "American Higher Education and the Federal Government," IN Keene 1975, 22-33. Original.

2181. Chambers, M. M., "The Point of Discourse," IN Goodall 1976, 241-249. HEFS (1970).

Professor Chambers explains why he is concerned with the trend toward centralization in higher education.

2182. Cohen, Wilbur J., "Higher Education and the Federal Government," IN Perkins 1972, 87-95. Original.

2183. Coombs, Philip H., "Some Issues Raised by Recent Legislation," IN Harris 1960, 83-87. Original.

Mr. Coombs speculates on the possible effects of the National Defense Education Act.

2184. Coor, Lattie F., "Making the Case for Higher Education," IN Heyns 1977, 186-192. Original.

An essay on the changing relationships between state governments and their colleges.

2185. Cosand, Joseph P., "Implementing the Education Amendments of 1972," IN Vermilye 1973, 190-196. Original.

2186. Crawford, Edwin M., "Government Relations: An Overview," IN Rowland 1977, 341-348. Original.

An overview of university communication and coordination with state and federal government.

2187. Davis, William E., "How to Work With State Legislatures," IN Heyns 1977, 192-198. Original.

2188. De Jouvenel, Bertrand, "Toward a Political Theory of Education," IN Cohen 1964, 55-74. Original.

2189. de Kiewiet, C. W., "Government, the Universities, and International Affairs: The Common Responsibilities," IN Shiver 1967, 22-43. Original.

Commentary by Paul R. Hanna follows on pages 58-62.

2190. Des Marais, Philip H., "Expectations from Federal Government of American Colleges and Universities," IN Donovan 1965, 85-97. Original.

2191. Distler, Theodore A., "Problems of the Washington Secretariat," IN Wilson 1965, 255-256. Original.

2192. Enarson, Harold L., "Pressures on Higher Education from the Federal Government," IN Smith 1965, 63-67. Original.

2193. Enlau, Heinz and Harold Quinley, "Legislators and Academicians," IN Goodall 1976, 108-123. SOHE (1970).

Commentary by David D. Henry follows on pages 124-131.

2194. Enlau, Heinz, "Political Norms Affecting Decisions Concerning Higher Education," IN Furniss 1971, 207-223. Original.

Commentaries by Patsy Y. Mink, Lyman A. Glenny, and David C. Knapp follow on pages 223-232.

2195. Fellman, David, "Confronting Current External Pressures on Colleges and Universities," IN Smith 1963, 124-127. Original.

2196. Fidler, William P., "Problems of the Professional Associations and Learned Societies," IN Wilson 1965, 250-254. Original.

2197. Finn Jr., Chester E., "Federal Patronage of the Universities: A Rose by Many Other Names?" IN Hook 1978, 7-49. Original.

Commentary by Martin Kramer follows on pages 95-96.

2198. Fishbein, Estelle A., "The Academic Industry--A Dangerous Premise," IN Hobbs 1978, 57-64. Original.

The author believes that in many respects life at public universities has been transformed into a more legalistic and procedural fashion than is justified by the requirement to meet federal regulation.

2199. Fleming, Robben W., "Who Will be Regulated and Why?" IN Hobbs 1978, 11-24. Original.

The major difficulty in government regulation of higher education is to acknowledge the complexity and diversity of the institutions within the higher education community.

2200. Frankel, Charles, "Government and Universities," IN Shiver 1967, 15-21. Original.

2201. Freelen, Robert E., "The Federal Network," IN Rowland 1977, 375-385. Original.

An excellent brief overview of the congressional process in considering bills related to higher education.

2202. Gardner, John W., "Government and the Universities," IN Wilson 1965, 286-292. Original.

2203. Gellhorn, Ernest and Barry B. Boyer, "The Academy as a Regulated Industry," IN Hobbs 1978, 25-56. Original.

2204. Gladfelter, Millard E., "State Aid for Private Institutions in Pennsylvania," IN Harris 1960, 91-92. Original.

2205. Gladieux, Lawrence E. and Thomas R. Wolanin, "Federal Politics," IN Breneman 1978, 197-230. Original.

2206. Glenny, Lyman A., "Coordination and Planning Despite Competition and Confusion," IN Riley 1977, 183-191. AAPWG (1975).

A review of the social and political climate at the state level in reference to their support of higher education.

2207. Glenny, Lyman A., "Politics and Current Patterns in Coordinating Higher Education," IN Minter 1966, 26-46. Original.

2208. Goldwin, Robert A., "How 'Different' Are Universities?" IN Hook 1978, 215-220. Original.

The author suggests that universities are unique in many aspects and, therefore, federal regulation cannot be applied the same way to them as it is to other types of organizations and institutions.

2209. Goodall, Leonard E., "Emerging Political Issues for State Coordinating Boards," IN Goodall 1976, 250-263. JHE, 45 (March 1974), 219-228.

2210. Goodall, Leonard, James B. Holderman, and James D. Nowlan, "Legislature and University: The Uneasy Partnership," IN Goodall 1976, 132-140. ER, 52 (Winter 1971), 36-40.

2211. Gould, Samuel B., "The University and State Government: Fears and Realities," IN Minter 1966, 2-15. Original.

2212. Gove, Samuel K., "Pressures on Higher Education: State and Local Governments," IN Smith 1965, 68-71. Original.

2213. Green, Edith, "Congress and Higher Education--Let's Look at the Whole Picture," IN Smith 1962, 30-36. Original.

2214. Green, Edith, "Higher Education Problems and Congress," IN Donovan 1964, 95-106. Original.

2215. Harrington, Fred H., "The Federal Government and the Future of Higher Education," IN Smith 1963, 22-28. Original.

2216. Hartman, Robert M., "The Rationale for Federal Support for Higher Education," IN Solmon 1973, 271-292. Original.

2217. "Harvard and the Federal Government," IN Mayhew 1967, 191-214.

(Note: This essay was taken from a report to the Faculty and Governing Boards, Harvard University, September 1961.)

2218. Hatfield, Mark O., "Public Pressures on Higher Education," IN Smith 1970, 75-84. Original.

2219. Henry, David D., "A Program of Action for Higher Education," IN Dobbins 1963, 99-116. Original.

An excellent assessment of the future (written in 1963) prospects for federal support of post-secondary education.

2220. Hetzel, Ralph D., "The Public Control of Public Universities," IN Smith 1967, 211-214. Original.

2221. Heyns, Roger W., "The Education Amendments and the Future," IN Vermilye 1973, 197-203. Original.

2222. Hicks, John W., "Lobbying for Limited Resources," IN Vermilye 1973, 21-24. Original.

2223. Hicks, John W., "Lobbying for Limited Resources," IN Goodall 1976, 141-145. FM (1973).

2224. Hill, Norman L., "Democratic and Other Principles of Empowerment on Campus," IN Robertson 1978, 21-40. Original.

2225. Hobbs, Walter C., "The Theory of Government Regulation," IN Hobbs 1978, 1-8. Original.

2226. Hook, Sidney, "The State and Higher Education," IN Hook 1978, 227-236. Original.

2227. Horing, Donald, "The Costs of Government Regulation," IN Hook 1978, 103-113. Original.

2228. Horn, Stephen, "The Higher Education Climate: Separating Facts from Myths," IN Heyns 1977, 199-206. Original.

> Dr. Horn outlines some of the current problems in attempting to shape public policy in regard to higher education.

2229. Hornback, Ray R., "State and Local Jurisdictions," IN Rowland 1977, 362-374. Original.

2230. Ikenberry, Stanley O., "The Public Interest and Institutional Autonomy," IN Anderson 1976, 309-325. Original.

2231. Ketter, Robert L., "By Hemp or by Silk, The Outcome is the Same," IN Hobbs 1978, 65-70. Original.

> A concise assessment of how higher education is adjusting to the requirements of federal regulation.

2232. Keyes, Richard, "Educational Dialogue and Power Conflict," IN Altman 1970, 117-121. Original.

> Mr. Keyes asserts that there is no internal communications problem between students and faculty, but rather that problems stem from attempts at control from "external political and economic interests."

2233. Kroepsch, Robert H., "Public Colleges and Outside Pressures," IN Smith 1964, 238-241. Original.

2234. Kurtz, Paul, "Should the Patron Be the Master?: The Autonomy of Public Universities and Colleges," IN Hook 1978, 287-291. Original.

2235. Ledbetter, Beverly, "Implementing the Regulations," IN Heyns 1977, 176-180. Original.

> This article presents several problems in complying with federal and state regulations.

2236. Lederle, John W., "Governors and Higher Education," IN Goodall 1976, 43-50. AGBP (1972).

2237. Little, J. Kenneth, "Federal Programs of Education and Training," IN Dobbins 1963, 66-75. Original.

2238. Longenecker, Herbert E., "A Time for Assessment," IN Dobbins 1963, 1-7. Original.

An essay on the nature and quality of federal involvement in higher education.

2239. McConnell, Thomas R., "State Systems of Higher Education," IN McGrath 1966, 19-39. Original.

2240. McGrath, Brian A., "Government and the College," IN Donovan 1964, 200-209. Original.

2241. Mace, George, "Political Considerations for Financial Aid Administrators," IN Keene 1975, 177-183. Original.

2242. Mallan, John P., "Current Proposals for Federal Aid to Higher Education: Some Political Implications," IN Orwig 1971, 303-330. Original.

2243. Marland Jr., Sidney P., "A Strengthening Alliance," IN Wilson 1972, 210-219. Original.

An overview of the academic community's view of relationships between higher education and government.

2244. Mather, J. Paul, "Federal and State Aid," IN Harris 1960, 88-90. Original.

2245. Miller, Gene S., "Federal Programs," IN College 1975, 92-117. Original.

An overview of student loan programs sponsored by the federal government.

2246. Millett, John D., "State Administration of Higher Education (The Perspectives of Political Science)," IN Wingfield 1970, 37-52. Original.

2247. Moor, Roy E., "The Federal Government Role in Higher Education," IN Mushkin 1962, 202-217. Original.

2248. Moos, Malcolm and Francis E., Rourke, "The State Story: Administrative Centralization," IN Goodall 1976, 93-105. CAS (1959).

2249. Morse, John F., "The Federal Government and Higher Education: Old Answers Breed New Questions," IN Minter 1966, 48-60. Original.

2250. Morse, Wayne L., "The Congress and Higher Education," IN Smith 1962, 25-29. Original.

2251. Muelder, Walter G., "Empowerment and the Integrity of Higher Education," IN Robertson 1978, 1-19. Original.

An engrossing essay that deals with the exercise of power by the highly educated which is sometimes in conflict with cultural values. This condition is felt both inside the university and between the university and its environment.

2252. Murphy, Thomas P. and Elizabeth Knipe, "The Federal Government and Urban Higher Education," IN Murphy 1975, 353-379. Original.

2253. Musgrave, Richard A., "Higher Education and the Federal Budget," IN Harris 1960, 96-101. Original.

2254. Mushkin, Selma J., "State Financing of Higher Education," IN Mushkin 1962, 218-249. Original.

2255. Newman, Frank, "Divining the Proper Federal Role," IN Godwin 1972, 181-184. Original.

2256. Norton, James A., "The Interaction of State and Federal Policy," IN Hook 1978, 73-76. Original.

2257. O'Hara, James G., "It's Time to Blow the Whistle," IN Young 1974, 141-150. Original.

The question of supporting low tuition schemes is presented in political terms by Congressman O'Hara.

2258. O'Neil, Michael, "A Case for Human Intelligence," IN Margolis 1969, 355-373. TMD (1967).

An excellent analysis of the "political realities" that constitute the background to any discussion of higher education.

2259. Orwig, M. D., "The Federal Government and the Finance of Higher Education," IN Orwig 1971, 331-360. Original.

2260. Paulsen, F. Robert, "Educators and Legislators in Partnership," IN Paulsen 1970, 171-179. Original.

2261. Perkins, John A. and Daniel W. Wood, "Issues in Federal Aid to Higher Education," IN Knight 1960, 140-175. Original.

2262. Post, A. Alan, "The View from California," IN Goodall 1976, 176-188. Original.

Mr. Post provides insight into the problems some state legislators have concerning university work loads, cost efficiency, etc.

2263. Powell, Arthur G., "Harvard's School of Education and the Federal Government: Institutional Effects of Interaction in the 1960s," IN Hook 1978, 51-72. Original.

Commentary by Robert F. Sassen follows on pages 87-93.

2264. Pusey, Nathan M., "The Carnegie Study of the Federal Government and Higher Education," IN Dobbins 1963, 17-29. Original.

2265. Quattlebaum, Charles A., "Federal Policies and Practices in Higher Education," IN Knight 1960, 29-75. Original.

2266. Quie, Albert H., "How Can a Legislator Become an Educational Leader?" IN Smith 1967, 46-52. Original.

2267. Quie, Albert H., "The View from the Hill," IN Vermilye 1973, 3-12. Original.

An overview of congressional interest in higher education from a member of the House of Representatives.

2268. Renne, Roland R., "Pressures on Higher Education from Political, Nongovernmental Groups," IN Smith 1965, 80-83. Original.

2269. Rusk, Dean, "Common Concerns of the Government and the Universities," IN Shiver 1967, 10-14. Original.

2270. Sanders, Edward, "History of Federal Involvement in Financial Aid," IN College 1975, 84-91. Original.

2271. Seabury, Paul, "HEW and the University," IN Gross 1977, 97-112. Comm, 53 (February 1972), 38-44.

2272. Shils, Edward, "Governments and Universities," IN Hook 1978, 177-204. Original.

2273. Shive, John N., "The Creation of New Relationships Among Employers, Educational Institutions, and Professional and Technical Societies," IN Smith 1963, 143-145. Original.

2274. Spark, Eli, "A Minority Report," IN Hook 1978, 245-248. Original.

The author comments on critics who attempt to blame outside institutions and organizations for many of the problems faced by universities and suggests that these critics should be more concerned with analysis that "begins at home."

2275. Steiger, William A., "Congress and the Campus," IN Smith 1970, 85-93. Original.

2276. Sunley Jr., Emil M., "Federal and State Tax Policies," IN Breneman 1978, 281-319. Original.

An analysis of federal, state, and local tax subsidies in support of philanthropy and general subsidy for higher education.

2277. Sykes, Gary W., "Images of Power in Academia: A Critical View," IN Robertson 1978, 79-105. Original.

2278. Thackrey, Russell I., "National Organization in Higher Education," IN Wilson 1965, 236-249. Original.

2279. Thackrey, Russell I., "Services of Higher Education Meeting National Needs for Which the Federal Government has Special Responsibility," IN Dobbins 1956, 44-61. Original.

2280. Thomas, Helen, "Reporting from the White House," IN Hughes 1975, 332-338. Original.

2281. Todorovich, Miro M., "Would a Reorganized Federal Department of Education Mean Better Higher Education?" IN Hook 1978, 265-275. Original.

2282. Tollett, Kenneth S., "What Is All the Shouting About?" IN Hook 1978, 77-85. Original.

The author presents a rather positive view of federal assistance to higher education, especially as applies to minority related programs.

2283. Turnbull, William W., "Special Institutions in Systems of Higher Education," IN Perkins 1972, 121-130. Original.

This essay touches on the influence of five higher education related organizations: (1) College Entrance Examination Board, (2) Educational Testing Services, (3) Carnegie Foundation for the Advancement of Teaching, (4) Teachers Insurance and Annuity Association, and (5) College Retirement Equities Fund.

2284. Vasconcellos, John and Patrick Callan, "The Public and Higher Education in California," IN Smelser 1974, 265-273. Original.

2285. Vickerey Jr., James F., "Principles for Effective Government Relations," IN Rowland 1977, 349-361. Original.

2286. Waldo, Dwight, "The University in Relation to the Governmental-Political," IN Wingfield 1970, 19-36. Original.

2287. Weinberger, Caspar W., "The Federal Stimulus in Postsecondary Education," IN Hughes 1975a, 86-92. Original.

2288. Wenberg, Stanley J., "State and Federal Legislative Relations," IN Wilson 1965, 282-285. Original.

2289. Wilson, Logan, "A Better Partnership for the Federal Government and Higher Education," IN Wilson 1965, 272-281. ER, 44 (April 1963), 137-144.

2290. Wilson, Logan, "Institutional Autonomy and Heteronomy," IN Dobbins 1968, 134-144. Original.

2291. Wilson, O. Meredith, "Private Systems of Education," IN Perkins 1972, 99-108. Original.

A short history of three important private (non-governmental) associations: (1) The National Association of State Universities and Land-Grant Colleges, (2) The American Association of Universities, and (3) The American Council on Education.

2292. Wofford Jr., Harris L., "Agent of Whom?" IN Minter 1968, 13-24. Original.

Professor Wofford makes a strong plea that the university should not take political stands on noneducational issues.

17 CURRICULUM AND INSTRUCTION—GENERAL

2293. Abercrombie, M. L. J., "Teaching in Small Groups," IN Butcher 1972, 119-130. Original.

2294. Allen, J., "Personal Observations on Effective Teaching," IN Buxton 1975, 132-139. Original.

2295. Anastasio, Ernest, "A Preview of the Evaluation of PLATO and TICCIT," IN Harrison 1975, 160-163. Original.

A brief overview of the evaluation of two computer assisted instructional programs.

2296. Anderson, Harold H., "Creativity and Education," IN Rice 1964, 41-49. Original.

2297. Anderson, Howard R., "How Can a More Realistic and Up-to-Date World View be Injected Into Teaching at the Elementary, Secondary, Higher, and Adult Levels?" IN Smith 1962, 177-180. Original.

Commentary by Oliver J. Caldwell follows on pages 181-184.

2298. Arbolino, Jack N., "Establishing and Maintaining Better Curricular Articulation Between Secondary and Higher Education," IN Smith 1961, 148-150. Original.

Commentary by James D. Logsdon follows on pages 150-152.

2299. Arrowsmith, William, "The Future of Teaching," IN Lee 1967, 57-71. Original.

2300. Arrowsmith, William, "The Future of Teaching," IN Eurich 1968, 116-133. ICT (1967).

2301. Astin, Alexander W. and Calvin B. T. Lee, "Current Practices in the Evaluation and Training of College Teachers," IN Lee 1967, 296-311. ER, 47 (Summer 1966), 361-375.

2302. Avakian, A. Nancy, "Writing a Learning Contract," IN Vermilye 1974, 50-56. Original.

2303. Axelrod, Joseph, "The Creative Student and the Grading System," IN Heist 1968, 117-143. Original.

2304. Axelrod, Joseph, "The Undergraduate Curriculum and Institutional Goals: An Exploration of Means and Ends?" IN Smith 1964, 126-128. Original.

2305. Banks, James A., "Teaching Black Studies for Social Change," IN Johnson 1974, 89-111. Original.

2306. Barton, Paul E., "Learning Through Work and Education," IN Keeton 1976, 119-130. Original.

2307. Baskin, Samuel, "Independent Study: Methods, Programs, and for Whom?" IN Smith 1962, 65-68. Original.

2308. Baskin, Samuel, "Innovations in College Teaching," IN Lee 1967, 181-196. Original.

Commentaries by Esther Raushenbush, Robert F. McDermott, and Nils Y. Wessell follow on pages 197-210.

2309. Beard, Ruth M., "Empirical Studies of Teaching Methods," IN Butcher 1972, 103-118. Original.

2310. Becker, Hellmut, "Theory and Practice," IN Henderson 1968, 125-134. Original.

Mr. Becker desires education which has achieved better unity between theory and practice.

2311. Bereiter, Carl and Mervin B. Freedman, "Fields of Study and the People in Them," IN Sanford 1962, 563-596. Original.

2312. Berman, Arthur I., "Field Studies of Small Media-Activated Learning Groups," IN Verreck 1974, 397-425. Original.

2313. Bernstein, Alison R., "How Big Is Too Big?" IN Vermilye 1976, 18-28. Original.

Mr. Bernstein discusses the impact of increasing enrollments on the quality of education received in our colleges and universities.

2314. Bess, James, "Latent Environmental Effects of Educational Technology," IN Harrison 1975, 72-78. Original.

A concise essay that deals with the measurement of effects of new instructional technology.

2315. Bilorusky, John A., "Selection of Student-Initiated Courses: Student Autonomy and Curricular Innovation," IN Feldman 1972, 453-462. Original.

2316. Blake Jr., Elias, "A Case Study in Producing Equal Educational Results: The Thirteen College Curriculum Program," IN Harcleroad 1971, 56-61. Original.

2317. Bolin, John G., "Honors Inflation," IN Vermilye 1975, 144-149. Original.

2318. Boyer, Ernest L., "Changing Time Requirements," IN Vermilye 1975, 14-22. Original.

2319. Boyer, Ernest L., "Shorter Time for Undergraduate Degrees," IN Godwin 1972, 57-66. Original.

2320. Brademas, John, "What is the Obligation of Higher Education to Prepare Students for Participation in Political Affairs?" IN Smith 1962, 141-145. Original.

Commentary by Abraham Holtzman follows on pages 146-149.

2321. Bradley Jr., A. Paul, "Faculty Roles in Contract Learning," IN Vermilye 1975, 66-74. Original.

2322. Braun, Ludwig, "Mini-Computers in Education," IN Harrison 1975, 166-167. Original.

2323. Brennan, Robert L., "A Model for the Use of Achievement Data in an Instructional System," IN Harrison 1975, 144-159. Original.

This paper outlines the type and collection of achievement data and how they can be used to measure the cognitive aspects of an instructional system.

2324. Briand Jr., Paul L., "Turning Students on Through Multimedia," IN Smith 1971, 34-38. Original.

2325. Buehrig, Edward H., "Implications for the Undergraduate Curriculum of the Growing Importance of International Affairs and the Mounting Need to Understand World Cultures," IN Smith 1961, 153-156. Original.

2326. Bunderson, C. Victor, "The TICCIT Project: Design Strategy for Educational Technology," IN Harrison 1975, 91-111. Original.

A case study of the application of television, cable technology, and minicomputers as aides in the teaching of English and mathematics.

2327. Burn, Barbara, "The American Academic Credit System," IN OECD 1974, 113-144. Original.

2328. Burris, Russell, "What Objectives of General Education Could be Realized Through Teaching Machines and Programmed Learning?" IN Smith 1962, 214-217. Original.

Commentary by Chester A. Lawson follows on pages 217-220.

2329. Bush, Robert R., "Mathematical Models of Learning," IN Smith 1963, 222-225. Original.

2330. Buxton, Thomas H., "A Humanistic Approach to Teaching," IN Buxton 1975, 120-127. Original.

2331. Cadbury Jr., William E., "Challenging the Superior Student in the Small Private College," IN Cohen 1966, 191-218. Original.

2332. Caffrey, John, "The Role of Computers in the Individualization of Education," IN Minter 1967, 123-136. Original.

2333. Cahn, Meyer M., "Teaching Through Student Models--City College of San Francisco," IN Runkel 1969, 36-50. Original.

2334. Carpenter, C. R., "Toward a Developed Technology of Instruction--1980," IN Eurich 1968, 236-253. Original.

2335. Carpenter, C. R. and L. P. Greenhill, "Providing the Conditions for Learning: The 'New' Media," IN Baskin 1965, 128-152. Original.

2336. Carter, Launor F., "The Computer and Instructional Technology," IN Smith 1967, 253-259. Original.

2337. Cartter, Allan M., "University Teaching and Excellence," IN Lee 1967, 149-163. ER, 47 (Summer 1966), 289-302.

2338. Centra, John A., "Problems of Evaluating Learning," IN Smith 1966, 261-264. Original.

2339. Chamberlain, Philip C., "Resistance to Change in Curriculum Planning," IN Brann 1972, 250-262. Original.

2340. Chavarría, Jesús, "Chicano Studies," IN Altman 1970, 173-178. Original.

2341. Chickering, Arthur W., "Developmental Change as a Major Outcome," IN Keeton 1976, 62-107. Original.

Dr. Chickering reviews current research on individual development, styles, competency and character and relates the findings to the purposes and processes of higher education.

2342. Chisholm, Margaret E., "The Media Paradox," IN Hughes 1975, 294-302. Original.

2343. Cohen, J. W., "Development of the Honors Movement in the United States," IN Cohen 1966, 9-24. Original.

2344. Cohen, J. W., "The First Coordinated Effort: The ICSS," IN Cohen 1966, 25-49. Original.

Describes the history and development of the Inter-University Committee on Superior Students.

2345. Conley, William H., "Resources for Good Teaching," IN Deferrari 1961, 123-134. Original.

2346. Cooper, Kenneth S., "Did You Ever Think of Aristotle as a College Freshman?" IN Buxton 1975, 86-93. Original.

2347. Cooper, Russell M., "Improving College Teaching and Administration," IN Baskin 1965, 196-222. Original.

2348. Coopmans, J. and Q. van der Meer, "A Strategy for Curriculum Innovation," IN Verreck 1974, 197-217. Original.

2349. Crawford Jr., Norman C., "The Salisbury Experience," IN Heyns 1977, 104-109. Original.

A case study of grading and academic standards at Salisbury State College.

2350. Crockett, Campbell, "College Teaching Today and Tomorrow: What Is Involved?" IN Smith 1964, 108-110. Original.

2351. Crookston, Burns B., "A Design for an Intentional Democratic Community," IN De Coster 1974, 55-67. Original.

The author talks about a "democratic community" within an institution of higher learning as the means to achieve an environment conducive to free and creative intellectual expression.

2352. Crookston, Burns B., "Education for Human Development?" IN Warnath 1973, 47-65. Original.

The author asserts that at least one cause that has led to the "diminution of general education" was the separation of student personnel from faculty responsibility. A possible solution to this problem is the creation of "education for human development." By this the author means the creation of "learning environments within which individuals, teachers, and social systems interact and utilize developmental tasks for personal growth and social betterment."

2353. Cross, K. Patricia, "The Instructional Revolution," IN Vermilye 1976, 49-61. Original.

The "pursuit of egalitarian ideals" has been responsible for much of the change in higher education over the past few decades. Once the goal of "education for all" is achieved, the next, and more difficult reform, will be the "improvement of instruction" to meet the needs of these new students.

2354. Cross, K. Patricia, "Learner-Centered Curricula," IN Vermilye 1975, 54-65. Original.

2355. Cross, K. Patricia, "New Forms for New Functions," IN Vermilye 1974, 86-92. Original.

The author would broaden the objectives of higher education to include three major functions: (1) work with data, (2) work with people, (3) work with things. This reorganization would then better match education with the needs of society.

2356. Dean, Ernest H., "Needed: Preparation for the Occupations," IN Altman 1971, 21-27. Original.

2357. Dearing, Bruce, "How Can the Continuity in the Study of the Language Arts, the Social Sciences, and the Humanities in High School and the First Years of College be Improved?" IN Smith 1960, 77-78. Original.

Several reactions to the various elements of Dr. Dearing's paper are included on pages 79-90.

2358. Dearing, Bruce, "Pressures Jeopardizing Quality of Undergraduate Teaching," IN Smith 1965, 115-118. Original.

2359. Dearing, Bruce, "The Student on His Own: Independent Study," IN Baskin 1965, 49-77. Original.

2360. Diamond, Robert M., "Individualizing Student Learning," IN Vermilye 1973, 142-146. Original.

2361. Dixon, James P., "Personalized Higher Education: Ideas and Issues," IN Minter 1967, 3-19. Original.

2362. Donohue, Thomas C., "Maintaining Curricular Balance in an Era of Expanding Governmental Activity and Financing, Growing Industrial-Business Interest and Financing, Periodic International Crises, and Strongly Held Societal Values," IN Smith 1961, 161-166. Original.

2363. Donovan, George F., "Traditional Methods of Teaching in College," IN Deferrari 1961, 3-20. Original.

2364. Dorp van, Cees, "Methodological Versus Empirical Rationales of Educational Objectives," IN Verreck 1974, 45-55. Original.

2365. Dressel, Paul L., "Comprehensive Examination Programs," IN Dressel 1961, 253-300. Original.

2366. Dressel, Paul L., "Development of Critical Thinking," IN Smith 1963, 79-83. Original.

2367. Dressel, Paul L., "The Essential Nature of Evaluation," IN Dressel 1961, 3-26. Original.

2368. Dressel, Paul L., "Goals for the Future of Undergraduate Education," IN Smith 1961, 144-147. Original.

2369. Dressel, Paul L., "A Look at New Curriculum Models for Undergraduate Education," IN Smith 1964, 143-145. Original.

2370. Dressel, Paul L., "Methods of Evaluation and Research," IN Mayhew 1960, 162-189. Original.

This paper outlines a series of conceptions concerning curriculum evaluation.

2371. Dressel, Paul L. and Clarence H. Nelson, "Testing and Grading Policies," IN Dressel 1961, 227-252. Original.

2372. Drosnin, Michael, "College Teachers and Teaching: A Student's View," IN Lee 1967, 252-255. ER, 47 (Summer 1966), 407-409.

2373. Eckert, Ruth E. and Daniel C. Neale, "Teachers and Teaching," IN Milton 1968, 71-90. RER, 35 (October 1965), 304-317.

2374. Entwistle, Noel, "Approaches to Teaching and Learning: Guidelines from Research," IN Entwistle 1976, 9-26. Original.

2375. Ericksen, Stanford C., "Earning and Learning by the Hour," IN Morris 1970, 1-37. Original.

The question addressed in this essay is: ". . . how can the instructor best utilize the available resources to direct the academic progress of students?"

2376. Erickson, Clifford G., "Introducing New Technology Into Institutions of Higher Education," IN Smith 1963, 108-111. Original.

2377. Estvan, Frank J., "New Perspectives on Teaching the Disciplines," IN Smith 1962, 79-81. Original.

Following this general essay, on pages 82 to 109, are specific short notes on teaching techniques in English, Music, Geography, Psychology, Philosophy, Chemistry, Mathematics, Biology, and Fine Arts.

2378. Ewing, Wallace, K., "Reshaping the Curriculum: What It Means After All," IN Vaccaro 1975, 9-17. CU, 49 (Spring 1974), 251-261.

2379. Fenton, Edwin, "Honors Programs in the Secondary Schools," IN Cohen 1966, 219-252. Original.

2380. Filep, Robert T., "Learning, Technology, and the Potential Increase of Productivity in Higher Education," IN Harrison 1975, 14-19. Original.

The author provides rationale for three basic approaches to utilizing educational technology in higher education.

2381. Finlay, Gilbert C., "How Can the Continuity in the Study of the Natural Sciences and Mathematics in High School and the First Two Years of College be Improved?" IN Smith 1960, 91-92. Original.

Commentaries on both elements of Mr. Finlay's paper follow on pages 93-102.

2382. Flaherty, Sister Mary R., "What Are the Marks of a Good College Teacher?" IN Deferrari 1961, 135-149. Original.

2383. Fleege, Urban H., "Individualization of Instruction," IN Deferrari 1961, 21-37. Original.

2384. Forbes, Jack D., "Native American Studies," IN Altman 1970, 159-171. Original.

2385. Frank, Glenn W., "'On My Honor I Will . . .,'" IN Buxton 1975, 140-146. Original.

A personal account of the circumstances that are required to achieve an excellent classroom teaching environment.

2386. Fransson, Anders, "Group Centred Instruction: Intentions and Outcomes," IN Entwistle 1976, 44-64. Original.

2387. Frost, James A., "Time-Shortening and Articulation," IN Godwin 1972, 67-74. Original.

2388. Gambino, Richard, "Ethnic Studies in Cultural Perspective," IN Vermilye 1976, 178-187. Original.

2389. Gardner, John W., "Quality in Higher Education," IN Mayhew 1967, 147-153. Current (1958).

2390. Garner, Ambrose, "Performance-Based Campus," IN Vermilye 1974, 62-66. Original.

A critique of the assumptions concerning performance-based education.

2391. Goldschmidt, Marcel L. and Bruce M. Shore, "The Learning Cell: A Field Test of an Educational Innovation," IN Verreck 1974, 218-236. Original.

The authors believe that peer-teaching offers an alternative to the large impersonal undergraduate class and present a detailed procedure they call the "learning cell."

2392. Goodman, Paul, "In What Ways Does the Present Marking and Credit System Inhibit or Promote Learning?" IN Smith 1964, 123-125. Original.

2393. Gordon, Shelia C., "Campus and Workplace as Arenas," IN Keeton 1976, 108-118. Original.

This essay deals with the arguments in favor of more closely relating college programs to "postcollegiate life and work."

2394. Greely, Andrew M., "The Teaching of Moral Wisdom," IN Smith 1968, 209-213. Original.

2395. Groombridge, Brian, "The Mass Media and Higher Education," IN Stephens 1978, 77-88. Original.

The author uses the experience of the Open University to discuss the positive and negative aspects of the application of mass media to higher education.

2396. Gustad, John W., "Evaluation of Teaching Performance: Issues and Possibilities," IN Lee 1967, 265-281. Original.

Commentaries by Neill Megaw, Bill J. Priest, James A. Johnson, and Edward J. Shoben, Jr. follow on pages 282-295.

2397. Gwynn, Frederick L., "And Sadly Teach," IN Dennis 1966, 196-201. Original.

The author's thesis is that: "The ineffectiveness of much college teaching may well be the major cause of the crisis (in higher education) . . ."

2398. Hamilton, Charles V., "Relevance of Black Studies," IN Smith 1969, 69-73. Original.

2399. Hankin, Joseph N., "Assessing Quality, Excellence, and Honesty," IN Peltason 1978, 86-94. Original.

2400. Hansen, Duncan, "Computer-Based Higher Education: A Five-Year Research Program," IN Harrison 1975, 128-143. Original.

Commentary by Robert J. Seidel follows on pages 164-165.

2401. Harbo, Torstein, "The Means-End Model in Curriculum Development and Research--A Cautionary Note," IN Verreck 1974, 56-74. Original.

2402. Harcleroad, Fred F., "Introducing New Technology and Procedures Into Institutions of Higher Education," IN Smith 1963, 112-115. Original.

2403. Hardin, Garrett, "A Path to Relevant Teaching," IN Morris 1970, 87-93. Original.

2404. Harding, Vincent, "The Future of Black Studies," IN Smith 1970, 212-219. Original.

2405. Hare, Nathan, "The Battle for Black Studies," IN Johnson 1974, 65-87. Original.

2406. Harmon, Lindsey R., "Are Respective Patterns of Undergraduate Education Reflected in Distinctive Achievements at the Graduate Level?" IN Smith 1964, 204-207. Original.

2407. Harrington, Fred, "Goals, Practices, and Procedures for Implementing Joint Responsibility for Institutional Policy Formation and for Instructional Evaluation and Improvement," IN Smith 1961, 112-114. Original.

2408. Harris, Robert G., "External Agencies: Roadblocks to Career Education," IN Vermilye 1972, 245-249. Original.

2409. Harrison, Roger, "Classroom Innovation--A Design Primer," IN Runkel 1969, 302-340. Original.

2410. Hart, Francis R., "Toward the Discipline of Humane Teaching," IN Buxton 1975, 189-206. Original.

2411. Haswell, Harold A., "Curriculum Patterns Survey Covering Sixteen Baccalaureate Degree Programs," IN Smith 1964, 180-181. Original.

2412. Healy, Timothy J., "The University and Career Education: Resolving an Ambiguity," IN Peltason 1978, 61-65. Original.

2413. Heist, Paul, "Evaluating Honors Programs: History, Problems, and Prospects," IN Cohen 1966, 253-281. Original.

2414. Henle, R. J., "Collegiate Education for Modern Culture," IN Lee 1967, 382-388. ER, 47 (Summer 1966), 340-346.

Father Henle suggests ways institutions resist major curriculum change, especially those attempts to "modernize" education.

2415. Hilberry, Conrad, "Learning Environments," IN McGrath 1972, 99-114. Original.

2416. Hill, Walker H. and Paul L. Dressel, "The Objectives of Instruction," IN Dressel 1961, 27-53. Original.

2417. Hodgkinson, Harold L., "Alternative Functions and Structures in Credentialing," IN Hughes 1975, 253-260. Original.

2418. Hodgkinson, Harold L., "Evaluation to Improve Performance," IN Vermilye 1975, 116-125. Original.

2419. Hodgkinson, Harold L., "Walden U," IN Hodgkinson 1971a, 77-90. Soundings, 52 (Summer 1969), 172-185.

An extremely interesting essay that creates a "utopian" university based entirely on a firm commitment to learning as inquiry.

2420. Hofstee, Willem K. B., "The Scrutiny of Educational Practice," IN Verreck 1974, 338-351. Original.

The author deals with assessment in education concerning both the individual and the institution.

2421. Holmes, Darrell, "Evaluating Teacher Effectiveness," IN Harcleroad 1971, 35-40. Original.

2422. Holt, Charles C., "External Testing Programs and the Schools," IN Smith 1961, 77-80. Original.

Commentary by John C. Palmer follows on pages 81-85.

2423. Holtzman, Wayne H., "Education for Creative Problem Solving," IN Messick 1976, 23-37. Original.

2424. Horn, Robert E., "Experiment in Programmed Learning--Columbia University," IN Runkel 1969, 68-87. Original.

2425. Horrigan, Alfred F., "Causes of Inefficient Teaching," IN Deferrari 1961, 88-100. Original.

2426. Howe II, Harold, "Less Teaching, More Conversation," IN Lee 1967, 259-264. Original.

2427. Hoyt, Donald P., "The Criterion Problem in Higher Education," IN Milton 1968, 125-135. NCNB, 25 (May 1966), 3-16.

A literature review on college grading practices.

2428. Humphries, Frederick S., "Effective Education for the Unprepared," IN Heyns 1977, 110-118. Original.

2429. Hurst, Robert N., "The Audio-Tutorial System of Instruction," IN Harrison 1975, 43-62. Original.

2430. Kadish, Mortimer R., "The Desirability of Pulling in One's Horns," IN Hook 1975, 205-209. Original.

Professor Kadish believes that curricular problems stem from educator's inflated expectations of what formal education can accomplish. A rejoinder to this paper by Dr. Sidney Hook follows on pages 211-215.

2431. Katz, Joseph, "Personality and Interpersonal Relations in the College Classroom," IN Sanford 1962, 365-395. Original.

2432. Katz, Joseph and Nevitt Sanford, "The Curriculum in the Perspective of the Theory of Personality Development," IN Sanford 1962, 418-444. Original.

2433. Keeton, Morris, "The Climate of Learning in College," IN Rice 1964, 23-31. Original.

2434. Keller, W. D., "On Teaching and Learning," IN Buxton 1975, 62-66. Original.

2435. Kent, Laura, "Student Evaluation of Teaching," IN Lee 1967, 312-343. ER, 47 (Summer 1966), 376-406.

2436. King, Edmund, "The Level of Education and Training," IN Holmes 1971, 202-215. Original.

The author reviews the concept of "training" (occupational) as a responsibility of the modern university.

2437. Kirk, Grayson L., "College Shouldn't Take Four Years," IN Bellman 1962, 19-34. SEP, 232 (March 26, 1960), 21; 108-112.

2438. Kirkwood, Robert, "Importance of Assessing Learning," IN Keeton 1976, 150-160. Original.

2439. Klare, G. R., "Readability and the Behavior of Readers," IN Harrison 1975, 235-240. Original.

2440. Klemp Jr., George O., "Career Development Through Job Competency Assessment," IN Peltason 1978, 72-80. Original.

2441. Klemp Jr., George O., "Three Factors of Success," IN Vermilye 1977, 102-109. Original.

Mr. Klemp, director of research for a behavioral science consulting firm, describes what his research has identified as the "kind of knowledge, skills, abilities, and other characteristics that are tied to effective performance" in a post-college work situation.

2442. Kogan, Nathan, "Sex Differences in Creativity and Cognitive Styles," IN Messick 1976, 93-125. Original.

Commentaries by Eleanor B. Sheldon, David Jenness, and Ravenna Helson follow on pages 120-133.

2443. Kurland, Norman, "Automation and Technology in Education," IN Mayhew 1967, 423-429. Original.

2444. Lange, Phil C., "Theory of Programed Instruction and Development of Programs," IN Smith 1963, 95-98. Original.

2445. Langford, Thomas A., "The Conveyance of Personal Knowledge," IN Buxton 1975, 147-153. Original.

2446. Lansky, Leonard M., "Changing the Classroom--Some Psychological Assumptions," IN Runkel 1969, 292-301. Original.

2447. Layard, Richard, "The Cost-Effectiveness of the New Media in Higher Education," IN Lumsden 1974, 149-173. Original.

2448. Lee, Calvin B. T., "Improving College Teaching: Inquiry and Quest," IN Lee 1967, 1-3. Original.

2449. Lee, Calvin B. T., "Knowledge Structure and Curriculum Development," IN Lee 1967, 389-402. ER, 47 (Summer 1966), 347-360.

2450. Lehmann, Irvin J., "Evaluation of Instruction," IN Dressel 1961, 330-359. Original.

2451. Lerner, Abba, "An Economist's View," IN Hook 1974, 123-124. Original.

Mr. Lerner believes colleges have increased in size because of the tendency to inflate educational requirements for entry into many jobs that do not need the added "certification."

2452. Lesser, Gerald S., "Cultural Differences in Learning and Thinking Styles," IN Messick 1976, 137-160. Original.

Commentaries by Michael Cole and Edmund W. Gordon follow on pages 161-174.

2453. Leyden, Ralph C., "Residence Halls as an Integral Part of the Learning Environment," IN Smith 1966, 253-256. Original.

2454. Lindquist, Jack, "Strategies for Contract Learning," IN Vermilye 1975, 75-89. Original.

2455. Lubell, Samuel, "The Fragmentation of Knowledge," IN Hook 1974, 93-96. Original.

2456. Luehrmann, Arthur, "Reading, Writing, Arithmetic and Computing," IN Harrison 1975, 33-42. Original.

> The author provides examples of the creative use of computers as an aide to traditional instructional modes.

2457. Lunine, Myron J., "Outward Forms of Inward Values," IN Heyns 1977, 118-125. Original.

> Dr. Lunine asserts that curricula innovation in higher education depends on the incorporation of existing academic values along with planning for changes in organizational structure and institutional priorities.

2458. Lusterman, Seymour, "Education in Industry," IN Vermilye 1977, 79-86. Original.

2459. McClatchy, Joseph D., "A Student Looks at the Curriculum," IN Dennis 1966, 185-188. Original.

2460. McGlynn, James V., "Curriculum Innovation Need Not Be Expensive," IN Brann 1972, 245-249. Original.

2461. McGrath, Earl J. and L. Richard Meeth, "Organizing for Teaching and Learning: The Curriculum," IN Baskin 1965, 27-48. Original.

2462. McKeachie, Wilbert J., "Effective Teaching: The Relevance of the Curriculum," IN Dennis 1966, 189-191. Original.

2463. McKeachie, W. J., "Procedures and Techniques of Teaching: A Survey of Experimental Studies," IN Sanford 1962, 312-364. Original.

2464. McKeachie, W. J., "Research in Teaching: The Gap Between Theory and Practice," IN Lee 1967, 211-239. Original

> Commentaries by Arthur A. Lumsdaine, N. L. Gage, and Donald D. O'Dowd follow on pages 240-251.

2465. McKeachie, Wilbert J., "Significant Student and Faculty Characteristics Relevant to Personalizing Higher Education," IN Minter 1967, 21-35. Original.

2466. McKeachie, Wilbert J., "What Do the Research Findings from Behavioral Sciences Suggest Concerning the Improvement of Teaching and Learning?" IN Smith 1960, 128-131. Original.

2467. MacKinnon, Donald W., "Characteristics of the Creative Person: Implications for the Teaching-Learning Process," IN Smith 1961, 89-92. Original.

2468. Maddi, Salvatore R., "Fostering Achievement and the Cost of So Doing," IN Smith 1966, 106-109. Original.

> The author uses the findings of David McClelland's book The Achieving Society to arrive at an understanding of values and motivation. He then discusses the implications of value formation for programs within institutions of higher education.

2469. Mahoney, Colette, "Curricula to Develop Conscience and Consciousness," IN Heyns 1977, 125-133. Original.

2470. Mann, Richard D., "The Multiple Goals of Teaching," IN Buxton 1975, 39-47. Original.

2471. Manning, Duane, "In Search of Substantive Change," IN Buxton 1975, 239-245. Original.

> Dr. Manning presents some common errors that seem to persist in efforts to change the learning environment.

2472. Marble, Samuel D., "College Teaching Today and Tomorrow: What is Involved?" IN Smith 1964, 110-112. Original.

2473. Marcus, Irwin, "Observations on Teaching," IN Buxton 1975, 67-69. Original.

2474. Maslach, G. J., "Educational Articulation, the Transfer Process, and the Transfer Student," IN Smelser 1974, 243-250. Original.

2475. Mattfeld, Jacquelyn, "The Perceptive Eye," IN Hughes 1975, 302-308. Original.

> This essay is a case study of institutional change in relation to instructional technology and classroom teaching.

2476. Mayhew, Lewis B., "The Future Undergraduate Curriculum," IN Eurich 1968, 200-220. Original.

2477. Mayhew, Lewis B., "Institutional Factors and the Learning Environment," IN Dennis 1966, 211-230. Original.

2478. Mays, Nebraska, "Development of Urban-Related Programs in Black Colleges," IN Johnson 1974, 215-220. Original.

2479. Messick, Samuel, "Personal Styles and Educational Options," IN Messick 1976, 310-326. Original.

2480. Messick, Samuel, "Personality Consistencies in Cognition and Creativity," IN Messick 1976, 4-22. Original.

This essay identifies core personality dimensions that underlie our typical modes of cognitive and creative functioning.

2481. Michael, Lloyd S., "How Can the Undergraduate College Best Meet Curricular Pressures from Graduate and Professional Schools and From New Developments in Secondary Education?" IN Smith 1964, 74-77. Original.

2482. Miller, David C., "Low-Cost Educational Technology," IN Harrison 1975, 63-71. Original.

2483. Miller, Wilbur C., "Internship in College Teaching," IN Smith 1964, 116-118. Original.

2484. Mills, Ted, "Work as a Learning Experience," IN Vermilye 1977, 87-101. Original.

2485. Milton, Ohmer, "Curriculum Reform," IN Smith 1970, 220-228. Original.

2486. Milton, Ohmer, "The State of the Establishment," IN Milton 1968, 1-11. Original.

Dr. Milton presents the conditions that require our reconsideration of the current arrangement of the college curriculum.

2487. Molnar, Andrew R., "The Computer and the Fourth Revolution," IN Harrison 1975, 79-87. Original.

A reflection on the growth of computer applications in higher education over the past two decades.

2488. Morehouse, Ward, "What Should be the Role of Area Programs in the 60s?" IN Smith 1960, 190-193. Original.

2489. Morrow, Ralph, "Preparation and Internship of College Teaching," IN Smith 1964, 119-122. Original.

2490. Moss, Warren, "To What Extent Should the Faculty, Administration, Trustees, Students, Federal Government, Accrediting Bodies, or Others Control the Curriculum?" IN Smith 1960, 49-51. Original.

Several reactions to specific elements of Mr. Moss' speech follow on pages 51-61.

2491. Murphy, Thomas P., "Interships in Urban Government," IN Murphy 1975, 71-92. Original.

2492. Nixon, James, "The Learners' View About Personalizing Higher Education--The Experimental College at San Francisco State," IN Minter 1967, 57-70. Original.

2493. Noonan, John F., "Curricular Change: A Strategy for Improving Teaching," IN Vermilye 1972, 191-201. Original.

2494. North, R. Stafford, "Technology Rewards Its Teachers," IN McGrath 1972, 86-98. Original.

A summary of how instructional technology can effect teaching and the college curriculum.

2495. Norvel, Smith, "Black Studies," IN Altman 1970, 179-188. Original.

2496. Novak, Michael, "Academic Teaching and Human Experience," IN Averill 1971, 126-135. Harper's, 223 (October 1961), 173-178.

2497. Nyquist, Ewald B., "Grading as a Factor in Good Teaching," IN Deferrari 1961, 38-58. Original.

2498. Odishaw, Hugh, "Undergraduate Education for the Next Century," IN Smith 1964, 146-148. Original.

2499. Oettinger, Anthony G. and Nikki Zapol, "Will Information Technologies Help Learning?" IN Kaysen 1973, 293-358. Original.

2500. Orlans, Harold, "The Fatuity of Credentialing Everyone and Everything," IN Hughes 1975, 272-283. Original.

2501. Panuska, Joseph A., "Open-Endedness as an Educational Goal," IN Buxton 1975, 94-102. Original.

2502. Parlett, Malcolm, "Evaluating Innovations in Teaching," IN Butcher 1972, 144-159. Original.

2503. Parry, James, "PLATO," IN Harrison 1975, 112-116. Original.

A brief overview of the computer assisted instructional program called PLATO (Programmed Logic for Automated Teaching Operation).

2504. Paschal, Elizabeth, "Organizing for Better Instruction," IN Eurich 1968, 220-235. Original.

2505. Pattilo, Manning M., "Resolving the Conflict of Purpose Between the Search for Truth and the Teaching of Values," IN Smith 1966, 110-113. Original.

2506. Pelz, Donald, "Evnironments for Creative Performance Within Universities," IN Messick 1976, 229-247. Original.

Dr. Pelz lists security and challenge as two conditions needed for creative problem solving. He goes on to say that these two individual characteristics are of major importance to the environmental design of educational systems.

Commentaries by Norman Frederiksen and Harold M. Proshansky follow on pages 248-264.

2507. Perkins, Dexter, "College Teaching Then and Now," IN Lee 1967, 405-407. Original.

2508. Phenix, Philip H., "Teaching as Celebration," IN Buxton 1975, 22-29. Original.

2509. Pickett, Ralph E., "The Function and Role of the Administrator, the Teaching Faculty, the Nonteaching Faculty (such as Counselors and Librarians), the Student Body, and the Board of Control in Developing New and Modified Instructional Objectives," IN Smith 1962, 225-228. Original.

2510. Piel, Gerard, "The Acceleration of History," IN Mayhew 1967, 29-41. Current (1964).

The author addresses what he believes is a long stand fallacy--namely, that " . . . learning is divided into two separate provinces: the scientific and the humane."

2511. Plomp, Tjeerd, "The Statistical Basis for Aptitude--Treatment Interactions Research: Definitions and Techniques," IN Verreck 1974, 293-323. Original.

An extensive statistical analysis that attempts to discern the best instructional technique in relation to the desired outcomes.

2512. Porter, John W., "Articulation of Vocational and Career-Oriented Programs at the Postsecondary Level," IN Hughes 1975, 206-214. Original.

2513. Postlethwait, Samuel N., "Planning for Better Learning," IN Smith 1967, 110-113. Original.

The author presents seven conditions that effect the nature of the learning process and therefore, the process of curriculum development.

2514. Postlethwait, S. N., "Students, Teachers, and Technology," IN Buxton 1975, 220-231. Original.

2515. Pressey, Sidney L., "Two Basic Neglected Psycho-educational Problems, IN Milton 1968, 61-70. AP, 20 (June 1965), 391-395.

The "problems" are: (1) how long people should continue in school and (2) how progress through school might be made more efficient.

2516. Raushenbush, Esther, "The Climate of Sarah Lawrence College," IN Murphy 1960, 21-57. Original.

2517. Reckford, Kenneth J., "Teaching the Heroic Journey," IN Buxton 1975, 11-21. Original.

2518. Rees, Mina, "How Can the Undergraduate College Best Meet Curricular Pressures from Graduate and Professional Schools and from New Developments in Secondary Education?" IN Smith 1964, 70-73. Original.

2519. Riesman, David, "Innovation and Reaction in Higher Education," IN Cohen 1964, 182-205. Original.

2520. Riesman, David and Joseph Gusfield, "Styles of Teaching in New Public Colleges," IN Morison 1966, 242-265. Original.

2521. Rosen, Sherwin, "Measuring the Obsolescence of Knowledge," IN Juster 1975, 199-232. Original.

2522. Runkel, Philip J., "The Campus as a Laboratory--University of Oregon," IN Runkel 1969, 134-154. Original.

2523. Rusholme, Lord James, "Quantity and Quality in University Education," IN Smith 1964, 48-54. Original.

2524. Ryans, David G., "Programed Learning and Audio-instructional Devices in Relation to a Theory of Instruction," IN Smith 1963, 104-107. Original.

2525. Sanford, Nevitt, "Implications for Education and for Adjustment of Curricula to Individual Students," IN McGrath 1966, 40-64. Original.

2526. Saupe, Joe L., "Learning and Evaluation Processes," IN Dressel 1961, 54-78. Original.

2527. Seiler, John A., "Training Managers in the Laboratory--Harvard University," IN Runkel 1969, 234-253. Original.

The author discusses the concept and advantages of apprentice training through his experience at the Laboratory of Organizational Behavior, Harvard Business School.

2528. Sheldrake, Peter, "The Politics of the Curriculum," IN Verreck 1974, 89-104. Original.

A case study of the politics and pressures involved in the evaluation of a curriculum innovation.

2529. Sherwin, Robert, "The Presentation of Educational Self in the Classroom," IN Buxton 1975, 30-38. Original.

2530. Shoben Jr., Edward J., "Academic Standards: A Problem in Values," IN Vermilye 1973, 160-173. Original.

2531. Shoben Jr., Edward Joseph, "On Student-Initiated Courses: Some Reflections," IN Smith 1967, 178-181. Original.

2532. Sicherman, Barbara, "The Invisible Woman: The Case for Women's Studies," IN Furniss 1974, 155-177. Original.

2533. Siegel, Laurence, "The Contributions and Implications of Recent Research Related to Improving Teaching and Learning," IN Milton 1968, 136-157. Original.

2534. Skinner, B. F., "Teaching Machines," IN Harris 1960, 189-191. Original.

2535. Smith, Huston, "Two Kinds of Teaching," IN Buxton 1975, 207-219. Original.

2536. Snow, Richard E., "Aptitude-Treatment Interactions and Individualized Alternatives in Higher Education," IN Messick 1976, 268-293. Original.

Commentaries by Winton H. Manning and Brian N. Lewis follow on pages 294-308.

2537. Snygg, Donald, "The Fully Functioning Person," IN Smith 1963, 76-79. Original.

A definition of the creative individual and how various institutions can effect conditions best suited for creative thinking.

2538. Springer, Norman, "A Teacher in an Alien Field--Saint Mary's College," IN Runkel 1969, 88-111. Original.

An extremely interesting essay concerning the nature of college curricula as reflected in the author's experiment in teaching a course (Euclidean geometry) outside his training in English literature.

2539. Steimel, Raymond J., "What Can Systematic Testing Contribute to Good Teaching?" IN Deferrari 1961, 59-71. Original.

2540. Stern, George G., "Environments for Learning," IN Sanford 1962, 690-730. Original.

2541. Stice, James E. and Susan M. Hereford, "The PSI Project at the University of Texas at Austin," IN Harrison 1975, 116-129. Original.

The development and use of PSI (Personalized System of Instruction) a computer assisted learning package.

2542. Stickler, W. Hugh, "The College Calendar: What Kind of a School Year?" IN Baskin 1965, 223-245. Original.

2543. Stolurow, Lawrence M., "Personalized and Open Learning Environments," IN Harrison 1975, 241-249. Original.

A general summary of the possible directions for program development in educational technology.

2544. Stolurow, Lawrence M. and Shelley A. Harrison, "Educational Technologies: Recommendations for Research and Development," IN Harrison 1975, 253-272. Original.

2545. Strickland, Conwell G., "Students' Rights and the Teacher's Obligations in the Classroom," IN Buxton 1975, 80-85. Original.

2546. Taylor, Harold, "An Approach to Education," IN Murphy 1960, 1-20. Original.

An historical survey of curriculum development and innovation at Sarah Lawrence College.

2547. "To What Extent Will the Emerging New Instructional Techniques, Including Electronic Devices, Influence or Modify Curriculum and Instruction?" IN Smith 1964, 132-142. Original.

2548. Tobias, Sheila, "Women's Studies: Its Origin, Organization, and Prospects," IN Astin 1978, 80-94. Original.

2549. Toft, Robert J., "Designing a Module," IN Vermilye 1974, 57-61. Original.

2550. Toombs, William, "New Colleges for New Occupations," IN Anderson 1976, 266-285. Original.

2551. Torbert, William R. and J. Richard Hackman, "Taking the Fun Out of Outfoxing the System--Yale University," IN Runkel 1969, 156-181. Original.

An overview of problems in curricular change and innovation as reported in the authors' attempt to alter an undergraduate course at Yale University.

2552. Trow, Martin, "Undergraduate Teaching at Large State Universities," IN Lee 1967, 164-180. ER, 47 (Summer 1966), 303-319.

2553. Troy, William F., "How Should a Good College Teacher Be Trained?" IN Deferrari 1961, 113-122. Original.

2554. Turner, James, "Black Studies: Challenge to Higher Education," IN Smith 1970, 201-211. Original.

2555. Ubamadu, H. Oziri, "Developing a Relevant Afro-American Studies Program," IN Johnson 1974, 113-124. Original.

2556. Upton, Miller, "Acceptance of Minor Curricular Changes," IN Smith 1967, 101-105. Original.

2557. Vaags, D. W. and J. W. B. M. van Lieshout, "Computer Management of Individualized Instruction," IN Verreck 1974, 258-277. Original.

2558. van Woerden, Willem H. and Hans L. Knip, "An Intervention Strategy of Educational Development," IN Verreck 1974, 161-170. Original.

2559. Verreck, Will, "Instructional Programmes and Individualisation of Learning: A Review of Recent Research and Development," IN Entwistle 1976, 65-83. Original.

2560. Veysey, Laurence, "Stability and Experiment in the American Undergraduate Curriculum," IN Kaysen 1973, 1-63. Original.

2561. Waggoner, George R., "Departmental Honors at the University of Kansas," IN Cohen 1966, 137-165. Original.

2562. Warren, Jonathan R., "Awarding Credit," IN Cross 1974, 116-147. Original.

2563. Watson, Patricia A., "Career Planning for the Liberal Arts Undergraduate," IN Peltason 1978, 66-71. Original.

2564. Weir, Walter D., "Honors and the Liberal Arts Colleges," IN Cohen 1966, 75-95. Original.

2565. Werdell, Philip R., "Teaching and Learning: The Basic Process," IN Runkel 1969, 4-19. WGHE (1968).

2566. Werdell, Philip R., "Teaching and Learning: Whose Goals are Important Around Here?" IN Dobbins 1968, 19-38. Original.

Commentaries by Joseph P. Cosand, Kenneth Eble, Jonathan E. Rhoads, and Harris Wofford, Jr. follow on pages 39-53.

2567. Wertz, Richard, "An Experience of Curricular Change," IN Hodgkinson 1971a, 113-126. Original.

A case study of an attempt at curricular reform at MIT, grounded in the belief that the first objective is to get the university to become "self-conscious about what it was doing and why."

2568. Whaley, Randall M., "Pressures from the Exponential Increases in Knowledge," IN Smith 1965, 107-111. Original.

2569. Whaley, Randall M., "The Search for Truth," IN Smith 1966, 114-117. Original.

Mr. Whaley believes college should help students "define truth" and "values" by providing them with techniques and procedures whereby they can, by themselves, discriminate between valid and suspect values.

2570. White, David A., "The Time Has Come Today," IN Letter 1970, 68-77. Original.

A student's view of the proper role of the college faculty and curriculum.

2571. Wicke, Myron F., "Criteria for Governing Curricular Content," IN Smith 1964, 200-203. Original.

2572. Wildt, Johannes and Gerd Gehrmann, "Action Research as an Innovation Strategy in Higher Education," IN Verreck 1974, 130-142. Original.

Describes a system for institutional self study aimed at the development of new and innovative curricula.

2573. Wilson, O. Meredith, "Teach Me, And I Will Hold My Tongue," IN Lee 1967, 7-11. Original.

A wide-ranging essay on the conditions of education and teaching in the 1960's.

2574. Winsey, Valentine R., "World Game: An Education in Education," IN Vermilye 1973, 104-110. Original.

Professor Winsey is critical of the fragmentation of college curricula and suggests a reorganization along interdisciplinary lines.

2575. Wise, W. Max, "Evaluation and Utilization of the Informal Education of Students: Student-to-Student and Teacher-to-Student Relationships on Residential and Non-residential Campuses," IN Smith 1962, 76-78. Original.

2576. Wisner, Robert J., "Areas of Uniformity and Diversity in Curriculum Construction," IN Smith 1963, 213-214. Original.

2577. Wynn, Dudley, "Honors and the University," IN Cohen 1966, 96-136. Original.

2578. Zigerell, James J., "Chicago's TV College: A Television-Based Open Learning Model," IN Harrison 1975, 171-180. Original.

Commentary by G. R. Klare follows on pages 232-234.

18
CURRICULUM AND INSTRUCTION—THE SCIENCES AND TECHNOLOGY

2579. Allen, Donald S., "The Future of the Physical Sciences in the Liberal Arts College," IN Letter 1970, 59-67. Original.

2580. Atkin, J. Myron, "A Role for the University in Science Curriculum Improvement at the Elementary School Level," IN Smith 1964, 149-152. Original.

2581. Audo, Ishaya S., "Relevancy in Agriculture Education Systems," IN Bailey 1977, 74-82. Original.

2582. Baldwin, Lionel V., "Videotape Applications in Engineering Education," IN Harrison 1975, 181-201. Original.

Commentary by Stephen Yelon follows on pages 228-231.

2583. Brasted, Robert C., "The Introductory Course in Chemistry," IN Buxton 1975, 109-119. Original.

2584. Brooks, Harvey, "Relative Growth in Humanities and Science," IN Smelser 1974, 235-241. Original.

2585. Burhoe, Ralph W., "Human Values in an Age of Science and Technology," IN Smith 1964, 33-35. Original.

2586. Crawford, Bryce, "New Trends in Graduate Study in the Physical Sciences," IN Walters 1965, 216-222. Original.

2587. Davidson, William C., "The Role of Science in Peace and War: Implications for Higher Education," IN Smith 1961, 12-18. Original.

2588. Davis, Robert B., "Undergraduate College Education in Relation to the 'New Curriculum' in Mathematics," IN Smith 1964, 153-155. Original.

2589. Davis, Saville R., "The Role of Science in U.S. Policy: Implications for Higher Education," IN Smith 1961, 19-23. Original.

2590. Dorsey, Gray, "A Proposal for a New Division of the Curriculum," IN Hook 1975, 247-252. Original.

The author suggests a new specialty be included in the college curriculum that would concentrate on techniques to assess the impacts of technology.

2591. Doty, Paul and Dorothy Zinberg, "Science and the Undergraduate," IN Kaysen 1973, 155-218. Original.

2592. Fischer, Don A., "Changed in Engineer Education," IN Smith 1963, 140-142. Original.

2593. Francis, George, "A Degree Program in Environmental Education," IN Vermilye 1972, 202-210. Original.

2594. Ginsberg, Benson E., "To What Extent Should Laboratory Requirements be a Part of Science Education for Nonscience Majors?" IN Smith 1966, 70-72. Original.

2595. Goldenberg, I. Ira, "The Relationship of the University to the Community: Implications for Community Mental Health Programs," IN Mitchell 1974, 163-174. Original.

2596. Hall, Thomas S., "Student Values and the Teaching of Biology," IN Carpenter 1960, 36-44. Original.

2597. Hathaway, Dale E., "Applying American Science and Technology in Developing Countries," IN Bailey 1977, 63-73. Original.

2598. Holton, Gerald, "Science, Science Teaching, and Rationality," IN Hook 1975, 101-118. Original.

2599. Horsbrugh, Patrick, "Environmental Crisis and the University," IN Kertesz 1971, 131-150. Original.

2600. Jones, Thomas F., "Discovery Laboratories: An Alternative to 'Cookbook Labs,'" IN Buxton 1975, 103-108. Original.

2601. Lancaster, Otis E., "The Future of Engineering Education in Land-Grant Universities," IN Anderson 1976, 104-131. Original.

2602. Lawson, Chester A., "Updating General Education Courses in the Natural Sciences," IN Smith 1961, 133-135. Original.

2603. McBay, Shirley M., "Black Students in the Sciences: A Look at Spelman College," IN Willie 1978, 216-228. Original.

2604. Mills, Thomas J., "National Requirements for Scientists and Engineers: A Second Illustration," IN Mushkin 1962, 58-66. Original.

2605. Mumford, Lewis, "The Automation of Knowledge," IN Smith 1964, 11-21. Original.

2606. Nagel, Ernest, "In Defense of Scientific Knowledge," IN Hook 1975, 119-126. Original.

2607. Nelson, Clarence H., "Evaluation in the Natural Sciences," IN Dressel 1961, 113-156. Original.

2608. Rabin, Michael, "The Uses and Limitations of Science Teaching," IN Hook 1975, 127-136. Original.

2609. Rees, Mina, "Efforts of the Mathematical Community to Improve the Mathematics Curriculum," IN Wilson 1965, 228-233. Original.

2610. Reithel, Francis J., "Honors and the Sciences," IN Cohen 1966, 166-190. Original.

2611. Reswick, James B. and Ronald K. Boyer, "Experiments in Engineering Education," IN Smith 1964, 129-131. Original.

2612. Rice, Stuart A., "A Private View of Teaching Science," IN Buxton 1975, 128-131. Original.

2613. Robertson, H. Rocke, "How Best Can the University Help Solve the Health Problems?" IN Henderson 1968, 102-108. Original.

2614. Rossi-Doria, Manlio, "Present and Future Problems of Food and Poverty: What Higher Education Can Contribute to Their Solution," IN Henderson 1968, 94-101. Original.

2615. Schein, Richard D., "The Land-Grant University and Environmental Affairs," IN Anderson 1976, 178-189. Original.

2616. Seamans Jr., Robert C. and Robert Jastrow, "The Role of Higher Education in the Developing Space Age," IN Smith 1961, 44-59. Original.

2617. Shamos, Morris H., "The Art of Teaching Science," IN Morris 1970, 66-86. Original.

2618. Snyder, Benson R., "The Education of Creative Science Students," IN Heist 1968, 56-70. Original.

2619. South, Oron, "Creativity for Engineers--Vanderbilt University," IN Runkel 1969, 182-208. Original.

2620. Stoker, Warren C., "Factors Contributing to Obsolesence of Scientific and Technical Knowledge and Skills," IN Smith 1963, 145-147. Original.

2621. Teare Jr., B. Richard, "Engineering," IN Henry 1962, 120-139. Original.

2622. Theobald, Robert, "The Great Non-Debate on Automation and Cybernation," IN Smith 1965, 102-106. Original.

2623. Thimann, Kenneth V., "The Social Role of the University and Its Science Departments," IN Smelser 1974, 227-233. Original.

2624. Todorovich, Miro M., "Multilevel Teaching of the Natural Sciences," IN Hook 1975, 137-142. Original.

2625. Torpey, William G., "Specific Policies and Practices for Reducing Scientific and Engineering Manpower Obsolescence," IN Smith 1963, 148-150. Original.

2626. Vallance, Theodore R., "Home Economics and the Development of New Forms of Human Service Education," IN Anderson 1976, 79-103. Original.

2627. van der Klauw, Cor F. and Tjeerd Plomp, "The Construction and Evaluation of a Feedback System," IN Verreck 1974, 237-257. Original.

A case study of a learner feedback system for freshmen mathematics called Individualized Study System.

2628. van Hout, J. F. M. J. and C. T. C. W. Mettes, "The Course Development Project 'Engineering Design' at the Twente University of Technology--Some Aspects of Planned Change in Higher Education," IN Verreck 1974, 171-196. Original.

2629. Weiss, Paul, "Science in the University," IN Morison 1966, 152-185. Dae, 93 (Fall 1964), 1184-1218.

2630. Whaley, W. Gordon, "New Trends in Graduate Study in the Biological Sciences," IN Walters 1965, 202-215. Original.

2631. Wilder, R. L., "The Beginning Teacher of College Mathematics," IN Morris 1970, 94-103. Original.

19
CURRICULUM AND INSTRUCTION—THE HUMANITIES

2632. Abrams, M. H., "The Language and Methods of Humanism," IN Hook 1975, 89-97. Original.

2633. Ackerman, James S., "The Arts in Higher Education," IN Kaysen 1973, 219-266. Original.

2634. Andrews, John D. W., "Encounter in Freshman Writing--State University of New York at Buffalo," IN Runkel 1969, 112-133. Original.

2635. Arlt, Gustave O., "New Trends in Graduate Study in the Humanities," IN Walters 1965, 185-201. Original.

2636. Axelrod, Joseph, "Intercultural Study Versus the Foreign Language Requirement," IN Smith 1968, 241-250. Original.

2637. Axelrod, Joseph, "Teaching Styles in the Humanities," IN Morris 1970, 38-55. Original.

2638. Babbitt, Irving, "The Humanities," IN Hawkins 1970, 53-59. AtL, 89 (1902), 770-776; 779.

2639. Bain, Wilfred C., "How Important are the Applied and Performing Arts as a Part of a Liberal Arts Curriculum," IN Smith 1960, 67-69. Original.

2640. Bartley, Robert L., "A Role for Social Science?" IN Hook 1975, 169-173. Original.

2641. Berman, Ronald, "Justifying the Humanities," IN Hook 1975, 75-79. Original.

Observations on the role of the federal government and the National Endowment for the Humanities in support of the arts and humanities.

2642. Blitzer, Charles, "Should a National Foundation for the Humanities Be Established?" IN Smith 1964, 78-79. Original.

2643. Bowman, David J., "Religious Cooperation," IN Donovan 1965, 73-84. Original.

2644. Bush, Douglas, "The Humanities," IN Morison 1966, 186-205. Dae, 93 (Fall 1964), 1219-1237.

2645. Butterfield, Victor L., "Pressures on Higher Education for the Arts and the Humanities," IN Smith 1965, 123-125. Original.

2646. Cadoux, Remunda, "Trends in Language and Cultural Studies," IN Bailey 1977, 125-131. Original.

2647. Dirks, J. Edwards, "To What Extent Should the Study of Religion be Included in the Curriculum?" IN Smith 1960, 73-75. Original.

Commentary by A. L. Sebaly follows on pages 75-76.

2648. Dominic, Sister Rose, "Cooperation Among Colleges for Religious Education," IN Donovan 1965, 19-13. Original.

2649. Eliot, T. S., "Modern Education and the Classics," IN Margolis 1969, 54-62. S Ess (1964).

2650. Fitzsimons, M. A., "The Humanities and Education for Humanity," IN Kertesz 1971, 73-91. Original.

2651. Flautz, John T., "The Complete Works in English of W-- G--," IN Bellman 1962, 35-41. CE, 22 (April 1961), 511-513.

A case study of the writing ability of a freshman.

2652. Giannini, Vittorio, "Nurturing Talent and Creativity in the Arts," IN Heist 1968, 73-83. Original.

2653. Gleason, Ralph J., "The Education of the Jazz Virtuoso," IN Heist 1968, 84-98. Original.

2654. Goldberg, Maxwell H., "The Humanities and the Discovery of New Knowledge," IN Smith 1963, 226-229. Original.

2655. Good, Leonard, "What is General Education's Responsibility for Creativity in the Language Arts and the Humanities?" IN Smith 1960, 103-104. Original.

Commentaries on the Good paper follow on pages 105-114.

2656. Hall, T. William, "The Role of Philosophy in General Education," IN Smith 1961, 129-132. Original.

2657. Hardison Jr., O. B., "Teaching the Humanities," IN Morris 1970, 56-65. Original.

2658. Heckscher, August, "The Relationship of the Arts and Humanities to Higher Education," IN Smith 1966, 68-71. Original.

2659. Heenan, David K., "Evaluation in the Humanities," IN Dressel 1961, 157-191. Original.

2660. Himmelfarb, Gertrude, "Observations on Humanism and History," IN Hook 1975, 81-87. Original.

2661. Issawi, Charles, "The Economist Among the Social Scientists," IN Hook 1975, 159-164. Original.

2662. Joseph, Lois, "The Role of Higher Education in Improving the Curriculum in English," IN Smith 1964, 156-159. Original.

2663. Kristeller, Paul O., "The Humanities as Scholarship and a Branch of Knowledge," IN Hook 1975, 217-220. Original.

2664. Lowry, W. McNeil, "The Arts," IN Morison 1966, 206-216. Original.

2665. Monro, John U., "Teaching and Learning English," IN Willie 1978, 235-260. Original.

This essay deals with the teaching of English at predominantly black colleges.

2666. Olafson, Frederick A., "Humanism and the Humanities," IN Hook 1975, 51-74. Original.

2667. Olds, Glenn A., "Foreign Study as Crosscultural Learning," IN Smith 1968, 251-257. Original.

2668. Ong, Walter J., "Knowledge, Time, and Man," IN Smith 1963, 230-232. Original.

The author provides some suggestions concerning the accumulation and transmission of knowledge in the humanities.

2669. Packwood, William T., "Religion," IN Packwood 1977, 206-218. Original.

A concise overview of the campus ministry program.

2670. Palmer, Osmond E., "Evaluation of Communication Skills," IN Dressel 1961, 192-226. Original.

2671. Pearce, Roy H., "Humanistic Studies and the Large Public University," IN Smelser 1974, 221-226. Original.

2672. Robertson, D. B., "Notes on Departments of Religion," IN Robertson 1978, 59-78. Original.

2673. Ross, Ralph G., "Development of Knowledge, Understanding, and Appreciation of the Humanities," IN Smith 1963, 74-76. Original.

2674. Roundtree, Thelma, "Teaching in the Humanities," IN Willie 1978, 229-234. Original.

This essay deals with humanities teaching in predominantly black colleges.

2675. Ryan, Harold F., "Reflections of a Humanist on the University as a Medium," IN Kent 1970, 161-172. Original.

2676. Safer, Louis T., "Updating General Education Courses in the Fine Arts and Humanities," IN Smith 1961, 136-139. Original.

2677. Shattuck, Roger, "Contract and Credentials: The Humanities in Higher Education," IN Kaysen 1973, 65-120. Original.

2678. Slayton, William L., "The University, the City, and Urban Renewal," IN Dobbins 1964, 2-9. Original.

2679. Smith, Henry Nash, "The Humanities in the Multiversity," IN Smelser 1974, 209-220. Original.

2680. Sowell, Thomas, "Social Science and General Education," IN Hook 1975, 165-168. Original.

2681. Steinberg, Erwin R., "The Undergraduate Curriculum in English," IN Smith 1963, 209-212. Original.

2682. Stevens, Roger L., "Priorities for the Arts," IN Smith 1965, 49-54. Original.

20
CURRICULUM AND INSTRUCTION—THE SOCIAL SCIENCES

2683. Anderson, Archibald W., "The Teaching Profession: An Example of Diversity in Training and Function," IN Henry 1962, 140-167. Original.

2684. Berelson, Bernard, "The Place of the Behavioral Sciences in General and Liberal Education," IN Smith 1964, 165-167. Original.

2685. Berg, Harry D., "Evaluation in Social Science," IN Dressel 1961, 79-112. Original.

2686. Boulding, Kenneth G., "The Task of the Teacher in the Social Sciences," IN Morris 1970, 104-123. Original.

2687. Bruner, Jerome S., "On Teaching Teachers," IN Smith 1964, 97-99. Original.

2688. Chase, Francis S., "The Role of Higher Education in the Development of Effective Certification Standards of Secondary School Teachers," IN Smith 1961, 124-126. Original.

Commentary by William R. Viall follows on pages 127-128.

2689. Church, Robert L., "Economists as Experts: The Rise of an Academic Profession in the United States, 1870-1920," IN Stone II 1974, 571-609. Original.

2690. Culbert, Samuel A., "Training Change Agents for Business and Public Administration--George Washington University," IN Runkel 1969, 210-232. Original.

2691. Dunner, Joseph, "On the Condition of Political Science," IN Hook 1975, 253-255. Original.

2692. Engbretson, William E., "Curricular Relevance in Teacher Education," IN Smith 1968, 220-231. Original.

2693. Ericksen, Stanford C., "Application of Learning Theory to Teaching of Introductory Psychology," IN Smith 1963, 241-242. Original.

2694. Friedman, Renee C. and Robert S. Friedman, "Social and Behavioral Sciences in the 1970s," IN Anderson 1976, 160-177. Original.

2695. Glazer, Nathan, "The Social Sciences in Liberal Education," IN Hook 1975, 145-158. Original.

2696. Grennan, Sister M. Jacqueline, "Massive Curriculum Reform and Its Implications for Teacher Education," IN Smith 1964, 100-103. Original.

2697. Gross, Frank, "Thoughts on a Social-Science Curriculum," IN Hook 1975, 261-273. Original.

2698. Haggerty, William J., "Significance for High School and College Teacher Preparation," IN McGrath 1966, 174-192. Original.

2699. Hewett, Stanley, "The Futures of the Colleges of Education," IN Lawlor 1972, 19-34. Original.

2700. Jacob, Herbert, "Some Consequences of Scientific Social Sciences," IN Kertesz 1971, 92-110. Original.

2701. Johnson, Jack T., "Updating General Education Courses in the Social Sciences," IN Smith 1961, 140-143. Original.

2702. Kimble, Gregory A., "Content of the Introductory Psychology Course," IN Smith 1963, 243-246. Original.

2703. Kozelka, Richard L., "Business--The Emerging Profession," IN Henry 1962, 168-189. Original.

2704. Levine, Daniel U., "Urban Teaching Training," IN Murphy 1975, 259-284. Original.

2705. Macleod, Robert B., "The Teaching of Psychology," IN Morris 1970, 124-132. Original.

2706. Mayo, Charles G., "Trends in Political Science: Implications for Graduate Education," IN Kent 1970, 111-124. Original.

2707. Miller, John P., "New Trends in Graduate Study in the Social Sciences," IN Walters 1965, 171-184. Original.

2708. Novotny, Henry R., "The Logic of the Social Sciences: To Be, To Do, or To Describe?" IN Hook 1975, 235-246. Original.

2709. Page, Ralph C., "The Role of the Academic Division in Teacher Preparation," IN Smith 1963, 215-218. Original.

2710. Prichard, Keith W., "Teaching Education Courses: The Other Side of the Tracks," IN Buxton 1975, 70-79. Original.

2711. Roizen, Judy, "Black Students in Higher Education," IN Trow 1975, 113-181. Original.

2712. Senesh, Lawrence, "The Role of Universities in Curriculum Research in Economics," IN Smith 1964, 160-164. Original.

2713. Shipman, M. D., "Changing Colleges of Education," IN Butcher 1972, 335-344. Original.

2714. Smelser, Neil J., "The Social Sciences," IN Kaysen 1973, 121-154. Original.

2715. Smith, Charles U., "Teaching and Learning the Social Sciences in the Predominantly Black Universities," IN Willie 1978, 195-215. Original.

2716. Tyler, Priscilla, "The Responsibility of Academic Departments for Preparation of Elementary and Secondary Teachers," IN Smith 1963, 218-221. Original.

2717. Walker, Edward L., "Utilizing Student Motivation for Mastering Content in Psychology," IN Smith 1963, 246-250. Original.

2718. Wise, W. Max, "Who Teaches the Teachers?" IN Lee 1967, 77-89. Original.

Commentaries by John W. Atherton, James I. Armstrong, and John E. King follow on pages 90-98.

2719. Woodring, Paul, "A Century of Teacher Education," IN Brickman 1962, 154-165. Original.

2720. Zacharis, Jerrold R., "Massive Curriculum Reform and Its Implications for Teacher Education," IN Smith 1964, 104-107. Original.

2721. Zelan, Joseph, "Undergraduates in Sociology," IN Trow 1975, 183-198. Amer Soc, 9 (February 1974), 9-17.

21
THE LIBERAL ARTS AND GENERAL EDUCATION

2722. Averill, Lloyd J., "The Sectarian Nature of Liberal Education," IN Averill 1971, 74-84. Original.

2723. Averill, Lloyd J., "The Vulnerability and Viability of the Liberal Arts," IN Smith 1964, 55-62. Original.

2724. Barr, Donald, "The Colleges' Crisis of Integrity: A Headmaster's View," IN Lee 1967, 373-381. Original.

An extended review of D. Bell's, The Reforming of General Education.

2725. Barr, Strinfellow, "Liberal Education: A Common Adventure," IN Margolis 1969, 39-53. AR, 15 (1955), 300-312.

2726. Bell, Daniel, "The Reform of General Education," IN Goldwin 1967, 97-119. Original.

2727. Bell, Daniel, "Reforming General Education," IN Lee 1967, 347-359. RGE (1966).

Commentaries by Charles Muscatine, M. Margaret Ball, and Richard H. Sullivan follow on pages 360-372.

2728. Benson, Frank T., "General Education and the 'Pervasive' Outcomes: Creativity, Critical Thinking, Values and Attitudes," IN Smith 1962, 210-213. Original.

2729. Blackman, Edward B., "Guidelines for Evaluation of General Education," IN Rice 1964, 69-78. Original.

2730. Bledstein, Burton J., "Reassessing General Education," IN Vermilye 1977, 141-147. Original.

2731. Bloom, Allan, "The Crisis of Liberal Education," IN Goldwin 1967, 121-139. Original.

2732. Boyer, Ernest L., "The Core of Learning," IN Vermilye 1977, 148-153. Change, 9 (March 1977), 22-29.

A strong appeal for a return to liberal education with a common core curriculum.

2733. Brown, J. Douglas, "The Squeeze on the Liberal University," IN Margolis 1969, 197-211. AtL, 213 (May 1964), 85-87.

2734. Cahn, Steven M., "The Content of a Liberal Education," IN Hook 1974, 99-106. Original.

2735. Carlin, Edward A., "General Education for the Future," IN Rice 1964, 61-67. Original.

2736. Carlin, Edward A., "Is General Education for Export?" IN Smith 1962, 221-224. Original.

2737. Carpenter, Marjorie, "Depth: Third Dimension in Learning-Pontentialities in General Education," IN Rice 1964, 33-39. Original.

2738. Carpenter, Marjorie, "Materials for Teaching in General Education Courses," IN Mayhew 1960, 112-132. Original.

2739. Carpenter, Marjorie, "Practices in Value-Oriented Courses," IN Carpenter 1960, 23-35. Original.

2740. Chickering, Arthur W., "Vocations and the Liberal Arts," IN Vermilye 1977, 125-140. Original.

2741. Cooper, Russell M., "Curricular Programs in General Education," IN Mayhew 1960, 61-89. Original.

2742. de Bary, Theodore, "The Challenge of General Education," IN Hook 1974, 259-260. Original.

Commentary by Arthur Bestor follows on pages 261-262.

2743. de Bary, Theodore, W., "General Education and the University Crisis," IN Hook 1975, 3-25. Original.

2744. Dolbec, Vincent R., "Admissions and the Liberal Arts," IN Rich 1963, 75-103. Original.

2745. Doren, Mark Van, "The Educated Person," IN Margolis 1969, 5-17. L Ed (1959).

2746. Dressell, Paul L., "What Should be the Content of the Liberal Arts Curriculum," IN Smith 1960, 62-66. Original.

2747. Eliot, Charles W., "What is a Liberal Education?" IN Portman 1972, 23-46. Cent Mag, 28 (June 1884), 203-212.

2748. French, Sidney J., "Teaching in General Education," IN Mayhew 1960, 90-111. Original.

2749. Goldberg, Maxwell H., "Liberal Learning and the Land-Grant System: Futures and Optatives," IN Anderson 1976, 132-159. Original.

2750. Goldberg, Maxwell H., "General Education and the Explosion of Knowledge," IN Rice 1964, 13-22. Original.

2751. Griswold, A. Whitney, "Liberal Education and the Democratic Ideal," IN Margolis 1969, 78-83. LEDI (1959).

2752. Harvard University Committee on General Education, "General and Special Education," IN Margolis 1969, 31-38. GEFS (1945).

2753. Hatch, Winslow, "Contributions General Education Can Make to the Education of More Heterogeneous Groups," IN Smith 1963, 251-252. Original.

2754. Hawkins, David, "Liberal Education: A Modest Polemic," IN Kaysen 1973, 491-542. Original.

2755. Henderson, Algo D., "Liberal Education in the Mid-Twentieth Century," IN Paulsen 1970, 95-108. Original.

2756. Hook, Sidney, "General Education: The Minimum Indispensables," IN Hook 1975, 27-36. Original.

2757. Hutchins, Robert M., "The Aims of Education," IN Margolis 1969, 18-30. EFF (1943).

2758. Johnson, B. Lamar and James L. McKenney, "Developing the General Education Faculty," IN Mayhew 1960, 133-161. Original.

2759. Johnson, Jack T., "The Illusion of the Disciplines," IN Letter 1970, 24-34. Original.

> Professor Johnson presents a very convincing argument concerning the possible "demise" of the liberal arts college.

2760. Kabir, Humayum, "Humanistic Education in India," IN Cohen 1964, 111-119. Original.

2761. Kamm, Robert, "General Education and the Undergraduate Major," IN Smith 1962, 125-128. Original.

2762. Kamm, Robert B., "How Can Students be Motivated Toward General Education?" IN Smith 1960, 169-171. Original.

> Commentaries by Peter E. Siegle and Angie Thomas follow on pages 172-174.

2763. Keeton, Morris T., "Alternative Pathways to Liberal Education," IN McGrath 1972, 62-85. Original.

2764. Klein, Jacob, "The Idea of Liberal Education," IN Weatherford 1960, 26-41. Original.

2765. Kranzberg, Melvin, "The Liberal Curriculum in a Scientific and Technological Age," IN Dennis 1966, 177-184. Original.

2766. Kurtz, Paul, "Education for the Future: The Liberating Arts," IN Hook 1975, 197-204. Original.

> Professor Kurtz strongly supports a liberal arts curriculum adjusted to help "both the student and the social polity to deal with the new kinds of problems emerging."

2767. Leyden, Ralph C., "The Contribution of General Education to the Handling of Larger Numbers of Students," IN Smith 1963, 198-201. Original.

2768. "Liberal Learning in a Changing World," IN Mayhew 1967, 383-394. CWA (1964).

2769. McCune, George H., "Contributions General Education Can Make to the Education of More Heterogeneous Groups," IN Smith 1963, 253-257. Original.

2770. McGrath, Earl J., "New Vistas in Liberal Education," IN Letter 1968, 1-11. Original.

2771. McKeon, Richard, "The Future of the Liberal Arts," IN Smith 1964, 36-44. Original.

2772. McKeon, Richard P., "The Liberating Arts and the Humanizing Arts in Education," IN Cohen 1964, 159-181. Original.

2773. Mayhew, Lewis B., "The Future of General Education," IN Mayhew 1960, 190-205. Original.

2774. Mayhew, Lewis B., "General Education: A Definition," IN Mayhew 1960, 1-24. Original.

2775. Mayhew, Lewis B., "General Education: A Definition," IN Mayhew 1967, 217-235. GEAA (1960).

2776. Morse, Horace T., "Liberal and General Education: A Problem of Differentiation," IN Rice 1964, 7-12. Original.

2777. Murray, John Courtney, "On the Future of Humanistic Education," IN Cohen 1964, 231-247. Original.

2778. Pace, C. Robert, "Liberal Arts Education and Women's Development," IN Astin 1978, 68-79. Original.

2779. Rhinelander, Philip H., "General Education and Pressures for Specialization," IN Smith 1963, 258-260. Original.

2780. Rose, Mary C., "The Maintaining of the Liberal Arts Attitude: The Chairperson's Role," IN Mauer 1976, 166-177. Original.

2781. Rothwell, C. Easton, "The Reaffirmation of Liberal Education," IN Smith 1964, 45-47. Original.

2782. Schwab, Joseph J., "On Reviving Liberal Education--In the Seventies," IN Hook 1975, 37-48. Original.

2783. Shao, Otis H., "Experimentation and Innovation in the Liberal Arts College and Their Implications for Graduate Education," IN Kent 1970, 173-187. Original.

2784. Stickler, W. Hugh, "Administrative Structures and Practices in General Education," IN Mayhew 1960, 25-60. Original.

2785. Strauss, Leo, "Liberal Education and Mass Democracy," IN Goldwin 1967, 73-96. Original.

2786. Taylor, Harold, "Individualism and the Liberal Tradition," IN Weatherford 1960, 9-25. Original.

2787. Thomas, Russell, "The College Curriculum: Liberal Art and Professional--A Problem," IN Donovan 1964, 107-119. Original.

2788. Truman, David B., "The Relevance of the Liberal Arts to the Needs of Society," IN Smith 1966, 122-125. Original.

2789. Trytten, M. H., "What are the Implications, for Genera Education, of the Explosion of Knowledge," IN Smith 1960, 115-118. Original.

2790. Tugwell, Rexford G., "A Connected View of Things," IN Cohen 1964, 138-158. Original.

The purpose of education and the attributes of a liberally educated man are discussed in the context of modern society.

2791. Ward, F. Champion, "Principles and Particulars in Liberal Education," IN Cohen 1964, 120-137. Original.

2792. Warrington, Willard G., "The Contribution of General Education to the Handling of Large Numbers of Students," IN Smith 1963, 201-205. Original.

2793. West, Andrew F., "Must the Classics Go?" IN Portman 1972, 47-50. NAR, 138 (February 1884), 151-162.

2794. Wilson, O. Meredith, "The Dilemmas of Humanistic Education in the United States," IN Cohen 1964, 99-110. Original.

22
GRADUATE AND PROFESSIONAL EDUCATION

2795. Anderson, G. Lester, "Professional Education: Present Status and Continuing Problems," IN Henry 1962, 3-26. Original.

2796. Anderson, G. Lester and Merton W. Ertell, "Extra-institutional Forces Affecting Professional Education," IN Henry 1962, 235-253. Original.

2797. Ashton, John W., "Other Doctorates," IN Walters 1965, 62-73. Original.

An essay on awarded degrees other than the Doctor of Philosophy degree.

2798. Babcock, Henry H., "Special Problems Encountered at the Graduate School of Business Administration," IN Blain 1961, 201-216. Original.

An article dealing with the emotional problems of graduate business students.

2799. Baird, Leonard L., "Who Goes to Graduate School and How They Get There," IN Katz 1976, 19-48. Original.

2800. Beach, Leonard B., "The Graduate Student," IN Walters 1965, 118-128. Original.

2801. Becker, Howard S., "The Nature of a Profession," IN Henry 1962, 27-46. Original.

2802. Bent, Henry E., "Fellowships, Assistantships, and Traineeships," IN Walters 1965, 129-152. Original.

2803. Bergin, Thomas P., "Continuing Education in the United States--The Challenge and Responsibility," IN Kertesz 1971, 123-130. Original.

2804. Blauch, Lloyd E., "A Century of the Professional School," IN Brickman 1962, 138-153. Original.

2805. Bojar, Samuel, "Psychiatric Problems of Medical Students," IN Blain 1961, 217-231. Original.

2806. Breneman, David W., "New Quality Ratings: A Force for Reform," IN Heyns 1977, 134-138. Original.

This essay provides a series of arguments for quality ratings of graduate programs.

2807. Brickman, William W., "Professional Education Outside the U.S.A.," IN Henry 1962, 68-100. Original.

2808. Brubacher, John S., "The Evolution of Professional Education," IN Henry 1962, 47-67. Original.

2809. Burke, William J., "Graduate Education in the Decades Ahead: Accent on the Individual," IN Kent 1970, 17-29. Original.

2810. Bye, Carl R., "What Will be the Dimensions of the Ph.D. and the Professional Doctorates?" IN Smith 1960, 183-186. Original.

2811. Carmichael, O. C., "Improving the Quality of Graduate Education for Prospective College Teachers," IN Smith 1962, 202-205. Original.

Commentary by John D. Millett follows on pages 206-209.

2812. Carr, William D., "Doctoral-Level Graduates with Higher Education as a Specialized Field of Study," IN Harcleroad 1974, 47-77. Original.

2813. Cartter, Allan M., "The Decades Ahead: Trends and Problems," IN Walters 1965, 223-246. Original.

Trends and problems in the development of graduate education in America are reviewed in this essay.

2814. Cartter, Allan M., "Graduate Education and Research in the Decades Ahead," IN Eurich 1968, 254-278. GET (1965).

2815. Clark, Mary Jo, "The Meaning of Quality in Graduate and Professional Education," IN Katz 1976, 85-104. Original.

2816. Conant, James B., "Education for the Learned Professions," IN Goldwin 1967, 141-153. Original.

2817. Crowe, Lawson, "Will the Future Be Like the Past," IN Kent 1970, 30-34. Original.

The author provides what he believes are the likely trends in graduate education.

2818. Darley, John G., "The Graduate School as a Professional School," IN Henry 1962, 190-207. Original.

2819. Donovan, George F., "Admissions and the Graduate Schools," IN Rich 1963, 111-127. Original.

2820. Dressel, Paul L., "Survey of Higher Education Programs," IN Harcleroad 1974, 25-36. Original.

2821. Dubin, Robert and Fredric Beisse, "The Assistant: Academic Subaltern," IN Kruytbosch 1970, 271-292. ASQ, 11 (March 1967), 521-547.

The thesis of this essay is that student activism against professors and administrators had its "principal source in the position and function of the graduate assistants . . ."

2822. Dunham, E. Alden, "Rx for Higher Education," IN Smith 1970, 184-193. Original.

Dunham wants to change the nature of graduate education to emphasize teaching skills appropriate and compatible with undergraduate liberal education. He goes on to assert that the research-oriented PhD programs are not operated necessarily to produce "college teachers."

2823. Duryea, E. D., "Some Thoughts on the Service Role of Departments of Higher Education," IN Harcleroad 1974, 89-91. Original.

2824. Eble, Kenneth E., "Graduate Students and the Job Market," IN Vermilye 1973, 49-55. Original.

2825. Elder, J. Peterson, "Janus Revisited," IN Kent 1970, 35-38. Original.

Professor Elder believes that traditional departmental PhD programs will be weakened in the future, but that continuing education beyond the B.A. will expand.

2826. Feldman, Saul D., "External Constraints: Marital Status and Graduate Education," IN Trow 1975, 249-264. Original.

2827. Fitzgerald, Laurine E., "Reassessing Graduate Education," IN Heyns 1977, 138-142. Original.

2828. Forsyth, John D., "Collective Bargaining with Graduate Student 'Employees': The University of Michigan Experience," IN Tice 1976, 299-315. Original.

2829. Gardner, Eldon J., "Ph.D. Degrees in a Changing Scene," IN Kent 1970, 39-51. Original.

2830. Goodman, Eric K., "Medical School, Law School, and Beyond," IN Sacks 1978, 268-287. Original.

2831. Gorter, Wytze, "Some Thoughts on Graduate Education in the Year 2000," IN Kent 1970, 52-55. Original.

2832. Gottlieb, David, "American Graduate Students," IN Yamamoto 1968, 445-450. JEP, 52 (October 1961), 236-240.

2833. Graham, Patricia A., "Graduate Education as Liberal Education," IN Heyns 1977, 142-148. Original.

2834. Haber, Samuel, "The Professions and Higher Education in America: A Historical View," IN Gordon 1974, 237-280. Original.

2835. Hartnett, Rodney T., "Environments for Advanced Learning," IN Katz 1976, 49-84. Original.

2836. Hartnett, Rodney T. and Joseph Katz, "Past and Present," IN Katz 1976, 3-15. Original.

This essay includes an evolution of graduate and professional education in the U.S. with notes on some important trends.

2837. Heard, Alexander, "The Lost Years in Graduate Education," IN Yamamoto 1968, 451-465. LYGE (1963).

2838. Heiss, Ann M., "Preparing College Teachers," IN Smith 1970, 165-178. Original.

2839. Heist, Paul, "Professions and the Student," IN Yamamoto 1968, 161-178. EFP (1962).

2840. Henle, Robert J., "Possibilities for Improving the Master's Degree to Render It a More Effective Means of Preparing College Teachers," IN Smith 1961, 157-160. Original.

2841. Henle, R. J., "The Soundness of the American Ph.D. Program," IN Lee 1967, 72-76. Original.

2842. Hughes, Everett C., "Higher Education and the Professions," IN Kaysen 1973, 267-291. Original.

2843. Jordon, David S., "Pettifogging Law-Schools and an Untrained Bar," IN Portman 1972, 111-117. Forum, 19 (May 1895), 350-355.

2844. Jorgensen, A. N., "Graduate Education for the Public Services," IN Paulsen 1970, 79-93. Original.

2845. Katz, Joseph and Rodney T. Hartnett, "Recommendations for Training Better Scholars," IN Katz 1976, 261-280. Original.

2846. Kidd, Charles V., "Doctorate Output: Overproduction or Underconsumption?" IN Vermilye 1973, 41-48. Original.

2847. Lavine, Thelma Z., "The Motive to Achieve Limited Success: The New Woman Law School Applicant," IN Furniss 1974, 187-191. Original.

2848. Leslie, Larry L., "Updating Education for the Professions: The New Mission," IN Anderson 1976, 237-265. Original.

2849. Levitt, Morton, "That Bouillabaisse: Medical School Admissions," IN Sacks 1978, 239-267. Original.

2850. Lucki, Emil, "Graduate Education in the Next Three Decades," IN Kent 1970, 69-77. Original.

2851. McClothlin, William J., "Insights from One Profession Which May be Applied to Educating for Other Professions," IN Smith 1961, 120-123. Original.

2852. McConnell, T. R., G. Lester Anderson, and Pauline Hunter, "The University and Professional Education," IN Henry 1962, 254-278. Original.

2853. McGrath, Earl J., "The Ideal Education for the Professional Man," IN Henry 1962, 281-301. Original.

2854. Magoun, H. W., "Geographic and Institutional Aspects of Graduate Education and Research," IN Kent 1970, 78-99. Original.

2855. Marlowe, Donald E., "Admissions and the Professional Schools," IN Rich 1963, 104-110. Original.

2856. May, William W., "Changing Patterns of Graduate Education: One Suggested Model," IN Kent 1970, 100-110. Original.

A model Ph.D. program in Urban Studies at the University of Southern California is used to suggest change and innovation in graduate education.

2857. Mayhew, Lewis B., "Problems and Issues in Programs in Higher Education," IN Harcleroad 1974, 37-46. Original.

2858. Miller, George E., "Medicine," IN Henry 1962, 103-119 Original.

2859. Miller, John P., "Outputs of Higher Education: Graduate Education," IN Lawrence 1970, 105-109. Original.

2860. Nelson, Robert L., "Special Problems of Graduate Students in the School of Arts and Sciences," IN Blain 1961, 186-200. Original.

2861. Nichols, Roy F., "Administering Graduate Education," IN Walters 1965, 103-117. Original.

2862. Nowlis, Vincent, "Graduate Student as Teacher," IN Smith 1970, 179-183.

> A summation of a large report by V. Nowlis, Kenneth B. Clark, and Miriam Rock, titled The Graduate Student as Teacher. Washington, D.C.: American Council on Education, 1968.

2863. Onat, Etta S. and Angela S. Moger, "Gladly Would She Learn and Gladly Teach: The Female Graduate Student," IN Sacks 1978, 288-317. Original.

2864. Pellegrino, Edmund D., "Time-Shortening and Medical Education," IN Godwin 1972, 75-83. Original.

2865. Prior, Moody E., "The Doctor of Philosophy Degree," IN Walters 1965, 30-61. Original.

2866. Rees, Mina, "Graduate Education--A Long Look," IN Kent 1970, 139-151. Original.

2867. Rees, Mina, "The Graduate Education of Women," IN Furniss 1974, 178-187. Original.

2868. Ross, Naomi, "Characteristics of Several Current Doctoral Programs and of Members of Association of Professors of Higher Education," IN Harcleroad 1974, 79-83. Original.

2869. Sanford, Nevitt, "Graduate Education, Then and Now," IN Katz 1976, 243-258. Original.

2870. Sigmund, Paul, "Princeton in Crisis and Change," IN Riesman 1973, 249-269. Original.

2871. Smith, David W., "Graduate Education for the Health and Social Service Professions," IN Paulsen 1970, 63-78. Original.

2872. Snell, John L., "The Master's Degree," IN Walters 1965, 74-102. Original.

2873. Springer, George P., "Arltiana," IN Kent 1970, 1-16. Original.

> A conversation with Gustave O. Arlt, Dean Emeritus, Graduate Division, University of California at Los Angeles.

2874. Stevens, Carl M., "Medical Schools and the Market for Physicians' Services," IN Gordon 1974, 503-554. Original.

2875. Stewart, William H., "Health Manpower: An Illustration," IN Mushkin 1962, 47-57. Original.

2876. Thomas, James A., "Heavy Traffic on the Purple Brick Road: The Route to Law School," IN Sacks 1978, 212-238. Original.

2877. Wallach, Aleta, "A View from the Law School," IN Howe 1975, 81-125. Original.

An overview of the response of law schools and the legal profession to greater access for women.

2878. Wallach, Michael A., "Psychology of Talent and Graduate Education," IN Messick 1976, 178-210. Original.

Commentaries by Liam Hudson and Jacquelyn A. Mattfeld follow on pages 211-226.

2879. Walters, Everett, "Graduate Education, 1862-1962," IN Brickman 1962, 124-137. Original.

2880. Walters, Everett, "The Rise of Graduate Education," IN Walters 1965, 1-29. Original.

2881. Walters, Everett, "The Rise of Graduate Education," IN Mayhew 1967, 127-137. GET (1965).

2882. Walton, H. J., "Current Attitudes to Medical Education," IN Butcher 1972, 131-143. Original.

2883. Whitaker, Virgil K., "Graduate Study in the Humanities--Substance and Support," IN Kent 1970, 188-203. Original.

2884. Wilkening, Marvin H., "The Search for Frontiers," IN Kent 1970, 204-210. Original.

The author suggests areas where graduate education may profit by the selection of certain research topics.

23
ADULT AND CONTINUING EDUCATION

2885. Astin, Helen S., "Adult Development and Education," IN Astin 1976, 45-56. Original.

2886. Astin, Helen S., "A Profile of the Women in Continuing Education," IN Astin 1976, 57-88. Original.

2887. Bergevin, Paul, John McKinley, and Robert M. Smith, "The Adult Education Activity: Content, Processes, and Procedures," IN Jensen 1964, 270-289. Original.

2888. Bernard, Jessie, "Women's Continuing Education: Whither Bound?" IN Astin 1976, 109-128. Original.

2889. Carp, Abraham, Richard Peterson, and Pamela Roelfs, "Adult Learning Interests and Experience," IN Cross 1974, 11-52. Original.

2890. Charters, Alexander N., "Pressures on Higher Education for Adult Education Services," IN Smith 1965, 134-137. Original.

2891. Cless, Elizabeth L., "The Birth of an Idea: An Account of the Genesis of Women's Continuing Education," IN Astin 1976, 1-21. Original.

2892. Culbertson, David J., "Corporate Role in Lifelong Learning," IN Vermilye 1974, 29-33. Original.

2893. Essert, Paul L., "Concepts of the Organization and Administration of the Adult Education Enterprise," IN Jensen 1964, 177-200. Original.

2894. Gardner, David P., "What Will the Future Bring?" IN Peltason 1978, 100-106. Original.

An assessment of the potential effects on higher education from the growing trend toward recurrent or lifelong education.

2895. Goldberg, Maxwell H., "Expectations and Responsibilities of Higher Education for the Mature American," IN Smith 1966, 72-77. Original.

2896. Hallenbeck, Wilbur C., "The Role of Adult Education in Society," IN Jensen 1964, 5-25. Original.

2897. Havinghurst, Robert J., "Encouraging Personal Incentive for Higher Education Among Youth from Low-Income Groups," IN Brown 1960, 91-97. Original.

2898. Houle, Cyril O., "The Emergence of Graduate Study in Adult Education," IN Jensen 1964, 69-83. Original.

2899. Jensen, Gale, "How Adult Education Borrows and Reformulates Knowledge of Other Disciplines," IN Jensen 1964, 105-111. Original.

2900. Jensen, Gale, "Social Psychology and Adult Education Practice," IN Jensen 1964, 137-153. Original.

2901. Jones, H. A., "Holes in the Walls: University Adult Education," IN Lawlor 1972, 91-103. Original.

2902. Katz, Joseph, "Home Life of Women in Continuing Education," IN Astin 1976, 89-105. Original.

2903. Keyserling, Mary D., "Continuing Education for Women: A Growing Challenge," IN Smith 1967, 218-222. Original.

2904. Knowles, Malcolm S., "The Field of Operations in Adult Education," IN Jensen 1964, 41-67. Original.

2905. Knowles, Malcolm S., "Teaching-Learning Teams in Adult Education--Boston University," IN Runkel 1969, 254-264. Original.

2906. Leland, Carole, "The Case-Study Programs: Academic Misfits Which Lasted," IN Astin 1976, 23-41. Original.

A review of fifteen case-studies dealing with the development of adult education programs for women.

2907. Liveright, A. A., "Learning Never Ends: A Plan for Continuing Education," IN Eurich 1968, 149-175. Original.

2908. Liveright, A. A., "The Nature and Aims of Adult Education as a Field of Graduate Education," IN Jensen 1964, 85-102. Original.

2909. London, Jack, "The Relevance of the Study of Sociology to Adult Education Practice," IN Jensen 1964, 113-136. Original.

2910. Loring, Rosalind, "Expanding Opportunities Through Continuing Education," IN Furniss 1974, 199-204. Original.

2911. McClusky, Howard Y., "The Relevance of Psychology for Adult Education," IN Jensen 1964, 155-175. Original.

2912. Miller, Harry L., "Adult Education Objectives," IN Jensen 1964, 221-240. Original.

2913. Morris, Glyn, "Encouraging Personal Incentive for Higher Education Among Rural Youth," IN Brown 1960, 98-101. Original.

2914. Nolfi, George J., "The Case for Selective Entitlement Vouchers," IN Vermilye 1976, 130-138. Original.

2915. Nollen, Stanley D., "The Current State of Recurrent Education," IN Vermilye 1977, 65-78. Original.

2916. Plaut, Richard L., "Personal Incentives for Higher Education Among Deprived Groups," IN Brown 1960, 102-122. Original.

2917. Rink, Susan, "The Alchemy of Lifelong Learning," IN Peltason 1978, 106-114. Original.

2918. Spear, George E., "The University and Adult Education," IN Murphy 1975, 181-196. Original.

2919. Thiede, Wilson, "Evaluation and Adult Education," IN Jensen 1964, 291-305. Original.

2920. Thomas, Alan M., "The Concept of Program in Adult Education," IN Jensen 1964, 241-269. Original.

2921. Tress, Ronald C., "The Universities' Alternative in Quaternary Education," IN Stephens 1978, 13-31. Original.

The author, using as an example the situation in Great Britain, suggests that higher education institutions "shift their centre of gravity" toward the adult and away from their traditional reliance on the 18 to 25-year group.

2922. Verner, Coolie, "Definition of Terms," IN Jensen 1964, 27-39. Original.

The author provides definitions for a series of terms and concepts dealing with the study of adult education.

2923. Walton, Wesley W., "New Paths for Adult Learning," IN Cross 1974, 95-115. Original.

2924. Whipple, James B., "The Uses of History for Adult Education," IN Jensen 1964, 201-219. Original.

2925. White, Thurman J., "Adults: From the Wings to Center Stage," IN Furniss 1971, 173-182. Original.

2926. Ziegler, Jerome M., "Continuing Education in the University," IN Morison 1966, 130-151. Dae, 93 (Fall 1964), 1162-1183.

24 ADMISSIONS, ACCESS, AND ACCREDITATION

2927. "The Admissions Story--A CM (College Management) Survey: Misunderstanding, Misinformation, and Mistrust," IN Fitzgerald 1970, 255-262. Col Man, 1 (December 1966), 25-29.

2928. Aisner, Robert S., "The Changing Face of College Admissions," IN Vaccaro 1975, 53-65. Original.

2929. Arbolino, Jack N., "Not the Traditional Student but Almost Everyone Else," IN College 1968, 84-95. Original.

An overview of the College-Level Examination Program (CLEP) and its effect on admissions policies and curriculum.

2930. Astin, Alexander W., "College Admissions: A Systems Perspective," IN Smith 1971, 91-109. Original.

2931. Astin, Alexander W., "Racial Considerations in Admissions," IN Nichols 1970, 113-141. Original.

Commentaries by Cheryl D. Adams, Nicholas Hobbs, Lois D. Rice, and Peter M. Miller follow on pages 142-155.

2932. Astin, Alexander W., "Who Goes Where to College?" IN Yamamoto 1968, 144-160. WGW (1965).

2933. Bender, Wilbur J., "Admission Policies and the Purpose of Liberal Education," IN McGrath 1964, 62-70. Original.

2934. Birenbaum, William M., "Who Should Go To College?" IN Rever 1971, 27-36. Original.

Commentaries by Timothy S. Healy and Robert S. Babcock follow on pages 37-43.

2935. Bolton, Roger E., "Higher Education for Everybody: Who Pays?" IN Furniss 1971, 185-201. Original.

Commentaries by Robert W. Hartman and Frederic W. Ness follow on pages 201-206.

2936. Bowles, Frank, "Preliminary Findings of the International Study of University Admissions," IN Harris 1964, 99-108. Original.

2937. Brennan, Brendan J., "Recruiting in College Admissions," IN Rich 1963, 36-48. Original.

2938. Brookover, Wilbur B., "Selection and Admission Policies and Practices," IN Brookover 1965, 41-57. Original.

2939. Califano Jr., Joseph A., "The Era of Engagement," IN Peltason 1978, 9-15. Original.

Mr. Califano believes that higher education must respond to the need for greater access and to better relationships between colleges and the secondary schools.

2940. Campbell, James M., "The Philosophy of College Admissions. Some Basic General Principles to Be Considered in Admitting and Not Admitting Applicants," IN Rich 1963, 3-12. Original.

2941. Carter Jr., Lisle C., "What Standard for Equal Opportunity?" IN Peltason 1978, 94-99. Original.

2942. Clark, Burton R., "College Image and Student Selection," IN Yamamoto 1968, 178-190. SED (1960).

2943. Clark, Burton R., "The Open Door College," IN Yamamoto 1968, 477-482. ODC (1960).

2944. Cleveland, Harlan, "America's Two Societies," IN Smith 1970, 37-45. Original.

This essay deals with the topics of open-admissions and ethnic studies as they relate to "pride" as a necessary step toward eliminating racial discrimination.

2945. Commager, Henry Steele, "Social, Political, Economic, and Personal Consequences," IN McGrath 1966, 1-18. Original.

A review of the historical and social implications of attempting to achieve universal access to education.

2946. Corey, Arthur F., "Universal Educational Opportunity Beyond the High School," IN Smith 1964, 182-185. Original.

2947. Cox, Archibald, "Harvard College Amicus Curiae De Funis v. Odegaard," IN Gross 1977, 184-197.

A "friends of the court" brief (U.S. Supreme Court, 1973, No. 73-235) that supports the Harvard College approach to minority admissions policy.

2948. Cross, K. Patricia, "The Elusive Goal of Educational Equality," IN Hughes 1975, 191-201. Original.

2949. Dennis, Lawrence E., "Equalizing Educational Opportunity for the Disadvantaged," IN Smith 1964, 186-192. Original.

2950. Dennis, Lawrence E., "Equalizing Educational Opportunity for the Disadvantaged," IN Mayhew 1967, 297-304. Current (1964).

2951. Dickey, Frank G., "Student Assessment in the Accrediting Activity," IN Harcleroad 1971, 43-51. Original.

2952. Doermann, Humphrey, "Lack of Money: A Barrier to Higher Education," IN College 1971, 130-147. Original.

2953. Dominicé, P., "How Open Should the University Be?" IN Stephens 1978, 32-41. Original.

2954. Douglas, William O., "De Funis v. Odegaard, Dissenting Opinion (April 23, 1974)," IN Gross 1977, 198-207.

U.S. Supreme Court, 416 U.S. 312 (1974).

2955. Douvan, Elizabeth and Carol Kaye, "Motivational Factors in College Entrance," IN Sanford 1962, 199-224. Original.

2956. Dragositz, Anna, "Testing: Before Admission," IN Rich 1963, 148-159. Original.

2957. Dugan, Willis E., "Opportunity for All," IN Harcleroad 1970, 45-53. Original.

Commentaries by Leo A. Munday and Allan W. Ostar follow on pages 54-55.

2958. Dupont, Gerald E., "The Superior Student and Admissions," IN Rich 1963, 195-206. Original.

2959. Dyer, Henry S., "Recruiting the Disadvantaged: An Urgent Need," IN College 1968, 96-114. JNE, 36 (Summer 1967), 216-229.

2960. Etzioni, Amitai, "The Policy of Open Admissions," IN Smith 1971, 110-120. Original.

2961. Fitchen, F. C., "Salvaging Professional Accreditation," IN Mauer 1976, 104-110. Original.

2962. Flemming, Arthur S., "Closing the Gap Between the Ideal and Reality," IN Furniss 1971, 279-284. Original.

Why and how the academic community can support the concept of universal access.

2963. Frankel, Charles, "A Plea for Pluralism: A Dissenting Note," IN Hook 1974, 97-98. Original.

Dr. Frankel suggests that the university in America rests on public support, therefore it must respond in some positive form to the demands for universal access.

2964. Furniss, W. Todd, "Educational Programs for Everybody," IN Furniss 1971, 3-18. Original.

Commentaries by Joseph J. Schwab and Douglas M. Knight follow on pages 18-22.

2965. Gross, Mason W., "Issues of Equality and Equity," IN Furniss 1974, 248-260. Original.

2966. Gumbert, Edgar B., "Social Class, Race and Access to Higher Education," IN Holmes 1971, 191-201. Original.

2967. Hammond III, John S., "Bringing Order into the Selection of a College," IN Fitzgerald 1970, 247-254. PGJ, 43 (March 1965), 654-660.

2968. Hanford, George H., "A Look from the Twenty-First Century," IN College 1968, 166-175. Original.

A projection of college admissions policies and administration in the 1980's and beyond.

2969. Hanford, George H., "Testing: Wise Restraints," IN Wilson 1965, 225-227. Original.

An assessment of testing for admission to higher education.

2970. Hansen, W. Lee and David R. Witmer, "Economic Benefits of Universal Higher Education," IN Wilson 1972, 19-39. Original.

Commentaries by Ivar Berg, John D. Millett, and Kermit C. Morrissey follow on pages 39-48.

2971. Härnqvist, Kjell, "Individual Differences in Higher Education: Selection or Adaptation?" IN Verreck 1974, 278-292. Original.

2972. Hausman, Louis, "Pressures, Benefits, and Options," IN Wilson 1972, 1-15. Original.

The author is concerned with two questions: Who wants higher education? and Who profits from it?

2973. Healy, Timothy S., "The CUNY Experience," IN Vermilye 1976, 170-177. Original.

A review of the impact of open admissions on the City University of New York.

2974. Healy, Timothy S., "Open Admissions: Status, Trends, and Implications," IN College 1971, 44-52. Original.

Commentary by John D. Millett follows on pages 53-57.

2975. Heist, Paul and Harold Webster, "A Research Orientation to Selection, Admission and Differential Education," IN Sprague 1960, 21-40. Original.

2976. Henderson, Algo D., "Assessment of Current Trends of Opportunity for Higher Education," IN Brown 1960, 1-16. Original.

2977. Holland, John L., "What Every College President Should Know About Admissions Practices," IN McGrath 1967, 17-23. Original.

2978. Hook, Sidney, "Democracy and Higher Education," IN Hook 1974, 33-40. Original.

Professor Hook provides a operational definition of the construct presented in the phrase "universal higher education."

2979. Howe II, Harold, "How Will More Schooling Affect the High Schools?" IN McGrath 1966, 122-139. Original.

2980. Huckfeldt, Vaughn E., "A Federal Planning Model for Analysis of Accessibility to Higher Education: An Overview," IN Heinlein 1974, 69-89.

This paper was published in 1973 by the National Center for Higher Education Management Systems, Boulder, Colorado.

2981. Jaffe, A. J. and Walter Adams, "Two Models of Open Enrollment," IN Wilson 1972, 223-251. Original.

Commentaries by Werner Z. Hirsch, T. Edward Hollander, and James M. Mitchell follow on pages 251-264.

2982. Johnson, Dennis L., "Impact of Admissions on Financial Stability," IN Jellema 1972, 129-135. Original.

2983. Karabel, Jerome, "Perspectives on Open Admissions," IN Wilson 1972, 265-286. ER, 53 (Winter 1972), 30-44.

2984. Kasper, Daniel M., "Licensure: A Critical View," IN Vermilye 1977, 167-171. Original.

A case study of the problems of accreditation and licensing of professional study and graduates, especially in the area of medical education.

2985. Katz, Joseph, "The Admissions Process--Society's Stake and the Individual's Interest," IN Sacks 1978, 318-347. Original.

2986. Keeton, Morris, "Dilemmas in Accrediting Off-Campus Learning," IN Vermilye 1972, 139-148. Original.

2987. Keniston, Kenneth and Mark Gerzon, "Human and Social Benefits," IN Wilson 1972, 49-74. Original.

Human and social benefits of universal access to higher education are discussed.

Commentaries by G. Homer Durham and Fritz Machlup follow on pages 74-84.

2988. Krongelb, Irving, "The College Admissions Process," IN Siegel 1968, 117-136. Original.

2989. Kuh, George D., "Admissions," IN Packwood 1977, 3-50. Original.

A very thorough overview of the college admissions function with an extensive bibliography.

2990. McHale, Anthony I., "The Way to Improve College Admissions," IN Rich 1963, 207-212. Original.

2991. MacKinnon, Donald W., "Selecting Students with Creative Potential," IN Heist 1968, 101-116. Original.

2992. Machlup, Fritz, "The Illusion of Universal Higher Education," IN Hook 1974, 3-19. Original.

A rejoinder to critical comments on this paper by authors in the first section of the anthology follows on pages 53-57.

2993. Manning, Winton H., "Personal and Institutional Assessment: Alternatives to Tests of Scholastic Aptitude and Achievement in the Admissions Process," IN College 1971, 81-99. Original.

Commentary by Hugh W. Lane follows on pages 100-108.

2994. Marlowe, Donald E., "College-Secondary School Relationships," IN Donovan 1964, 194-199. Original.

2995. Mayer, Martin, "Higher Education for All? The Case of Open Admissions," IN Murphy 1975, 215-239. Comm, 55 (February 1973), 37-47.

2996. Meder Jr., Albert E., "Recent Trends in Accreditation and Their Significance for the Teaching Staff," IN Deferrari 1961, 190-197. Original.

2997. Mednick, Sarnoff A., "Development of Admission Criteria for Colleges and Universities That Will Eliminate Such Applicants as the Bright Nonconformist, the Underchallenged, and the Individual With Highly Specialized Ability," IN Smith 1961, 86-88. Original.

2998. Miller Jr., James L., "Who Needs Higher Education?" IN Furniss 1971, 94-105. Original.

> Commentaries by Bette J. Soldwedel, James S. Smoot, and John K. Folger follow on pages 105-111.

2999. Millett, John D., "Clear Institutional Objectives Essential to Admissions Function," IN College 1968, 52-65. Original.

3000. Moffitt, Joseph M., "The Admissions Process," IN Rich 1963, 13-22. Original.

3001. Monro, John U., "Problems and Responsibilities of Colleges in the Search for Talented Students: Report of a Colloquium," IN Brown 1966, 33-36. Original.

3002. Moon Jr., Rexford G., "Opportunity Must Follow Encouragement," IN Smith 1961, 97-100. Original.

> The author suggests certain general conclusions concerning educational opportunity for disadvantaged groups.

3003. Moon Jr., Rexford G., "Universal Higher Education in the United States: Kind, Access, Substance," IN Smith 1966, 56-59. Original.

3004. Morse, John F., "The Effect of Federal Programs on Admission Policies," IN College 1968, 23-39. Original.

3005. Morse, Wayne L., "Who Should Decide Who Goes to College?" IN Rever 1971, 5-16. Original.

> A commentary by Stephen J. Tonsor follows on pages 17-21.

3006. Moynihan, Daniel P., "On Universal Higher Education," IN Furniss 1971, 233-254. Original.

Commentary by Arthur S. Flemming follows on pages 255-257.

3007. Munday, Leo A. and Philip R. Rever, "Prespectives on Open Admissions," IN Rever 1971, 75-96. Original.

3008. Newcomb, Theodore M., "Campus Environment as a Factor in Admissions," IN College 1968, 126-136. Original.

3009. Newcomb, Theodore M., "Open Admissions: Before the Deluge," IN Rever 1971, 55-62. Original.

A commentary by Edmund W. Gordon on this and the paper by Peter Schrag follows on pages 63-70.

3010. Nickel, James W., "Preferential Policies in Hiring and Admissions: A Jurisprudential Approach," IN Gross 1977, 324-347. Col Law R, 75 (April 1975), 534-558.

3011. Norton, Eleanor H., "In Pursuit of Equality: New Themes and Dissonant Chords," IN Vermilye 1976, 200-211. Original.

3012. Nuñez, Rene, "Recruitment and Admission of Minority Students: The Glaring Reality," IN Altman 1970, 127-140. Original.

3013. Nyquist, Ewald B., "This Orbit of Mine," IN Rich 1963, 49-60.

Reflections of the Deputy Commissioner of Education for the State of New York on the current state of higher education, plus his views on what constitutes a well organized admissions function at a college or university.

3014. "The Objective," IN Mayhew 1967, 97-101. UOEBHS (1964).

Presents both idealistic and practical reasons for ensuring the widest possible opportunity for access to higher education.

3015. O'Neil, Robert M., "Beyond the Threshold: Changing Patterns of Access to Higher Education," IN Furniss 1971, 115-125. Original.

3016. O'Neil, R. M., "The Case for Preferential Admissions," IN Gross 1977, 66-83. DAD (1975).

3017. Pace, C. Robert, "Selective Higher Education for Diverse Students," IN McGrath 1966, 159-173. Original.

3018. Pearson, Richard, "Admission to College," IN McGrath 1966, 140-158. Original.

3019. Pellegrin, Jean-Pierre, "Admission Policies in Post-Secondary Education," IN OECD 1974a, 63-103. Original.

3020. Reagan, Donald J., "Admissions and the Secondary School," IN Rich 1963, 128-147. Original.

3021. Rever, Philip R., "The Dynamics of Admission to the Less-Selective Public and Private-Sector Colleges," IN Sacks 1978, 111-144. Original.

3022. Rogers, Martha P., "The Role of the Equal Employment Opportunity Commission," IN Furniss 1974, 219-223. Original.

3023. Rossi, Henry F., "Automation," IN Rich 1963, 169-176. Original.

> This essay explores the potential for automation of the admissions procedure.

3024. Sacks, Herbert S., "'Bloody Monday' The Crisis of the High School Seniors," IN Sacks 1978, 10-47. Original.

> A case study of the "psychodynamic features of the student and family response to the (college) admission crisis." The students under study were attempting to gain admission to "highly-selective colleges."

3025. Sanford, Charles W., "State Plans for Higher Education and Their Influence on Admissions," IN College 1968, 40-51. Original.

3026. Schrag, Peter, "Open Admissions to What?" IN Rever 1971, 49-53. Original.

3027. Selden, William K., "Accreditation--A Challenge and an Opportunity," IN Donovan 1964, 66-71. Original.

3028. Selden, William K., "Nationwide Standards and Accreditation," IN Wilson 1965, 212-221. Original.

3029. Selden, William K., "Struggles and Tensions in Accreditation of Higher Education," IN Smith 1965, 119-122. Original.

3030. Shimberg, Benjamin S., "Continuing Education and Licensing," IN Vermilye 1977, 154-166. Original.

3031. Silber, John R., "Standards Versus Opportunity: The Unnecessary Conflict," IN Peltason 1978, 81-86. Original.

3032. Sims, Albert G., "On the University, Admissions, and International Education," IN College 1968, 115-125. Original.

3033. Snyder, Rixford K., "Developing Nationwide Standards: Admissions," IN Wilson 1965, 222-224. Original.

3034. Steimel, Raymond J., "Testing: After Admission," IN Rich 1963, 160-168. Original.

3035. Sullivan, Richard H., "Who Should Go to College?" IN Weatherford 1960, 42-56. Original.

3036. Suppes, Patrick, "The Promise of Universal Higher Education," IN Hook 1974, 21-32. Original.

Commentary by Daniel P. Moynihan follows on pages 41-44.

3037. Thresher, B. Alden, "Frozen Assumptions in Admissions," IN College 1968, 9-22. Original.

3038. Thresher, B. Alden, "Uses and Abuses of Scholastic Aptitude and Achievement Tests," IN College 1971, 24-40. Original.

Commentary by Alexander W. Astin follows on pages 41-43.

3039. Tilley, David, "Opening Admissions and the Post-selective Era: A View from the Public Sector," IN Sacks 1978, 76-110. Original.

3040. Trow, Martin, "Admissions and the Crisis in American Higher Education," IN Furniss 1971, 26-52. Original.

Commentaries by Timothy S. Healy, Michael Clear, and A. J. Jaffe follow on pages 52-64.

3041. Trow, Martin, "U.S.A.," IN Archer 1972, 246-280. Dae, 99 (Winter 1970), 1-42.

A version of Dr. Trow's essay titled, "Reflections on the Transition from Mass to Universal Higher Education."

3042. Tyler, Ralph W., "Academic Excellence and Equal Opportunity," IN Harcleroad 1970, 166-183. Original.

3043. Van den Haag, Ernest, "Gresham's Law in Education," IN Hook 1974, 45-49. Original.

The author attributes the greatly increased demand for higher education as the source of many institutional problems.

Commentary by Ernest Nagel follows on pages 51-52.

3044. Volkmann, M. Fredric, "Researching the Market," IN Rowland 1977, 399-407. Original.

The author suggests the use of "market studies" to improve the effectiveness of student recruitment and related activities.

3045. Vroman, Clyde, "Problems and Issues Confronting the Admissions Community," IN College 1968, 1-8. Original.

3046. Wells, Peter, "Applying to College: Bulldog Bibs and Potency Myths," IN Sacks 1978, 48-75. Original.

3047. Wexler, Jacqueline G., "Educating a Whole People," IN Vermilye 1975, 23-29. Original.

President Wexler describes a psychological barrier to educational opportunity embodied in a "hierarchial philosophy" which suggests higher education is only for "the best and the brightest."

3048. Whitla, Dean K., "Candidate Overlap Studies and Other Admissions Research," IN College 1968, 137-165. Original.

3049. Willingham, Warren W., "Educational Opportunity and the Organization of Higher Education," IN College 1971, 1-23. Original.

3050. Willingham, Warren W., "Free-Access Colleges: Where They Are and Whom They Serve," IN Murphy 1975, 197-213. CBR, 76 (Summer 1970), 6-14.

3051. Wilson, Logan, "Alternatives to College for Everybody," IN Furniss 1971, 168-172. Original.

3052. Zimmerman, Marvin, "Equality and Quality in Education," IN Hook 1974, 229-232. Original.

25
MINORITIES AND WOMEN

3053. Adler, Nancy E., "Women Students," IN Katz 1976, 197-225. Original.

3054. American Council of Education, "Historical Notes on the American Council of Education's Involvement with the Concerns of Women in Higher Education," IN Astin 1976, 139-145. Original.

3055. Amprey Jr., Joseph L., "A New Black Coalition," IN Johnson 1974, 335-352. Original.

A sociological analysis of the attempt to provide black Americans with access to greater social and economic mobility.

3056. Angell, George W. and Edward P. Kelley, Jr., "Avoiding Discrimination Problems," IN Angell 1977, 294-309. Original.

3057. Apter, Julia T., "Increasing the Professional Visability of Women in Academe: A Case Study," IN Furniss 1974, 104-109. Original.

3058. Astin, Alexander W., "The Undergraduate Woman," IN Astin 1978, 95-112. Original.

A comprehensive profile of the undergraduate woman.

3059. Astin, Helen S., "Career Profiles of Women Doctorates," IN Rossi 1973, 139-161. Original.

3060. Astin, Helen S., "Where Are All the Talented Women?" IN Furniss 1974, 95-99. Original.

3061. Astin, Helen S. and Alan E. Bayer, "Sex Discrimination in Academe," IN Rossi 1973, 333-356. Original.

3062. Barasch, F. K., "HEW, The University, and Women," IN Gross 1977, 54-65. Dissent, 20 (Summer 1973), 332-339.

3063. Bar-Yosef, Rivka W., "What Kind of Equality for Women?" IN Bailey 1977, 143-155. Original.

3064. Bayles, Michael D., "Reparations to Wronged Groups," IN Gross 1977, 303-305. Analysis, 33 (June 1973), 182-184.

3065. Beach, Ruth, "A Case History of Affirmative Action," IN Wasserman 1975, 128-138. Original.

3066. Bernstein, Alison R., "Pluralism: Myths and Realities," IN Vermilye 1973, 131-141. Original.

Case studies of how two schools (Vassar and Staten Island Community College) responded to the concept of pluralism.

3067. Binger, Carl A. L., "Emotional Disturbances Among College Women," IN Blain 1961, 172-185. Original.

3068. Birenbaum, William M., "White Power and American Higher Education," IN Altman 1970, 3-17. Original.

3069. Bittker, Boris, "Identifying the Beneficiaries," IN Gross 1977, 279-287. CFBR (1973).

The author presents various rationale for determining who should qualify for benefits in the case where social and economic injustice has been identified and reparations are demanded.

3070. Blackwell, Gordon W., "The College and the Continuing Education of Women," IN Dennis 1963, 72-91. Original.

3071. Bond, Horace Mann, "A Century of Negro Higher Education," IN Brickman 1962, 182-196. Original.

3072. Bond, Julian, "We Hold These Truths," IN Nichols 1970, 10-15. Original.

Mr. Bond presents what the higher education community should do to eliminate race as an issue on the college campus.

3073. Bowles, Frank H., "The Dual Purpose Revolution," IN Smith 1966, 17-23. Original.

By increasing opportunity of access to higher education we accommodate more students, create new types of programs, and help to abolish poverty and improve racial problems. The motivation for this change is humanistic, but at the same time addresses serious economic issues.

3074. Bowles, Frank H., "Next Steps in Encouraging Personal Incentive Among Talented but Disadvantaged Youth," IN Brown 1966, 153-162. Original.

3075. Boxhill, Bernard, "The Morality of Reparation," IN Gross 1977, 270-278. Soc Th P, 2 (Spring 1972), 113-124.

The essay discusses both the justification for and the aims of reparation and compensation for social injustice and how they fit into a general theory of justice.

3076. Bracy Jr., Randolph, "Compensatory Educational Programs: Is There a Place in Higher Education?" IN Johnson 1974, 277-284. Original.

3077. Branson, Herman R., "Black Colleges of the North," IN Willie 1978, 149-154. Original.

3078. Brown, Janet Welsh, "Professional Development for Women," IN Vermilye 1976, 87-96. Original.

3079. Browning, Jane E. Smith and John B. Williams, "History and Goals of Black Institutions of Higher Learning," IN Willie 1978, 68-93. Original.

3080. Bruce, Beverlee, "A Philosophical Base for Minority Education," IN Altman 1970, 19-29. Original.

3081. Bundy, McGeorge, "'Justice as Fairness?' Between Men and Women," IN Furniss 1974, 237-247. Original.

3082. Bunting, Mary I., "Creating Opportunities for Women in Science," IN Wasserman 1975, 115-119. Original.

3083. Butler, Broadus N., "Pressures on Higher Education for the Education of Disadvantaged Groups," IN Smith 1965, 130-133. Original.

3084. Cambridge, Charlie, "The American Indian and the White Campus," IN Altman 1970, 79-81. Original.

3085. Campbell, Jean W., "Women Drop Back In: Educational Innovation in the Sixties," IN Rossi 1973, 93-124. Original.

3086. Carroll, Constance M., "Three's a Crowd: The Dilemma of the Black Woman in Higher Education," IN Rossi 1973, 173-185. Original.

3087. Cervantes, Frank D., "Chicanos and the Economic Problem of a College Education," IN College 1970, 22-23. Original.

3088. Chalmers, Hani, "The Psychology of Women: Implications for Interpersonal Relationships," IN De Coster 1974, 135-148. Original.

3089. Cheek Jr., King V., "The Black College in a Multiracial Society," IN Vermilye 1972, 67-77. Original.

3090. Chisholm, Shirley, "Of Course Women Dare," IN Vermilye 1972, 41-48. Original.

3091. Clark, Burton R., "The Wesleyan Story: The Importance of Moral Capital," IN Riesman 1973, 367-381. Original.

Recounts the story of black-white student confrontation and of the institutional reaction within a historical context of strong institutional "character."

3092. Clark, Kenneth B., "The Invisible Wall," IN Mayhew 1967, 19-27. DG (1965).

An essay on the social, economic, and educational consequences of urban ghettos.

3093. Cook, Alice H., "Sex Discrimination at Universities: An Ombudsman's View," IN Wasserman 1975, 120-127. AAUPB, 58 (September 1972), 279-282.

3094. Cook, Samuel Du Bois, "The Socio-Ethical Role and Responsibility of the Black-College Graduate," IN Willie 1978, 51-67. Original.

3095. Cowan, L. J., "Inverse Discrimination," IN Gross 1977, 291-293. Analysis, 33 (October 1973), 10-12.

3096. Cross, K. Patricia, "The Woman Student," IN Furniss 1974, 29-50. Original.

Commentary by Joan I. Roberts follows on pages 50-55.

3097. Doermann, Humphrey, "Financial Aid for Disadvantaged Students in Private Universities," IN College 1970, 24-32. Original.

3098. Duncan, Birt L., "Minority Students," IN Katz 1976, 227-242. Original.

3099. Egerton, John, "The White Sea of Higher Education," IN Altman 1970, 35-41. Original.

Mr. Egerton indicates some of the major reasons why non-whites do no enter higher education in the same proportions as whites.

3100. Ely, John H., "The Constitutionality of Reverse Racial Discrimination," IN Gross 1977, 208-216. U Chic Law R, 41 (Summer 1974), 723-741.

3101. Farmer, James, "To Be Black and American," IN Caffrey 1969, 191-201. Original.

3102. Fields, Carl A., "Black Students in a White University," IN College 1970, 33-37. Original.

3103. Fleming, Robben W., "The Implementation of Affirmative Action Programs," IN Furniss 1974, 224-228. Original.

3104. Freedom, Richard, "The Implications of the Changing Labor Market for Members of Minority Groups," IN Gordon 1974, 83-109. BE (1976).

3105. Freeman, Bonnie C., "Faculty Women in the American University: Up the Down Staircase," IN Altbach 1977, 166-190. HE, 6 (May 1977), 165-188.

3106. Freeman, Jo, "Women on the Move: The Roots of Revolt," IN Rossi 1973, 1-32. Original.

3107. Fuller, Ann L., "Liberating the Administrator's Wife," IN Furniss 1974, 145-152. Original.

3108. Fulton, Oliver, "Rewards and Fairness: Academic Women in the United States," IN Trow 1975, 199-248. Original.

3109. Furniss, W. Todd, "Racial Minorities and Curriculum Change," IN Nichols 1970, 69-85. Original.

Commentaries by Lawrence C. Howard, Robert A. Malson, and John U. Monro follow on pages 86-95.

3110. Gardner, Jo Ann Evans, "The Feminist Movement," IN Smith 1970, 46-53. Original.

3111. Gartner, Alan P., "Credentialing the Disenfranchised," IN Keeton 1976, 34-40. Original.

3112. Gary, Lawrence E. and Lee P. Brown, "Educating Blacks for the 1970's: The Role of Black Colleges," IN Johnson 1974, 371-390. Original.

3113. Gates Jr., Henry-Louis, "They Think You're an Airplane, but You're Really a Bird: The Education of an Afro-American," IN Sacks 1978, 193-211. Original.

3114. Glazer, Nathan, "The Emergence of an American Ethnic Pattern," IN Gross 1977, 132-155. ADEI (1975).

3115. Godard, James M., "Opportunity for the 'Culturally Distinct' Student," IN Smith 1969, 74-77. Original.

3116. Goldman, Alan H., "Reparations to Individuals or Groups?" IN Gross 1977, 321-323. Analysis, 35 (April 1975), 168-170.

3117. Gomez, Anna N., "A Chicano Student's Perspective of the White Campus," IN Altman 1970, 75-78. Original.

3118. Gordon, Edmund W., "The Culturally Different, Deprived or Economically Marginal Student: A Challenge to Education," IN Mayhew 1967, 363-381. Original.

3119. Gordon, Edmund W., "Programs and Practices for Minority Group Youth in Higher Education," IN College 1971, 109-126. Original.

Commentary by Edmund W. Gordon follows on pages 127-129.

3120. Gordon, Edmund W., "Programs and Practices for Minority Group Youth in Higher Education," IN Solmon 1973, 251-268. College Board (1971).

3121. Graham, Patricia Albjerg, "Status Transitions of Women Students, Faculty, and Administrators," IN Rossi 1973, 163-172. Original.

3122. Gross, Barry R., "Is Turn About Fair Play?" IN Gross 1977, 379-387. J Crit A, 5 (January-April 1975), 126-135.

Mr. Gross presents four interrelated series of reasons that suggest reverse discrimination is not justified.

3123. Hamilton, Charles V., "Minority Groups," IN Connery 1970, 15-27. Original.

3124. Harcleroad, Fred F., "Disadvantaged Students and Survival in College," IN Smith 1971, 138-148. Original.

3125. Harris, Patricia R., "Problems and Solutions in Achieving Equality for Women," IN Furniss 1974, 11-26. Original.

3126. Haubrich, Vernon F., "Education of Teachers for the Disadvantaged," IN Paulsen 1970, 17-39. Original.

3127. Hembrough, Betty L., "A Twofold Educational Challenge: The Student Wife and the Mature Woman Student," IN Fitzgerald 1970, 340-344. JNAWDC, 29 (Summer 1966), 163-167.

3128. Hesburgh, Theodore M., "Civil Rights and the Women's Movement," IN Astin 1978, 172-180. Original.

3129. Hirshleifer, Jack, "A Dangerous Precedent," IN Hook 1974, 251-252. Original.

Mr. Hirshleifer attacks the use of "quotas" as part of affirmative action programs.

3130. Hochschield, Arlie R., "Inside the Clockwork of Male Careers," IN Howe 1975, 47-80. Original.

3131. Hodgkinson, Harold L., "Subordination Squared--The Minority Student," IN Altman 1970, 51-58. Original.

3132. Hoffman, Robert, "Justice, Merit, and the Good," IN Gross 1977, 358-372. Original.

3133. Hook, Sidney, "The Bias in Anti-Bias Regulation," IN Gross 1977, 88-96. Measure, 14 (October 1971).

3134. Hook, Sidney, "Discrimination, Color Blindness, and the Quota System," IN Gross 1977, 84-87. Measure, 30 (November 1974).

3135. Hoover, Robert, "Meeting Community Needs," IN Altman 1970, 189-197. Original.

> A case study of the development of the "Nairobi schools" in East Palo Alto, California. The "Nairobi schools" were created to meet the special needs of the black community in East Palo Alto.

3136. Hornig, Lili S., "Affirmative Action Through Affirmative Attitudes," IN Wasserman 1975, 8-19. Original.

3137. Howard, Lawrence C., "Black Consciousness and Identity Crisis," IN Hodgkinson 1971a, 177-207. Original.

3138. Howe, Florence, "Women and the Power to Change," IN Howe 1975, 127-171. Original.

3139. Howe, Florence and Carol Ahlum, "Women's Studies and Social Change," IN Rossi 1973, 393-423. Original.

3140. Huber, Joan, "From Sugar and Spice to Professor," IN Rossi 1973, 125-135. Original.

3141. Hurst Jr., Charles G., "Pluralism and Peace on Campus," IN Altman 1970, 203-218. Original.

3142. Johnson, Roosevelt, "Compensatory Programs for Blacks: A Study," IN Johnson 1974, 257-275. Original.

3143. Johnson, Roosevelt, "Higher Education, Black Inmates and Corrections," IN Johnson 1974, 315-321. Original.

3144. Johnson, Roosevelt, "Special Programs: The Need for a Concept and Commitment, Not a Name!" IN Johnson 1974, 285-291. Original.

3145. Johnson, Roosevelt, "Vignettes on White Academia," IN Johnson 1974, 1-34. Original.

> A series of five brief essays on various aspects of the problems faced by black faculty and students at predominantly white institutions of higher education.

3146. Jones, Hardy E., "On the Justifiability of Reverse Discrimination," IN Gross 1977, 348-357. Original.

3147. Jones, J. B., "Minority Student Concerns and Cross-Cultural Relationships," IN De Coster 1974, 117-134. Original.

3148. Jones, Mack H., "The Responsibility of the Black College to the Black Community," IN Solmon 1973, 239-250. Dae, 100 (Summer 1971), 732-744.

3149. Kaplan, Susan Romer, "Women's Education: The Case for the Single-Sex College," IN Astin 1978, 53-67. Original.

3150. Kaurouma, Yusuf, "Right On! . . . Where? Historical Contradictions of the Black Student Movement," IN Altman 1970, 63-73. Original.

3151. Kendrick, S. A., "Minority Students on Campus," IN Altman 1970, 43-50. Original.

3152. Klotzburger, Katherine M., "Advisory Committee Role in Constructing Affirmative Action Programs," IN Furniss 1974, 229-233. Original.

3153. Klotzburger, Kay, "Political Action by Academic Women," IN Rossi 1973, 359-392. Original.

3154. Kreps, Junita M., "The Woman Professional in Higher Education," IN Furniss 1974, 75-94. Original.

3155. Lavell, Martha, "A New Partnership for Social Change: The Urban University and Suburban Women," IN Mitchell 1974, 87-105. Original.

3156. Leibowitz, Arleen, "Education and the Allocation of Women's Time," IN Juster 1975, 171-197. Original.

3157. Lewis, W. Arthur, "Black Power and the American University," IN Nichols 1970, 16-27. Univ, (Spring 1969), 8-12.

3158. Loeb, Jane W. and Marianne A. Ferber, "Representation, Performance and Status of Women on the Faculty at the Urbana-Champaign Campus of the University of Illinois," IN Rossi 1973, 239-254. Original.

3159. McClellan, Frank, "A Black Student's Reaction to the Present System of Financial Aid," IN College 1970, 16-19. Original.

3160. McKinney Jr., T. E., "The Black Revolt and the Student Revolt in Perspective," IN Nichols 1970, 293-295. Original.

3161. McPherson, James M., "The New Puritanism: Values and Goals of Freedmen's Education in America," IN Stone II 1974, 611-642. Original.

3162. Martin, Warren B., "Equality and Quality: An Introduction," IN Vermilye 1976, 1-7. Original.

3163. Mays, Benjamin E., "The Black College in Higher Education," IN Willie 1978, 19-28. Original.

3164. Merry, Margaret H., "Pilot Projects for Continuing Education for Women," IN Dennis 1963, 92-124. Original.

3165. Miner, Anne S., "Affirmative Action at Stanford University," IN Wasserman 1975, 139-162. Original.

Ms. Miner provides an introduction to the Stanford University affirmative action plan.

3166. Monro, John, "Teaching in a Black College," IN Smith 1971, 27-33. Original.

3167. Monsour, Karen J., "Education and a Woman's Life," IN Dennis 1963, 9-28. Original.

3168. Moore Jr., William, "Opportunity for the Disadvantaged," IN Smith 1968, 232-238. Original.

3169. Morlock, Laura, "Discipline Variation in the Status of Academic Women," IN Rossi 1973, 255-312. Original.

3170. Naughton, Ezra A., "What You See Is What You Get: Black Student/White Campus," IN Vermilye 1972, 49-66. Original.

3171. Neuman, Rebecca R., "The Educational Needs of Women," IN Yamamoto 1968, 470-476. JCP, 10 (Winter 1963), 378-383.

3172. Newton, Lisa H., "Reverse Discrimination as Unjustified," IN Gross 1977, 373-378. Ethics, 83 (July 1973), 308-312.

3173. Nickel, James W., "Discrimination and Morally Relevant Characteristics," IN Gross 1977, 288-290. Analysis, 32 (March 1972), 113-114.

3174. Nickel, James W., "Should Reparations Be to Individuals or to Groups?" IN Gross 1977, 314-320. Analysis, 34 (April 1974), 154-160.

3175. Nisbet, Lee, "Affirmative Action--A Liberal Program?" IN Gross 1977, 50-53. Original.

3176. Nunn III, William A., "Reverse Discrimination," IN Gross 1977, 306-309. Analysis, 34 (April 1974), 151-154.

3177. Oltman, Ruth M., "Women in Higher Education," IN Smith 1971, 129-137. Original.

3178. O'Neil, Robert M., "Beyond Title IX: Nondiscrimination Is Not Equality," IN Bailey 1977, 155-159. Original.

3179. Orbell, John M., "Protest Participation Among Souther Negro College Students," IN Feldman 1972, 409-426. APSR, 61 (June 1967), 446-456.

3180. Park, Rosemary, "Some Considerations on the Higher Education of Women," IN Astin 1978, 3-28. Original.

An excellent historical and social survey of the higher education of women.

3181. Patterson, Michelle, "Sex and Specialization in Academe and the Professions," IN Rossi 1973, 313-331. Original.

3182. Patterson, Michelle, "Some Limitations of Traditional Research on the Benefits of Higher Education: The Case of Women," IN Solmon 1973, 225-230. Original.

3183. Patterson, Michelle and Lucy Sells, "Women Dropouts from Higher Education," IN Rossi 1973, 79-91. Original.

3184. Peterson, Esther, "Needs and Opportunities in Our Society for the Educated Woman," IN Dennis 1963, 51-71. Original.

3185. Peterson, Martha E., "Women, Autonomy, and Accountability in Higher Education," IN Furniss 1974, 3-10. Original.

3186. Pifer, Alan and Avery Russell, "Responsibility and Public Policy: Is It a Moral Question," IN Astin 1978, 166-171. Original.

A review of the concept of equality as a factor in public policy dealing with women in higher education.

3187. Platt, Gerald M., "Financial Support of Higher Education So That the Poor May Learn," IN Solmon 1973, 341-349. Original.

3188. Pottinger, J. Stanley, "Race, Sex, and Jobs: The Drive Toward Equality," IN Wasserman 1975, 37-44. Change, 4 (October 1972), 24; 26-29.

3189. Pottinger, J. Stanley, "Race, Sex, and Jobs: The Drive Toward Equality," IN Gross 1977, 41-49. Change, 4 (October 1972), 24; 26-29.

3190. Proctor, Samuel D., "Land-Grant Universities and the Black Presence," IN Anderson 1976, 190-204. Original.

3191. Proctor, Samuel D., "Racial Pressures on Urban Institutions," IN Nichols 1970, 43-58. Original.

Commentaries by William R. Keast, Gwendolyn P. Woods, Charles D. Gelatt, and Norvel L. Smith follow on pages 59-68.

3192. Quidachay, Ronald, "The Hostile College Environment: An Asian-American Student's View," IN Altman 1970, 83-86. Original.

3193. Ralston, Richard D., "An Endangered Species: Black Students at White Universities," IN Johnson 1974, 221-239. Original.

3194. Rich, Adrienne, "Toward a Woman-Centered University," IN Howe 1975, 15-46. Original.

3195. Risco-Lozada, Eliezer, "The Communication Gap," IN Altman 1970, 107-115. Original.

This essay outlines what the author believes minority students are asking of college administrators and faculty in order to achieve a "relevant" education.

3196. Rivlin, Alice M., "Equality of Opportunity and Public Policy," IN College 1970, 6-11. Original.

3197. Roberts, Virgil, "Minority Interests in Value Change and Power Conflict," IN Minter 1969, 99-112. Original.

3198. Robinson, Lora H., "Institutional Variation in the Status of Academic Women," IN Rossi 1973, 199-238. Original.

3199. Roby, Pamela, "Institutional Barriers to Women Students in Higher Education," IN Rossi 1973, 37-56. Original.

3200. Rosenblatt, Louise, "The Importance of a Positive Appeal," IN Hook 1974, 257-258. Original.

This essay draws our attention to the problem among liberals on the proper course of action to take in cases of discrimination.

3201. Rosner, James M., "Higher Education and the Black American: An Overview," IN Johnson 1974, 241-255. Original.

3202. Ross, Dorothy, "A Modest Beginning and a Modest Proposal," IN Furniss 1974, 99-104. Original.

A case study of the development of a "talent pool" for women historians within the American Historical Association.

3203. Rothwell, C. Easton, "The Milieu of the Educated Woman," IN Dennis 1963, 29-50. Original.

3204. Rumbarger, Margaret L., "The Great Quota Debate and Other Issues in Affirmative Action," IN Furniss 1974, 207-214. Original.

3205. Rumbarger, Margaret L., "Internal Remedies for Sex Discrimination in College and Universities," IN Rossi 1973, 425-438. Original.

3206. Sack, Saul, "The Higher Education of Women, 1862-1962," IN Brickman 1962, 166-181. Original.

3207. Sandler, Bernice, "Equal Employment Opportunity on the Campus," IN Vladeck 1975, 333-355. Original.

3208. Sandler, Bernice, "Equity for Women in Higher Education," IN Vermilye 1972, 78-92. Original.

3209. Sandler, Bernice, "A Little Help from Our Government: WEAL (Women's Equal Action League) and Contract Compliance," IN Rossi 1973, 439-462. Original.

3210. Schleman, Helen B., "How is the Education of Women Different from the Education of Men?" IN Smith 1964, 80-82. Original.

3211. Schwartz, Pepper and Janet Lever, "Women in the Male World of Higher Education," IN Rossi 1973, 57-77. Original.

3212. Scott, Elizabeth L., "Developing Criteria and Measures of Equal Opportunities for Women," IN Wasserman 1975, 82-114. Original.

3213. Shepherd, Robert E., "Student Support and the Black Student," IN Keene 1975, 170-176. Original.

3214. Shiner, Roger A., "Individuals, Groups and Inverse Discrimination," IN Gross 1977, 310-313. Analysis, 33 (June 1973), 185-187.

3215. Sill, E. R., "Shall Women Go to College?" IN Portman 1972, 163-173. Cent Mag, 32 (June 1886), 323-326.

3216. Silvestri, Philip, "The Justification of Inverse Discrimination," IN Gross 1977, 294-295. Analysis, 34 (October 1973), 31.

3217. Singletary, Otis A., "Obligations and Services of Higher Education to the Disadvantaged and Underprivileged," IN Smith 1966, 78-81. Original.

3218. Smythe, Mabel M., "Feminism and Black Liberation," IN Furniss 1974, 279-281. Original.

3219. Sowell, Thomas, "'Affirmative Action' Reconsidered," IN Gross 1977, 113-131. PI, 42 (Winter 1976), 47-65.

3220. Stanley, Julian C., "Predicting College Success of Educationally Disadvantaged Students," IN College 1971, 58-77. Original.

Commentary by Kenneth B. Clark follows on pages 78-80.

3221. Stimpson, Catharine R., "Conflict, Probable; Coalition, Possible: Feminism and the Black Movement," IN Furniss 1974, 261-278. Original.

3222. Stowe, Harriet B., "The Education of Freedmen," IN Portman 1972, 175-191. NAR, 129 (July 1879), 81-94.

3223. Taylor, Paul W., "Reverse Discrimination and Compensatory Justice," IN Gross 1977, 296-302. Analysis, 33 (June 1973), 177-182.

3224. Thomas, Gerald E., "Resocialization of the Black Student Within a New Permissive Education System?" IN Johnson 1974, 45-63. Original.

3225. Thompson, Daniel C., "Black College Faculty and Students: The Nature of Their Interaction," IN Willie 1978, 180-194. Original.

3226. Thorne, Alison C., "Women and Higher Education," IN Paulsen 1970, 137-156. Original.

3227. Tidball, M. Elizabeth, "Equality and Success," IN Vermilye 1976, 192-199. Original.

> America's system of higher education gains its strength from diversity. This strength can be enhanced by new resolve in support of women faculty in the profession of teaching.

3228. Tinker, Irene, "Federal City College: How Black?" IN Riesman 1973, 99-126. Original.

3229. Truax, Anne T., "Maternity Leave Policies," IN Furniss 1974, 137-139. Original.

3230. Truman, David B., "The Women's Movement and the Women's College," IN Furniss 1974, 56-60. Original.

3231. Useem, Ruth H., "What Does Society Expect Higher Education to Do for Women: Who Knows and Who Cares?" IN Smith 1966, 136-140. Original.

3232. Wallin, Janet L., "Compliance With Federal Legislation Relating to Discrimination on the Basis of Sex and Race," IN Peterson 1977, 103-133. Original.

3233. Ward, Paul L., "Women's Share in College Enrollments," IN Smith 1965, 138-140. Original.

3234. Weitzman, Lenore J., "Affirmative Action Plans for Eliminating Sex Discrimination in Academe," IN Rossi 1973, 463-504. Original.

3235. Willie, Charles V., "Perspectives on Black Education and the Education of Blacks," IN Solmon 1973, 231-238. Original.

3236. Willie, Charles V., "Racism, Black Education and the Sociology of Knowledge," IN Willie 1978, 3-13. Original.

3237. Willie, Charles V., "Uniting Method and Purpose in Higher Education," IN Willie 1978, 263-270. Original.

An excellent and concise statement concerning the nature and goals of black colleges and how they fit into the scheme of American culture.

3238. Wilson, Logan, "Merit and Equality in Higher Education," IN Nichols 1970, 28-40. Original.

3239. Wilson, O. Meredith, "A Woman Is a Woman Is a Woman . . .," IN Dennis 1963, 1-8. Original.

President Wilson's thesis is that society needs to discover better ways to utilize the talents of women to improve culture and civilization.

3240. Windham, Thomas L., "The Black Student on the College Campus," IN Bloom 1975, 77-95. Original.

3241. Wisdom, Paul E. and Kenneth A. Shaw, "Black Challenge to Higher Education," IN Nichols 1970, 96-109. ER, 50 (Fall 1969), 351-359.

3242. Wright Jr., Nathan, "Serving Black Students: For What?" IN Johnson 1974, 35-44. Original.

3243. Young Jr., Whitney M., "Civil Rights--A Challenge to Higher Education," IN Smith 1965, 23-32. Original.

26
COUNSELING AND OTHER SPECIAL SERVICES

3244. Adams, Frank C., "Administering the Office of Student Work and Financial Assistance," IN Keene 1975, 214-228. Original.

3245. American College Health Association, "Recommended Standards and Practices for a College Health Program," IN Fitzgerald 1970, 305-313. Stu M, 10 (September 1961), 33-44.

3246. American Personnel and Guidance Association, "Ethnic Standards," IN Fitzgerald 1970, 390-397. PGJ, 40 (October 1961), 206-209.

3247. Baker, Roberta, "Placement Counseling," IN Siegel 1968, 189-212. Original.

3248. Baker, William, "The Financial Aid Office and Minority Students," IN Altman 1970, 149-154. Original.

3249. Banning, James H., "Improving Mental Health Services on Western Campuses--A Regional Action Program," IN Bloom 1975, 197-207. Original.

3250. Berdie, Ralph F., "Student Personnel Work: Definition and Redefinition," IN Fitzgerald 1970, 11-18. JCSP, 7 (May 1966), 131-136.

3251. Berrick, Myron E., "General, Academic, and Preprofessional Counseling," IN Siegel 1968, 137-152. Original.

3252. Berry, Jane B., "Women: Clients and Counselors," IN Warnath 1973, 173-190. Original.

3253. Blaska, Betty and Marlin R. Schmidt, "Placement," IN Packwood 1977, 368-421. Original.

A thorough history and overview of the college advising and placement function with an extensive bibliography.

3254. Bowman, Alden E., "The Financial Aid Counselor--A True Educator," IN Keene 1975, 276-283. Original.

3255. Brown, Richard A., "Counseling Blacks: Abstraction and Reality," IN Warnath 1973, 163-172. Original.

3256. Brown, William F. and Vernon G. Zunker, "Student Counselor Utilization at Four-Year Institutions of Higher Learning," IN Fitzgerald 1970, 297-304. JCSP, 7 (January 1966), 41-46.

3257. Canizales, Frank, "Orientation and Counseling Services for Minority Students," IN Altman 1970, 141-147. Original.

3258. Conley, William H., "Faculty Contributions to the Student Personnel Program," IN Donovan 1962, 98-107. Original.

3259. Conley, William H., "Role of the Individual Student in the Personnel Program," IN Donovan 1962, 108-114. Original.

3260. Cook, Patrick E., John Kalafat, and Mary Tyler, "Development of a Campus Telephone Counseling Service," IN Bloom 1975, 231-244. Original.

3261. Crowley, W. H., "Reflections of a Troublesome but Hopeful Rip Van Winkle," IN Fitzgerald 1970, 24-32. JCSP, 6 (December 1964), 66-73.

An overview of the important developments in student personnel work since the 1930's.

3262. Dannells, Michael and George D. Kuh, "Orientation," IN Packwood 1977, 102-124. Original.

A very thorough overview of freshmen orientation programs with an extensive bibliography.

3263. Davenport, Lawrence F., "Mandamus for Change in Student Services," IN Johnson 1974, 323-334. Original.

This essay deals with the opportunity and access to higher education for blacks, plus the need for counseling and other personnel services.

3264. Donovan, George F., "Meaning and Aims of the College and University Student Personnel Program," IN Donovan 1962, 3-18. Original.

3265. Dragositz, Anna, "Tests and Measurements in the Student Personnel Program," IN Donovan 1962, 182-196. Original.

3266. Evans, Wilson A., "Supervisors of Student Workers as Teachers," IN Keene 1975, 284-293. Original.

3267. Farnsworth, Dana L. and Preston K. Munter, "The Role of the College Psychiatrist," IN Blain 1961, 1-16. Original.

3268. Fawcett Jr., John R. and Jack E. Campbell, "New Dimensions in Junior College Student Personnel Administration," IN Herron 1970, 179-208. Original.

3269. Fishman, Joshua A., "Some Social-Psychological Theory for Selecting and Guiding College Students," IN Sanford 1962, 666-689. Original.

3270. Fitzgerald, Laurine E., "Faculty Perceptions of Student Personnel Functions," IN Fitzgerald 1970, 159-170. JCSP, 3 (June 1962), 169-179.

3271. Fitzpatrick, Richard, "The History of College Counseling," IN Siegel 1968, 3-14. Original.

3272. Fley, Jo Ann, "Changing Approaches to Discipline in Student Personnel Work," IN Fitzgerald 1970, 83-91. JNAWDC, 27 (Spring 1964), 105-113.

3273. Frankel, Ruth R., "Health Services Counseling," IN Siegel 1968, 301-324. Original.

3274. Garrett, Thomas A., "Organization of Student Personnel Services in Higher Education," IN Donovan 1962, 117-128. Original.

3275. Glick, G. Wayne, "Student Services," IN Jellema 1972, 93-103. Original.

3276. Gometz, Lynn and Clyde A. Parker, "Disciplinary Counseling: A Contradiction?" IN Fitzgerald 1970, 100-107. PGJ, 46 (January 1968), 437-443.

3277. Greenleaf, Elizabeth A., "The Role of Student Staff Members," IN De Coster 1974, 181-194. Original.

An excellent essay on the role, growth, and development of residence hall staff.

3278. Gruen, Richard E., "The Counseling Interview," IN Siegel 1968, 45-76. Original.

3279. Gruen, Richard E., "Vocational Career Planning," IN Siegel 1968, 215-239. Original.

3280. Halleck, Seymour, "Counselor as Double Agent," IN Warnath 1973, 82-93. Original.

3281. Harmon, Lenore W., "Credibility and the Counseling Center," IN Warnath 1973, 94-105. Original.

3282. Heist, Paul A., "Advising and Counseling--One Approach to Student's Problems," IN Smith 1966, 175-179. Original.

3283. Herron Jr., Orley R., "New Dimensions: An Overview," IN Herron 1970, 1-20. Original.

A comprehensive overview of the major issues and trends in student personnel services for the 1970's.

3284. Hills, David A., "A Small Center in the Blind," IN Warnath 1973, 227-243. Original.

A case study of the counseling center at Wake Forest University and its adjustment to the changes in student interests and demands during the late 1960's.

3285. Hocking, Thomas K., "A Center Survives a Crisis," IN Warnath 1973, 244-258. Original.

A case study of the student personnel unit at the University of Wisconsin at Oshkosh and its adjustments to declining enrollment and a "host of political and economic difficulties."

3286. Hopwood, Kathryn L., "Re-evaluation of Programs of Student Services in the Light of Social and Academic Changes," IN Smith 1962, 185-188. Original.

3287. Horowitz, Murray M., "The Teacher and the Counselor," IN Siegel 1968, 375-384. Original.

3288. Houtz, Patricia, "Internships in Student Personnel Programs," IN Fitzgerald 1970, 42-48. JCSP, 8 (September 1967), 322-326.

3289. Hoyt, Donald P. and James J. Rhatigan, "Professional Preparation of Junior and Senior College Student Personnel Administrators," IN Fitzgerald 1970, 33-42. PGJ, 47 (November 1968), 263-270.

3290. Hoyt, Donald P. and Philip A. Tripp, "Characteristics of ACPA (American College Personnel Association) Members," IN Fitzgerald 1970, 379-390. JCSP, 8 (January 1967), 32-39.

3291. Johnson, Walter F., "Student Personnel Work in Higher Education: Philosophy and Framework," IN Fitzgerald 1970, 6-11. Original.

3292. Keene, Roland, "Evaluation of Financial Aid Personnel and Programs," IN Keene 1975, 243-256. Original.

3293. Keene, Roland, "A Look at Diversity, Unity and Basic Beliefs," IN Keene 1975, 3-13. Original.

Provides several models that attempt to define the nature of financial aid personnel in colleges and universities.

3294. Keene, Roland, Frank C. Adams, and John E. King, "New Philosophy--New Profession," IN Keene 1975, 305-323. Original.

A summary of the changes in higher education and how they relate to the development of student support professionals.

3295. Kiell, Norman, "Counseling the Physically Handicapped," IN Siegel 1968, 283-299. Original.

3296. King, John E., "The Academic Preparation of Student Support Career Workers," IN Keene 1975, 294-301. Original.

3297. Kirk, Barbara A., "Relations Between Counseling and Placement," IN Fitzgerald 1970, 321-325. JCSP, 6 (September 1965), 289-292.

3298. Kirk, Barbara A., "What are Future Needs in Educational Counseling and to What Extent Can Automated Techniques be Used?" IN Smith 1962, 72-75. Original.

3299. Koch, Ernst, "Disciplinary Counseling," IN Siegel 1968, 337-354. Original.

3300. Kramer, Howard C., "Campus Community Mental Health," IN Warnath 1973, 116-136. Original.

3301. Krumboltz, John D., "Parable of the Good Counselor," IN Fitzgerald 1970, 287-296. PGJ, 43 (October 1964), 118-126.

3302. Larsen, Charles E., "A Student Development Center," IN Warnath 1973, 216-226. Original.

3303. Lewis, Edwin C., "Counselors and Girls," IN Fitzgerald 1970, 332-339. JCP, 12 (Summer 1965), 159-165.

3304. McDermott, John C., "Orientation in Student Personnel," IN Donovan 1962, 161-168. Original.

3305. Malnig, Lawrence R., "Role of Research in Student Personnel," IN Donovan 1962, 169-181. Original.

3306. Miller, Theodore K., "College Student Personnel Preparation: Present Perspective and Future Directions," IN Fitzgerald 1970, 48-53. JNSAPA, 4 (April 1967), 171-176.

3307. Miller, Theodore K., "Professional Preparation and Development of Residence Educators," IN De Coster 1974, 164-180. Original.

3308. Moore, Leila V., "Some Problems in the Study of Students' Perception of Personnel Services," IN Fitzgerald 1970, 171-174. JNAWDC, 30 (Fall 1966), 33-36.

3309. Morrill, Weston H. and James H. Banning, "Counseling Outreach Programs on the College Campus," IN Bloom 1975, 209-218. Original.

3310. Morris, Sumner B., "Innovative Group Work," IN Warnath 1973, 204-215. Original.

3311. Mueller, Kate H., "The Future of the Campus Personnel Work," IN Fitzgerald 1970, 18-23. JNAWDC, 31 (Spring 1968), 132-137.

3312. Nelson, Theodore M., "Guidance and Relevance," IN Harcleroad 1970, 98-104. Original.

Commentaries by Elias Blake, Jr., Carl B. Wiemann Jr., and H. Kenneth Barker follow on pages 104-107.

3313. Newsome, Audrey, "Student Services in Britain," IN Warnath 1973, 259-274. Original.

3314. Niblack, Mason L., "A Canadian View," IN Warnath 1973, 275-285. Original.

An overview of student personnel services in Canada.

3315. North, Walter M., "The Role of the Aid Officer in the Institution," IN Keene 1975, 259-275. Original.

3316. O'Bannon, Terry U., "Organizations for Student Personnel Workers," IN Fitzgerald 1970, 376-379. JCJ, 37 (September 1966), 19-20.

3317. Osmon, William R., "Information Systems in Student Personnel Administration," IN Herron 1970, 139-155. Original.

3318. O'Sullivan, John J., "Religious Counseling," IN Siegel 1968, 325-335. Original.

3319. Packwood, William T., "Graduation," IN Packwood 1977, 422-427. Original.

A concise history of the college graduation ceremony.

3320. Packwood, William T., "Health," IN Packwood 1977, 298-339. Original.

A thorough overview of college student health services with an extensive bibliography.

3321. Packwood, William T., "Ombudsman," IN Packwood 1977, 219-231. Original.

A concise overview of the concept of a campus ombudsman.

3322. Palmer, David W., "Confusions of Counseling," IN Warnath 1973, 66-81. Original.

3323. Powell, John R., "Inservice Education for Student Staff," IN De Coster 1974, 195-208. Original.

An overview of inservice education programs for residence hall staff.

3324. Raines, Max R., "Student Personnel Development in Junior Colleges," IN Fitzgerald 1970, 59-67. JNASPA, 4 (April 1967), 153-161.

3325. Riegel, Paul S., "Counseling for Post-Baccalaureate Study," IN Fitzgerald 1970, 350-356. JCSP, 7 (March 1966), 86-89.

3326. Riker, Harold C., "The Role of Residence Educators," IN De Coster 1974, 151-163. Original.

The skills and qualifications of the residence hall advisor are discussed in the context of effecting broad educational goals.

3327. Robinson, Donald W., "Evaluation as a Function of Student Personnel Administration," IN Fitzgerald 1970, 155-158. JCSP, 4 (October 1962), 20-22.

3328. Robinson, Donald W. and Richard C. McKee, "Expenditures for Student Services in Higher Education," IN Fitzgerald 1970, 142-147. JCSP, 6 (September 1965), 259-262.

3329. Rose, Harriet A., "Use of Research," IN Warnath 1973, 191-203. Original.

An analysis of the direction of research on student personnel and counseling functions of colleges and universities.

3330. Russel, John H., "Some Points of Concern in Student Services Administration," IN Fitzgerald 1970, 73-78. JCSP, 7 (June 1966), 241-245.

3331. Ryle, Anthony, "Student Health and Counseling," IN Butcher 1971, 211-220. Original.

3332. Samler, Joseph, "The Counseling Service in the Administrative Setting: Problems and Possible Solutions," IN Fitzgerald 1970, 277-286. PGJ, 44 (March 1966), 715-722.

3333. Schlossberg, Nancy K., "Community-Based Guidance," IN Vermilye 1974, 113-119. Original.

3334. Schmalzried, Beverly, "Day Care Services for Children of Campus Employees," IN Furniss 1974, 140-144. Original.

3335. Schneider, Lynette D., "Counseling," IN Packwood 1977, 340-367. Original.

A thorough history and overview of college student counseling services.

3336. Schneider, Lynette D., "Junior College Services," IN Packwood 1977, 450-486. Original.

An extensive overview of student personnel services at the junior college level.

3337. Seeley, John R., "Guidance and the Youth Culture," IN Yamamoto 1968, 60-70. PGJ, 41 (December 1962), 302-310.

3338. "Selected Bibliographies of Student Personnel Programs," IN Fitzgerald 1970, 416-473. Original.

3339. Shaffer, Robert H., "Meeting the Challenge of Today's Students," IN Fitzgerald 1970, 54-58. JNASPA, 4 (April 1967), 177-182.

The author suggests that the "social forces" that face today's (1967) college student require a reassessment of traditional college student personnel programs.

3340. Shaw, Phillip B., "Reading and Other Academic Improvement Services," IN Siegel 1968, 355-371. Original.

3341. Siegel, Max, "Group Techniques in Education, Counseling, and Psychotherapy," IN Siegel 1968, 99-113. Original.

3342. Siegel, Max, "Student Services: Administration and Structure," IN Siegel 1968, 419-426. Original.

3343. Southworth, J. Alfred and Theodore Slovin, "Outreach Programing: Campus Community Psychology in Action," IN Warnath 1973, 137-162. Original.

3344. Strowig, R. Wray, "Helping the Student Understand Himself," IN Herron 1970, 94-106. Original.

3345. Stubbins, Joseph, "Social Context of College Counseling," IN Warnath 1973, 21-46. Original.

3346. Summerskill, John and John Osander, "Educational Passport," IN Vermilye 1974, 93-96. Original.

The educational passport is a document that would contain a student's credentials from high school, college, and work.

3347. Thomas, William G., "Placement's Role in the University," IN Fitzgerald 1970, 314-320. J Col P, 26 (April-May 1966), 87-92.

3348. Thoreson, Richard W. and Charles J. Krauskopf, "Relevant Training for Counselors," IN Warnath 1973, 106-115. Original.

3349. Truitt, John W. and Richard A. Gross, "In-Service Education," IN Herron 1970, 209-229.

This essay was originally published as a monograph, Inservice Education for College Student Personnel by the National Association of Student Personnel Administrators (Bulletin No. 1, 1966).

3350. Van Houten, Peter S., "A Positive Approach to Better Student Conduct," IN Fitzgerald 1970, 108-111. JNAWDC, 28 (Winter 1965), 88-91.

3351. Walker, C. Eugene, "The Changing Role of the Counselor in Modern Society," IN Herron 1970, 86-93. Original.

3352. Warnath, Charles F., "Can Counselors Make a Difference?" IN Warnath 1973, 286-298. Original.

3353. Warnath, Charles F., "Who Does the College Counselor Serve?" IN Warnath 1973, 1-20. Original.

3354. Weiner, Max, "Psychological Testing and the College Counselor," IN Siegel 1968, 77-98. Original.

3355. Wilson, Robin S., "Toward a National Counseling System," IN Vermilye 1974, 108-112. Original.

3356. Wise, W. Max, "Counseling Individuals in Liberal Arts Colleges," IN McGrath 1966a, 72-79. Original.

3357. Wolpin, Milton and C. Eugene Walker, "The Behavior Therapies: Alternatives and Additions to Traditional Counseling Approaches," IN Herron 1970, 107-119. Original.

3358. Wrenn, C. Gilbert, "The Development of Student Personnel Work in the United States and Some Guidelines for the Future," IN Minter 1967, 101-121. Original.

3359. Wrenn, C. Gilbert, "The Development of Student Personnel Work in the United States and Some Guidelines for the Future," IN Fitzgerald 1970, 401-414. IAS (1967).

27
LEGAL ISSUES

3360. Alstyne, William Van, "Financial Exigency: Avoidance of Litigation and Friction," IN Hughes 1975, 17-29. Original.

3361. Bakken, Clarence J., "Legal Aspects of In Loco Parentis," IN Fitzgerald 1970, 94-97. JCSP, 8 (July 1967), 234-236.

3362. Bedau, Hugo A., "Free Speech, the Right to Listen, and Disruptive Interference," IN Pincoffs 1972, 191-211. Original.

3363. Black, Virginia, "The Erosion of Legal Principles in the Creation of Legal Policies," IN Gross 1975, 163-183. Ethics, 84 (January 1974), 93-115.

> The author presents legal theory concerning the counterproductive aspects of "reverse discrimination" laws.

3364. Brown, George K., "Release of Student Records," IN Fitzgerald 1970, 139-141. JNASPA, 3 (October 1965), 3-6.

3365. Byse, Clark, "Procedural Due Process and the College Student: Law and Policy," IN Dennis 1966, 305-317. JCSP, 4 (March 1963), 130-143.

3366. Callis, Robert, "Educational Aspects of In Loco Parentis," IN Fitzgerald 1970, 91-93. JCSP, 8 (July 1967), 231-233.

3367. Chambers, M. M., "The Courts and the Colleges Since Mid-Century," IN Fitzgerald 1970, 124-133. ER, 45 (Spring 1964), 182-189.

3368. Chambers, M. M., "Legal Developments in Higher Education, 1862-1962," IN Brickman 1962, 32-49. Original.

3369. "A Court Looks at University Autonomy," IN Goodall 1976, 25-31.

A "judicial analysis of the constitutional autonomy of universities."

From: University of Michigan et al. V. State of Michigan and State Board of Education. 47 Mich. App. 43; 208 NW2d871 (1973).

3370. Daane, Roderick, "The Law in Higher Education: Issues and Trends," IN Peterson 1977, 1-13. Original.

3371. Fishbein, Estelle A., "Administration of Equal Employment Opportunity Law on Campus," IN Hughes 1975, 3-11. Original.

3372. Glenny, Lyman A. and Thomas K. Dalglish, "Higher Education and the Law," IN Perkins 1973, 173-202. Original.

3373. Gove, Samuel K. and Susan Welch, "The Influence of State Constitutional Conventions on the Future of Higher Education," IN Goodall 1976, 9-24. ER, 50 (Spring 1969), 206-212.

3374. Greenawalt, Kent, "Judicial Scrutiny of 'Benign' Racial Preference in Law School Admissions," IN Gross 1977, 217-238. Col Law R, 75 (April 1975), 559-602.

3375. Johnson, Alan W., "Double Jeopardy: A Misnomer: The Relations of the Student to the College and the Courts," IN Fitzgerald 1970, 117-124. JHE, 37 (January 1966), 16-23.

3376. Johnson, Annette R. and Stephen R. Ripps, "Tort Liability of College and University Faculty, Administrators, and Trustees," IN Peterson 1977, 14-45. Original.

3377. Joughin, Louis, "Academic Due Process," IN Baade 1964, 143-171. LCP, 28 (Summer 1963), 573-601.

3378. Joyce, Walter A., "Student Discipline in Higher Education and the Courts: A Study of the Absence of Due Process," IN Fitzgerald 1970, 111-116. JNASPA, 5 (January 1968), 253-258.

3379. Kanowitz, Leo, "Some Legal Aspects of Affirmative Action Programs," IN Furniss 1974, 215-218. Original.

3380. Katenbach, Nicholas de B., "Demonstrations, Freedom, and the Law," IN Dennis 1966, 298-304. Original.

3381. Liethen, Michael A., "Institutional Liabilities," IN Peltason 1978, 43-51. Original.

A concise review of student litigation concerning the quality of the education that they received at a particular institution.

3382. McIlhenny, Edmund, "Due Process and the 'Private' Institution," IN Dennis 1966, 326-332. Original.

3383. Morris, Arval A., "Academic Freedom and Loyalty Oaths," IN Baade 1964, 57-84. LCP, 28 (Summer 1963), 487-514.

3384. Mundinger, Donald C., "Campus Life in a Litigious Age," IN Dennis 1966, 318-322. Original.

3385. Murphy, William P., "Academic Freedom--An Emerging Constitutional Right," IN Baade 1964, 17-56. LCP, 28 (Summer 1963), 447-486.

3386. Nordby, Virginia B., "Due Process for Students: Converting Legal Mandates Into Workable Institutional Procedures," IN Peterson 1977, 76-91. Original.

3387. O'Neil, Robert M., "Law and Higher Education in California," IN Smelser 1974, 191-207. Original.

3388. O'Neil, Robert M., "Law and Higher Education in California," IN Riley 1977, 168-182. PHEC (1974).

3389. Packer, Joel, "A Student's View of Consumerism in Postsecondary Education," IN Peltason 1978, 52-60. Original.

3390. Perry, Richard R., "Faculty Contracts: Major Concerns," IN Peterson 1977, 46-75. Original.

A concise synopsis of the legal and administrative ramifications of faculty contracts.

3391. Ripps, Stephen R., "So You've Been Sued! Components of the Lawsuit," IN Peterson 1977, 92-102. Original.

3392. Rosenblum, Victor G., "Changes in Faculty Status and Responsibility: The Impact of Recent Court Decisions," IN Vaccaro 1975, 78-92. Original.

3393. Sandalow, Terrance, "Racial Preferences in Higher Education: Political Responsibility and the Judicial Role," IN Gross 1977, 239-264. U Chic Law R, 42 (Summer 1975), 653-703.

3394. Sandler, Bernice, "Sex Discrimination, Educational Institutions, and the Law: A New Issue on Campus," IN Wasserman 1975, 20-36. JLE, 2 (October 1973), 613-635.

3395. Shaul, Dennis, "Due Process: A Student's Viewpoint," IN Dennis 1966, 323-325. Original.

3396. Van Alstyne, William W., "The Specific Theory of Academic Freedom and the General Issue of Civil Liberty," IN Pincoffs 1972, 59-85. Annals, 404 (November 1972), 140-156.

3397. Weitzman, Lenore J., "Legal Requirements, Structures, and Strategies for Eliminating Sex Discrimination in Academe," IN Wasserman 1975, 45-81. Original.

3398. Wilms, John H., "Medical Aspects of In Loco Parentis," IN Fitzgerald 1970, 98-99. JCSP, 8 (July 1967), 237-238.

3399. Young, D. Parker, "The Legal Implications of Student Independence," IN College 1974, 27-41. Original.

Commentary by David J. Hanson follows on pages 42-44.

28 RESEARCH— INSTITUTIONAL AND FACULTY

3400. Anderson, G. Lester, "Center for the Study of Higher Education: A Consultant in Residence Role?" IN Harcleroad 1974, 93-97. Original.

A case study of activities of the Center for the Study of Higher Education, The Pennsylvania State University.

3401. Anderson, Robert C. and Robert A. McRorie, "Sponsored Research, Graduate Training, and Academic Growth," IN Strickland 1967, 26-32. Original.

3402. Allen, Harry S., "Research and Planning," IN Budig 1970, 137-147. Original.

3403. Andrews, Frederick N., "The Purdue Research Foundation," IN Strickland 1967, 142-146. Original.

3404. Arcuri, F. William, Thomas R. Mason, and Mark Meredith, "The Impact of Academic Program Structure on the Utilization of Space and Time Resources of Colleges and Universities: A Research Model," IN Johnson 1969, 145-162. Original.

3405. Astin, Alexander W., "An Empirical Characterization of Higher Educational Institutions," IN Feldman 1972, 149-164. JEP, 53 (October 1962), 224-235.

3406. Astin, Alexander W., "The Professor-Policy Analyst," IN Harcleroad 1974, 13-16. Original.

3407. Bacon, Arthur L., "Research in Traditionally Black Schools," IN Johnson 1974, 153-158. Original.

3408. Bazerman, Charles, "The Grant, the Scholar and the University Community," IN Hook 1978, 221-225. Original.

3409. Blume, Stuart, "New Teaching-Research Relationships in Mass Post-Secondary Education," IN OECD 1974, 7-63. Original.

3410. Boggs Jr., Nathaniel, "Research: To Do or Not To Do, That Is The Question," IN Johnson 1974, 175-190. Original.

A concise essay dealing with the relationship between faculty research and teaching effectiveness, especially as applies to faculty at black colleges and universities.

3411. Boykin, Leander L., "Research in Black Colleges and Universities: Administrative Perspectives, Prospectives and Challenges," IN Johnson 1974, 125-151. Original.

3412. Brademas, John, "A Time for Reassessment," IN Strickland 1967, 47-56. Original.

Congressman Brademas presents his view concerning the federal role in support of college and university research.

3413. Burroughs, Robert E., "The Administration of Research at the University of Michigan," IN Strickland 1967, 129-141. Original.

3414. Cagel, Fred R., "A Revised System of Government Support," IN Strickland 1967, 236-247. Original.

A very interesting analysis of the problems that stem from the nature of federally funded research such as the greatly increased "service functions" of universities versus their more traditional roles.

3415. Churchman, C. West, "R^2 on E: Some Suggestions for Research on the Role of Research in Higher Education," IN Lawrence 1970, 41-49. Original.

3416. Clark, Burton R., "The Professor-Disciplinarian," IN Harcleroad 1974, 5-7. Original.

A brief overview of how faculty in various disciplines have contributed to the "study of higher education."

3417. Dressel, Paul L., "A Comprehensive and Continuing Program of Institutional Research," IN McGrath 1964, 37-49. Original.

3418. Du Bridge, Lee A., "Research and Academic Policy," IN Strickland 1967, 9-17. Original.

3419. Dupont, Gerald E., "The Relation Between Teaching and Research," IN Deferrari 1961, 101-112. Original.

3420. Edgerton, Russell, "Education, Work, and FIPSE," IN Vermilye 1977, 110-124. Original.

> Mr. Edgerton gives ". . . a brief overview of what the Fund for the Improvement of Postsecondary Education (FIPSE) has done with $42 million . . . to 380 separate improvement projects . . . relating education and work."

3421. Entwistle, N. J., "Complementary Paradigms for Research and Development Work in Higher Education," IN Verreck 1974, 75-88. Original.

3422. Eurich, Alvin C., "Reflections on University Research Administration," IN Strickland 1967, 1-6. Original.

3423. Folger, John K., "How Can Institutional Research Facilitate Continuous Planning and Progressive Change Required by Our Colleges?" IN Smith 1960, 150-152. Original.

3424. Furnas, C. C., "Coping with Sponsored Research: A Special Word to Presidents," IN Strickland 1967, 33-43. Original.

3425. Gilmore, Robert B., "Challenging an Assumption," IN Strickland 1967, 125-128. Original.

> Mr. Gilmore challenges the idea that government/private foundation sponsored research versus other faculty academic activities require separate and distinct administration.

3426. Gunnell, James B. and Carol A. Shepard, "Educational Research and Development: A Training Model Proposed for Predominantly Black Institutions," IN Johnson 1974, 159-174. Original.

3427. Hallowell, Burton C., "Sponsored Research at Wesleyan University," IN Strickland 1967, 175-179. Original.

3428. Haswell, Harold A., "Containing the Information Explosion," IN Smith 1967, 286-289. Original.

3429. Heist, Paul A., "Research in Higher Education: Current Status and Future Needs," IN Smith 1962, 154-157. Original.

3430. Humphrey, Richard A., "The Plane of Government-Academic Dialogue: An Introduction," IN Humphrey 1967, 1-17. Original.

> An historical and program review of American university support of research and related assistance to foreign countries, especially in the "Third World."

3431. Jamrich, John X. and Paul L. Dressel, "Surveys and Studies of Higher Education Needs and Problems," IN Dressel 1961, 360-392. Original.

3432. Kidd, Charles V., "A Turbulent Dependency," IN Strickland 1967, 57-65. Original.

An assessment of the changing relationships between the federal government and universities, especially concerning government support of faculty research.

3433. Kidd, Charles V., "The Implications of Research Funds for Academic Freedom," IN Baade 1964, 183-194. LCP, 28 (Summer 1963), 613-624.

3434. Killian Jr., J. R., "University Research," IN Connery 1970, 38-43. Original.

3435. Kruytbosch, Carlos E. and Sheldon L. Messinger, "Unequal Peers--The Research of Researchers at Berkeley," IN Kruytbosch 1970, 247-270. ABS, 11 (May-June 1968), 33-43.

3436. McCormack, James and Vincent A. Fulmer, "Federal Sponsorship of University Research," IN Knight 1960, 76-139. Original.

3437. Martin, Warren B. and Dale Heckman, "Understanding Maladies and Effecting Cures," IN Smith 1969, 213-227. Original.

A summary of 50 research projects on higher education relating to the themes of Agony and Promise. Also, the authors provide comments on higher education as a field of study.

3438. Mason, Clarence T., "Sponsored Research at Tuskegee Institute," IN Strickland 1967, 170-174. Original.

3439. Mason, Thomas R., "Institutional Research," IN Jellema 1972, 31-36. Original.

3440. Meeth, L. Richard, "Selected Literature of 1968," IN Smith 1969, 228-240. Original.

3441. Mosley, Philip E., "The Universities and Public Policy--Challenges and Limits," IN Kertesz 1971, 34-51. Original.

The bulk of this essay deals with the role of the university in the development of knowledge through research.

3442. Niblett, W. R., "The Scope and Use of Research in Higher Education," IN Verreck 1974, 1-15. Original.

3443. Pow, Alex S., "The University of Alabama Approach to Sponsored Research," IN Strickland 1967, 156-169. Original.

3444. Reinhard, Karl R. and John F. Sherman, "Administration: Continuing Challenges, Maturing Capabilities," IN Strickland 1967, 76-90. Original.

This essay deals with the problems and challenges of administering government and non-government sponsored university research programs.

3445. Roseman, Alvin, "The University and Its Field Mission," IN Humphrey 1967, 57-77. Original.

3446. Rossi, Peter H., "Researchers, Scholars and Policy Makers: The Politics of Large Scale Research," IN Morison 1966, 110-129. Dae, 93 (Fall 1964), 1142-1161.

3447. Rudd, Ernest, "The Pressures Towards Research," IN Butcher 1972, 305-324. Original.

3448. Sanford, Nevitt, "Higher Education as a Field of Study," IN Sanford 1962, 31-73. Original.

3449. Sanford, Nevitt, "Research and Policy in Higher Education," IN Sanford 1962, 1009-1034. Original.

3450. Scanlon, T. M., "Academic Freedom and the Control of Research," IN Pincoffs 1972, 237-254. Original.

3451. Schauer, Charles H., "The Foundation-College Relationship: A Special Role," IN Strickland 1967, 119-124. Original.

3452. Silverman, Robert J., "The Professor-Editor," IN Harcleroad 1974, 17-22. Original.

3453. Smelser, Neil, "The Place and Role of Basic Research in the Future Structures of Post-Secondary Education," IN OECD 1974, 66-88. Original.

3454. Smuckler, Ralph, "University Responsibilities and International Development Research," IN Humphrey 1967, 110-133. Original.

3455. Smull, Thomas Leland K., "Agencies, Institutions, and Research: Other Frontiers," IN Strickland 1967, 66-75. Original.

Mr. Smull presents the role of the federal government in support of university based research by emphasizing the fact that the nature of research support varies greatly among federal agencies. He also suggests that universities should be permitted more discretion in shaping the direction and speed of research.

3456. Spalding, Keith, "Sponsored Research in the Liberal Arts College," IN Strickland 1967, 18-25. Original.

3457. Spencer, Lyle M., "The Research Function and the Advancement of Knowledge," IN Dobbins 1968, 54-66. Original.

Commentaries by Keith Spalding, W. Eugene Groves, Kermit Gordon, and E. Peter Volpe follow on pages 67-82.

3458. Stecklein, John E., "Institutional Research: Current Status and Future Requirements," IN Smith 1962, 249-252. Original.

3459. Strickland, Stephen, "The Conflict-of-Interest Problem: A Case Study in Cooperation," IN Strickland 1967, 214-227. Original.

A case study that illustrates the potential for problems involving faculty and federal government funded research.

3460. Strickland, Stephen, "Research Grants and Middlemen," IN Strickland 1967, 185-195. Original.

3461. Strickland, Stephen and Theodore Vallance, "Classified Research: To Be or Not To Be Involved," IN Strickland 1967, 196-213. Original.

3462. Thomson, Judith J., "Academic Freedom and Research," IN Pincoffs 1972, 255-264. Original.

3463. Thorp, Willard L., "101 Questions for Investigation," IN Mushkin 1962, 345-356. Original.

The author presents 101 questions that represent major research topics on all aspects of higher education.

3464. Trow, Martin and Oliver Fulton, "Research Activity in American Higher Education," IN Trow 1975, 39-83. Original.

3465. Turner, W. Homer, "Private Sponsorship, Public Gains," IN Strickland 1967, 91-118. Original.

An excellent overview of college and university research programs that are supported by non-governmental philanthropic funds from private foundation grants.

3466. Weaver, John C., "The Federal Research Endeavor and Higher Education," IN Dobbins 1963, 55-65. Original.

3467. Weidner, Edward, "Evaluation of the Impact of University Contracting Abroad," IN Humphrey 1967, 134-179. Original.

3468. Wescoe, W. Clarke, "The Use of University Resources," IN Connery 1970, 44-57. Original.

3469. Wile, Howard P., "The Human Element in Research Administration," IN Strickland 1967, 180-184. Original.

3470. Woodrow, Raymond J., "Sponsored Research at Princeton University," IN Strickland 1967, 147-155. Original.

3471. Woodrow, Raymond J. and Neil O. Hines, "Cost Sharing in Government-Sponsored Research," IN Strickland 1967, 228-235. Original.

3472. Zachrisson, Bertil, "The Role of Research and Development in Higher Education: A Minister's View," IN Entwistle 1976, 4-7. Original.

(Mr. Zachrisson is Swedish Minister of Education)

29
THE PHYSICAL PLANT—
LIBRARIES AND OTHER
INSTRUCTIONAL FACILITIES

3473. Bergen, Dan, "'Knowledge and Library-College Integration,'" IN Bergen 1966, 81-84. Original.

3474. Brubaker, Charles W., "Cooperative Planning for New Campus Facilities by Educator and Architect," IN Smith 1964, 220-224. Original.

3475. Caudill, William W., "Housing the Educational Program: The Physical Plant as Educational Environment," IN Knorr 1965, 53-63. Original.

3476. Creese, James, "How Can Colleges and Universities Make Most Effective Use of New Knowledge Concerning Educational Facilities?" IN Smith 1960, 197-199. Original.

Commentaries on the Creese paper follow on pages 199-208.

3477. Davis, Brody and Associates, "User Requirements: Analytic Techniques for Academic Architecture," IN Ritterbush 1972, 97-112. Original.

3478. Eltin, Mel, "Classrooms," IN Mayhew 1967, 341-361. BM (1964).

3479. Ely, Donald P., "The Design of Large Spaces for Instruction-Learning Processes," IN Smith 1963, 84-87. Original.

3480. Goettelmann, Paul A., "Development of the Physical Plant," IN Donovan 1964, 155-163. Original.

3481. Gores, Harold B., "Bricks and Mortarboards," IN Smith 1963, 29-38. Original.

> This essay provides the reader with seven questions of specific importance concerning the process of decision-making on physical plant expansion.

3482. Green, Alan C., "Architectural Implications of the New Technologies," IN Smith 1963, 88-90. Original.

3483. Haas, Warren J., "Future Developments in Library Facilities in Independent Liberal Arts Colleges," IN Letter 1968, 61-72. Original.

3484. Hallenbeck, Edwin F., "The College Campus--Workplace for Learning," IN Smith 1964, 224-227. Original.

3485. Horn, Francis H., Jonathan King, and James J. Morisseau, "Facilities and Learning: An Overview of Developments," IN Baskin 1965, 153-173. Original.

3486. Jordan, Robert T., "The 'Library-College,' A Merging of Library and Classroom," IN Bergen 1966, 37-60. Original.

3487. Knapp, Patricia, "Involving the Library in an Integrated Learning Environment," IN Bergen 1966, 21-35. Original.

3488. Kortendick, James J., "Cooperative Role of the College Library," IN Donovan 1965, 47-52. Original.

3489. Kortendick, James J., "Library--A New and Expanding Campus Institution," IN Donovan 1964, 25-35. Original.

3490. Levi, Julian H., "Ground Space for the University," IN Dobbins 1964, 9-15. Original.

> The author provides a series of political and economic considerations to be used in determining the location of new facilities, especially for urban institutions.

3491. Lewis, Philip, "Instructional and Communication Systems," IN Smith 1963, 101-103. Original.

> This essay examines language laboratories and the instructional technology that has resulted from their use.

3492. Martin, Warren B., "A Conservative Approach to Radical Reform," IN Minter 1967, 37-54. Original.

The author suggests that we must change the total educational environment through the reform of our philosophy of education by appeal to "purposes that transend the self" and by curriculum innovation away from subject-matter specialization toward education of the "whole person," and finally we must transform the architecture of colleges based on "dissimilarity (more) than similarity with existing models."

3493. Morisseau, James J., "Bricks and Mortarboards," IN Smith 1964, 227-229. Original.

3494. Mushkin, Selma J. and W. Robert Bokelman, "Student Higher Education and Facilities of Colleges and Universities: Projections," IN Mushkin 1962, 173-197. Original.

3495. Perkins, Lawrence B., "New Institutions 'on the Drawing Board': Campus Layouts and Physical Facilities for the Future," IN Smith 1962, 229-232. Original.

3496. Rovetch, Warren, "Architecture for the Urban Campus," IN Smith 1969, 78-81. Original.

3497. Schneider, Lynette D., "Housing," IN Packwood 1977, 125-152. Original.

An excellent and concise overview of college student housing programs and services with an extensive bibliography.

3498. Taubin, Harold, "The University Environment," IN Dobbins 1964, 26-31. Original.

The experience and problems of planners at the University of Pennsylvania in developing the physical plant within state and local constraints.

3499. Tharp, Charles D., "The Learning and Instructional Resources Center at the University of Miami," IN Smith 1963, 91-94. Original.

3500. Williams, Kenneth R., "Capsules, Carrels, and Computers," IN Smith 1963, 136-139. Original.

A case study of the impact of libraries on the development of an experimental university (Florida Atlantic University).

30
INSTITUTIONAL GOALS, REFORM, INNOVATION, AND CHANGE

3501. Adams, John C., "The Hofstra Experiment for Commuters," IN Harris 1960, 136-139. Original.

3502. Ashby, Eric, "Reconciliation of Tradition and Modernity in Universities," IN McMurrin 1976, 13-27. Original.

3503. Baldridge, J. Victor, "Organizational Change: Institutional Sages, External Challenges, and Internal Politics," IN Riley 1977, 123-144. MCEO (1975).

3504. Baldridge, J. Victor and Terrence E. Deal, "Change Processes in Educational Organizations," IN Riley 1977, 80-98. OVEI (1974).

3505. Bartecki, Jayne, "Institutional Goal Setting," IN Wattel 1975, 146-217. Original.

3506. Benezet, Louis T., "Continuity and Change: The Need for Both," IN Caffrey 1969, 15-29. Original.

> Commentaries by Harry S. Broudy, Ferrel Heady, Samuel D. Proctor, Kermit C. Morrissey, and Albert W. Dent follow on pages 30-43.

3507. Birenbaum, William M., "Lost Academic Souls," IN Smith 1969, 18-24. Original.

> An essay speculating on the changes that are needed to revitalize our institutions of higher learning, especially in large urban areas.

3508. Birenbaum, William M., "Something for Everybody Is Not Enough," IN Furniss 1971, 65-82. Original.

An historical and sociological analysis of higher education and the process of change in response to social demands.

Commentaries by Andrew M. Greeley, Jacqueline Wexler, and Harris Wofford, Jr. follow on pages 82-93.

3509. Boyer, Ernest L., "The Changing World and Higher Education," IN Peltason 1978, 1-8. Original.

The author provides an explanation of three areas that are critical if institutions of higher education are to respond to changing social contexts and changing students.

3510. Caffrey, John G., "Alternative Models," IN Smith 1970, 248-259. Original.

The author presents a series of "models" or alternatives to the present structure of higher education.

3511. Case, Charles W., "Trials and Tribulations of University Reorganization: Initial Steps Toward a Matrix Organization," IN Mauer 1976, 33-42. Original.

3512. Cater, Douglas, "Leadership and Change in Higher Education," IN Smith 1967, 35-40. Original.

3513. Caws, Peter, "The Goals and Governance of Universities Regarded as Institutions of Learning," IN Rittenbush 1972, 7-34. Original.

3514. Cerych, Ladislav and Dorotea Furth, "The Search for a Global System: Unity and Diversity of Post-Secondary Education," IN Holmes 1971, 108-119. Original.

The authors view the period of 1950-1970 as dominated by three developments concerning higher education: (1) "quantitative expansion," (2) "reform of individual institution and/or specific aspects of higher education," and (3) "reform of the higher education as a whole."

3515. Chickering, Arthur W., "Social Change, Human Development, and Higher Education," IN McGrath 1972, 13-29. Original.

3516. Clark, Terry N., "Institutionalization of Innovations in Higher Education: Four Models," IN Baldridge 1971, 75-96. ASQ, 13 (June 1968), 1-25.

3517. Cordier, Andrew W., "The United Nations and the Winds of Change," IN Smith 1962, 44-50. Original.

3518. Curle, Adam, "Universities in a Changing World: Innovation and Stagnation," IN Lawlor 1968, 3-24. Original.

3519. Dale, Edgar, "The Innovator and the Establishment," IN Smith 1967, 88-91. Original.

3520. Dalin, Per and Milbrey McLaughlin, "Strategies for Innovation in Higher Education," IN Entwistle 1976, 133-155. Original.

3521. Darley, John G., "Our Larger Purposes," IN Brown 1960, 17-32. Original.

> Dr. Darley believes that higher education ". . . has not adequately fulfilled its larger purposes and that some of its own spokesmen do not clearly understand them."

3522. Dearing, Bruce, "Experiment and Reform in the State of New York," IN McLeod 1973, 169-170. Original.

3523. de Grott, Andriaan D., "To What Purpose, To What Effect? Some Problems of Methods and Theory in the Evaluation of Higher Education," IN Verreck 1974, 16-44. Original.

3524. Drake, George A., "The Politics of Reform," IN Mauer 1976, 73-77. Original.

3525. Franz Jr., Paul J., "The Management of Goals and Objectives," IN Rowland 1977, 464-469. Original.

3526. Gardner, David P., "Forces for Change in American Higher Education," IN McMurrin 1976, 103-123. Original.

3527. Goodman, Paul, "A Simple Proposal," IN Margolis 1969, 313-327. COS (1962).

> Mr. Goodman does not advocate a reforming of the university but, instead, suggests that small groups leave the university and form their own academic communities.

3528. Gould, Samuel B., "Leadership in a Time of Educational Change," IN Smith 1967, 125-134. Original.

3529. Gould, Samuel B., "Less Talk, More Action," IN Vermilye 1972, 177-187. Original.

> Dr. Gould, Chairman of the Commission on Non-Traditional Study, discusses the dangers associated with a non-discriminate view of educational innovations.

3530. Gould, Samuel B., "A New Objective," IN Dobbins 1968, 220-229. Original.

The author presents a rationale for developing goals and objectives for higher education.

3531. Gross, Edward, "Universities as Organizations: A Study of Goals," IN Baldridge 1971, 22-57. ASR, 33 (August 1968), 518-544.

3532. Hatfield, Mark O., "A Nation on the Move," IN Herron 1970, 21-28. Original.

Senator Hatfield believes that the solution to contemporary social problems must begin with a change in people's attitudes and values. Some of this change can be accomplished through alterations in institutions, including colleges and universities.

3533. Hefferlin, J. B. Lon, "Ritualism, Privilege and Reform," IN Smith 1970, 146-152. Original.

In this essay the author asserts that most colleges and universities are "inherently antithetical to change and that reform must come from the 'outside.'"

3534. Henderson, Algo D., "College and Universities as Agents of Social Change: Goals and Conflicts," IN Minter 1968, 57-74. Original.

3535. Hesburgh, Theodore M., "The Nature of the Challenge--Traditional Organization and Attitudes of Universities Toward Contemporary Realities," IN Kertesz 1971, 3-11. Original.

3536. Heyns, Roger W., "The University as an Instrument of Social Action," IN Minter 1968, 25-40. Original.

3537. Hickman, C. Addison, "What Happens to the Social Structure and Inner Dynamics of a College in the Process of Change?" IN Smith 1962, 129-132. Original.

3538. Hodgkinson, Harold L., "Walden U.: A Working Paper," IN Brann 1972, 105-117. ICH (1971).

Dr. Hodgkinson's paper suggests the need for new ways of viewing the context and process of higher education if meaningful reform is to be achieved.

3539. Jervis, Frederick M. and Janis W. Jervis, "Change in Higher Education: Piecemeal or Comprehensive?" IN Vaccaro 1975, 123-143. Original.

3540. Jones, Thomas F., "On Turning the Innovation Crank," IN Mauer 1976, 153-159. Original.

3541. Keeton, Morris T., "Reform and Red Tape," IN Vermilye 1975, 30-36. Original.

3542. Kerr, Clark, "The Frantic Race to Remain Contemporary," IN Margolis 1969, 156-178. Dae, 93 (Fall 1964), 1051-1070.

3543. King, Jonathan, "Campus Cultures and the Cultured Campus," IN Lunsford 1963a, 129-138. Original.

> The author points to the fact that there are conflicting objectives of institutions themselves as well as those of their students.

3544. Kirk, Russell, "American Colleges: A Proposal for Reform," IN Mayhew 1967, 103-112. IPOCS (1965).

3545. Knoell, Dorothy M., "How Can Two- and Four-Year Colleges Provide Articulation in the Face of Rapid Changes?" IN Smith 1964, 216-219. Original.

3546. Lee, Calvin B. T., "Whose Goals for American Higher Education," IN Dobbins 1968, 1-15. Original.

3547. Lee, Sang M. and Laurence J. Moore, "Goal Programing for Administrative Decisions in Higher Education," IN Heinlein 1974, 121-129. Original.

3548. Loeb, Martin B., "How Can the Undergraduate College Introduce Innovations and Effect New Developments Which Reflect Present and Future Responsibilities Without Destroying Institutional Balance?" IN Smith 1964, 63-65. Original.

3549. Longsworth, Charles R., "Policies as Reflectors of Institutional Goals," IN Heyns 1977, 43-50. Original.

> This essay suggests that a college's personnel policies should be designed in response to "changing institutional goals."

3550. Lumsden, Keith, "Technological Innovation in a Hostile Environment: Problems of Increasing Productivity in Higher Education," IN Harrison 1975, 5-13. Original.

3551. McConnell, T. R., "Colleges and Universities as Agents of Social Change: An Introduction," IN Minter 1968, 1-12. Original.

3552. McCune, Shannon, "The College of the 60's: The Imperative of Major Departures," IN Smith 1960, 32-35. Original.

> Dr. Shannon lists several changes he feels will take place in the 1960's and states how these changes will impact on the institutions of both private and public higher education.

3553. Maguire, John David, "Strategies for Academic Reform," IN Hodgkinson 1971a, 91-112. Original.

3554. Mangelsdorf Jr., Paul, "Swarthmore Knocks on Wood," IN Riesman 1973, 323-342. Original.

The author provides an assessment of the effect of student activism on Swarthmore, especially in the area of "academic egalitarianism."

3555. Martin, Charles E., "Conflict Between Policy and Institutional Purpose," IN Mauer 1976, 78-91. Original.

3556. Newman, Frank, "The Transformation of the American University," IN Entwistle 1976, 107-123. Original.

3557. Perkins, James A., "Reform of Higher Education: Mission Impossible?" IN Furniss 1971, 148-158. Original.

Commentaries by Warren B. Martin, Scott W. MacCoy, and Don Davies follow on pages 158-167.

3558. Randel, William, "How Can Meritorious Rather than Efficently Promoted Purpose be Translated Into Practice?" IN Smith 1964, 215-216. Original.

3559. Schwartz, Edward, "The New University," IN Hodgkinson 1971a, 127-150. Original.

Mr. Schwartz wants to create a new kind of higher education institution based on a "radical communiversity" where loyalty is primarily among those who share objectives, especially radical objectives designed to change society.

3560. Sessums, T. Terrell, "Legislating Educational Change," IN Godwin 1972, 176-180. Original.

3561. Silber, John, "Campus Reform: From Within or Without?" IN Altman 1971, 39-49. Original.

3562. Snyder, Benson, "Change Despite Turmoil at MIT," IN Riesman 1973, 155-171. Original.

3563. Stadtman, Verne A., "Governmental Strategies for Educational Reform and Innovation," IN Hughes 1975a, 95-112. Original.

Commentaries by John Vasconcellos and Elias Blake, Jr. follow on pages 113-119.

3564. Swim, Dudley, "Why Not Genuinely Reform Education?" IN Altman 1971, 29-36. Original.

Mr. Swim's reform would emphasize the "depoliticizing of education," "career orientation," and the "evolution . . . of private enterprise" in higher education.

3565. Thompson, Kenneth W., "Education For What? The Debate Over Goals," IN Kertesz 1971, 23-33. Original.

3566. Trippet, Byron K., "Are Fundamental Changes Required in Higher Education?" IN Smith 1961, 24-29. Original.

3567. Uhl, Norman P., "Identifying Institutional Goals," IN Ritterbush 1972, 83-91. Original.

3568. Waes, Robert Van, "Student Freedoms and Educational Reform," IN Smith 1968, 73-76. Original.

3569. Ward, F. Champion, "University Initiative in Response to Change," IN Niblett 1970, 159-171. Original.

Commentary by John Deutsch follows on pages 172-180.

3570. Watson, Goodwin, "Reward Systems for Innovation," IN Brann 1972, 238-244. Original.

3571. Weingart, Peter, "The Integration of Learning and Research In Mass Higher Education: Towards a New Concept of Science," IN OECD 1974, 89-112. Original.

Mr. Weingart argues that the problems of higher education must be considered in a much wider context if we are to see the contradictions between existing structures and the means to reform and innovation.

3572. Wilson, Logan, "Setting Institutional Priorities," IN Smith 1965, 33-39. Original.

3573. Wilson, Logan, "Setting Institutional Priorities," IN Milton 1968, 25-35. Current (1965).

3574. Yarmolinsky, Adam, "Civil Defense and Security Measures: Responsibilities of Institutions of Higher Education and Their Staffs," IN Smith 1962, 233-237. Original.

Commentary by David Inglis follows on pages 237-241.

31
THE FUTURE OF POSTSECONDARY EDUCATION

3575. Armytage, W. H. G., "In Lieu of Delphi: What?" IN Lawlor 1972, 3-16. Original.

3576. Ashby, Eric, "The Case for Ivory Towers," IN Henderson 1968, 6-17. Original.

A prediction concerning the nature and use of universities in the future.

3577. Benne, Kenneth D., "The Idea of a University in 1965," IN Stroup 1966, 1-51. Original.

An extremely well reasoned essay that projects the future of the university based on a thorough sociological analysis of the institution in the mid-1960's.

3578. Blough, Roger M., "Agenda for the 1970's," IN Connery 1970, 175-184. Original.

3579. Bowen, Howard R., "Teaching and Learning in 2000 A.D.," IN Vermilye 1975, 154-165. Original.

3580. Bowen, Howard R., "Technological Change and the Future of Higher Education," IN Smith 1966, 42-48. Original.

3581. Breneman, David W. and Chester E. Finn, Jr., "An Agenda for the Eighties," IN Breneman 1978, 411-450. Original.

A projection of public interest and public policy relating to higher education for the 1980's.

3582. Brewster Jr., Kingman, "Campus 1980," IN Connery 1970, 58-65. Original.

3583. Brumbaugh, A. J., "New Institutions 'on the drawing board': Concepts and Programs for Higher Education in the Future," IN Smith 1962, 133-136. Original.

Commentary by C. R. Carpenter follows on pages 137-140.

3584. Caffrey, John, "The Future Academic Community?" IN Caffrey 1961, 1-12. Original.

3585. Caffrey, John, "Predictions for Higher Education in the 1970s," IN Caffrey 1969, 261-293. Original.

Commentaries by Robert H. Kroepsch, William H. Sewell, and Joseph E. Slater follow on pages 293-304.

3586. Commager, Henry Steele, "The University and the Community of Learning," IN Stroup 1966, 76-94. Original.

3587. Diebold, John, "The New World Coming," IN Mayhew 1967, 63-67. SR, 49 (July 23, 1966), 17-18.

The author believes that computers will "revolutionize business, education, communications, science--in ways only dimly forseen."

3588. Eurich, Alvin C., "Higher Education in the 21st Century," IN Margolis 1969, 101-112. AtL, 211 (June 1963), 51-55.

3589. Eurich, Alvin C., "Managing the Future: Some Practical Suggestions," IN Caffrey 1969, 233-247. Original.

Commentaries by Martin Meyerson, Murray H. Block, Theodore M. Hesburgh, Theodore Walker, and Franklin Patterson follow on pages 248-260.

3590. Eurich, Alvin C., "A Twenty-First Century Look at Higher Education," IN Smith 1963, 39-46. Original.

3591. Eurich, Alvin C., "A Twenty-First Century Look at Higher Education," IN Mayhew 1967, 443-453. Current (1963).

3592. Gardner, John W., "America in the Twenty-Third Century," IN Margolis 1969, 377-381.

This essay first appeared in the New York Times (NYT) on July 27, 1968, p. 26+.

3593. Gores, Harold B., "The American Campus--1980," IN Eurich 1968, 279-298. Original.

3594. Green, Edith, "Through a Glass Darkly: Campus Issues in 1980," IN Smith 1968, 280-290. Original.

3595. Harman, Willis W., "Future Work, Future Learning," IN Vermilye 1977, 236-249. Original.

3596. Henry, David D., "An Assessment of the Future of Higher Education," IN Harcleroad 1971, 65-75. Original.

3597. Hesburgh, Theodore M., "Resurrection for Higher Education," IN Wilson 1972, 327-336. Original.

3598. Hodgkinson, Harold L., "A Look Ahead," IN Hodgkinson 1971, 206-208. Original.

3599. Lane, Hugh W., "The Seventies, Eighties, and Beyond," IN Vermilye 1973, 96-103. Original.

3600. Martin, Warren B., "A Conspiracy for the Future," IN Altman 1971, 63-68. Original.

The author predicts a future in which "higher education" has helped to change society toward, among other things, socialism and "meritocratic oligarchies."

3601. Marvel, William W., "The University and the World," IN Eurich 1968, 64-91. Original.

3602. Mayhew, Lewis B., "Faith and Despair," IN Smith 1968, 265-279. Original.

The author presents a series of propositions about the present and the future of higher education.

3603. Myrdal, Gunnar, "The Future University," IN Stroup 1966, 95-111. Original.

3604. Nason, John W., "American Higher Education in 1980--Some Basic Issues," IN Mayhew 1967, 397-422. AHE (1966).

3605. Niblett, W. R., "Ahead--But in What Direction?" IN Niblett 1970, 1-5. Original.

Introductory remarks concerning the future of higher education and the assumptions that have historically effected decision-making in this area.

3606. Niblett, W. R., "Insight and Foresight in Higher Education," IN Niblett 1970, 243-256. Original.

3607. Niblett, W. Roy, "Issues and Choices," IN Niblett 1972, 3-13. Original.

The author discusses some of the more important issues that colleges and universities will have to face in the near future.

3608. Sarnoff, David, "No Life Untouched," IN Mayhew 1967, 57-61. SR, 49 (July 23, 1966), 19-23.

A speculation on the wide effect of computers on all aspects of society towards the end of this century.

3609. Schaff, Adam, "The Future of the University," IN Henderson 1968, 31-40. Original.

3610. Smith, Allan F., "Four Challenges for Higher Education," IN Henderson 1968, 49-55. Original.

The challenges are: (1) the integration of multiple purposes, (2) to integrate developing knowledge into a meaningful whole that is available to the non-expert (3) how institutions can teach a value system, and (4) how higher education can foster excellence in a society strongly committed to egalitarian ideals.

3611. Spaulding, Seth and Joseph Herman, "Speculations from an International Perspective," IN Niblett 1972, 45-59. Original.

A projection concerning the issues that will be of greatest concern for higher education in the future.

3612. Tickton, Sidney G., "The Magnitude of American Higher Education in 1980," IN Eurich 1968, 9-22. Original.

3613. Ulich, Robert, "Higher Education and the Future of Mankind," IN Smith 1961, 38-43. Original.

3614. Vacarro, Louis C., "The Future Shpae of American Higher Education," IN Vacarro 1975, 1-8. PDK, (February 1975), 387-389.

3615. Visalberghi, Aldo, "Changes in Higher Education: Two Possible Futures," IN Bailey 1977, 132-142. Original.

3616. Wilson, Logan, "American Higher Education Confronts Its Future," IN Wilson 1965, 1-5. Original.

3617. Zurayk, Constantine K., "Universities and the Making of Tomorrow's World," IN Henderson 1968, 18-30. Original.

AUTHOR INDEX

SUBJECT INDEX

ABOUT THE COMPILER

Richard H. Quay is assistant social science librarian and educational bibliographer at the King Library of Miami University in Oxford, Ohio. His previous books include *Research in Higher Education: A Guide to Source Bibliographies*, *In Pursuit of Equality of Educational Opportunity*, and *The Costs and Benefits of a College Degree.*